POLARISING DEVEI

Polarising Development

Alternatives to Neoliberalism and the Crisis

Edited by
Lucia Pradella
and
Thomas Marois

PlutoPress
www.plutobooks.com

First published 2015 by Pluto Press
345 Archway Road, London N6 5AA

www.plutobooks.com

British Library Cataloguing in Publication Data
A catalogue record for this book is available from the British Library

ISBN 978 0 7453 3470 7 Hardback
ISBN 978 0 7453 3469 1 Paperback
ISBN 978 1 7837 1181 9 PDF eBook
ISBN 978 1 7837 1183 3 Kindle eBook
ISBN 978 1 7837 1182 6 EPUB eBook

Library of Congress Cataloging in Publication Data applied for.

This book is printed on paper suitable for recycling and made from fully managed and sustained forest sources. Logging, pulping and manufacturing processes are expected to conform to the environmental standards of the country of origin.

10 9 8 7 6 5 4 3 2 1

Typeset by Curran Publishing Services, Norwich
Text design by Melanie Patrick
Simultaneously printed digitally by CPI Antony Rowe, Chippenham, UK
and
Edwards Bros in the United States of America

Contents

Foreword

This book is the result of a collaborative research project that started in 2011 with a debate on the theoretical premises of development studies. After initially attempting, but ultimately failing, to organise a research seminar that involved both Marxist and new developmentalist scholars, we thought it more productive to focus on clarifying our own Marxian-inspired approach to development. This opportunity seemed especially important. Ten years had passed since the height of the alter-globalisation movement and some four years had gone by after the eruption of the global economic crisis. Yet remarkably little Marxist research had been produced on international and collective strategies to move beyond neoliberalism and the crisis.

We thus organised two research seminars at SOAS, University of London – the first in May 2012 and the second one year later in 2013. Here we discussed the various aspects of the project, issues of solidarity, and some grounds for our Marxian approaches to alternatives. This book meets our initial objectives to varying degrees. It is a first and important step in the elaboration of a distinctively Marxian-inspired approach that sees labour and social movements as core determinants of development outcomes and of alternatives to the ravages of capitalism. It is for this reason that the book does not want to, nor does it pretend to, offer a neutral analysis. Rather, as a diverse collection inspired by critical and socially progressive frameworks, the book seeks to provide existing movements of all shapes and sizes with some tools and lessons for the active transformation of society.

We would like to thank Ben Fine for his support throughout this project, beginning with the first seminar, and Benjamin Selwyn for his essential role in bringing forward this initial idea. We are also grateful to Dae-oup Chang, Adam Hanieh, Abelardo Mariña-Flores, Tim Pringle, Alfredo Saad-Filho and John Smith for their inputs and help during various stages of the project, and to the SOAS Department of Development Studies for its financial support.

As a final word, we wish to dedicate this book to all those movements that, by resisting neoliberalism and imperialism, create the conditions for realising progressive alternatives to capitalism.

Lucia Pradella and Thomas Marois

Polarising Development – Introducing Alternatives to Neoliberalism and the Crisis

Thomas Marois and Lucia Pradella

Polarising the Debate on Alternatives

Neoliberal economic policies, with their emphasis on market-led development and individual rationality, have been exposed as bankrupt not only by the global economic crisis but also by increasing social opposition and resistance. Social movements and critical scholars in Latin America, East Asia, Europe and the United States, alongside the Arab uprisings, have triggered renewed debate on possible different futures. While for some years any discussion of substantive alternatives has been marginalised, the global crisis since 2008 has opened up new spaces to debate, and indeed to radically rethink, the meaning of development. Debates on developmental change are no longer tethered to the pole of 'reform and reproduce': a new pole of 'critique and strategy beyond' neoliberal capitalism has emerged.

Despite being forcefully challenged, neoliberalism has proven remarkably resilient. In the first years since the crisis erupted, the bulk of the alternative literature pointed to continued growth in the BRICS (Brazil, Russia, India, China and South Africa) and in other big emerging market countries to affirm the necessary role for the state in sustaining capitalist development. New developmental economists have consequently reasserted themselves. Their proposals converged into a broader demand for global Keynesianism (Patomäki, 2012) – a demand that is proving to be less and less realistic in the face of a deepening global economic crisis.

Advocates of 'reform and reproduce' – be they new developmental or neo-Keynesian – share deep commitments to capitalism and the subordination of workers to the needs of accumulation. In contrast, this book represents a collaborative attempt by a group of Marxian-inspired scholars to explore real and potential alternatives to the exploitative reality of neoliberal capitalism. Despite varying approaches, contributors to this book understand that neoliberalism and the ongoing crisis are an expression of the fundamental contradictions of capitalism. They reflect on the alternatives that workers, women, peasants and oppressed peoples have defended and struggled to create. At the same time the book seeks to provide an analysis of capitalism, and its crisis, as a global phenomenon, and in doing so overcome academic divisions between development studies of the South and the study of neoliberalism in the North.

Importantly, a guiding theme helping to shape the book has been a refusal to accept nation-states as self-contained units of analysis: that is, the 'methodological nationalism' found in much of the developmental literature. Contributors instead seek to understand the case-specific dynamics of neoliberalism in ways that capture the global tendencies of capitalist accumulation as an integrated whole. In this approach contemporary development is not separated from existing labour and social movements, just as concrete alternatives depend on real social mobilisations. Capitalist development is taken as an inherently antagonistic and polarising process shaped by class struggle. Alternatives are assessed by the extent to which they enable the fulfilment of social aspirations for an equal and just existence free from exploitation and oppression. The contributors' critical analyses thus seek to reveal the contours of different and better possible forms of social development.

The book is structured as follows. Part I, Alternative Themes, develops a broad analysis of capitalist relations of production, social reproduction, climate change, crisis and alternatives. Part II, Alternative Cases, explores the specificities of capitalist development in Latin America, Asia, Africa, the Middle East, North America and Western Europe. The remainder of this Introduction is intended to orient the reader to the book's key concepts, with reference to specific contributors as relevant. It is organised around four sections. The first explores neoliberalism in historical and conceptual terms. The second considers the current crisis and the alternative opportunities it may or may not have opened up. The third questions the extent to which new developmentalist approaches offer substantive alternatives to neoliberalism. The final section then pulls together some of the vital theoretical and practical elements of what our contributors pose as alternatives. As a whole, the book intends to spur debate on the nature and varieties of neoliberalism, the social impacts of its crises, and the forms alternatives must take.

Interpreting and Resisting Neoliberalism

Neoliberalism is a historical phenomenon. In the early 1970s firms began to feel acutely the impact of falling profitability. Many managers and owners believed the mounting power of organised labour was responsible. Indeed, this emerging structural crisis of capitalism was amplified by increasing labour militancy and social opposition, and by the rising challenge of socialism and nationalism from the Global South – the greatest wave of decolonisation in world history (Arrighi, 2007: 136). The power of the United States reached its nadir with its defeat in Vietnam (1975), with the Iranian Revolution in the late 1970s, and with the spread of revolutionary struggles, notably in Latin America. It is against this backdrop that the rise of neoliberalism becomes understandable.

Neoliberalism's set of pro-market and anti-labour policies were first implemented by the brutal US-backed Pinochet dictatorship in Chile (1973). The monetarist economic principles of the infamous 'Chicago Boys' guided the process. At this time, however, many other governments in the South resisted initial demands by the Northern-dominated international financial institutions (IFIs), notably the World Bank and International Monetary Fund (IMF), to implement rapid 'shock therapy' structural adjustment programmes.

The 1979 to 1982 Volcker Shock changed matters dramatically. Paul Volcker, then head of the US Federal Reserve, allowed US interest rates to skyrocket from around 5 per cent to over 20 per cent, ostensibly to halt persistent inflation and to shock the US economy out of stagnation. This move sparked a global rise in interest rates and a wave of profound economic crises in Africa, Asia, Latin America and the Soviet bloc. Governments in these countries lost the ability to service their debts because of the dramatic falls in the prices received for and the quantity of their primary goods exported. This triggered the 1980s debt crisis, which opened an opportunity for governments North and South to press more systematically for neoliberal transformation.

Instead of mobilising workers and peasants against this new form of economic imperialism, governments in the South began to reorient their economies toward intensified export production in order to earn the foreign currency needed to repay their loans. With the fall of the Soviet Union, neoliberal shock therapy was also extended to Russia and other Eastern European countries. In the former Yugoslavia, Iraq and Afghanistan, Western governments mobilised their military power to facilitate the entrenchment of neoliberal policies at a terrible human cost.

Neoliberalism has entailed processes of contested socio-economic transformation. Amidst great popular resistance and economic instability, post-war state-led strategies of development gave way to market-oriented neoliberal ones, or the so-called 'Washington consensus'. The economist John Williamson identified ten policies characteristic of the consensus: fiscal discipline, reduction in public expenditure, tax reform, financial liberalisation, market-determined exchange rates, trade liberalisation, an open door to foreign direct investment, privatisation of public service and state-owned enterprises, deregulation, and secure property rights. These policies have led to higher unemployment, worsening social inequalities, widespread impoverishment, peasant land dispossessions, unsustainable urbanisation and increased worker exploitation.

Contributors to this book describe many of the specific developmental transformations in the Global South, and how neoliberal processes have led to an expansion of the global reserve army of workers and accelerated international migration. At the same time, financial and trade deregulation have enhanced the power of finance capital and multinational corporations, which they have used to pursue the outsourcing and offshoring of many industrial and service activities. This globalisation of production has brought with it intensified processes of ecological destruction.

Women and the poor are the most negatively impacted by the neoliberal privatisation of public services. As women increasingly enter into the workforce, the privatisation of public services magnifies their 'double burden'. Such transformations have been global, having negative impacts on workers in the South and, increasingly, in the North.

The neoliberal policies shaping these transformative processes are derived from neoclassical economic theory. Neoclassical theory obscures and naturalises the exploitative foundations of capitalism because it reduces labour to just another factor of production, not unlike other 'technical inputs' like land and capital. The social reproduction of workers is further assumed to be a private, genderless process restricted to the household, when it is in fact vital to overall capital accumulation processes. In not dissimilar ways, neoclassical economics tends to treat the environment as an externality. Further embedded in this kind of approach is a tendency towards methodological nationalism. Certain models presuppose that capital and labour do not move internationally and that international trade represents merely exchange of commodities between national units. It follows, in theory, that by promoting domestic specialisation according to a given country's comparative advantage, free trade would spontaneously stabilise participating 'national' economies at an equilibrium level, maintaining employment and growth in all of them.

With its emphasis on liberal, market-based notions of individual equality and freedom, neoclassical economics conceals underlying social polarisations and exploitative relationships characteristic of capitalism. In reality, neoliberal transformation favours the interests of the strongest capitals internationally (see Shaikh, 2005). Despite the proclaimed spontaneity of the market, moreover, neoliberalism does not lead to a retreat of the state. Rather, neoliberalism is marked by the class-based restructuring of the state apparatus in ways that have responded to the evolving needs of capital accumulation (for example, around new financial imperatives). What is more, as today's capitalism is dominated by Northern powerhouses like the United States and Western European countries, the extension of capitalist relations globally embodies these imperialist powers' aspirations to retain supremacy in the hierarchy of states.

Neoliberalism, in fact, has always occurred through and within states, never in the absence of states. Actually existing neoliberal transformations are mediated by the hierarchical position of a given state within the world market and by specific social struggles. Consequently, neoliberal transition in the United States is not the same as neoliberalism transition in India or Iraq, and each entails specific national, class, racial and gendered dimensions. Yet contributors to this book recognise that neoliberalism is a class-based political and economic project, defined by the attack of capital and neoliberal state authorities on the collective capacity of organised labour, the peasantry and popular classes to resist the subordination of all social, political, economic and ecological processes to accumulation imperatives. The subsequent consolidation of neoliberalism globally has thus been to the benefit of global capital, and has come at the expense of workers, women and the poor. Relations of imperialist domination, environmental exploitation, racial and gender oppression are constitutive dimensions of this class struggle.

Neoliberal consolidations nonetheless generate new social resistances. Many contributors to this book identify continuing processes involving the recomposition of working classes and the formation of important social movements. With the 1999 demonstrations in Seattle, these struggles assumed an inter-American character. Various indigenous groups, trade unionists, faith-based and women's organisations marched alongside environmentalists and farmers in a collective bid to shut down the World Trade Organization (WTO) talks (Burbach, Fox and Fuentes, 2013: 2). In the new millennium, the 'alter-globalisation' movement has attained a truly global scale. Yet the movement has not been without problems. Notably, the activists and organisations have failed to produce precise sets of collective demands or a coherent international political programme. Pre-existing antagonisms among workers and peoples across lines of national and social oppression were not overcome. The movement, as a result, failed to articulate collective resistance across national, regional and international levels (Prashad, 2013: 235). After the huge demonstrations against the war on Iraq (2003), it gradually faded away.

Still, resistances to neoliberalism grew thereafter, especially in the Global South. In some cases these made significant advances. For example, while the United States and other Western states were bogged down with military aggressions in the Middle East, US control over Latin America eased. Social mobilisations there enjoyed new spaces for action, which helped give rise to a variety of progressive governments less subservient to imperialist interests and the competitive imperatives of neoliberal development. In this book, Abelardo Mariña-Flores suggests that progressive income redistribution and the reinforcement of regional integration processes are among the most significant achievements. Susan Spronk and Sarah Miraglia highlight the progressive, albeit imperfect, gendered dimensions of the Bolivarian transformative movement in Venezuela.

Neoliberal transformations also create new socio-economic conditions that may undermine US and Western hegemony. As several authors attest, for example, the relocation of industrial production towards East Asia has generated new centres of accumulation. Consequently, Western imperial powers now face a major challenge with the rise of China and India. So too have other big emerging capitalisms, like Brazil, Russia, South Africa, Indonesia and the Gulf States, become ever more important centres of accumulation. This has lent support to arguments suggesting global hegemony has started to shift from the West to the East.

To be sure, these emerging capitalisms, China in particular, offer alternative sources of foreign direct investment, international aid, developmental loans and technological know-how to countries in Asia, Africa and Latin America. Leaders of the BRICS have, for example, called for a 'multipolar' reform of the financial system and of the IFIs, which includes the establishment of a new multilateral Development Bank, the 'BRICS Bank'. Yet the extent to which these changes offer an alternative at all has everything to do with the extent to which South–South relations and flows of know-how do not serve to extend and reproduce exploitative class relations of domination, even be they under novel forms of sub/ Southern imperialism. This remains to be seen, and indeed the global crisis is affecting the terms of this debate.

The Global Crisis and the Resilience of Neoliberalism

The global crisis that emerged in the United States in 2007 was rooted in the preceding decades of neoliberal restructuring. Its immediate trigger, however, was the subprime mortgage lending debacle. The US subprime crisis then took a global turn in late September 2008 with the collapse of the US investment bank Lehman Brothers. As investors scrambled to preserve their wealth and dump any toxic assets they had bought into, otherwise liquid US credit markets seized up, bringing the global financial system to the edge of ruin. Only massive and sustained state intervention prevented the system's implosion. Many Western governments rolled out financial Keynesianism. This entailed nationalising failed private banks and industries and adding trillions of dollars to the public debt. The governments thus staved off global economic collapse but only by incurring massive increases in new public debts. This gave rise to the sovereign debt crises in the 'peripheral' EU countries. A number of developing countries also incurred new public debts as governments rolled out economic stimulus packages to help sustain domestic investment, maintain employment and buttress internal demand.

On the one hand, the privileges and powers gained by global capital under neoliberal transformation remain largely intact. Indeed, imperialist governments have done everything in their power to reinforce the current system. Such is the aim of the quantitative easing and zero interest rate policies being pursued by the US Federal Reserve, the Banks of England and Japan, and increasingly the European Central Bank. These actions are intended to prop up the financial markets, support the prices of financial assets and make these countries' exports more competitive. Throughout it all neoliberal technocrats remain unwavering in their ideological commitments to market-oriented development. For example, the World Bank's *Global Financial Development Report 2013* attempts to reframe the global crisis not as a fundamental problem of 'market failure' and capitalism, but instead as essentially about 'state failure' and flawed human nature. The solution? More of the same neoliberal policies implemented since the 1980s, but now guided and sustained by a more robust state apparatus that ensures better market discipline. Despite such socially costly crisis and recovery processes, neoliberalism remains largely intact and unscathed among the globe's major international policymakers (Marois, 2012: 208–13).

On the other hand, the interests of those workers, peasants and women who did not cause the crisis have been targeted and undermined in efforts to overcome the crisis. By socialising the costs through the state apparatus, governments have forced workers and popular classes to pay for the crisis (Marois, 2014). In Western countries, austerity has reinforced preceding trends towards increased poverty and social inequality, disproportionately impacting workers, especially immigrant workers, and women. This is discursively framed around the need to renew growth. In this narrative, the banker, the bureaucrat and the baker's helper are all in it together. Nothing is further from the truth. The point is, as David McNally argues in his chapter on the United States, that in a context of sluggish profitability, austerity is necessary for capital to increase labour exploitation and profits. Likewise, Lucia Pradella investigates the global political economic roots and social impacts of the crisis in Western Europe. Other contributors focus attention on the Middle East, Africa, Latin America and Asia.

Workers and popular classes may be down, but they are not out. In response to the rank injustice meted out by those in power wishing to preserve capitalism in the wake of the crisis, social resistances have arisen anew. Contributors to this book highlight their spectacular range and diversity, starting from the development of a revolutionary movement in the Arab world, presented by Adam Hanieh. Yet this book's contributors are under no illusion that economic crisis alone will launch the collapse of neoliberalism or capitalism. So long as neoliberal advocates are able to push the costs of crisis systematically onto workers, women and oppressed peoples, capitalists will find means of reproducing this exploitative system. That said, the crisis and the movements emerging in response have reopened an opportunity to envision, and fight for, substantial alternatives.

The Limits of New Developmental Alternatives

The immediate aftermath of the global crisis raised the spectre of global Keynesianism. The long-standing institutionalist thesis necessitating the extra-market role of the state in sustaining capitalist growth and stability seemed vindicated. In the Global South too, new developmentalist strategies appeared justified. The rejuvenated developmental state was contributing to an apparent post-crisis global recovery, nowhere more visible than in China with its massive capital infusions.

There is an internal logic to their reassertion of the state. New developmental scholars understand neoliberalism primarily through an institutional lens as various manifestations of the Washington consensus policies. As new developmentalists see it, then, the real problem is that these market-oriented policies have failed to produce stable growth and reduce inequality. Rather, recurrent crises and instability have created boom/bust growth cycles and worsened inequality. It follows that neoliberalism is essentially a 'policy error' characterised by excessive regulatory slippage. By implication, a break with neoliberalism can be achieved by a 'return of the state' (Grugel and Riggirozzi, 2012). However, as this debate is only concerned with how to best achieve virtuous cycles of capitalist growth, capitalism itself is never in question. Merely the pace, timing and institutional strength of changes in the regulatory environment of 'national' capitalisms are questioned. New developmentalism, advocates argue, would allow a return to an 'original' development path devoid of the labour repression, climate change, gender inequality and state bureaucratisation characteristic of the first developmentalism (Kahn and Christiansen, 2011: 5; 255–7).

New developmentalists present one pole of the debate over alternatives. Contributors to this book present another, radically opposite pole. From our perspective, and for present purposes, we signal four main limitations to the new developmentalist approach to alternatives.

First, new developmentalists ignore the exploitative nature of capitalist production relations. For example, many stress that national progressive competitiveness strategies should drive up domestic productivity. In this thesis, poverty is reduced to a symptom of interrupted cycles of otherwise virtuous growth. Yet, as both Benjamin Selwyn and Dae-Oup Chang argue in this book, new developmentalist strategies obscure the systematic repression of workers' rights, wages and human aspirations through the state apparatus. Focusing more on growth and mitigating economic inequality, most developmentalists set aside capitalism's inherent tendency towards social polarisation. Consequently, constitutive issues of social reproduction and of the deepening ecological crisis remain largely on the sidelines.

Second, new developmentalists uphold an idealised understanding of the state. In this paradigm, states are understood as autonomous and elite institutions that can moderate capitalist development for the overall 'social good'. The underlying historical social relations of class, gender and race constitutive of the state apparatus are typically papered over in this framework, and how change is achieved and consolidated, and who benefits from it, are thus distorted.

Third, new developmentalism also rests on methodologically nationalist assumptions, and reproduces the same state/market and national/international dualisms characteristic of neoclassical economics (see Pradella, 2014). Primacy is given to the 'extra-market' coordinating role of the state in instituting national comparative advantages in the world market. If achieved, then free trade can once again positively benefit all participating countries. Concretely, scholars point to the national developmental successes of East Asia, and more recently China, as dehistoricised, decontextualised and discrete developmental models seemingly transferable to all developing countries.

Fourth, it follows that new developmentalists underestimate imperialist relations and capitalism's tendency towards uneven and combined development. As Alfredo Saad-Filho illustrates in this book, mainstream expectations of global economic convergence are exaggerated since the underlying driving forces of neoliberal globalisation, which lead towards persistent economic polarisation, are still operating. Development in the South continues to be very uneven and characterised by complex hierarchical patterns of international integration and deindustrialisation. Looking to Africa, Baba Aye's contribution points to the 'new scramble for Africa' as emerging capitalisms like China are solidifying their place in Africa as new trade and financial partners, thus intensifying international competitive imperatives on the continent. Similar patterns of uneven and combined development in the Middle East, East Asia and Latin America are documented elsewhere in the book. Jerome Klassen, moreover, discusses how the weakening of US and Western hegemony is intensifying international rivalries and military tensions.

In the final assessment, new developmentalism admirably targets some of neoliberalism's economic failures, seeks to craft virtuous cycles of stable growth and to alleviate poverty. The structural power of capital and the systematic exploitation of workers are nonetheless repackaged and reproduced. New developmentalism only modifies neoliberalism as a form of class rule responding to labour and social mobilisations. At the same time the post-crisis consolidations of what have been defined as new developmentalist governments have given rise to new social tensions. As Tim Pringle argues in the book, there is a mounting sense of collective consciousness and power arising within the Chinese working class. And China is by no means the only case. Over the last several years significant protest waves and movements have erupted in Russia, India, South Africa, Brazil, Mexico, Thailand and Turkey. The crisis is indeed global. Despite much rhetoric, the BRICS countries have not formed a real alliance and they remain dependent on exports to and financial relations with imperialist countries, with their economic growth now decelerating or stopping altogether. There is a great need, therefore, to elaborate on real alternatives to neoliberal capitalism.

What Makes for Substantive Developmental Alternatives?

Contributors to this book share an understanding that many societies are in dire need of substantive alternatives to both neoliberal capitalism and its new developmentalist variants. But what does this mean? While we do not ascribe to a single, shared vision (nor need we), each contributor has tried to identify and signal various progressive tendencies that arise from the specific contexts, cases and struggles they have dealt with – be it from women's struggles in Turkey, Cambodia or Venezuela, from revolutionary lessons in Latin America and the Middle East, or from the many labour resistances discussed. We accepted at the start of the project that alternatives cannot and do not simply arrive pre-formed from outside existing society. In other words, the struggle to break with neoliberal capitalism necessarily begins within the historical confines of neoliberalism. Consequently, alternatives must be sought in everyday and actually existing struggles.

To recognise the necessarily historical specificity of struggles to overcome neoliberal capitalism is not to abandon universal aspirations for social justice or common strategies of resistance. On the contrary, by analysing how capitalism works, contributors to this book have tried to provide an analytical framework within which a strategy of change can be shaped. To this end, we share a baseline understanding of what is needed to constitute an alternative. That is, any alternative must stand in sharp contrast to any form of exploitation and oppression, and it must be achieved through working and popular class agency. There is no evidence that capitalists and their advocates will relinquish their accumulated institutional and material power and control willingly. Progressive change must be achieved from below.

Given this shared baseline, it is worth highlighting some of the concrete strategies and principles that emerge throughout the book.

- **Worker-led resistances and aspirations**: Various contributors point to how the gains made by workers and popular classes are due to their collective mobilisations. Many argue that the sustainability of struggles for progressive alternatives depends on the capacity of labour and social movements to build local, national, regional and international movements oriented toward structural transformation. Abelardo Mariña-Flores and Jeffery Webber discuss this perspective with regard to Latin America. Rohini Hensman, Dae-oup Chang and Tim Pringle highlight the potential of the massive working classes in Asia and their capacity to disrupt capitalist production globally. Other contributors highlight the importance of establishing cooperative productive and economic capacity as a prerequisite for more solidarity-based and worker-led social economies. Leandro Vergara-Camus, in particular, discusses the successes of the regional Zapatista movement in Mexico and national Landless Movement in Brazil, but questions the extent to which these forms of peasant resistance are generalisable. Other contributors identify the length of the working day as a key terrain of social transformation, and affirm the centrality of creating autonomous working class political organisations with an internationalist and anti-imperialist perspective. If the global restructuring of production and international migration potentially strengthens the working class internationally, various contributors reflect on the strategies needed to unify workers across the North/South divide and beyond national and racialised divisions (see John Smith, Pietro Basso, Laura Horn and Angela Wigger). For Klassen, an effective anti-war movement has to be based on a new solidarity of working class and oppressed peoples' struggles.
- **Equitable social reproduction**: Various contributors highlight the crucial importance of women's agency in challenging the gendered inequalities of neoliberal production and social reproduction. Drawing on socialist feminist tenets, Demet Özmen Yilmaz (in the case of Turkey) and Susan Spronk and Sarah Miraglia (in the cases of Venezuela and Cambodia) explore women's agency in these societies. Their contributions point to the need to fight for

renewed public services to alleviate the unequal burdens women face day in and day out. Contributors also highlight the need to radically question allegedly natural gender roles in the domestic sphere. At the same time, the differential exploitation of women workers needs to be addressed, defending women's rights as women and as workers. Various contributors highlight the enormous potential for these struggles, including the crucial role of women in the Arab uprisings and in the struggles sparked by the Rana Plaza disaster in Bangladesh (see Hanieh and Smith in this book).

- **Renewing and democratising the public sector:** There is no escaping the struggle to substantively democratise the public sector. To the extent that new developmentalists seek alternatives to neoliberalism, state-owned and public services are presented as alternatives simply because they are not privately owned. Contributors to this book share no such illusions: public services can be aggressively neoliberal in their operations. To recognise this is not to reject the public sector as a necessary, if not sufficient, condition for breaking with neoliberalism. Public ownership can provide a powerful stimulus towards more collective social ownership and the democratisation of political and economic processes. Yet this is no straightforward process. David McDonald's chapter points to many struggles aiming to protect public service provisioning globally. In doing so he proposes a clearer definition of 'publicness' and an alternative methodology by which we can critically evaluate and improve public services for the social good. Likewise, Thomas Marois points to the massive capacity that still-existing state banks hold globally. He argues that capturing and democratising these public sources of credit, along with the dispossession of the accumulated wealth and power of financial capital, are necessary features of any sustainable alternative to neoliberalism. The knock-on benefits of exerting democratic control over society's monetary resources are substantial: solidaristic funding for public services, public infrastructure and cooperatives, as well as for gendered and green social developmental initiatives.

- **Social and environmental justice:** Many contributors to this book accept that environmental struggles are intimately tied to workers' and women's aspirations. Andreas Malm's contribution investigates the links between struggles against climate change and for social justice. He highlights the strategic role of industrial workers for realising this transformation, potentially unifying the entire working class and its social allies, including women's and peasant-based struggles against dispossession and environmental destruction. Hugo Radice's contribution further argues that an alternative, socialist society must be characterised by the material equality of all its members as the basis for free and equal participation in processes of production and reproduction, respectful of the environment.

By criticising neoliberalism and by reflecting on the forms alternatives have taken and are taking, this book tries to 'polarise development'. This direction is meant not just to criticise existing social polarisations, but also to recognise the seeds of material interdependence and class power existing within the present society. In different ways, workers, women and social movements all over the world are trying to oppose the exploitative and oppressive social relations of capitalist rule. As the crisis continues to unfold and deepen, it is increasingly imperative that any realistic alternatives to neoliberalism move beyond the pole of 'reform and reproduce' and toward a radical break with capitalism itself. None of the strategies and principles presented in this book, on their own, are assumed to be sufficient to realise such a break. Nevertheless, in important and transformative ways, they each may contribute to advancing in this direction. We do not wish for this book to remain at the level of debate. Rather, we see it as a contribution to the struggles of workers and social movements, who are the real forces that can polarise development and subordinate it to real social needs.

Select bibliography

Arrighi, G. (2007) *Adam Smith in Beijing: Lineages of the Twenty-First Century*. London: Verso.

Burbach, R., Fox, M. and Fuentes, F. (2013) *Latin America's Turbulent Transitions: The Future of Twenty-First-Century Socialism*. Winnipeg and New York: Fernwood and Zed Books.

Grugel, J. and Riggirozzi, P. (2012) 'Post-neoliberalism in Latin America: rebuilding and reclaiming the state after crisis', *Development and Change*, 43(1): 1–21.

Kahn, S. R. and Christiansen, J. (eds) (2011) *Towards New Developmentalism: Market as Means Rather Than Master*. Abingdon and New York: Routledge.

Marois, T. (2012) *States, Banks, and Crisis: Emerging Finance Capitalism in Mexico and Turkey*. Cheltenham, Glos.: Edward Elgar.

Marois, T. (2014) 'Historical precedents, contemporary manifestations: crisis and the socialization of financial risk in neoliberal Mexico', *Review of Radical Political Economics*, 46(3).

Patomäki, H. (2012) *The Great Eurozone Disaster: From Crisis to Global New Deal*. London: Zed Books.

Pradella, L. (2014) 'New developmentalism and the origins of methodological nationalism', *Competition and Change*, 18(2): 180–93.

Prashad, V. (2013) *The Poorer Nations: A Possible History of the Global South*. London: Verso.

Shaikh, A. (2005) 'The economic mythology of neoliberalism', pp. 41–49 in A. Saad-Filho and D. Johnston (eds), *Neoliberalism: A Critical Reader*. London: Pluto.

Part I

Alternative Themes

CHAPTER TWO

Beyond Impoverishment: Western Europe in the World Economy

Lucia Pradella

In Western Europe, in the wake of the crisis that erupted in 2007–08, unemployment is rising well above the 'natural rate' expected by neoliberals, real wages are declining, inequality is skyrocketing and attacks on the working class have intensified. According to Eurostat, in 2012 almost 25 per cent of the EU-15 population, totalling nearly 92 million people, was at risk of poverty or social exclusion – nearly 8.5 million more people than in 2007. These processes are taking place unevenly, but in all Western European countries. Conditions of poverty, precarity and super-exploitation traditionally associated with the Global South are becoming increasingly widespread in the rich parts of Europe. The speed and depth of these transformations has been dramatic.

The working class has fought back throughout the crisis, especially in the countries hit most by it. The scale of its resistance, however, has nowhere been equal to the scale of the assault. This chapter starts from the assumption that a strengthening of the labour movement and the fight against the crisis requires an understanding of the root causes of impoverishment and a capacity to think about real alternatives. Even though it is much measured, however, poverty is little theorised. Neoliberal and neo-Keynesian economists equate work with monetised economic activity. Living labour is conceptualised as a commodity and as a factor of production at the aggregate level of the national economy, while outsourcing, offshoring and international migration are considered as external variables. This approach renders workers invisible, depicting them as passive and adaptive, and also obscures gender and social reproduction. Productivity increases are supposed to aim at improving living standards, while poverty typically results from insufficient access to resources. The alternatives in this approach consist of reducing rather than eliminating poverty, and the debate tends to revolve around whether market-led growth is sufficient or whether state intervention is necessary to this end.

By contrast, this chapter examines the relation between labour, development and impoverishment. It argues that Marx's *Capital* presents the necessary categories for understanding the process of workers' impoverishment in Western Europe under neoliberalism and after the outbreak of the global economic crisis.

Offering an analysis of capital as a social relation, Marx's main work also presents a reflection on the development of the working class and its potential for social transformation. Since the working class is the only source of social wealth, it has the potential power not only to mitigate but also to eliminate the root causes of impoverishment, laying the foundations for a social system in which increases in productive forces aim at the free development of individuality. Any realistic strategy against impoverishment, the chapter concludes, must be as systemic and international as the crisis we are facing.

Labour, Development and Impoverishment

Any interpretation of development is closely linked to the question of 'what has to be done' with it. Marx's projection beyond capitalism allowed him to conceive of accumulation as a synonymous with an overall impoverishment of the working class. This thesis may seem counterintuitive: capitalism, after all, has fostered unprecedented technological progress and led to substantial improvements in living standards for at least a minority of the world population, as it is still doing in some 'developing' countries. But impoverishment, for Marx, is not just a question of consumption levels: it involves both quantitative and qualitative aspects of workers' labour and living conditions, in their gendered and environmental dimensions. Impoverishment has to be measured in relation to the profits of the capitalist class, and to the potential for individual emancipation created by the development of productive forces. Very importantly, moreover, impoverishment has to be analysed at the international, not at the national level. Poverty, as a consolidated and protracted situation of need, is an extreme expression of impoverishment, which is a social and therefore essentially relative phenomenon.

Impoverishment is the underlying premise for the existence of a working class, which presupposes a continual process of dispossession of independent producers, and the result of the production of wealth as capital. Industrialisation in Western Europe presupposed a process of concentration of mercantile and usurious capitals that took place through robbing, pillaging and conquering colonised peoples, determining an unprecedented increase in international inequalities (see Saad-Filho, Chapter 6 of this book). The violent expropriation of the peasants' land laid the premises for the formation of a class of workers forced to sell their labour-power in exchange for a wage. By selling their labour capacity, workers necessarily impoverish themselves. The wage, in fact, corresponds (ideally) to the value of the commodities necessary for workers' reproduction, and is necessarily lower than the value they produce. The development of productive forces aims at increasing this gap – that is, their exploitation – and renders human activity a source of self-sacrifice, not of self-fulfilment.

Even if we focus on wages, impoverishment is not synonymous with extreme poverty. The wage has three forms: nominal, real and relative. The nominal wage (the sum of money for which workers sell their labour-power) does not correspond to the real wage (the quantity of commodities that workers can buy with their wages), and even less to the relative wage, which expresses the relation between value appropriated and value produced by the working class. The relative wage is for Marx the real indicator of the distribution of social wealth. Under certain conditions, growing productivity may permit increases in nominal and real wages, which can coexist however with a reduction of the relative wage. Historical elements have an impact in determining the value of the labour-power and the amount of taxes spent in reproductive services. In the decades after the end of the Second World War, for example, high growth rates in Western Europe made it possible for organised working classes to obtain real wages increases, reductions in working hours, universal public services provisioning and extended political rights. Nevertheless, workers generally appropriated a declining share of the social wealth they produced: their relative wage declined, therefore.

The centrality attributed to labour exploitation allowed Marx to identify the driving force of capitalism in its globalising tendency (Pradella, 2010). As living labour is the only source of value, its declining relative role in production as a result of mechanisation – and the consequent tendency of the rate of profit to fall[1] – compels capital periodically to destroy constant capital and to increase labour exploitation to the utmost. The internationalisation of production is one of the chief means of achieving increasing labour exploitation. This internationalisation is made possible by having permanent recourse to state intervention and methods of so-called primitive accumulation like commercial policies and colonial wars. Supposedly extra-economic forms of value extraction, such as plunder and pillaging, and commercial and usurious forms of exploitation, also have a permanent role.

Accumulation produces international inequalities as it tends to concentrate high value-added production and capital in the system's most competitive centres, determining a forced specialisation of dependent countries in low value-added sectors, repatriating profits extracted in these countries, and leading to forms of unequal exchange between nations with different productivity levels. Capitalism is an imperialist system that integrates different forms of exploitation and impoverishment, and leads to a continual process of proletarianisation of peasants, artisans and the self-employed.

In *Capital*, however, Marx does not focus on these differences but rather on the unitary trend of the system that, despite and through these differences, determines the impoverishment of the working class internationally. Impoverishment, in his view, is not a consequence of a lack of development but its very result. Technological development itself leads to a relative reduction in the demand for labour-power and to the growth of the global industrial reserve army of unemployed and underemployed workers. These workers put pressure on the employed, limiting their claims and creating the conditions for the compression of workers' wages. Low wages and poverty force the employed population to accept the

---

1   The rate of profit is the ratio of the mass of profit to the total capital advanced.

prolongation of the working day, which in turn reduces the demand for labour power and releases a greater labour supply to the market. Unemployment, under-employment and overwork thus feed off one another in a vicious circle wherein workers make themselves relatively redundant as members of their class.

This socially devastating process, in Marx's view, makes it necessary to establish an alternative form of society in which production meets individual and social needs. This necessity for an alternative social system becomes more and more feasible since industrial development is based on the increasing cooperation of labour. Cooperation lays the premises for the reciprocal reinforcement of workers' struggles internationally. The industrial working class, for Marx, could also lead the struggles of small peasants and proletarianised petty commodity producers (Marx, 1996 [1867]: 750). Marx, in fact, was not indifferent toward the peasant question. What is more, he came to recognise the centrality of anti-colonial and peas-ant-based struggles as part and parcel of the international proletarian movement. While capitalist development created the premises for relative improvements in the material conditions and the social integration of the working classes in imperialist countries, anti-colonial struggles and independent national development in the periphery could accelerate the tendency towards crisis.

Marx, for example, unconditionally supported the Sepoy Uprising in India, the Chinese Taiping Revolution and the Irish anticolonial struggle, which he thought of as the precondition of the emancipation of the working class in Britain. Had these national revolutions been successful, the situation of the masses would have depended on their appropriation of the fruits of their countries' independent development.

At this point, it is worth emphasising that Marx's late support for developmen-talist projects does not make him a developmental economist. This myth derives from an economistic reading that separates Marx's economic analysis from his revolutionary perspective. Marx examined development in the periphery, in fact, as an integral part of his revolutionary critique of capitalism as an exploitative and imperialist system.

Global Impoverishment under Neoliberalism

Marx's *Capital*, therefore, allows us to understand the structural and international dimension of impoverishment in its multifaceted aspects. Such a structural and international dimension became even more evident after the crisis of profitability erupted in the mid-1970s and the implementation of neoliberal policies interna-tionally. These policies – promoted by North-dominated institutions such as the International Monetary Fund (IMF), the World Bank and the General Agreement on Tariffs and Trade (GATT)/World Trade Organization – were aimed at subordi-nating the industrialisation and national developmental projects of countries in the Global South and the former Soviet bloc. These neoliberal policies determined a sharp increase in global poverty and social inequalities, and an acceleration of the process of concentration of agricultural production, land dispossession and rural–urban migration. The result was an unprecedented growth in the global industrial reserve army of vulnerable, unemployed and inactive workers, which now comprises some 2.4 billion people, according to the International Labour Organization. At the same time, financial deregulation, alongside information and transport innovations, has allowed for the outsourcing and offshoring of many industrial and service activities.

Since the mid-1970s the Southern industrial workforce has rapidly outgrown that in the North. According to World Bank's estimates, which surely underestimate the real extent of global poverty (Bush, 2007: 14–8), between the 1980s and early 2000s the absolute number of people in *extreme* poverty increased, when China is excluded, whilst the number of people in *ordinary* poverty increased substantially in every developing region except East Asia. In 2010 an estimated 942 million working poor – nearly one in three workers worldwide – lived below the US$2/day poverty line.

Western European capital has benefited enormously from the expansion of the global industrial reserve army through outsourcing, offshoring and immigration. In Western Europe, the global restructuring of production led to a concentration of capital-intensive production and services in Northern member states and of low capital-intensive production in Southern member states. Lowering transaction costs and eliminating exchange rate uncertainties, the introduction of the euro accelerated the process of production relocation. This caused a substantial increase in unemployment in Western Europe. The Organisation for Economic Co-operation and Development (OECD) reports that while there were 8 million registered unemployed workers in 1970, by 1994 that number had risen to 35 million. Unemployment was only initially compensated by the development of non-standard forms of employment and by the expansion of the service sector, where outsourcing and offshoring have also accelerated since the 2000s. Immigration led to further increases in the labour supply. Restrictive and selective migration policies did not aim at stopping immigration. Rather, these policies produced illegality and a differential system of rights, creating stratifications and divisions in order to hinder working class organisation (see Basso, Chapter 8 of this book).

Since the 1980s, in Western Europe neoliberal reforms have encountered social opposition: from the Fiat struggle in Italy (1980) to the miners' strike in Britain (1984) and to the pension strike in France (1995). Although in some cases workers' struggles have been successful in limiting the negative impact of specific policies, they did not halt neoliberalism as such and the overall worsening of their situation. Because of their national approach, trade union strategies have been largely ineffective in the face of processes of neoliberal restructuring of production and against ruling classes' attempts at dividing and weakening the working class. Trade unions were thus unable to stop the introduction of reforms that reduced the scope for trade union activity and promoted labour market liberalisation, privatisations and increased labour market participation (through pension reforms, internship and workfare).[2] These processes caused a general decrease in union density and in collective bargaining coverage, growing segmentation and casualisation of employment, and increasing low pay and wage inequalities. This led to downward pressure on workers' wages and working conditions which did not affect only low-skilled and unprotected workers, but also more skilled and unionised ones. Indeed, neoliberalism in Western Europe has been characterised by real wage moderation and a decreasing wage share of GDP, which indicates that workers have appropriated a smaller part of the value they produced.

This trend appeared first in the United Kingdom – where a surge in poverty in the 1980s was accompanied by a massive increase in income and wage inequality – and only later in countries like Italy and Germany. According to OECD data, by the mid-2000s the incidence of low wages (in the formal sector) in Italy (9.5 per cent) was still lower than in Germany, which exhibited the second highest share of low-wage work in the EU-15 (20.2 per cent), following closely the United Kingdom (20.6 per cent). Italy, however, exhibited one of the highest percentages of working poor in Western Europe (around 10 per cent), also because labour market reforms were introduced without any welfare compensation.

As Marx explained, unemployment, poverty and low wages play a fundamental disciplining role in production. The processes allow for an increasing exploitation of the employed population, and this in turn fuels unemployment, underemployment and poverty in a vicious circle. Indeed, under neoliberalism, working hours have been extended and unequally distributed (Basso, 2003). While the 35-hour week has been everywhere abrogated, in 2008 EU employment ministers allowed for exceptions to the 48 weekly hour limit to as high as 60 or even 65 hours a week. The spread of Toyotaism, moreover, intensified work in all branches of social organisation, generating a work environment much more stressful, tiring, insecure and harmful than the Fordist one.[3] Workfare and the victimisation of the unemployed contribute to the increasing brutalisation of work experienced by workers in the neoliberal period.

And Then, the Crisis …

Undermining the historical, colonial division of labour between industrialised countries and producers of raw materials in the South, the neoliberal restructuring of industrial production has led to an approximation of the completely globalised system presupposed by Marx in *Capital*, and allowed for an even harsher imposition of the law of impoverishment of the working class.

The neoliberal processes of global impoverishment, however, did not entail

---

2   Workfare policies force individuals to undertake low-paid work, if paid at all, in order to retain their benefit payments.

3   Fordism is an industrialised system of mass production introduced by Henry Ford in his auto plants at the beginning of the 20th century. Toyotaism is a new system of labour organisation aimed at removing any dead time from the labour process.

a simplistic 'race to the bottom'. In the neoliberal period, countervailing effects mitigated the decline in real wages and the growth of poverty in Western Europe: in addition to the increasing exploitation of workers domestically, the differential exploitation of workers in the South and the international transfer of profits supported domestic profitability. The hypertrophy of public and private indebtedness sustained consumption, and cheaper manufactured imports helped to reduce inflation and to maintain income levels. Social policies did contribute to keeping down poverty rates but did not help those with bad job prospects to integrate into the regular, formal labour market (shaped by contracting and regulation). On the contrary, social policies made possible a progressive erosion of the regular labour market, and replaced the universalism of social protection with social assistance directed at the 'deserving poor'. These policies thus impeded a sudden and sharp fall in workers' living standards, which was initially politically unfeasible given the presence of organised working classes.

Neoliberalism, however, has created the economic, social and political premises for a crisis of even greater proportions. Neoliberalism has multiplied the risks of a crisis of overproduction[4] while allowing for an only partial recovery of the rate of profit for capital. Neoliberalism is also characterised by chronic patterns of financial instability. The globalisation of industrial production contradictorily laid the premises for the emergence of new centres of accumulation. The relocation of industries such as textiles, electronics, furniture making and steel, and increasingly services, has laid the conditions for the growth of new working classes, and these have started to raise social and political demands (Silver, 2005). In Eastern Europe and some Asian countries, for example, workers' struggles obtained increases in real wages. As detailed elsewhere in this book, since the late 1990s social movements in many Latin American countries have brought to power a wide range of progressive governments. Mass resistance from Iraq to Afghanistan, from Palestine to Lebanon, hindered the expansion of Western imperialism. These movements started to question the expansion of imperialism and neoliberalism, increasing the factors of crisis.

The rise of China represents another source of contradictions for Western capital. In China, despite increasing social inequalities and a declining wage share of GDP, industrial development and modifications in class balances of forces allowed for a reduction in the rate of extreme poverty and some increases in real wages, leading to a growth of internal markets. Chinese capital, moreover, started to expand to the rest of the Global South (see Pringle, Chapter 17 and Aye, Chapter 19). As a result, since 2000 the European Union has lost market shares to countries such as Brazil, India and China. This is especially true for China, which has become the largest exporter of goods and is moving up the global value chain. In doing so, China has put increasing pressure on both low-tech and high-tech production in the European Union.

---

4   Overproduction is an accumulation of commodities and capital beyond the consumption capability of society.

Cambridge Econometrics (2011) has shown that if we include Brazil, India and China within the range of countries considered as competitors, the scale of deterioration of EU competitiveness in manufacturing appears to be even bigger. These processes affect all EU-15 countries, the Southern member states in particular, which are stuck at a middle level of technology and increasingly compete with emerging markets. Foreign direct investment (FDI) flows from the EU-15, moreover, are shifting to non-EU emerging markets. According to the UN Conference on Trade and Development (UNCTAD), for the first time in 2010 developing economies absorbed close to half of global FDI flows, in both production and research and development. A consolidation of global production networks has been registered, and also the growth of South–South trade.

These processes help to explain the uneven effects of the crisis in Western Europe. According to Eurofound, between 2008 and 2013 over 4.5 million industrial jobs have been lost in Europe and production levels are more than 12 per cent below the pre-crisis levels. The situation is highly differentiated between sectors and between member states. In 2013, general unemployment levels within the European Union showed unprecedented inter-country differences: from 5.4 per cent in Germany to 27 per cent in Spain and Greece. In the last three years, real wages only nominally increased in Germany, while they declined by more than 3 per cent in Italy and the United Kingdom, by almost 7 per cent in Portugal and Spain, and by 23 per cent in Greece (Schulten, 2013).

Austerity policies aim not only at reducing public debt and government spending as such, but also at supporting competitiveness and profitability by cutting government spending, reducing welfare-related benefits, extending the privatisation process and generalising precarious working relations. This is how governments demonstrate the creditworthiness of states in the eyes of financial capital. The crisis is thus reducing the capacity for social policies to mitigate the effects of the labour market, manifesting trends towards impoverishment and declining real wages that have been in place since the mid-1970s. Indeed, while nearly 25 per cent of the population is now at risk of poverty, material deprivation is rising and in-work poverty is increasing both in Southern member states (9.8 to 15.1 per cent) and in countries where official unemployment is lower, such as Germany and the United Kingdom (7.8 and 9 per cent).[5] When dealing with these data we should always bear in mind that they surely underestimate the real extent of poverty, and its class, gendered and racialised dimensions (see Pradella, 2013).

We can reasonably expect that things will worsen even further in the future. In countries with macro-economic imbalances, in fact, the European Union has developed a new form of wage policy interventionism (Euro Plus Pact, Six Pack), which is leading to an erosion of collective bargaining systems and to a convergence towards the much more strongly enterprise-oriented negotiating structures previously completed in other EU states. And in countries that performed best

---

5   Source: Eurostat.

in preserving employment, this is also shifting into the precarious labour market. This is the case in the United Kingdom, even though the proportion of fixed contracts there is lower than in the other Western European countries, probably since 'permanent' workers in the United Kingdom enjoy far less job security. The Liberal–Conservative coalition government's reductions of labour market regulations, welfare spending and public services, moreover, are going to worsen poverty in the country.

In Germany, the agreement by the Grand Coalition on a national minimum wage indicates how low pay has become a crucial political issue. Yet it is doubtful whether this will reduce poverty among workers – as in the example of the United Kingdom, where the minimum wage was introduced in 1998. In all countries, moreover, inflation is rising faster than GDP, and the main items driving it upwards have been food, commodity prices and energy, which disproportionally affect low-income households.

Reaffirming Marx's analysis of the function of impoverishment under capitalism, these processes are triggering more intense pressures towards market and workplace discipline, thus further increasing labour exploitation in workplaces. This is contributing to rebalancing the external positions in Eurozone countries: the combined account of Greece, Ireland, Italy, Portugal and Spain narrowed from a deficit of 7 per cent of GDP in 2008 to a deficit of 0.6 per cent at the end of 2012. What is more, in most Western European countries – with the exception of Italy – this has helped to raise profitability, which is however still below its peak in 2007 (see Roberts, 2013). This is the main reason why investment has not resumed. Despite their recovery, moreover, exports do not compensate for the decrease in domestic demand. Although they generate a spiral of depression, austerity policies are not absurd or irrational, but seek to support capital accumulation and profitability.

Fighting Impoverishment

This chapter argues that the global economic crisis is not a temporary aberration that will eventually and peacefully end with the 'old good times' coming back. No, this crisis manifests a structural tendency towards impoverishment, and bears on deep economic and geopolitical dynamics. The crisis is linked to a persistent crisis of profitability and to the growth of new competitors, mainly from emerging countries. In the face of these dynamics, social-democratic strategies – aimed at maintaining a balance between class and national interests – have proved to be completely bankrupt for workers. In the post-war period, despite declining relative wages, the power and mobilisations of organised working classes in Western Europe compelled commitments to full employment, increasing real wages and social rights. In the neoliberal period the social-economic conditions for making these gains have been eroded, leading to 40 years of 'reformisms without reforms' in which even left-wing parties have implemented neoliberal policies and supported Western European imperialism, leading to widespread popular loss of trust in institutional politics and formal democracy.

In the late 1990s and early 2000s, the 'alter-globalisation' protest seemed to represent a moment of convergence between different movements, able to reinforce resistance nationally and internationally. Against the neoliberal mantra 'There is no alternative', the streets of Seattle, Porto Alegre, Genoa and Nairobi proclaimed that a different world was possible. But this convergence did not find an adequate political direction. Influential currents questioned the centrality of the working class in favour of an undefined multitude, and proclaimed the autonomy of the movement from political organisations while maintaining its links with, if not actual subordination to, institutional left-wing parties. The February 2003 mobilisations, when about 10 million people demonstrated in over 60 countries against the aggression on Iraq, represented the peak of the international mass protests, and the beginning of their decline. The movement, in fact, proved to be ill equipped to respond to the 'permanent war' declared by Western imperialism against the people of the Global South. The movement did not pursue a unitary struggle against neoliberalism and imperialism rooted in workplaces and grassroots activism. The lack of real solidarity with people resisting imperialism and with immigrant workers facing increasing racism and Islamophobia weakened the movement, while its eventual involvement in mainstream politics had catastrophic effects on it.

The economic crisis erupted at this moment of decline of the alter-globalisation movement, but has laid the basis for the emergence of a potentially stronger movement rooted in workplace resistance. Especially in the Western European countries hit most by the crisis, working class, public sector and unemployed workers have taken up the struggle. Drawing inspiration also from the Arab uprisings which started to occur at this time, labour and social movements developed outside the established trade union structures, such as the Indignados (or M-15 movement) in Spain, or in complex dialogue with unions, as in Greece and Portugal. In the majority of Northern countries, however, the crisis has not led to any significant response on behalf of the working class. This is certainly owing partly to the uneven impact of the crisis in Western Europe, and also to the internal divisions of the working class – especially along national, gender and employment status lines – and the shortcomings of its main trade union and political organisations. The 2005 banlieu rebellions in France, echoed in the clashes during the 2010 general strike against the pension reform, and the 2011 riots in the United Kingdom show that social discontent against neoliberalism and state racism increasingly erupts outside the main unions.

Up to now, however, not even the powerful reaction of Greek workers – with more than 25 general strikes, hundreds of demonstrations, mobilisations, occupations and a huge social movement – has been able to stop the devastating effects of crisis. The day of European trade-union mobilisation in November 2012 remained confined within Southern Europe and did not lead to more systematic coordination. European trade union bureaucracies appealed to the 'sense of civic responsibility' of the Troika (the European Commission, the European Central Bank and the IMF), asking it to reconsider its policies. The few initiatives for bargaining coordination at the EU level and for international actions have been largely unsuccessful. Not even the European radical left is sufficiently aware of the systemic and international character of the crisis, and of the necessary response to it (see Wigger and Horn, Chapter 22). Debates within the left have tended to focus around leaving the Eurozone or not, while the rise of Syriza in Greece has renewed debates around building a governmental alternative, channelling the movement into an alleged realist strategy of renegotiating austerity and limiting impoverishment. In times of crisis such as the present one, the prospect of assuming government without a programme for a radical break with capitalism leads to moderation and retreats, dispersing the potential for struggle existing among workers, and dangerously, leaving room to the far right. The results of the European elections in May 2014 are a proof of this danger.

The point is that reformist and neo-Keynesian agendas cannot offer any realistic and progressive alternative to the crisis. The crisis, in fact, is exposing the structural antagonisms of capitalism and the link between processes of impoverishment in the North and South. The labour and social movements that have emerged in Western Europe against the crisis have shown the necessity, and the possibility, of breaking down divisions within the working class and developing alternative forms of power to institutional politics. In order to advance in these struggles, and break the vicious circle of downward competition opened up by neoliberal capitalism, workers need to oppose the logic of competitiveness and question the very origin of their impoverishment, namely capitalist production relations. International solidarity is the most powerful weapon they have in their hands. By creating organisations that are equal in geographical scope to those of capital, workers can actualise their increasing potential power at the point of production. Despite its fragmentation, the working class has never been as numerous as it is today. Since mechanisation makes capital more and more dependent on the exploitation of living labour, moreover, the more globalised the networks of production, the wider and stronger is the potential of disruptions (Silver, 2005).

An international organisation also strengthens the working class at the national level and reinforces its demands on governments. The rejection of the logic of competitiveness enhances and substantiates processes of solidarity-building between immigrant and native-born, precarious and less precarious, unemployed and employed, male and female workers. An important step in this direction is the demand for a general reduction in working hours and workloads for the same pay, and the fight against unemployment. Equally urgent are the abrogation of the racist legislation against immigrant workers that facilitates their super-exploitation; the fight against state racism and Islamophobia; the opposition to gender discrimination and women's oppression; the struggle for the defence of the public sector and social benefits, and for a programme of public works. All this has to be funded by the capitalist class and the state, and can be achieved only by rejecting the payment of the national debt and by opposing imperialism.

As struggles in the Global South have inspired struggles in Western Europe, the reinforcement of struggles in Western Europe can strengthen struggles elsewhere and further weaken Western European imperialism, fostering a process of international class recomposition. The fate of workers is also, and above all, linked by an enormous potential for struggle of a growing global working class – an alternative in the making.

Select Bibliography

Basso, P. (2003) *Modern Times, Ancient Hours: Working Lives in the Twenty-first Century.* London and New York: Verso.

Bush, R. (2007) *Poverty and Neoliberalism: Persistence and Reproduction in the Global South.* London and Ann Arbor, Mi.: Pluto Press.

Cambridge Econometrics (2011) *Study on the Competitiveness of European Industry in the Globalisation Era: Final Report.* Cambridge.

Marx, K. (1996) [1867] *Capital,* Vol. I (*Collected Works,* Vol. 35). London: Lawrence & Wishart.

Pradella, L. (2010) *L'attualità del 'Capitale': Accumulazione e impoverimento nel capitalismo globale* [The current relevance of Marx's *Capital*: accumulation and impoverishment in global capitalism]. Padua: Il Poligrafo.

Pradella, L. (2013) 'The working poor in Western Europe: a global political economy perspective', unpublished manuscript.

Roberts, M. (2013) 'Profitability, the euro crisis and Icelandic myths', March 27. Available at: thenextrecession.wordpress.com

Schulten, T. (2013) 'Wages and the euro crisis', paper presented at the ILERA European Conference, Amsterdam.

Silver, B. (2005) *Forces of Labor: Workers' Movements and Globalization since 1870s.* Cambridge: Cambridge University Press.

CHAPTER THREE

Banking on Alternatives to Neoliberal Development

Thomas Marois

It is a far from widely shared proposition that banks should have anything to do with any alternative to neoliberalism in the developing world, let alone facilitate any substantive break with capitalism's social relations of power, production and oppression. This is despite 25 per cent of all financial institutions globally remaining state-owned (and hence potentially more open to democratic control) and despite banks continuing to play a central role in developing and emerging capitalist societies. There has been a near systemic neglect of banking and financial alternatives in the field of development, most strikingly among radicals. Many scholars, activists, unions and social forces that take the question of alternative development seriously focus on workers' control of the productive apparatus. Yet neither in historical practice nor in theory is there much basis for this financial blind spot. From the experiences and experiments of 'less-than-liberal-capitalist' banking systems in societies as diverse as China, Cuba, Vietnam and Venezuela to the analytical works of Marxists like Rudolf Hilferding, V. I. Lenin, Makoto Itoh and Costas Lapavitsas, banking systems not fully subordinated to profit and competitive imperatives have been understood as integral to potentially socialist projects.

It is time to revive this debate, to unearth actually existing potential alternatives, and to strategise the anti-capitalist role that banking and finance can serve in alternative development. To this end this chapter seeks to make a modest contribution. It does so by suggesting that the struggle for the democratised control of banks is a necessary, if not sufficient, condition for any substantive anti-capitalist break with neoliberal financial capitalism. I argue this by first exploring what financial capital looks like in relation to development today, thus setting the basis of why finance must be confronted in any strategy of change. Second, I consider what needs to be done by drawing on some past and present examples suggestive of alternative democratic and sustainable banking alternatives. This is followed by a brief conclusion.

The Current Situation of Finance in Development

Speaking of developmental alternatives in banking and finance can be voluntaristic if prevailing structural features are not recognised. For present purposes three features stand out: the quantitative significance of *financial capital* (defined as both money capital and the institutions money capitalists control) to global capitalism, the centrality of *developing and emerging capitalisms* to world market stability, and the fact that *recurrent crises* have reinforced rather than undermined the power of financial capital.

First, for over three decades flows of money capital have grown quantitatively and reached an increasingly important position in the neoliberal world market. This rise occurred out of the capitalist crises of the 1970s. Private firms everywhere were suffering from waning profitability and the mounting power of organised labour. In response, neoliberal advocates challenged the material foundations of post-war working class power, including state-owned enterprises, public services and unionisation as well as hitherto stricter restrictions on international flows of capital. The opening of the public sector and international borders gave rise to unprecedented opportunities for new private investment. As one indicator (others follow below), the global supervisory institution and sort of 'bank of central bankers', the Bank for International Settlements (BIS), reports that the daily turnover of global foreign exchange (that is, the conversion of one currency into another), which had topped a record US$1.5 trillion in the late 1990s, was just shy of $4 trillion by 2010. Economist James Crotty of the Political Economy Research Institute reports that during this same time period, the financial share of corporate profits (that is, 'who benefits' from new financial opportunities) increased fourfold, or from 10 per cent in the 1980s to 40 per cent in the new millennium.

The quantitative expansion of the financial world market has been materially and institutionally supported by powerful international financial institutions (IFIs) such as the International Monetary Fund (IMF), World Bank and BIS, which are themselves institutions dependent on the support of the world's advanced capitalist states. Chief among all, the US Treasury has authored this financial expansion, not least through its role as a global lender of last resort willing to provide public resources to overcome financial crises, maintain open world markets, and underwrite continued US financial supremacy. The financial world market, while composed of ever-greater flows of capital, is therefore also defined by imperial relations and a hierarchy of states: the United States sits at the top followed by other advanced capitalisms, the rising powerhouse China, other important emerging capitalisms, and finally the rest of the world. In development studies, then, when we speak of financing development we must account for these societies' subordinate position within the hierarchy of states.

Second, despite being subordinate, developing and emerging capitalisms have assumed greater importance in and responsibility for protecting the financial world market. Since the 1980s neoliberal advocates (domestic capital and technocrats in collaboration with foreign capital and IFIs) have championed pro-capital and market-oriented political and economic restructuring within emerging capitalisms. Consequently, these societies have become more important profit-making destinations for financial capital.[1] Between 1980 and 2010, for example, private financial flows to emerging and developing capitalisms have grown from about $15 billion to over $600 billion. Portfolio flows, the most volatile 'hot money' flows, likewise grew from negative $1.25 billion to over $240 billion. Governing elites and domestic capitalists in developing and emerging capitalisms have led a corresponding shift to debt-led growth strategies: external debt increased nearly ten-fold or from nearly $570 billion in 1980 to nearly $5.5 trillion in 2010. The cost of external debt servicing (tantamount to a transfer of value from South to North through interest payments) has grown from $89.4 billion in 1980 to $1.74 trillion in 2010.

In the wake of the 2008–09 global crisis and with the quantitative easing programmes of the United States and the United Kingdom, money capital flowed into the emerging capitalisms where the cheap US credits could be invested at much higher rates of return. This 'carry trade' has led to the overindebtedness of domestic corporations – debts that carry huge exchange rate risks. Emerging capitalist governments, too, remain heavily indebted to foreign finance.

In many cases after the crisis the stimulus packages and corporate tax cuts did nothing to relieve public debt burdens. As quantitative easing tapered into 2014, foreign capital has also begun to slow financial flows to the emerging capitalisms, with highly destabilising effects. This reflects a typical pattern of North to South boom/bust funding since the 1990s. To help offset the damaging financial crises that have been increasingly recurrent since the 1990s, developing country governments have built up colossal war chests of foreign reserves as a form of self-insurance, which state authorities use at times of financial threats to appease globally mobile capital. The IMF reports that in emerging and developing countries, foreign reserves grew from about $162 billion in 1980 to about $7.4 trillion in 2012. The IMF too has increased its available resources to aid crisis and recovery by doubling country quotas from about $358 billion to about $715 billion in 2011. The South is inextricably linked to patterns of global accumulation and to the reproduction of global capitalism.

The last three decades of financial restructuring have also led towards the privatisation of state-owned banks alongside the concentration and centralisation of bank capital in fewer and larger institutions in the developing world. Whereas in the 1970s state ownership of banks in developing countries was commonly in the 60 to 70 per cent range, this has fallen to between 20 and 40 per cent. Whereas in the post-war period of state-led development, the banking sector would have dozens of banks that operated locally, regionally and at the national level, today banks have centralised operations into larger and more powerful units, with a few

---

1   The data that follow are drawn from IMF online, World Economic Outlook (2012) and International Financial Statistics (2013).

large and increasingly foreign banks controlling the lion's share of domestic assets. In 2012 the five largest global banks (Deutsche Bank, Mitsubishi UFJ Financial Group, the state-owned Industrial & Commercial Bank of China, HSBC Holdings, and Barclays) collectively controlled over $13.6 trillion in assets, which is nearly double the annual gross domestic product (GDP) of China and just shy of total US GDP. The banks' chief executive officers (CEOs) see developing countries as extremely lucrative spaces of accumulation.

None of this global explosion would have been possible without the restructuring and strengthening of the state's financial apparatus in emerging capitalisms to privilege market-oriented imperatives (Marois, 2012). Notably, the treasury has assumed a place of prominence in the state apparatus. Through the state treasury, governing elites and neoliberal technocrats have centralised and taken control of state power through financial means. At the same time, neoliberal advocates have restructured developing country central banks (the bank of domestic banks). Neoliberals have forced through so-called central bank independence to ensure price stability and inflation targeting, which institutionally elevates the needs of financial capital over all other developmental considerations – from employment to planned investment – and insulates the central bank from democratic input. Central bank and governing authorities subsequently created other new state institutions to further support financial accumulation, including for example capital market boards, bank insurance funds, and specialised banking and financial regulatory institutions. The roles and responsibilities of these vary from case to case depending on the specific division of labour between the central bank, treasury and other governing institutions. Yet in most cases full or near complete independence from popular, let alone governmental demands, is the essential ingredient of international financial credibility nowadays.

Further, these state financial institutions actively sign memorandums of understanding with other countries' bank regulators enabling the interpenetration of bank capital and cross-border regulation premised on international best practices (typically modelled after US and European standards). The point is that the quantitative growth in the financial world market and prosperity of financial capital have not transcended the state apparatus. Instead, financial capital has ascended in power alongside and thanks to more muscular state financial apparatuses in both the advanced and emerging capitalisms.

Third, contrary to what we might expect, the increasingly recurrent and costly financial crises over the last three decades have reinforced rather than reversed the power of financial capital globally. In Mexico the 1994–95 crisis cost 20 per cent of GDP, Brazil's 1994 crisis cost 13 per cent, Thailand's 1997 crisis cost 44 per cent, Russia's 1998 crisis 6 per cent, Argentina's 2001 crisis 10 per cent, and Turkey's 2001 crisis 30 per cent. These are but the tip of the iceberg, with IMF researchers recording more than 120 banking crises globally since 1980. On average (and before the Great Recession) the IMF reports that these crises cost just over 13 per cent of GDP to rescue and resolve, with only about 18 per cent of these public costs ever being recovered. Because state authorities socialise the costs of financial crisis and recovery through the state apparatus, which results in austerity measures and taxes being diverted to financial capital, the costs of crisis and recovery are borne disproportionately by the general working populace, to the benefit of financial capital.

Yet far from sparking an academic rethink or substantive political break in neoliberalism, such crises have led developing country state authorities to further bolster the financial state apparatus by building new institutions and accumulating more foreign reserves, as noted. This has been absolutely vital to the survival of the financial world market, as responsibility for systemic persistence is diffused internationally as developing country authorities take responsibility for protecting their corner of the world market. Domestically, authorities also took charge of rationalising the failed financial sectors around new market imperatives and so-called international best practices, ensuring, as always, creditworthiness and their attractiveness as an investment destination.

This also holds true in the advanced capitalisms. Since the unfolding of the US-based subprime crisis, state authorities in advanced capitalisms (notably the United States) have mobilised some $13 trillion to resurrect the global financial system and created the new Financial Stability Board in 2009. Yet no substantive structural changes have been demanded from financial capital. Instead we have entered the 'age of austerity' wherein public resources are gutted and sovereign debt limits abandoned to ensure financial capital endures despite worsening global inequality and growing numbers of desperately poor and overworked people.

Consequently, neoliberalism – defined in class terms as capital's systematic attack on the capacity of organised labour and the popular classes to resist market-oriented structural adjustment since the 1980s – persists today. Since the 1990s neoliberalism has taken on an increasingly finance-led form, as financial capitalists have attained the capacity to institutionally push the costs of financial crises onto the state apparatus and, by extension, onto workers in general. This, as I argue elsewhere, suggests we have entered into a phase of capital accumulation defined by the fusion of the interests of domestic and foreign financial capital in the state apparatus, as the institutionalised priorities and overarching social logic guiding the actions of state managers and government elites, often to the detriment of labour (Marois, 2012). The quantitative rise in financial flows, the importance of emerging capitalisms to the financial world market, and that crises have deepened not weakened finance capitalism illustrate some of the barriers to be faced.

What Has Been Done, What Is To Be Done? Banking on Alternatives

The power of financial capital simply cannot be avoided. Moreover, the centrality of banking and the financial system to all aspects of capitalist accumulation, exchange relations and contemporary social reproduction means that changes here will affect all workers everywhere. Thus, the struggle for democratised social control over banking and finance has the unique potential to connect all resistances to neoliberalism and transcend capitalism. This begins by overcoming immediate working class barriers. The transition to neoliberalism is replete with the financial conditionalities of loans, taken to bridge bouts of instability, aimed at undermining the public ethos of public services in preparation for privatisation *cum* accumulation by dispossession.

Continuing struggles to protect public services or to gain and sustain workers' collective control today name the lack of supportive financing as a serious problem. The democratised social control of banking and financing eliminates such barriers posed by the power of private financial capital over society. This immediately raises the question of 'What is to be done?' which is as much a historical and practical question as it is a strategic one. I broach this by illustrating some necessarily imperfect past and present examples of banking alternatives and by highlighting some strategic lessons for collective action.

Bertolt Brecht's play *The Days of the Commune* aptly captures the primordial fears of Europe's bourgeoisie in his character de Ploeuc, the director of the Central Bank of France and sly adversary of the nascent Paris Commune. While energetically defending the sanctity of the Bank's independence to the Communards, behind closed doors, de Ploeuc admits that if the 'vaults are taken', what he understands as the 'nerve centre' of everything, then the 'Communards will have won, whatever else happens'.

Marx, too, well understood from the Paris Commune that the proletariat couldn't simply adopt the capitalist state ready-made for socialist purposes. Rather, what is *objectively* capitalist must be laid to waste and replaced by egalitarian socialist structures crafted (that is, institutionalised) in the interests of the workers. Indeed, this was the stated intent when the Bolsheviks nationalised the private Russian banks in December 1917. It was none other than Lenin who staunchly advocated bank nationalisation, writing that the financial apparatus 'must not, and should not, be smashed' but be '*subordinated* to the proletarian Soviets'. He continues:

> Capitalism has created an accounting apparatus in the shape of the banks ....
> *Without big banks socialism would be impossible.* The big banks *are* the 'state apparatus' which we need to bring about socialism, and which we *take ready-made* from capitalism; our task here is merely to *lop off* what *capitalistically mutilates* this excellent apparatus, to make it *even bigger*, even more democratic, even more comprehensive. Quantity will be transformed into quality.
> (Lenin, 1977 [1917]: 106; emphasis in original)

Lenin, following Hilferding, did not equate banks with capital itself. Banks are posed as rather more historically malleable institutions which, should they be politically subordinated, could perform important accounting and regulatory duties in the new workers' economy. In line with Marx, banks were not *objectively* capitalist but historically and politically *subjected* to capitalist imperatives. This formulation opens bank operations up to historical rather than transhistorical determinations.

There are also historical precedents that illustrate alternative logics to what predominates now. Yet in presenting these I would caution that these examples are very much illustrative of specific cases requiring further in-depth study. I find no benefit in suggesting that any of these banks existed outside of the generalised post-war thrust towards capitalism in peripheral societies. As we see, many potential alternatives have become subordinated to neoliberal competitive imperatives, albeit in highly modified ways. Still, recognising the obvious today is not to relinquish the historical potential accorded to 'revolutionary' banking for socialist and anti-imperialist struggles.

There are many variations of alternative banking institutions among developing capitalisms. In its post-National Revolution period of state-led capitalist transition, the first Turkish government (formed out of the defunct Ottoman Empire) created state-owned banks in the 1920s and 1930s with institutionalised social developmental missions attached to, for example, funding agriculture, cooperatives and small traders. These banks were understood as equally anti-imperialist given the Ottoman Empire's experiences with the 'odious' debt administration of the European-owned Ottoman Bank, which had controlled state finances.

Some decades later, the post-revolutionary People's Republic of China (1949) mobilised the People's Bank of China (PBC, est. 1948) to fund communist development plans. The PBC functioned under the Ministry of Finance and was the lone bank in China until 1978. The PBC served as a central bank, collected revenues from other state-owned enterprises (SOEs), and channelled investment funds into different sectors and infrastructure projects.

Around the same time, the Vietnamese were mired in an anti-imperialist war against the French. To help fund the war of resistance the Democratic Republic of Vietnam established the State Bank in 1951. Much like the PBC, the State Bank issued money and managed payment services while providing credits and funds to administer the state budget. With the pushing-out of the French in 1954 the government transformed the State Bank into a funding institution for domestic trade, industry, handicrafts, cooperatives, agriculture, and other SOEs and organisations. After 1959 the post-revolutionary Cuban authorities also nationalised the banks. The February 1961 Law No. 930 then centralised the central banking and commercial banking functions within the Banco Nacional de Cuba. The Socialist Federal Republic of Yugoslavia differed insofar as it initiated a system of competitive worker self-management and banking. At a national level, the National Bank of Yugoslavia employed a system of credit limits and preferential interest rates to promote certain sectors. Yet competition determined much in the allocation of credits to worker cooperatives, undermining many socialist aspirations.

However imperfect, these historically diverse institutional arrangements each pooled domestic money so as to channel resources into developmental priorities in nationally differentiated ways which, if not fully independent, were not fully subordinate to global capitalist and imperialist tendencies. The point is that these banks are suggestive of a socially malleable social content.

There remain potentially important and substantial state-owned banking options in many developing and emerging capitalisms. For example, the World Bank reported in 2010 that Argentina and Brazil had 44 per cent, Costa Rica 54 per cent, and Venezuela over 33 per cent of bank assets under state control.[2] Outside of Latin America, Russia reported 41 per cent, Turkey nearly 32 per cent, Egypt around 50 per cent, and Indonesia over 38 per cent state-owned. In Africa, Sierra Leone state bank ownership is nearly 38 per cent and in Burundi it is nearly 49 per cent. In India and China more than 75 per cent of all bank assets are majority state controlled. This is only a sample of what quantitatively exists, which illustrates no lack of potential state banking alternatives despite three decades of neoliberalism.

To be sure, the institutional frameworks, material foundations, daily operations and normative orientations vary dramatically between countries and among banking institutions even within countries. Moreover, all state banks exist within the capitalist and deeply 'financialised' world market today and alongside domestic political priorities, all of which exert structural and conjunctural political limits on each country's governing elites, financial authorities, individual state bank management and frontline workers. This is not to be forgotten or set aside. Yet radical scholars have largely bypassed such a potentially powerful material and institutional basis of social power. Resist healthcare privatisation, yes! Push back against the sell-off of water, a must! The fate of state banks and bank workers? Relative to their central location in capitalist accumulation and development processes, surprisingly little has been said.[3]

It is worth pausing to explore some contemporary variations among state-owned banks in emerging capitalisms. Since the late 1970s the Chinese Communist Party initiated market-oriented changes in its banking sector. While these were initially framed as strengthening socialism, over time social forces in the Communist Party have mobilised the state banks to support China's particular capitalist transformation. This has entailed creating a number of massive, more specialised banks like the Agricultural Bank of China, the China Construction Bank, the Bank of China, and the Industrial and Commercial Bank of China. The opening of China's new specialised banks meant SOEs would finance operations through retained earnings and from the state banks directly, with authorities

---

2   State control will vary in each case, with some being fully state-owned and others majority state-owned but with private and foreign share participations.

3   For example, radical left assessments of privatisation and development typically do not include any discussion of state bank privatisations (for example, Bayliss and Fine, 2008; McDonald and Ruiters, 2012). Additionally, while Marxists have called for some form of bank nationalisation, especially since the 2008–09 crisis, this is often made at the level of general strategy (Harvey, 2010; Albo, 2012). With the exception of Marois (2012), it is remarkable that there are practically no contemporary case studies of state banks or bank workers undertaken within the Marxian tradition.

reasoning that repayable interest charges would encourage greater efficiency in the factories. In 1994 the authorities created three more specialised banks, the Agricultural Development Bank of China, the China Development Bank and the Export-Import Bank of China, to further fund market development. Many of China's state banks have now been opened to foreign ownership participations but the state retains majority control. This has brought newly institutionalised profit and efficiency imperatives such that these state banks act increasingly as if they were private profit-seeking banks.

Brazil has had a rather different, and initially decentralised, experience with state-owned banks. For example, in 1990 there were some 35 different state (provincial) publicly owned banks. Two decades later only a few large nationwide state banks remain alongside five smaller ones. The large state-owned commercial banks, including the Banco do Brasil (est. 1808), the Caixa Econômica Federal (est. 1861), and the Banco do Estado do Rio Grande do Sul (Banrisul, est. 1928), maintain extensive retail commercial operations but also provide federal government services such as social benefit and unemployment payments. The large Brazilian development bank, Banco Nacional de Desenvolvimento Economico e Social (BNDES, est. 1952) has gone through different operational phases, from initially promoting national capitalist development to being subsumed under military rule after 1964, to facilitating privatisation and neoliberal transformation after the mid-1980s (as Mexican authorities did with its nationalised banks after 1982), to supporting new developmentalism since 2003.

Venezuela offers a sharper example of social forces trying to carve an alternative out of current circumstances (albeit still subject to capitalist imperatives). On 31 July 2008, the Chavez government nationalised the Bank of Venezuela from the Spanish-owned Santander Group. Rather than rescuing the banks to rescue capitalism (the form advocated by the World Bank), the political intent was to subordinate the once private bank's operations to national developmental strategies and to strengthen the Bolivarian revolutionary process by bolstering the public financial sector. Shortly thereafter a corruption scandal in late 2008 led the government to extend state ownership, with the liquidation and takeover of eight smaller private banks. Four of these were merged into the state-owned bank Banfoandes to craft a new, powerful, state investment bank, the Banco Bicentario (controlling about 20 per cent of deposits). The bank now supports alternative productive processes, and in particular more accessible housing credits. The state banks also fund the central government budgeting process by purchasing state bonds, and have institutionalised requirements to lend to the public sector. Social and political forces understand the government's move into banking as necessary to mitigate the power of financial capital in Venezuela and as a way to mobilise domestic resources in the service of the Bolivarian revolutionary process.

Several points need to be drawn out here. First, while diverse and often contradictory, there are historical and contemporary examples of sufficiently anti-imperialist and/or anti-neoliberal alternative banking arrangements to lay to rest the popular myths that (a) there are no alternatives to private banks and (b) socialism doesn't need banks. Second, leftist social forces should take note that there remains substantial material and institutional state banking capacity today. This potential stronghold should not be lightly relinquished. Third, and contrary to most heterodox accounts, state bank ownership can by no means be taken as a sufficient condition in determining whether a state bank offers an alternative to neoliberalism. State-owned banks can and do act as if they were private profit-seeking entities, given the neoliberal will to do so. That is, state banks have no transcendental logic outside of prevailing economic and political imperatives. As both a methodological and strategic issue, state banks are historically specific institutions of prevailing class and power relations, and are thus open to politically organised change. Hilferding made this point in his seminal work *Finance Capital* (2006 [1910]).

We must remember that bank workers are not, by default, antagonistic to socialist forces. Many of these working people struggle under the neoliberal intensification of labour, flexibilisation, privatisation and so on. Not recognising a potential ally, and one located in the most powerful economic sector, is a strategic mistake. Indeed, there are notable, if sporadic, examples of bank workers collectively organising and mobilising within emerging capitalisms and elsewhere. For example in Turkey, where bank workers lack the legal right to strike, many state bank workers resisted closures and privatisations during the 2000–01 banking crisis through work-to-rule actions and even by occupying a state bank's headquarters. More recently in 2013, Bank-Sen, a radical bank workers' union, launched an anti-privatisation campaign to halt the further sell-off of Turkey's state banks. Other countries have more militant bank worker unions. Over the last decade Brazilian bank workers have repeatedly shut down state and private banks, most recently in September 2011 and September 2012, in defence of decent wages and working conditions. Argentinean bank workers followed suit and struck in December 2012.

Europe has also witnessed a rise in bank worker activism. In Greece in response to forced austerity and the restructuring of their banks, bank workers held strikes in mid-2012. Cypriot bank workers held a strike in April 2013, fearing the impact of their banking crisis on jobs and pensions. During this same time Spain saw its first strike by bank workers (in a newly nationalised bank) since the 1990s. Still, perhaps the most militant of all are the Indian bank worker unions. Following a number of strikes in recent years, around 1 million bank workers walked out of their workplaces for two days in February 2013, effectively shutting down the country's banking sector. What these examples show is that bank workers can and do assert their collective rights and will.

Drawing on this analysis, but also on recent studies identifying diverse public alternatives to privatisation (see McDonald, Chapter 11) and my own research, I see six necessary if not sufficient strategies for alternative banking and the breaking of neoliberalism:

- The posing of radically democratised social banking as a complex and integral process that must neither necessarily precede nor follow broader strategies of socialist transformation.

- The organisation of workers within banks (both state and private): any substantive change will have to have popular support from within the banks rather than simply being imposed top-down.
- The substantive linking of bank workers to other private and public sector workers' unions as well as to non-governmental organisations and civil society: perhaps more than in any other sector, the successful transformation of banking will depend on broad-based social support and solidarity.
- The move towards a coordinated, multi-sector resistance against all bank privatisations understood as a common, if intermediate, socialist goal.
- The strategising of resistance to privatisation beyond merely legislative or constitutional-based strategies to one that systematically pushes for socialised banking foundations.
- The collective formulation of end goals that transcend banking as a public utility under government control, Rather, a progressive financial system must be formally subordinated to democratic and collective ownership in the pursuit of social developmental goals shaped by bank workers in collaboration with other collective sectoral demands.

Conclusion

Change, in the context of moving beyond neoliberal capitalism, must involve a collective struggle to dispossess financial capital of its accumulated power, wealth and institutions. Change must also involve a concurrent popular restructuring process of the banking and financial apparatus operations around socially efficient, equitable and solidaristic foundations. In this understanding I accept, not uncritically or unrealistically, that banks are needed to effectively manage social resources and facilitate socialist social reproduction. To this end the banks themselves will need to be reconfigured as semi-autonomous worker collectives. Such a strategy of transformation, in the short term, promises relief from contemporary imperial financial relations perpetuated through the US, EU, IMF and World Bank nexus of material and institutional financial power.

In the long term, alternative banking provides extra-market means to reverse all forms of historic inequalities generated by capitalist profit and competitive imperatives. This includes having the capacity to reverse the transferring of wealth from the poor rural areas to the already wealthy urban centre, to effectively fund green and gendered strategies of social development, and to support democratic developmental aspirations without fear of reprisal from financial capital. All this, as a matter of necessity, must be articulated within an internationalist solidarity framework for facilitating trade and financial relations among socialist societies.

Still, as we know, people make history but never in the conditions of their own choosing. The conditions we must face today include the overwhelming power of financial capital. There are nodes, pockets, and potentially significant material and institutional bases for progressive social developmental alternatives to private banking and financial capitalism. But these nodes have so far been too isolated and too neglected. There is an urgent need to place the struggle over banking and the agency of bank workers at the heart of anti-neoliberal, anti-capitalist, and anti-imperialist strategies. This will mean, in addition to preserving existing public banks, directly confronting financial capital, taking democratic control of the banking institutions and resources they control, and reorienting these to democratic and collective interests. Clearly any such strategy of radical change must be prepared for the savage responses of financial capital to any remotely popular or democratic challenge. The enormity of this challenge only substantiates its necessity.

Select Bibliography

Albo, G. (2012) 'The crisis and economic alternatives', in L. Panitch, G. Albo and V. Chibber (eds), *Socialist Register 2013: The Question of Strategy*. Pontypool, Wales: Merlin Press.

Bayliss, K. and Fine, B. (eds) (2008) *Privatization and Alternative Public Sector Reform in Sub-Saharan Africa: Delivering on Electricity and Water*. New York: Palgrave Macmillan.

Harvey, D. (2010) *The Enigma of Capital and the Crises of Capitalism*. London: Profile.

Hilferding, R. (2006) [1910] *Finance Capital: A Study of the Latest Phase of Capitalist Development*. London: Routledge.

Itoh, M. and Lapavitsas, C. (1999) *Political Economy of Money and Finance*. New York: St. Martin's Press.

Lenin, V. I. (1977) [1917] 'Can the Bolsheviks retain state power?' in *Collected Works*, Vol. 26, Sept. 1917–Feb. 1918. Moscow: Progress. Trans. Y. Sdobnikov and G. Hanna, ed. G. Hanna. Accessed digital reprint provided by 'From Marx to Mao' (2011).

Marois, T. (2012) *States, Banks, and Crisis: Emerging Finance Capitalism in Mexico and Turkey*. Cheltenham, Glos.: Edward Elgar.

McDonald, D. A. and Ruiters, G. (eds) (2012) *Alternatives to Privatization: Public Options for Essential Services in the Global South*. Cape Town: HSRC Press.

CHAPTER FOUR

The Political Economy of Development: Statism or Marxism?

Benjamin Selwyn

The central objective of development theory and practice is to find ways to alleviate the conditions of the world's poor. Neoliberalism has failed in this regard. For many students of development, statist political economy (SPE) is the natural and obvious alternative to neoliberalism. The rise of formerly peripheral powers, in particular China, increases the attraction of statist over free market models of development.

This chapter discusses the merits and demerits of SPE. Key thinkers in the SPE tradition include Ha-Joon Chang, Robert Wade, Alice Amsden, Atul Kohli, Eric Reinert and Mehdi Shaffaedin. These writers have shown how, from the 1960s onwards, the East Asian states of South Korea and Taiwan, and now increasingly China, have been able to transform themselves from predominantly poor, agricultural economies to rich industrialised economies. These thinkers are indebted to Friedrich List; his *National System of Political Economy*, first published in 1841, is widely considered to represent the founding text of SPE. List's infant industry argument is represented in much contemporary development studies as constituting an anti-imperialist, pro-poor strategy that enables nations of the Global South to pursue meaningful socio-economic development. For example, according to Ha-Joon Chang, most countries will be better off in the long run with a more activist development strategy than with the bankrupt Washington orthodoxy.

Despite the attractions of SPE to opponents of neoliberalism, this chapter argues that List's political economy, and SPE more generally, does not represent a genuine human developmental alternative to neoliberalism, because it rests upon and requires the repression and exploitation of labour. This represents a fundamental contradiction within SPE – that while it advocates state actions to achieve economic growth and catch-up development to improve the lot of the poor, doing so requires the exploitation and repression of the latter.

This chapter also argues that Marxism provides an alternative, political economy of development – the political economy of labour – which holds that the uplifting and development of the poor – from poverty elimination, to improvements in human development indicators (health, life expectancy, literacy), to participation in, influence and control within and over the economy and the democratic process – must be achieved by their own means. This conception of development prevents us falling into the contradiction where the elite minority advocate the repression and exploitation of the majority in the name of the latter's benefits.

The fundamental differences between SPE and the political economy of labour are that the former represents a top-down political economy, in which state authorities in conjunction with capitalist entrepreneurs are identified as key developmental actors and their policies are to be achieved through manipulating labouring classes, with the latter denied any developmental role apart from the provision of their labour power as a cheap commodity input. The latter represents a bottom-up political economy, in which labouring classes are the key developmental actors, and their actions take the form of struggles against capitalist classes and states. SPE has historically been associated with imperialist expansion, while the political economy of labour requires anti-imperialist and internationalist solidarity between labouring classes of different countries. While SPE seeks to establish competitive capitalist economies under the auspices of strong, centralised national states, the political economy of labour seeks to win developmental gains for labouring classes under capitalism, while generating the movements and institutions capable of transcending capitalism nationally and internationally.

Following this introduction, I discuss Friedrich List's work and then outline the contemporary application of his ideas. I conclude with first a critique of SPE and then an alternative, rooted in Marx's conception of the political economy of labour.

Friedrich List and the Foundations of Statist Political Economy

Friedrich List was writing at a time when Britain's industrial revolution was enabling its capitalist class to dominate world markets. He was acutely aware that countries or regions (such as his own German confederation of states) that did not employ protective counter-measures would experience industrial decimation at the hands of more competitive British industrial exports. He formulated the infant industry argument, based on historical cases, to guide economically backward countries as they sought to catch up with economically advanced countries. Mehdi Shafaeddin notes how List's infant industry argument 'has been the basis of most new trade theories for the industrialisation of developing countries ... no country has developed its industrial base without resorting to infant industry protection' (2005: 42).

List characterised the then (and now) dominant conception of free trade (grounded in the theory of comparative advantage) as based on double standards. For example, he accused Britain of attempting to 'kick away the ladder' from those attempting to emulate it in order to preserve its role as sole producer of high value manufactures:

> It is a vulgar rule of prudence for him [sic] who has reached the pinnacle of power to cast down the ladder by which he mounted, that others may not follow .... A nation which by protective duties and maritime restrictions has built up a manufacturing industry and a merchant marine to such a point of strength and power as not to fear the competition of any other, can pursue no safer policy than to *thrust aside the means of elevation*, to preach to other nations the advantages of free trade.
>
> (List, 1856 [1841]: 440; emphasis added)

In contrast with free trade, List advocated infant industry promotion, in which states in economically backward countries shield their firms from competitors, while providing them with direct assistance (ranging from investment and funding provision to research and development – R&D) in order to establish a strong national economic system that can eventually compete successfully in international markets.

Central to the infant industry strategy is List's conception of productive power. He argued that:

> The causes of wealth are quite a different thing from wealth itself. An individual may possess wealth, that is, exchangeable values; but if he [sic] is not able to produce more values than he consumes, he will be impoverished. An individual may be poor, but if he can produce more than he consumes, he may grow rich.
>
> (List, 1856 [1841]: 208)

For List, the ability of states to engender productive power enables them to participate in world trade on a value-adding basis, through producing goods that embody relatively high levels of skills and command relatively high prices on international markets.

Productive power comprises three types of capital: natural, material and mental. The first comprises land, sea, rivers and mineral resources. The second comprises all objects that are used directly or indirectly in the production process, such as raw materials and machines. The third comprises skills, training, enterprises, industry and government. The creation of wealth is the outcome of the interaction between these three types of capital within a nation, leading to enhanced productive power. In particular, List prioritised mental (in today's terms 'human') capital formation as a key component of states' attempts at catching up with their more advanced competitors. The creation of a skilled workforce and managerial cadre was central to the production of higher-value goods. List's focus on mental/human capital was complemented by an analysis of the state's role in coordinating different economic sectors (for example industry and agriculture) in order to enhance the country's productive power. Infant industry protection required an adequate system of infrastructure, communication and transport. This technical coordination was to be complemented by an ideological 'coordination' designed to pull a country's population behind the development project.

SPE: Contemporary Applications

Ha-Joon Chang's *Kicking Away the Ladder: Development Strategy in Historical Perspective* (2002) does much to popularise List's political economy. He shows how, in order to accelerate development, developed countries used the same infant industry strategies that they now deny to today's developing countries. Robert Wade, Chang and Alice Amsden provide empirical accounts of how the East Asian states of Japan, South Korea and Taiwan purposively managed and facilitated industrialisation and economic catch-up. They demonstrate how they tightly managed foreign trade and foreign direct investment, and how they regulated domestic firms – subjecting them to performance requirements as well as providing supportive subsidies.

These states implemented sectoral upgrading programmes using technology transfer, facilitated by well-educated managerial cadres, based on the shop floor and in R&D agencies, and hence closely coordinating firm requirements with state investments. State authorities used price controls to prevent domestic monopolies from benefiting at the expense of national catch-up objectives. In their accounts, these authors dismantle neoliberal explanations of 'market-friendly' East Asian growth (as argued by the World Bank in its 1993 report). All of these states benefited from preferential incorporation into the United States' imperial structure – with the latter assisting their state authorities in the combatting of internal labour opposition, and through providing generous trade agreements, contracts for the US army in the Vietnam War, and military 'protection' against the Chinese Communist threat.

Derived from their analysis of successful late industrialising countries, Chang and Grabel (2004: 66–188) propose a set of policies that contemporary developing countries could use to facilitate economic catch-up. These include:

- protection of strategic industries to ensure long-term national growth
- prioritising organisational reforms over privatisation
- prioritising the education of the population and specifically the workforce as a means of stimulating intellectual advance (as opposed to supporting rigorous intellectual property rights)
- tying foreign direct investment (FDI) to a national development strategy, rather than allowing it free rein
- subordinating the financial sector to national development needs via, for example, currency and capital controls and state-directed lending
- using monetary policy to pursue growth rather than (as under the contemporary orthodoxy) to reduce inflation.

SPE provides a more plausible comprehension of the strategies necessary for the pursuit of successful late industrialisation than advocates of neoliberalism. However, SPE conceives of workers' labour power as a commodity input to production, to be used to generate as much value as possible at the lowest cost. This can only be achieved through labour repression and exploitation.

In his *State-Directed Development: Political Power and Industrialization in the Global Periphery*, for example, Atul Kohli (2004) explains that disciplining the labour force, through keeping wages down and precluding or at least minimising the political independence of labour organisations, is necessary to successful late industrialisation as it both increases capital's profits, hence enabling further accumulation, and prevents organised working class influence on state expenditures (diverting resources away from capital accumulation). He observes how states such as South Korea successfully combined 'repression and profits' where the former 'was a key component in enabling private investors … to have a ready supply of cheap, "flexible" and disciplined labour' (Kohli, 2004: 13). In a similar vein, Alice Amsden recognises how 'high profits in Korea's mass-production industries have been derived not merely from investments in machinery and modern work methods … but also from the world's longest working week' (1990: 13–14, 18).

These examples of heightened labour exploitation illustrate the uncomfortable disjuncture between the political regimes that SPE aspires to (democratic and liberal) and those they assert are required for late industrialisation (authoritarian). Kohli concludes his study by stating that authoritarian regimes are a necessary component of late industrialisation, and summarises their core characteristics:

> Generally right-wing authoritarian states, they prioritize rapid industrialization as a national goal, are staffed competently, work closely with industrialists, systematically discipline and repress labour, penetrate and control the rural society, and use economic nationalism as a tool of political mobilisation.
>
> (Kohli 2004: 381)

Wade (2004) comes to similar conclusions about the exclusion of labour, albeit with significant reservations. He advocates developing 'corporatist institutions as or before the system is democratized' (2004: 375). The necessity of such institutions is rationalised as follows:

> Inclusion of labour is obviously desirable in principle. But note that if labour exclusion is part of a set of arrangements which generate high-speed growth, workers are protected to some extent by high labour demand. Labour exclusion also gives a government more room to manoeuvre when austerity comes, and that latitude can be used to restore fast growth more quickly.
>
> (Wade, 2004: 376n18)

Note the irony here, of a statist political economist turning to the market as a source of labour protection.

Why does SPE require labour repression and exploitation? Marx answers this question, and provides an alternative, labour-centred conception of the political economy of development.

SPE: A Marxist Critique

Four years after the publication of the *National System*, Marx wrote a rarely commented on draft critique of List's book (first published in Russian in 1971). Marx regarded List as a representative of the rising German bourgeoisie, who as their organic intellectual was inherently antithetical to the German working class. For Marx, List's political economy articulates the ideology of the aspirant German bourgeois who:

> puffs himself up into being the 'nation' in relation to foreign countries and says: I do not submit to the laws of competition ... the German philistine wants the laws of competition ... to lose their power at the ... barriers of his country! He is willing to recognise the power of bourgeois society only insofar as it is in accord with his interests, the interests of his class!
>
> (Marx, 1975 [1845]: 278)

To be realised, these aspirations required protection from more competitive foreign trade, heightened exploitation of labour at home and imperialist expansion. Marx identified how List's ideology of late development required the partial negation of the laws of free-trade capitalist competition (through tariffs and other 'uncompetitive' measures), but only in order for late-developing states to compete profitably and more effectively once such policies had achieved their objectives – of building up an internationally competitive industrial economy. As part of this strategy, List favoured German colonisation of South-Eastern Europe and Central and South America as a means of expanding markets and population from which to generate productive power. Marx characterised List's understanding of relations between German and foreign capital as:

> We German bourgeois do not want to be exploited by the English bourgeois in the way that you German proletarians are exploited by us and that we exploit one another. We do not want to subject ourselves to the same laws of exchange value as those to which we subject you. We do not want any longer to recognise outside the country the economic laws which we recognise inside the country.
>
> (Marx, 1975 [1845]: 278)

The German bourgeoisie needed state authorities to do their work for them because they were too weak to generate the capital to invest in industry in the face of superior competition from British manufacturing. And domestically they existed as subordinate political actors to the landlord class and nobility. They also required state assistance in regulating domestic political relations in their favour, as opposed to the interests of landlords and labourers. The former stood to benefit from integration into the world economy based on principles of comparative advantage, as under such arrangements they would preside over the most productive and valuable sectors of the economy. The latter needed to be 'convinced' that industrial capital represented the 'national interest', rather than a sectional, exploitative class interest.

Acceptance of the economic role of the state in presiding over and (re)producing capitalist social relations required elevating it into an institution representing the 'general interest' of the nation, as opposed to the narrow, sectional interests of manufacturers or capital more generally. Marx noted how the development of manufacturing requires 'making the majority of people in the nations into a "commodity"' (1975: 278) – where workers are reduced to their ability to labour (what Marx calls their labour power) – to be purchased and applied as effectively as possible by capitalists without consideration of, and often through the denial of their broader human needs.

In his conception of productive power, List argued for the need for the development of 'mental capital', entailing industrial training to establish a cadre of skilled workers. But he was deliberately vague as to how this would impact on new industrial working classes. To this Marx responded:

> Under the present system, if a crooked spine, twisted limbs, a one-sided development and strengthening of certain muscles, etc., make you more capable of working (more productive), then your crooked spine, your twisted limbs, your one-sided muscular movement are a productive force.
>
> (Marx, 1975 [1845]: 300)

Furthermore, Marx argued that the identification and subdivision of distinct human actions (mental and mental capital in List's terms) was an outcome of the alienation of labour – where workers lost control over their labour as it became organised and directed by managers, themselves responding to the pressures of competitive capital accumulation.

The Political Economy of Labour

In his analysis of the English industrial working class, Marx developed his conception of the political economy of labour, which had been introduced in his 1864 Inaugural Address to the First International. Here he revealed a rival political economy to that of capital and the state. He began his address by criticising the then (and now) commonly held assumption of the causal relationship between economic growth and enhanced human well-being. Speaking about the English experience, he argued that:

> It is a great fact that the misery of the working masses has not diminished from 1848 to 1864, and yet this period is unrivalled for the development of its industry and the growth of commerce.
>
> (Marx, 1974a [1864]: 73)

Rather than capital accumulation generating trickle-down mechanisms leading to distribution of wealth amongst workers, Marx presented an altogether different picture. In an ideal world for fast-expanding capital:

> What the lot of the labouring population would be if everything were left to isolated, individual bargaining, may be easily foreseen. The iron rule of supply and demand, if left unchecked, would speedily reduce the producers of all wealth to a starvation diet.
>
> (Marx, 1974b [1867]: 137)

However, workers' organisations contradict these rules and potentially represent an alternative political economy. Collective gains against capital are won through engaging in planned cooperation in order to negate the laws of supply and demand.

Marx provides three examples of the political economy of labour in his inaugural address to the first International. The first example, the Ten-Hours Act (introduced in England in 1847 which legally reduced the working day to a maximum of ten hours), was the first time that 'in broad daylight the political economy of the [capitalist] class succumbed to the political economy of the working class' (Marx, 1974a: 75). The second example was the creation of worker-run cooperative factories. The latter were of great significance because:

> by deed instead of by argument... [such organisations]... have shown that production on a large scale, and in accord with the behests of modern science, may be carried on without the existence of a class of masters employing a class of hands.
>
> (Marx, 1974a [1864]: 75)

Marx's crucial insight here, which contradicts fundamentally neoliberal and statist comprehensions of development, is that while capitalists always need workers the reverse is not the case.

In the third example, Marx identified how the European working class, in its support for the struggle for abolition of slavery during the US Civil War, had effectively formulated its own foreign policy – a policy of international labouring-class solidarity. Other principles of the political economy of labour include negating competition between workers (for example, between workers of different 'race', ethnicity or gender, or in geographically separated workplaces), and restricting capital's coercive control in the workplace.

Marx's conception of labour-centred development embraced struggles by diverse labouring classes around the world, and their interconnections, for the amelioration of their conditions. For example, he understood the struggles in situations as diverse as colonial Australia, rural Russia, urban Paris (in the form of the Paris Commune), and industrial England as all containing the potential to enhance the livelihoods of these countries' labouring classes under capitalism, but also potentially contributing to struggles that would generate a post-capitalist future (Selwyn, 2013).

In his analysis he identified how labouring-class struggles could generate shorter and longer-term developmental gains – where the former entailed better conditions under capitalism and the latter entailed the transcendence of capitalism. These struggles were, for Marx, inextricably interlinked and united. They unified labouring classes against capital and capitalist states, in the process illuminating the possibilities and the strategies necessary for immediate and longer-term gains. Put differently, these struggles generated the conditions where labouring classes were able to understand their constitutive role in the development process, rather than the passive role allocated to them by SPE and liberal conceptions of development.

The political economy of labour embodies a conception of development that is fundamentally different from, and opposed to, SPE. Marx demonstrated how workers do not need to wait for an unspecified time in the future for benefits to trickle down to them. Moreover, the political economy of labour is one based upon international solidarity (also see Pradella, Chapter 2), rather than the international competitive accumulation that rests at the heart of SPE. Such solidarity took the form of the support of European working classes for the abolition of slavery, and also the spread of labouring-class organisational forms, such as trade unions and political parties which were then potentially able to articulate further labouring-class objectives and strategies.

Contemporary China illustrates vividly the clash between SPE in conjunction with private capital and the political economy of labour. On the one hand Chinese industrialisation is based upon the intense exploitation and repression of its vast industrial working class as a source of business profits. On the other hand Chinese workers are attempting to ameliorate their conditions through direct struggles against firms and Chinese state agencies (see Pringle, Chapter 17).

While China's one-party system leaves little room for dissenting political organisation or expression, Chinese workers have engaged in mass struggles and have been able to defend, and in many cases ameliorate, their conditions. The nature of these mass incidents across China has started to change (China Labour Bulletin, 2012: 13, 17). While the majority of actions are defensive (seeking to retain established rights), offensive actions – seeking to establish new rights, better conditions and better pay – have increased, from between 9 and 17 per cent of mass incidents prior to 2010, to around 30 per cent of 'mass incidents' in 2010. One consequence of these struggles have been that, as the *Economist* (29 June 2010) reported, manufacturing wages increased by 17 per cent between 2009 and 2010.

Strikes are workers' main method of articulating and achieving their demands. Strikers use picket lines to prevent the delivery of goods in and out of factories, and they often block roads and use sit-ins in city centres to gain media attention. They utilise mobile communication technology and social media to broadcast and communicate their demands, organise further strikes, and report progress in negotiating them with factory managers (China Labour Bulletin, 2012).

Beyond wage increases, Silver and Zhang (2009: 176) argue that these protests have made the Chinese government increasingly fearful of political instability and socio-political breakdown. In response:

> Between 2003 and 2005, the central government and the Chinese Communist Party began to move away from a single-minded emphasis on attracting foreign capital and fostering economic growth at all costs to promoting the idea of a 'new development model' aimed at reducing inequalities among classes and regions as part of the pursuit of a 'harmonious society' ... Likewise... the [state run] All China Federation of Trade Unions, amended its constitution to 'make the protection of workers' rights a priority' in 2003.
>
> (Chan and Kwan, 2003, in Silver and Zhang, 2009: 176)

Labouring-class struggles are beginning to transform China's political economic landscape. The balance of class power, between labouring-class organisations, the state, and foreign and domestic capital, will determine whether Chinese workers are able to continue to improve their living standards, or are continually subordinated to the needs of profit maximisation and international competitiveness.

Conclusion

This chapter outlined the roots and contemporary applications of SPE, and showed it to be based on labour repression and exploitation. SPE suffers from a fundamental contradiction – that an elite few (whether statist political economists, or state bureaucrats) want and claim to be able to improve the lot of the poor, but can only do so by exploiting and repressing them. The chapter proposed an alternative labour-centred political economy of development, rooted in the political economy of labour. The latter rests upon the self-activity of labouring classes in their resistance to attempts by states and capital to increase their exploitation. Its objectives – the amelioration of workers' lives through shortening the working day, improving the conditions of work, and increasing the democratic control of workers over their labour – contradict the objectives of states and capital who view workers only as a commodity input to the production process, to be utilised most efficiently at lowest cost. It is no surprise then, that open class struggles are particularly visible in the situation of attempted state-led industrialisation.

It might be objected that arguing for labouring-class organisations to ameliorate their conditions through class struggles against capital presupposes an already-accumulated sum of wealth (held by capital and the state) which can be partly or fully expropriated by labour. If this is correct, then labouring-class organisations in poor countries must bide their time until such wealth has been generated, before struggling to get hold of it. Such arguments ignore (and sometimes purposefully occlude) the fact that the establishment of capitalist social relations was and is itself a process and outcome of (successful) class struggles from above, by states and capital. Within SPE these struggles from above are interpreted as developmental strategies. They are, but only for the state and capital. They are not developmental for the disposed peasantries or for the 'disciplined' labouring classes. While SPE invites students of development to support such struggles from above, a political economy of labour perspective argues that the peasants and workers who resist their dispossession and subjection to discipline are, in fact, articulating an alternative developmental vision and process.

Just as proponents of capitalist development are clear about their support for the creation of structures which facilitate capital accumulation, so a labour-centred conception of development supports labouring-class attempts to extract as many concessions as possible from capital and the state within capitalism, and their attempts to challenge and supersede capitalism. The argument that labouring classes should wait for, or actively assist in, large-scale capital accumulation before pressing their claims upon the state and capital is one designed (often purposefully) to demobilise workers and to transform them into a commodity-input within the accumulation process. In stark opposition to SPE, the political economy of labour identifies a way of organising the generation, distribution and consumption of social wealth from the perspective of labouring classes, within and potentially beyond capitalism.

Select Bibliography

Amsden, A. (1990) 'Third World industrialisation: Global Fordism or a new model?' *New Left Review*, 1(182): 5–31.

Chang, H.-J. (2002) *Kicking Away the Ladder: Economic Development in Historical Perspective.* London: Anthem.

Chang, H.-J. and Grabel, I. (2004) *Reclaiming Development – An Alternative Economic Policy Manual.* London: Zed.

China Labour Bulletin (2012) *A Decade of Change: The Workers' Movement in China 2000– 2012.* Hong Kong: China Labour Bulletin.

Kohli, A. (2004) *State-Directed Development: Political Power and Industrialization in the Global Periphery.* Cambridge: Cambridge University Press.

List, F. (1856) [1841] *The National System of Political Economy.* Philadelphia, Pa.: J. Lippencott (republished by University of Michigan Library).

Marx, K. (1974a) [1864] 'Inaugural Address of the International Working Men's Association', in K. Marx and F. Engels, *Selected Works, Vol. 3.* London: Penguin/New Left Review.

Marx, K. (1974b) [1867] 'Address of the General Council of the International Working Men's Association to the Members and Affiliated Societies', 9 July 1867, *Minutes of the General Council of the First International, 1866–68.* Moscow: Progress.

Marx, K. (1975) [1845] 'Draft of an article on Friedrich List's book *Das Nationale System Der Politischen Oekonomie*', in K. Marx and F. Engels, *Collected Works, Vol. 4.* Moscow: Progress.

Selwyn, B. (2013) 'Karl Marx, class struggle and labour-centred development', *Global Labour Journal*, 4(1): 48–70.

Shaffaedin, M. (2005) 'Friedrich List and the infant industry argument', in K. S. Jomo (ed.), *The Pioneers of Development Economics*. London: Zed.

Silver, B. and Zhang, L. (2009) 'China as an emerging epicentre of world labour unrest', in Ho-Fung Hung (ed.), *China and the Transformation of Global Capitalism*. Baltimore, Md.: Johns Hopkins University Press.

Wade, R. (2004) *Governing the Market*, 2nd edn. Princeton, N.J.: Princeton University Press.

CHAPTER FIVE

The Globalisation of Production and the Struggle for Workers' Unity: Lessons from Bangladesh

John Smith

Declining profitability was at the heart of the last system-threatening crisis to afflict the major imperialist economies in the 1970s. The relocation of wide sectors of industrial production to low-wage countries played a crucial, yet insufficiently acknowledged, role in the restoration of profits and exit from that crisis. The outsourcing of production – or 'export-oriented industrialisation' looked at from a Southern perspective – gave the capitalist system a respite that was to last for barely 25 years, all the time preparing the ground for the eruption of a new, even bigger crisis.

I begin by discussing how the fundamental force driving and shaping the globalisation and southwards shift of production is the effort of Northern capitalists to cut production costs, wage costs in particular, by substituting relatively high-paid domestic labour with low-paid workers in 'emerging nations', taking advantage not only of lower wages but of higher rates of exploitation. This very capitalist form of imperialism has grown rapidly since the 1970s to become the defining feature of neoliberal globalisation. And it has transformed the face of the world working class, which – through the internationalisation of production and the increasing influx of women into the industrial workforce – now much more closely resembles the face of humanity.

I then consider some fundamental problems in the collection and interpretation of data on international wage differentials, productivity and gross domestic product (GDP). Particular attention is given to the 'GDP illusion': 'GDP', it is argued, does not measure 'domestic product', that is, the total value *produced by* firms in a given nation, as economists claim it does. Rather, GDP measures that part of total value that firms *capture*. Much of the value generated by, for example, Bangladeshi garment workers or Chinese iPhone assemblers, is captured by Northern 'lead firms' and appears in Northern GDP. Thus 'GDP' underestimates the real contribution of Southern labour to global wealth and obscures the transfer of large portions of it to firms, governments and consumers in 'developed' countries.

I conclude with a case study of Bangladesh's garment industry. This industry epitomises the export-oriented industrialisation strategy also pursued by other countries in the Global South, and starkly exemplifies challenges facing working people in these countries. The death of 1,127 garment workers on 24 April 2013 in the collapse of Rana Plaza, one of the worst workplace 'accidents' in world history – termed 'mass industrial slaughter' by Jyrki Raina, general secretary of IndustriALL – shone a bright light on three issues of universal relevance to working people of all countries: *the living wage, workplace safety* and *union organisation*. It also serves as a useful case study of attempts by activists and trade unions to give practical solidarity to those in countries like Bangladesh most lacking these essential needs. The chapter finishes with some brief conclusions concerning working class solidarity in a time of global crisis.

The Globalisation of Industrial Production and of the Working Class

During the neoliberal era, efforts by capitalists in imperialist nations to cut costs and boost profits by substituting higher-wage labour with lower-wage labour have been the principal force driving and shaping the globalisation of industrial production. Stephen Roach, a senior economist at Morgan Stanley, expressed this with unusual clarity, arguing that 'extracting product from relatively low-wage workers in the developing world has become an increasingly urgent survival tactic for companies in the developed economies' (2003: 5–6). There are in fact two ways for Northern capitalists to 'extract product' from low-wage workers: by migrating their production processes to low-wage economies or by employing workers who have migrated to the imperialist nations. The International Monetary Fund (IMF) explained this quite precisely: 'the global pool of labour can be accessed by advanced economies through imports and immigration', observing that outsourcing 'is the more important and faster-expanding channel, in large part because immigration remains very restricted in many countries' (2007: 180).

Many antecedents of modern cross-border, wage-driven production outsourcing can be found in previous phases of capitalist development. Yet only during the neoliberal era has it become prevalent as a vastly increased source of surplus value that has provided crucial support to the rate of profit in imperialist countries. Production outsourcing has also reshaped the world working class: the share of the world's industrial workers living in 'emerging nations' grew from 50 per cent in 1980 to 80 per cent in 2010. In that year, according to the International Labour Organization (ILO), 541 million industrial workers lived in 'less developed' and 145 million in 'more developed' regions.

The true extent of this shift of production and of the producers is even greater than these numbers suggest. In 1980 much of the South's industrial proletariat produced for protected domestic markets. Neoliberal reforms dismantled these protections and destroyed many of these jobs, while the numbers employed in export-oriented industries surged. Since then, the growth of the South's industrial workforce has been a function of its integration into global value chains dominated by 'lead firms' headquartered in Europe, North America and Japan. The scale of this shift can be seen starkly in the changing composition of Southern trade. In 1980, 80 per cent of African, Asian and Latin American exports were 'primary commodities', that is, natural resources and agricultural products. By 1995, manufactured goods had risen from 20 per cent of rapidly expanding Southern exports to 66 per cent, a flood-tide since swollen by China's integration into global supply chains.

Neoliberalism's triumph was not inevitable since it was not the only possible outcome to capitalism's systemic crisis of the 1970s. Deepening class struggle in the imperialist countries and revolutions in Vietnam, Iran, Nicaragua, Grenada and elsewhere could have opened the door to an anti-imperialist and socialist path of development. Many factors, however, including disunity and poor leadership, led to missed opportunities and defeats. Revolutionary Cuba was left to pursue this path alone. The only capitalist way out of the crisis for ruling classes in low-wage nations was to submit to 'structural adjustment' – the neoliberal recipes concocted by imperialist governments and administered by the IMF and World Bank – and to take the road of export-oriented industrialisation by offering up their living labour to multinational corporations and 'global buyers'.

A striking feature of wage-driven globalisation of production has been the massive influx of women into industrial production in low-wage countries. As a UN report noted, 'industrialisation in the context of globalisation is as much female-led as it is export-led' (1999: 29). Profound poverty, the desire for economic independence and expanding social horizons explain why, in the most diverse cultures and societies, poor women have sought employment with multinational corporations or their local suppliers. What explains the demand for their labour? Labour economists widely cite the perceived cheapness, docility and dexterity of women workers. The ILO reports that the liberalisation of trade and investment led to wider gender pay gaps, suggesting this resulted from women's 'weaker ability to negotiate terms and conditions of employment' (2006: 10–32).

Stephanie Seguino notes that economies with the widest gender wage gaps grew most rapidly (2000: 55). For example, South Korea's rapid growth was assisted by the world's highest gender pay gap: in 1980, women's wages were just 44.5 per cent of men's. Yet women's militant resistance to low pay and long hours spearheaded the mass movement that toppled the US-backed military dictatorship in that country, blazing the trail for the massive labour struggles of the 1980s.[1] Female factory workers also led the struggle that toppled the Suharto dictatorship in Indonesia in 1998, and at the time of writing are in the front lines of strikes and demonstrations in Bangladesh and Cambodia, in both cases standing up to soldiers, police and company goons. These and many other

---

1   South Korea continues to have one of the widest gender pay gaps in the world, with estimated female earnings just 52 per cent of male earnings (see World Economic Forum, 2013).

examples demonstrate (see also Chapters 9 and 21 of this book) that, contrary to capitalists' hopes and expectations, the potential fighting strength of the working class movement is greatly increased by the influx of women into its ranks.

Wages, Productivity and the GDP Illusion

Since global wage differentials have played such an important role it is worth reminding ourselves just how wide these differentials are. Data on average wages mask growing wage inequality within nations and are especially suspect in low-wage countries, where they typically count only those in formal employment, ignoring widespread underpayment and illegally low wages. Data on Chinese wages often exclude migrant workers and ignore significant regional variations. Bearing this in mind, the US government's Bureau of Labour Statistics reports that, despite decades of wage stagnation in the United States and years of above-inflation wage rises in China, average hourly 'labour compensation' (wages plus benefits) of US manufacturing workers in 2010 was 20 times greater than in China (US$34.74 per hour versus $1.71 per hour). This actually underestimates the global picture, since labour compensation in countries such as Canada, France and Germany is higher than in the United States, while wages in India, Sri Lanka, Indonesia and Vietnam are even lower than in China. Bangladeshi wages are lowest of all. In Bangladesh the minimum textile workers' wage is just 32¢ per hour, and this is after a 77 per cent increase wrested by waves of strikes and mass demonstrations that followed the Rana Plaza disaster.

Underlining why even these miserably low wages must not be taken at face value, Dhaka's *Daily Star* reports that workers in Bangladesh's tea plantations are paid just 71¢ *per day*. Widely touted statistics on unemployment in poor countries also suffer from poor data collection and political manipulation. These statistics often take no account of the fact that, in the absence of social security, workers simply cannot afford to be unemployed and are compelled to find work in the burgeoning informal economy. Thus the World Bank reports Bangladesh's rate of unemployment to be a ludicrously low 5 per cent, yet ILO data shows that in 2010, 23.26 per cent of all Bangladeshi workers were in 'precarious/casual employment', with men earning just $2.20 per week and women less than $1 per week (2013: 34).

Clearly, wages are profoundly affected by conditions in labour markets – for example, the repression of unions, massive unemployment and underemployment, extreme rural poverty, the manipulation of gender and ethnic divisions – none of which have any direct bearing on the productivity of workers when at work. This is one reason to question the widespread belief of mainstream economists that low wages in 'emerging economies' merely reflect the low productivity of their workers. That Western firms are so keen to outsource production to the other side of the world is compelling evidence that the low wages they find so attractive are not cancelled out by low productivity. Why is this important?

Because, to the considerable extent that international wage differentials do not reflect differences in productivity, they must reflect international differences in the rate of exploitation. And a higher rate of exploitation signifies that a greater portion of the wealth created by these workers is captured by capitalists and, through competition, turned into profit. It is vitally important to understand how this happens, and how it is rendered invisible in standard interpretations of economic data.

Statistics on GDP, trade and productivity suffer from even more severe defects than those afflicting wages and employment. Here the problems are conceptual, not technical. Bangladesh's garment-exporting industry provides a glaring illustration. Few would deny that Primark, Wal-Mart, M&S and other major UK retailers profit from the exploitation of Bangladeshi garment workers. A moment's thought reveals other beneficiaries: the commercial capitalists who own the buildings leased by these retailers, the myriad of companies providing them with advertising, security and other services; and also governments, which tax their profits and their employees' wages and collect VAT on every sale. Yet, according to trade and financial data, *not one penny* of UK firms' profits or their government's tax revenues derives from the sweated labour of the workers who made their goods. The huge mark-up on the costs of production, typically 60–80 per cent and often more, instead appears as 'value added' in the United Kingdom and other countries where these goods are consumed, expanding their GDP by far more than that of the country where they are produced.

Value added, defined as the difference between the prices a firm pays for its inputs and the prices it receives for its output, is the content of GDP – the total value-added generated by all firms within an economy; and also of *productivity* – 'value added per worker'. According to mainstream economic theory, 'value added' is identical to the value generated within the firm's own production process, which presumes that none of it may leak to other firms or be captured from them. The production process is thus not only a black box, where all we know is the price paid for inputs and the price received for outputs; it is also hermetically sealed from all other black boxes in that no value can be transferred or redistributed between them.

Marxist political economy rejects this absurdity and advances a radically different conception: 'value added' is really *value captured*. It measures the share of total value generated by all workers that is captured by a firm, which does not in any way correspond to the value generated by the living labour employed within that firm. Indeed, many firms supposedly generating value added are engaged in nonproduction activities, such as finance, security and advertising, which produce no value at all.

If, within a national economy, value produced by workers in one firm (that is, in one production process) can be redistributed through competition to other firms, it is irrefutable that, in the era of globalised production, such value-transfers also occur between firms in different countries. To the extent that it does, GDP departs ever further from being an objective, more-or-less accurate approximation of a nation's product. Rather, GDP becomes a veil that conceals greatly expanded exploitation by Northern capitalists of Southern living labour.

Redefining 'value added' as value captured transforms our perception of the global economy. It allows us to see that the lion's share of the value produced by low-wage workers in China, Bangladesh and elsewhere is captured by corporations and governments in the imperialist countries.

Migration and Labour Market Conditions in Bangladesh

Bangladesh provides a telling example of how, during the neoliberal era, outsourcing and migration have become two aspects of the same wage-differential driven transformation of global production. Speaking of 1980s and 1990s Bangladesh, Tasneem Siddiqui reported that the continuous outflow of people of working-age played a major role in keeping the unemployment rate stable (2003: 2). According to the International Organisation for Migration, 5.4 million Bangladeshis work overseas, more than half in India, with the rest spread between Western Europe, North America, Australasia and the Middle East, especially Saudi Arabia. Some $14 billion of remittances flowed into house-holds in Bangladesh in 2012, equivalent to 11 per cent of Bangladesh's GDP. In the same year, Bangladesh received $19 billion for its garment exports (80 per cent of Bangladesh's total exports), but this includes the cost of imported cotton and other fabrics, typically 25 per cent of the production cost. In other words, net earnings from garment exports in 2012 approximately equalled total remit-tances from Bangladeshis working abroad. And while only a small fraction of export earnings are paid out in wages, all of the latter flows directly into poor households.

The World Bank reports that each of 210,000 UK-based Bangladeshi migrant workers, the largest concentration of all imperialist countries, sent home an average of $4,058, close to the average for other imperialist countries. In compar-ison, average wages following the 2013 increase in Bangladesh's textile industry were $115 per month, or $1,380 per year. It follows that each Bangladeshi working in the United Kingdom remits in one year what it would take his (most Bangladeshi migrant workers are male) wife, sister or daughter three years to earn working in a garment factory.

Between 2004 and 2012 Bangladesh's GDP growth barely moved from its range of between 6 and 7 per cent, briefly dropping to 5.7 per cent in 2009. Yet this was only enough to generate an average annual 1.4 per cent increase in employment, barely enough to soak up new entrants into the labour market. Two factors account for this discrepancy: an increase in the length of the working week, already among the highest in the world, and an increase in labour produc-tivity not matched by higher wages. The ILO observed that 'the proportion of employed people working excessive hours increased, while little progress was observed in adequate earnings.' (2013: 23) The extremely adverse and deteriorating conditions faced by Bangladeshi workers are also reflected in the prevalence of informal employment, that is, employment that is unregulated by minimum wage and maximum working day legislation and provides no compensation for workplace injury, maternity leave, paid holidays and so on. According to the ILO, its incidence in Bangladesh increased from an already sky-high 76.2 per cent in 2000 to 87.5 per cent in 2010 (2013: 8). Within this, the double oppression of women workers is evident: 92.3 per cent of women workers were informally employed in 2010, compared with 85.5 per cent of men.

Employment in garment factories (85 per cent female) is widely credited with raising the social status of Bangladeshi women, freeing them from domestic confinement and increasing their economic independence. Yet employers prefer women's labour precisely because of their downtrodden status. According to the ILO, the average wage of female 'machine operators and assemblers' is 73 per cent of their male counterparts, and, despite the massive influx of women into garment factories, female participation in the labour force in Bangladesh as a whole remains one of the lowest in the world. In 2010, 33.9 per cent of working-age women were employed compared with 79.2 per cent of working-age men.

Building Solidarity and International Workers Unity – Lessons from Bangladesh

Bangladeshi workers epitomise not only extreme exploitation but also the growing militancy, accumulating experience of struggle and budding political consciousness of millions of workers employed in export-oriented manufacturing in China, Cambodia, Indonesia, Vietnam and so on – each part of a broader process of political awakening across the global South. Bangladesh has seen waves of militant struggles by the 3.9 million workers in the clothing industry, particularly in 2006, 2010, 2012 and in May 2013 following the Rana Plaza disaster. These struggles, which at times have resembled mini-insurrections, have centred on the demand for wage increases, the right to form unions and the enforcement of widely ignored health and safety legislation. The Bangladeshi government, many of whose top officials are factory owners, has responded with brutal repression, using the regular police, the *ansars* (village-based militias) and the 'anti-terrorist' Rapid Action Battalion against recent workers protests – along with the Industrial Police, formed in the midst of the 2010 strike wave, whose sole task is to police garment districts and repress workers' protests. Its 2,900 officers contrast with the grand total of 51 inspectors who, at the time of the Rana Plaza disaster, were charged with enforcing health and safety, minimum age and minimum wage laws in all of Bangladesh's 200,000 workshops and factories, including 5,000 in the garment sector.

Within a fortnight of the factory collapse, intense discussions between non-governmental organisations (NGOs), international union federations

(IndustriAll and UNI) and representatives of western clothing giants resulted in the 'Accord on Fire and Building Safety in Bangladesh' (available at www.clean-clothes.org). A 6 June 2013 IndustriALL press release defined the Accord as its 'strong response to the recent horrific catastrophes in the Bangladeshi garment industry'. Negotiated between the IndustriALL Global Union, UNI Global Union and over 40 global fashion brands, the Accord would not be 'just another voluntary initiative, [but] a binding agreement with a complaints mechanisms and real consequences for non-compliance'.

The Accord's centrepiece was the formation of a new factory inspectorate overseen by a Steering Committee, chaired by the ILO, comprising three representatives from international unions and three from international companies. The parties to the Accord agreed to make 'all reasonable efforts to ensure that an initial inspection of each factory covered by this Agreement shall be carried out within the first two years', and provides for publication of safety reports, remediation and safety training. Supplier companies are required to form health and safety committees made up of managers and workers, the latter to be selected by unions or by 'democratic election' where no union is present. Touted as 'legally binding', the Accord only envisages penalties – that is, loss of orders – against supplier companies. The whole programme is to be financed by the western 'brands', through a subscription related to the size of their business in the country.

Thus quick-moving trade unions and NGOs succeeded in persuading 40 or more 'of the most progressive global fashion brands' into taking some responsibility for the lethal conditions in their suppliers' factories. Yet there is no mention in the Accord about excessive overtime, a key health and safety issue, nor are supplier factories required to allow trade unions to organise – despite shop-floor union organisation being the most important line of defence against dangerous working practices. Before Rana Plaza collapsed, hundreds of garment workers were crammed into hot and poorly ventilated rooms – unhealthy and unsafe working conditions that will not be prohibited by the 'Accord on Fire and Building Safety'.

A key clause in the Accord responds to complaints by factory owners that ruthless price-gouging by international retailers forces them to cut corners, specifically, that 'participating brands and retailers will negotiate commercial terms with their suppliers which ensure that it is financially feasible for the factories to maintain safe workplaces'. Yet neither the Steering Committee nor anyone else is tasked with monitoring this clause.

Several months of lobbying of US and European retail giants resulted in the endorsement of the Accord by over 40 leading brands, with GAP and Walmart being notable exceptions. Jyrki Raina described the Accord as 'historic', while Philip Jennings, general secretary of UNI, defined it as a 'turning point', marking 'the end of the race to the bottom in the global supply chain'. Yet we have been here before – in the 1990s, waves of campus-based anti-sweatshop activism resulted in the formation by US President Bill Clinton of the 'Apparel Industry Partnership' (AIP), which later morphed into the 'Fair Labor Association' (FLA).

This brought together US labour unions and retail giants with the declared aim of eliminating sweatshops and improving labour rights. Yet it has been criticised for allowing ruthless profiteers such as Nike and Apple to masquerade as 'labour-friendly'. These corporations finance the FLA and pay the generous salaries of its officers, a small price to pay for the 'fair labour' label their products receive in return. The Bangladeshi 'Accord' is also to be financed by its corporate endorsers. Though too early to judge its results, we can expect that some blood money will be paid, some improvements will be made and some lives will be saved – but this Accord does not 'mark the end of the race to the bottom' and participation in it does not mean that a firm is 'most progressive'.

Turning to the fight for a living wage, the 77 per cent increase in garment workers' wages conceded in November 2013 was a significant victory, but far short of the 170 per cent wage increase they demanded and for which they continue to struggle. It leaves their wages a long way below all estimates of what is needed to feed, clothe and house their families. According to the Asia Floor Wage Alliance, an alliance of Asian trade unions and activist groups such as the Clean Clothes Campaign, the new basic wage is barely one-fifth (!) of what is necessary to nourish, house and clothe a garment worker, one adult and two child dependants (see 'Calculating a living wage', www.cleanclothes.org). The 2013 wage hike was the first increase since 2010, since when inflation has raised overall prices by 28 per cent, and basic necessities like food and cooking oil by much more. Landlords have already moved to jack up rents, while past experience suggests that many employers will resist paying wage increases in full.

Concerning union rights, blacklisting, state repression and intense competition for jobs have impeded the formation of workplace unions, which formally exist in only a few dozen factories across Bangladesh. Their absence has lent an explosive character to garment workers' struggles, leading the US government and the European Union to put some pressure on Bangladesh's rulers to relax anti-union laws and provide a safety valve for workers' discontent. The Bangladeshi government responded in July 2013 with amendments to its labour legislation. Yet the amendments have been condemned by Bangladeshi unions as cosmetic and even regressive. To form a union, 30 per cent of the workforce must sign up, which remains unchanged despite unions' demands for a reduction. Prior to July 2013 employers invariably used the list of signatories to identify union members for mass sackings. The new law denies employers access to the list, but workers know that the payment of a small bribe will easily get around this. The law also bans union organisation in the export processing zones, where many of the biggest garment factories are located, and denies union rights to most public sector workers. Rickshaw drivers and other workers in the informal economy are not recognised as workers and have no right to form unions.

After Rana Plaza, Jyrki Raina pledged to 'use the global muscle of IndustriALL to create sustainable conditions for garment workers, with the right to join a union, with living wages, and safe and healthy working conditions'. Yet unions in Western Europe and North America left the organisation of protests to anti-sweatshop activists and campaigning charities and did nothing to mobilise their members in solidarity. Unions in North America added their names to an 'international day of action against deathtraps' in June 2013, but there is no evidence of serious effort to build this action. Instead, their reflex has been to act in partnership with imperialist governments and international brands. The UK trade union Unite and North America's United Steel Workers, both of which are affiliated to IndustriALL, issued a joint statement a few days after the Rana Plaza disaster urging the US and European governments 'to immediately suspend Bangladesh's market access under the Generalized System of Preferences' and 'to enact laws ... that would ban the importation of goods produced under sweatshop conditions'. This thinly veiled protectionism is opposed by Bangladeshi trade unions and labour activists, and for this reason is not promoted by IndustriALL or UNI, which include Bangladeshi trade union affiliates.

Conclusion

The first part of this chapter argued that firms' profits and governments' tax revenues in imperialist economies have, during the neoliberal era, become increasingly dependent on the super-exploitation of Southern workers through both outsourcing/offshoring and migration. Furthermore, as an abundant literature has shown (see e.g. Hale and Wills, 2005, and Pradella, Chapter 2 in this book), this expanded super-exploitation helps capitalists and their governments to attack rights and to increase workers' exploitation in the North. As detailed in Chapter 8, moreover, racial and national divisions and the super-exploitation of migrant workers in the imperialist nations induces a deterioration in the conditions of the whole working class. But this is only one side of a complex picture. Access to ever-cheaper consumer goods has mitigated the effects of austerity and wage repression on workers' living standards in imperialist countries, while greatly increased competition between workers North and South leads to a reflexive protectionism, fatal to any prospect of building international working class unity. Attempts to defend living standards and social provision at home by pursuing 'national' solutions are not only ineffective, they strengthen xenophobia and dovetail with efforts by capitalist politicians to play on national, racial and gender divisions.

I then moved on to consider the adverse conditions, brave struggles and only modest gains won by Bangladeshi workers since the Rana Plaza disaster in April 2013. Particular attention was given to workplace safety, where activity by anti-sweatshop campaigns and international union federations has been most intense and has yielded some tangible results. The Accord on workplace safety struck between international unions and international brands may result in some improvements. Time will tell. The brands will trumpet their new-found concern for worker safety. But women and men in Bangladesh and other low-wage countries will continue to work long hours in unhealthy workplaces for starvation wages, boosting the profits of western corporations and governments.

The most important achievements of the struggles sparked by the Rana Plaza disaster are the sense of potential power they have given to participants, the impetus they have imparted to union organisation, and the sympathy they have won from working people around the world. In order for this sympathy to become real solidarity, and in order not to compete with their sisters and brothers in the South, workers in imperialist countries must join with them in the struggle to abolish the racial hierarchy of nations and the tremendous disparities associated with it. This is the condition for achieving an authentic globalisation – a world without borders – in which no one has more right to a job, an education or a life than anyone else. As Malcolm X said, 'Freedom for everybody, or freedom for nobody!'

Select Bibliography

Hale, A. and Wills, J. (eds) (2005) *Threads of Labour: Garment Industry Supply Chains from the Workers' Perspective*. Malden, Mass.: Blackwell.

International Labour Organization (ILO) (2006) *Report of the Director General: Changing Patterns in the World of Work*. Geneva: ILO.

ILO (2013) *Decent Work Country Profile – Bangladesh*, Geneva: ILO.

International Monetary Fund (IMF) (2007) *World Economic Outlook 2007 — Spillovers and Cycles in the Global Economy*. Washington DC: IMF.

Roach, S. S. (2003) 'The World Economy at the Crossroads: Outsourcing, Protectionism, and the Global Labor Arbitrage.' Speech Before the Boao Forum for Asia Annual Conference 2003, Hainan Province, People's Republic of China.

Seguino, S. (2000) 'Accounting for gender in Asian economic growth', *Feminist Economics*, 6(3): 27–58.

Siddiqui, T. (2003) *Migration as a Livelihood Strategy of the Poor: The Bangladesh Case*. Dhaka: Refugee and Migratory Movements Research Unit, Dhaka University.

Smith, J. (2012) 'The GDP illusion: value added versus value capture', *Monthly Review*, 64(3): 86–102.

United Nations (UN) (1999) *World Survey on the Role of Women in Development: Globalization, Gender and Work*. New York: United Nations Publications, Department of Economic and Social Affairs.

World Economic Forum (2013) *Global Gender Gap Report 2013*. Geneva: World Economic Forum.

CHAPTER SIX

The 'Rise of the South'

Alfredo Saad-Filho

Recent debates about the 'Rise of the South' (RoS), global convergence and North–South decoupling have been driven by the perception of far-reaching transformations in the global economy in the last 30 years. These views have been supported by the impressive economic performance of several developing economies (DEs) recently, especially the so-called BRICS (Brazil, Russia, India, China and South Africa), and by the relatively shallow downturn experienced by the latter in the wake of the global crisis starting in 2007, in contrast with the deep contraction and the protracted slowdown in many advanced economies (AEs).

The size, importance and perceived success of the larger DEs, and the striking growth achievements of many smaller economies, have lent support to the argument that the world is 'turning upside down': the economic and political supremacy of the West is being eroded rapidly, changes in global governance will inevitably follow, and the next generation of world-leading economies can already be identified.

Many political scientists and international relations scholars have expressed concerns about the potentially destabilising implications of these transformations. This chapter does not address these issues (see Klassen, Chapter 7 in this book). It focuses instead on the economic debates around global convergence. It shows that, despite the potential significance of the RoS, the conventional narrative of this process and its implications is flawed. In contrast, a critical political economy analysis suggests that the global economy is defined by shifting patterns of unevenness at the levels of firms, production chains, countries and regions, and that there is no automatic tendency for countries to converge. Outcomes depend on circumstances, economic policies, the strength of social movements and global constraints. Examination of the structures and processes included in the 'RoS' can help to illuminate the achievements, limitations and contradictions of economic development policy in the age of neoliberalism, and inform the search for democratic alternatives.

This chapter has six sections. The first reviews the mainstream literature on economic growth and convergence, and the evidence of long-term convergence. The second summarises the long-term patterns of divergence in the world economy, in the light of the concepts of primary and secondary uneven and combined development. The third focuses on the development policies implemented in the post-war period, their impact on global inequality, and recent DE growth performance. The fourth assesses the period since the onset of the global crisis, and discusses the predictions of North–South 'decoupling'. These sections show that moments of convergence have often been decontextualised and exaggerated in support of a neoliberal policy agenda. The fifth examines three possible drivers of convergence: transnational production networks, the 'flying geese' paradigm and industrial policy. The final section discusses the conditions for promoting democratic (pro-poor) development strategies in the South, supporting a socially desirable process of convergence.

Long-Term Patterns of Growth

Evidence of sustained economic growth in the Northern 'core' of the world economy since the Industrial Revolution, in contrast with slow growth or even decline in the Southern 'periphery', has triggered several waves of debate about the scope for global convergence.

In the early and mid-20th century, Thorstein Veblen and Alexander Gerschenkron advanced the intuitively appealing idea that early developers create technologies which others can learn, purchase or steal. Since the adaptation of new methods of production is likely to be cheaper than their discovery, latecomers have an inbuilt advantage and can fast-track their development process. Consequently, capitalist economies can converge rapidly in terms of per capita income, living standards, productivity and technology, dispensing with the need for socialist revolutions or even large-scale state intervention. These insights were incorporated into the growth literature through the work of Evsey Domar, Roy Harrod, and especially Robert Solow. Solow's influential growth model became especially prominent, and was associated with the notion of *unconditional convergence* (for a more detailed presentation, see Saad-Filho, 2014).

Despite their econometric sophistication, most mainstream studies of unconditional convergence have been unpersuasive. They tend to suffer from several limitations, including questionable data sets, inadequate models, and the mutual determination of parameters and outcomes. Their closed economy assumptions rule out international trade, flows of capital and labour, technology transfers and institutional learning (including the effect of Washington consensus-type policy conditionalities), even though neoclassical theory claims that global integration is a key driver of growth.

By the mid-1970s most observers had accepted that poor countries were not actually converging; moreover, the distribution of income was clearly deteriorating across the developing world. Despite these obvious limitations, the Solow model has remained influential, because it is simple, optimistic, and follows directly from the postulates of mainstream economics.

The weaknesses of traditional growth theory and increasing recognition of global divergence helped to popularise the alternative mainstream view that convergence is both rare and policy-dependent, or that it is *conditional*: each economy tends towards its own income level in the long run, depending on their policies, institutions and circumstances. In order to converge, DEs must adopt the 'correct' economic policies and implement the 'necessary' structural reforms, which are invariably inspired by mainstream economics. These insights have been incorporated into competing variants of endogenous (new) growth theory since the mid-1980s.

The controversies between supporters of conditional and unconditional convergence have been inconclusive, and, while some authors estimate progressive reductions in global inequality since the Second World War, others find a large increase in the dispersion of global per capita income. These disagreements are partly because of differences in their models, and partly because of the difficulty of combing national accounts data with household surveys in order to obtain comparable income estimates. New growth theory has also been criticised for its vagueness, unrealistic assumptions (for example, that technology is freely available and usable everywhere), and poor empirical results.

Long-Term Divergence

While mainstream studies remain mired in methodological and empirical difficulties, historical analyses provide an incontrovertible picture of long-term divergence. Five hundred years ago, Asia, Africa and Latin America had 75 per cent of the world's population and a similar percentage of world income. By 1950, their population share had declined to 66 per cent, and their income share had tumbled to 27 per cent. In contrast, the population share of the AEs had risen from 25 per cent to 33 per cent, and their share of world income had reached 73 per cent. These trends were reversed only marginally in the following decades. For example, although the DE share in world gross domestic product (GDP) rose from 15 to 22 per cent between 1970 and 2005, the ratio of the average gross national product (GNP) per capita of the richest quintile of the world's population to the poorest quintile increased from 31:1 in 1965 to 60:1 in 1990, and 74:1 in 1997 (Nayyar, 2009: 2, 6, 13). Similarly, in his careful examination of long-term global growth, Pritchett concludes that:

> Divergence in relative productivity levels and living standards is the dominant feature of modern economic history. In the last century, incomes in the 'less developed' ... countries have fallen far behind those in the 'developed' countries, both proportionately and absolutely.
>
> (Pritchett, 1997: 3, 10)

The observed pattern of global development – at once *uneven* (because it is unequal, with the patterns of inequality changing over time) and *combined* (because countries are economically integrated in multiple ways) – was initially recognised by Leon Trotsky in the early years of the 20th century. Later work, especially by John Weeks (2001), has identified two levels of uneven and combined development (UCD): *primary UCD* and *secondary UCD*.

Primary UCD derives from the geographically localised emergence of capitalism in Europe and North America between the late middle ages and the 19th century, and the consolidation of manufacturing production in this region. These processes consolidated the division of the world into a small, economically dynamic, highly integrated and militarily aggressive set of 'core' capitalist countries, which set out to dominate a much larger and comparatively slower-changing (in economic terms) set of 'peripheral' regions. In the latter, capitalist relations of exploitation were imposed on top of the pre-existing non-capitalist social relations, leading to complex, but invariably highly exploitative, colonial or semi-colonial relations.

These relationships of international exploitation supported the acceleration of capitalist development in the 'core', and consolidated peculiar social and economic structures in the 'periphery'. While some of these social structures and modalities of exploitation supported the transition to capitalism in the 'periphery', others were inimical to it. As a result of these tensions and the subordinate integration of the 'periphery' into the global economy, primary UCD generates an enduring global pattern of divergence: production, trade, finance and markets expand rapidly among the 'core' economies, while simultaneously the DEs become structurally dependent on 'core' inputs, markets, finance and technology.

Within the 'core' economies, intra-sectoral competition led to rapid productivity growth and the spread of technical advances, simultaneously with the diffusion of new modalities of labour control, while inter-sectoral competition and the expansion of finance supported capital flows that created strong equalising tendencies within and between these economies: 'core' industries and countries tended to move together and grow increasingly similar, in terms of productivity, innovations, institutions and output per capita, forging ahead of the 'periphery'.

Competition within the capitalist areas generates a secondary process of UCD, as it fosters cyclical processes of convergence and divergence across sectors, regions and countries, as new technologies and industries are introduced, expand and eventually decline. These processes are modified by economic and social policies, shifts in income levels, and the mobility and activism of the wage-workers in each economy, which can promote growth or accelerate processes of relative or even absolute decline. Since the ensuing movements of convergence and divergence within capitalist areas are ultimately driven by competition for profits, it is reasonable to assume that they contain a tendency towards convergence, while the counter-tendencies towards divergence are the result of technological lags, sectoral decline, social conflicts and deficient policy implementation.

The interaction between primary and secondary UCD suggests a long-term tendency towards the convergence of capitalist countries and regions, in parallel with a long-term tendency of divergence between these (capitalist) countries and regions and those areas where social relations are largely, or predominantly, non-capitalist. Examination of the interaction between primary and secondary UCD also suggests that, in periods of rapid accumulation, capitalist countries and regions will tend to converge faster, while in times of crisis they tend to converge more slowly or even to diverge. In contrast, the non-capitalist countries and regions may not converge at all with the 'core', regardless of the speed of global economic growth – unless capitalist relations of production penetrate more deeply in these regions.

Development in the Age of Neoliberalism

The patterns of growth, integration and global convergence have changed recently. After two or more decades of rapid economic growth led by the diffusion of capitalist relations, the expansion of the wage-working class, and the spread of manufacturing, most DEs were heavily penalised by the international debt crisis starting in 1982, and by exceptionally low commodity prices between the mid-1980s and the early 2000s. Under strong pressure from the International Monetary Fund (IMF), the World Bank and the US administration, working in close association with domestic capital and home-grown neoliberal technocrats, dozens of DEs and former socialist economies discarded their developmentalist economic strategies, which tended to stress manufacturing growth, and introduced policies inspired by the Washington (and later post-Washington) consensus.

In many countries, these policies led to one and, sometimes, two 'lost decades' with little if any per capita income growth, rising inequality, deindustrialisation, and the proliferation of precarious forms of employment. These destructive processes have supported the rapid spread of capitalist relations of production and 'core' economic domination around the world. Neoliberal 'adjustment' strategies and 'market-led' policy reforms have supported the expansion of global capitalism into hitherto inaccessible areas of the world, including the former Soviet Bloc, China, India, and vast regions of Asia, sub-Saharan Africa and Latin America.

Dismay with the macro-economic performance of most DEs since the early 1980s was supplanted by a wave of optimism in the mid-1990s, which intensified in the early 2000s as most DEs recovered smoothly from the bursting of the dotcom bubble, and soon achieved annual GDP growth rates around 5 percentage points higher than the AEs (Akyüz, 2012: 10). This process was widely celebrated. For example: 'the world's economic centre of gravity has moved towards the East and South, from OECD members to emerging economies .... This realignment ... represents a structural change of historical significance' (OECD, 2010: 15).

Despite the historical significance of these transformations, commonly held views of global convergence are often supported by questionable data and the arbitrary extrapolation of recent performance differences, leading to simplistic and often exaggerated expectations of imminent and unproblematic convergence.

First, claims of convergence are generally based on purchasing power parity (PPP$) measures of DE output. Although these estimates can help us compare living standards in different countries, it is the market value of domestic output (measured in current dollars) that determines the contribution of each economy to global supply and demand, and the expansionary and deflationary impulses that it transmits to the rest of the world.

Second, recent DE growth was fuelled by the commodity price bubble in the early and mid-2000s, which in turn was caused by rapid global growth, especially in China, the financialisation of commodity markets, the recovery of Latin America after two decades under the (post-) Washington consensus, the stabilisation of several African countries, and the gigantic US-centred speculative bubble which burst in 2007. These conditions are hardly replicable, much less over several decades.

Third, and despite the hype, claims of global convergence hinge almost entirely on the performance of two countries, China and India.

Fourth, regardless of the achievements of several DEs, the distribution of income remains increasingly unequal both globally and within most countries (UNCTAD, 2012). At all these levels, claims of convergence need a strong dose of realism, as well as clearer analytical underpinnings.

Convergence After the Crisis

With the outbreak of the global crisis, the international economic environment deteriorated rapidly in all areas that had previously supported the expansion of the DEs: net capital flows turned negative, commodity prices tumbled and economic activity contracted rapidly in most AEs, leading to a sharp drop in DE exports.

The policy responses in most AEs were based on state-sponsored financial sector stabilisation, fiscal spending and monetary policy activism. In contrast, DE policies tended to be both more varied and proportionately larger. This was partly because of the more diversified sources of disruption affecting the DEs, and partly because most DEs had sounder macroeconomic, balance of payments and financial positions than the AEs, giving them additional policy space. The fiscal stabilisation package in 15 Asian DEs reached 7.5 per cent of 2008 GDP, almost three times the average level in G7 countries, and China's fiscal response alone reached US$600 billion (13 per cent of GDP). Large stimuli were also introduced in Argentina, Brazil, Korea, Malaysia, Singapore and Thailand (Akyüz, 2012).

These aggressive responses were supported by the rapid recovery of North–South capital flows. This was an unintended consequence of the fiscal and monetary policy relaxation in the AEs, which was meant to support their own banking systems and restore domestic lending. Yet a large part of the resources created by AE fiscal deficits and central bank asset purchases slipped to more dynamic (and higher interest rate) economies in the South. The rapid recovery of most DEs reinforced the perception of global convergence, and gave credence to the view that the South had 'decoupled': it could now grow faster than the North, and independently of the latter's tribulations.

Despite its superficial plausibility, examination of the decoupling hypothesis reveals significant weaknesses. First, Wälti (2009) assessed business cycle synchronicity between 34 DEs and four groups of AEs, and concluded that it has not declined recently. These results support the view that 'globalisation brings national business cycles closer together' (p. 3), rather than 'decoupling' them. Second, while decoupling (just like the earlier notion of convergence) has drawn support from DE ability to avoid the worst of the global crisis, it subsequently lost credibility as the prolonged AE slowdown eventually exhausted the potential sources of DE growth. Finally, current debates and the trajectory of leading DEs show that decoupling is incompatible with global financial integration. In other words, if the South intends to decouple from the North – in the sense of being able to sustain growth independently of AE cycles, by pursuing appropriate development policies and neutralising external shocks – it must reduce its degree of exposure to global financial flows, and make greater efforts towards regional and South–South integration of production, trade and finance.

In the longer term, as was shown above, it is impossible to restore the growth-promoting conditions of the pre-crisis global economy. Consequently, unless fundamental changes take place in DE policy making and in their global integration, the recent spurt of convergence is likely to exhaust itself, as part of a cyclical pattern of secondary UCD.

The limitations to growth in China are the most significant example, because of the size and importance of the country's economy, and its influence on global commodity demand. Despite its extraordinary economic achievements in the last decades, China suffers from severe under-consumption because of the low share of household income in GDP (that is, extremely low wages) and high precautionary savings (for example, the dismantling of social provision compels families to save in order to meet their health, education and housing needs). Consumption growth lagged GDP growth throughout the 2000s; in the eve of the crisis, private consumption was only 36 per cent of GDP, and it declined further subsequently (in contrast, in AEs consumption often exceeds 70 per cent of GDP). In 2009, investment accounted for 50 per cent of the country's GDP, and for a staggering 80 per cent of China's growth. However, this will inevitably lead to immense overcapacity and a vast problem of non-performing loans.

The global implications of the unavoidable economic shifts in China will be compounded by the conventional adjustment programmes being imposed in several countries simultaneously, most notably in the Eurozone periphery. These programmes compress demand, support the illusion that all countries can export their way to growth, promote global deflation, and foster persistent and regionally uneven regressive patterns of development.

Drivers of Convergence

In addition to the diffusion of capitalist relations around the world, and the neoliberal economic reforms, three other – more concrete – drivers of convergence have been identified in the literature. They deserve closer examination.

Global Trade and Global Production Networks

No area has been as powerfully symbolic of the RoS as international trade. As late as 1990, North–North exchanges still accounted for nearly 60 per cent of global trade, while South–South trade barely reached 8 per cent and the DE share of global exports reached only 23 per cent. In contrast, by 2008 North–North trade had declined to 40 per cent, South–South trade had reached 20 per cent, and the DE export share was 37 per cent (OECD 2010: 71).

The exceptionally rapid growth of DE trade can be attributed to several factors, including faster growth in most DEs than in the AEs, the commodity price boom, and the rapid opening to trade in many DEs, leading to a steep climb in their export-to-GDP and import-to-GDP ratios.

Although impressive, trade growth data can exaggerate DE performance and its potential developmental impact. First, although higher commodity prices lift national income, they do not directly imply economic 'success', except tautologically. Second, while GDP includes only value added domestically, total exports (X) and imports (M) include value added in other countries; consequently, trade growth tends to inflate the X/GDP and M/GDP ratios without any implications for local income or welfare. This effect is especially significant in countries joining transnational production networks, which involve large imports of inputs for domestic processing and the subsequent export of finished goods, largely for consumption in AE markets. Third, trade growth is a poor indicator of development, because trade generally responds to, rather than leads, economic growth.

Beyond the 'Flying Geese' Paradigm

The vertical integration of production in East Asia has been called the 'flying geese' pattern of development (see Chang, Chapter 16 in this book). It has often been suggested that this modality of regional integration could be generalised as a paradigm for North–South interaction, with the Northern AEs as the leading goose bringing along a flock of Southern DEs, bound together by (almost invariably Northern) trade-promoting foreign direct investment (FDI).

Although this scenario is superficially plausible, the combination of historical interpretation and policy prescription underpinning the flying geese paradigm is insufficient at four levels. First, East Asian development has included both tighter integration of production networks within the region and the incorporation of East Asia into the global economy, largely through production for AE markets. Consequently, the growth of regional trade is due not generally to the flow of final products, but instead to the flow of inputs into increasingly complex transnational production chains for processing for extra-regional consumption. Historically, the movements of capital, technology and manufacturing capacity within the region, and the upward mobility of countries, were predicated on access to AE markets, which may not be available to newer generations of DEs after the crisis.

Second, it is implicitly assumed that transnational corporations (TNCs) are benevolent conveyors of industrial knowledge, that are willing to share their technologies through FDI, licensing, subcontracting, technical assistance and joint projects, that local firms in countries down the chain can absorb these technologies smoothly, and that local firms can expand and diversify their output mix despite the competitive pressures from firms based in more advanced economies. However, this may not be the case, because their competition might instead throttle relatively smaller and undercapitalised firms in the peripheral countries.

The upshot may be a complex pattern of transnational integration with deindustrialisation, which can be understood in terms of secondary UCD. To the extent that manufacturing development takes place in the periphery, it is likely to increase local dependence on imported capital, technologies and components, with limited linkages across local suppliers. This helps to explain why poorer countries entering the East Asian regional division of labour often run trade deficits with Japan, South Korea, Taiwan and China.

Third, instead of being either the outcome or the harbinger of growing cooperation between increasingly autonomous DEs, East Asian integration closely resembles the hierarchical trade and investment relations between North and South.

Fourth, and more prosaically, it is not clear that significant tranches of manufacturing production will move out of China any time soon. Given the country's rapidly improving infrastructure and vast reserves of unskilled labour, manufacturing production is just as likely to migrate within China for many years, drastically reducing the scope for 'flying geese' with other DEs.

In sum, expectations that flying geese provide a realistic depiction of East Asian industrialisation, and that this model can support the convergence of new DE economic blocs, gloss over the analytical and historical shortcomings of the model, and greatly exaggerate its policy relevance. Despite the limitations of this particular model, it remains true that South-centred production networks can diversify the sources of DE growth, expand the scope for DE manufacturing production and open new export markets. This process can be supported by the production of low-tech goods or host assembly operations in poorer DEs, while the more advanced countries provide them with markets, technology, capital, and trade and investment credit. These arrangements can be supported by monetary and financial policy integration and the expansion of regional infrastructure. This would not amount to a BRICS-centred flying geese strategy, because the production networks, markets and sources of capital would be diversified, rather than being centred in one leading economy; the physical and financial infrastructure should include a range of countries, rather than connecting ever more closely a given hierarchy of countries, and manufacturing development should be closely connected with national industrial policies, rather than simply accommodating TNC strategies.

Industrial Policy and Manufacturing Growth

Historically, the countries that have converged with the 'core' have managed to dislocate binding cost, technological, labour market and balance of payments constraints, through the diffusion of capitalist social relations and the expansion of high-productivity manufacturing activities. As a result of these processes, the DE share in world manufacturing value added (at 1975 prices) increased from 8 to 11 per cent between 1960 and 1980. In the following decade, this share (at 1980 prices) rose only from 14 to 15 per cent, but between 1990 and 2007 this share (at 2000 prices) shot up from 16 to 27 per cent (Nayyar, 2009: 20). It was explained above that overcoming primary UCD is both complex and costly; it is, then, unsurprising that these achievements were concentrated in a small number of countries, especially Brazil, China (including Hong Kong and Taiwan), India, Indonesia, Korea, Malaysia, Mexico, Singapore, South Africa, Thailand and Turkey.

Their achievements depended on rapid capital accumulation, the careful selection of sectoral priorities, technological learning and institutional adaptation, and a conducive financial, institutional and regulatory framework, which can be encapsulated in the notion of industrial policy. These experiences confirm the heterodox economics view that economic growth is sectorally biased: a unit of value added can have a very different impact on long-term growth, depending on the sector where it is produced.

The manufacturing sector plays a key role in rapid growth and development for five reasons. First, manufacturing growth fosters diversification, backward and forward linkages, agglomeration economies and dynamic economies of scale through learning-by-doing. Thus, manufacturing tends to 'pull' the other economic sectors, even when they are initially larger. Second, manufacturing offers greater scope for productivity growth than agriculture or services, especially through the development and adaptation of new technologies. These innovations are subsequently diffused across the economy through the spread of new skills and production methods and the sale of manufactured inputs. Third, manufacturing productivity tends to rise with the rate of growth of manufacturing output, potentially creating virtuous circles of growth across the economy. Fourth, manufacturing fosters export diversification and the production of import substitutes, which can alleviate the balance of payments constraint. Fifth, manufacturing sector wages tend to be relatively high, which can support demand growth and improvements in living standards. Hence, intersectoral shifts of labour and other resources towards manufacturing can help to raise productivity and growth rates in DEs. Conversely, economic structures narrowly determined by static comparative advantages, as is envisaged by mainstream economics, are sub-optimal for long-term growth and for global convergence.

Successful policies supporting manufacturing sector growth are almost invariably heterodox. Nowhere did markets spontaneously conjure the conditions for long-term manufacturing growth, and economic planning has been extensively used in all converging countries (see Selwyn, Chapter 4 in this book). However, growth for growth's sake is an insufficient economic strategy; the goal of economic development must be the improvement of the living conditions of the vast majority of the population. This type of growth pattern – known as pro-poor growth (Saad-Filho, 2007) – is defined by a faster increase in the incomes of the poor than in the incomes of the rich; in other words, growth is pro-poor when it reduces not only absolute poverty but also relative poverty (that is, the distance between the rich and the poor in terms of income). This is best achieved through a democratic development strategy, which improves the incomes as well as the bargaining position of the workers and the poor, potentially supporting a self-sustaining process of economic, social and political inclusion.

The Way Forward

Convergence is essential for the achievement of a more equal and balanced world economy, and decoupling would help the South to converge. Despite encouraging signs recently, decoupling and convergence remain elusive. Much of the catch-up in the last 30 years is attributable to fast growth in a small number of DEs, and more recently to the impact of high commodity prices; most DEs remain heavily dependent on the AEs, performance disparities within the South continue to be significant, and over the long term most DEs have underperformed relative to the AEs.

Two more immediate challenges also demand a rethink of DE development strategies. The first is the risk of further global slowdown, which could be triggered by continuing stagnation or another finance-led slump in Western Europe, Japan or the United States. Second, DEs cannot expect the return of the growth pattern they enjoyed during the early 2000s boom, even after an eventual economic recovery in the AEs.

The challenges of stable, rapid and pro-poor economic growth in the DEs can be addressed only through a careful choice of economic policies supporting rapid accumulation and productivity growth, and the coordinated expansion of employment and demand, assisted by greater South–South integration and cooperation initiatives. Convergence and decoupling are important for these countries, and progress towards these goals would facilitate distributional improvements, employment creation and poverty alleviation. Faster progress along these lines is essential, although it remains conditional on unconventional policy choices and improvements in the living conditions of the majority of the population.

Acknowledgement

This chapter draws on Saad-Filho (2014).

Select Bibliography

Akyüz, Y. (2012) *The Staggering Rise of the South?* South Centre Research Paper 44. Geneva: UN Conference on Trade and Development (UNCTAD).

Nayyar, D. (2009) *Developing Countries in the World Economy: The Future in the Past?* WIDER Annual Lecture 12.

OECD (2010) *Perspectives on Global Development: Shifting Wealth.* Paris: OECD Development Centre.

Pritchett, L. (1997) 'Divergence, big time', *Journal of Economic Perspectives*, 11(3): 3–17.

Saad-Filho, A. (2007) 'There is life beyond the Washington consensus: an introduction to pro-poor macroeconomic policies', *Review of Political Economy*, 19(4): 513–37.

Saad-Filho, A. (2014) 'The 'Rise of the South': global convergence at last?' *New Political Economy*, 19(4): 578–600.

UNCTAD (2012) *Trade and Development Report.* New York and Geneva: United Nations.

Wälti, S. (2009) *The Myth of Decoupling.* Vox. Available at: www.voxeu.org/index. php?q=node/3814 (accessed 1 June 2014).

Weeks, J. (2001) 'The expansion of capital and uneven development on a world scale', *Capital and Class*, 74: 9–30.

CHAPTER SEVEN

Hegemony in Question: US Primacy, Multi-Polarity and Global Resistance

Jerome Klassen

Since the end of the cold war, the United States has led the international political economy as an uncontested superpower. With the disintegration of the Soviet Union and various strands of Third World nationalism, and with the subordinate cooperation of Western Europe and Japan, the United States was free to advance the twin goals of US grand strategy since the Second World War: the globalisation of capitalism and preeminent power for the United States itself. To these ends, the neoliberal project of financial globalisation was activated through the economic, political and military means of Washington.

In recent years, however, US primacy has been called into question in two key respects. First, the economic crisis of 2008–09 revealed the fundamental contradictions of the 'Washington consensus' on financial liberalisation, free trade and deregulated markets (see McNally, Chapter 23 of this book). The bursting of the US housing bubble sent shockwaves across the US economy and exposed the degree to which US capitalism had been built on risky debt financing. In this context, elites around the world increasingly questioned the strength of US capitalism compared with its competitors, particularly in Asia. For some, the crisis was symbolic of a long-term decline of US corporate power, and of a long-term rise of China as an economic powerhouse.

If the first setback for US primacy was economic in nature, the second was geopolitical. By 2008, the military occupations of Iraq and Afghanistan had entered a terminal stage of crisis, as insurgencies in both countries challenged US military forces and their local allies in government. The over-extension of US forces in Iraq and Afghanistan limited the means of US militarism elsewhere. In Latin America, a wave of left-wing governments came to power, promising a reversal of neoliberal policies and an opposition to US dominance. Similarly in Asia, China was building networks of trade and finance as a counterweight to US influence. In Africa as well, China was beginning to invest heavily in aid and infrastructure. China also helped to form the BRICS (Brazil, Russia, India, China and South Africa) bloc as a means of institutionalising a new global agenda. Thus, as the US economy was breaking down, so too was the US agenda for primacy in political and military affairs.

In this context, commentators from across the political spectrum began to ask: Is *Pax Americana* ending? In particular, is the United States in decline economically and geopolitically, and is a multi-polar or 'post-American' world emerging? If so, how will the United States respond? Will it double down on a strategy of primacy by exploiting its military edge? Will it accommodate emerging powers in US-led institutions of global governance? Or will it retrench as a leader of North America? Finally, will such a transition proceed peacefully or, as occurred in the first half of the 20th century, through cataclysmic warfare?

The purpose of this chapter is to map out several answers to these questions, and to survey the key dynamics of power, crisis and conflict in the contemporary global order. The first section reviews the principal theories of international political economy, including realism, liberalism and Marxism. It examines how each theory comes to terms with power, crisis and conflict in the world economy and interstate system. The second section then analyses the grand strategy of US foreign policy since the Second World War, a project of globalising capital and US political leadership. The third section considers the current crisis of US primacy and the new tendencies towards multi-polarity globally. The chapter closes with a reflection on the prospects for popular resistance. The key argument is that a global movement for socialism is necessary for challenging – and eventually transcending – the military conflicts and social inequalities of the capitalist world system.

Theories of International Political Economy (IPE)

Across the field of IPE, there is general agreement that the world order of the past few decades is undergoing a process of crisis and transformation, and that such dynamics are responsible for new configurations of power and conflict. However, in the key theories of the discipline – realism, liberalism and Marxism – the logic of crisis and transformation is understood in different ways.

Consider, first, the realist paradigm wherein *states* are the primary units of analysis and the *balance of power* between them drives geopolitical conflicts. This is because the nation-state system is constituted by *anarchy* in that no sovereignty exists beyond states themselves. As a result, states must practise *self-help* – they must rely upon their own resources for defending themselves and their national interests. In particular, states must prepare for war on a systematic basis. For realists, three conclusions follow. First, a hegemonic or dominant state can help stabilise the balance of power by securing trade routes and imposing discipline globally. Second, hegemonic states will nevertheless be challenged eventually by rising states. And third, hegemonic transitions tend to occur through Great Power warfare, as contender states seek a new balance of power.

In the present, realists are divided on the question of US primacy. For 'offensive realists,' the United States still commands absolute primacy in all registers of global power, and thus should work to contain or suppress any challengers, especially China. By contrast, 'defensive realists' tend to focus on the relative decline of US power and thus on the need for diplomatic and military retrenchment.

Although realism draws attention to patterns of rivalry and conflict in international politics, it offers no conceptualisation of its fundamental unit of analysis, namely the state. Realism views the state solely from the standpoint of the global balance of power and thus ignores domestic sources of state formation and policy choices. Related to this, realism fails to make sense of the state as anything but a military agent of the 'national interest.' In doing so, it obfuscates the class relations of the capitalist state.

Liberalism, as the second major paradigm, offers a different perspective. Here the fundamental agent is the *individual* as an actor in free-market exchanges. The market is seen as the ultimate space of human freedom – the site in which self-seeking individuals buy and sell goods on an equal basis and thus satisfy their wants and needs. In liberalism, the law of supply and demand regulates the exchange of commodities and guarantees equilibrium. It follows that the state must be limited to protecting private property, enforcing law and order, and defending the nation from outside threats. For liberal theory, the international exchange of commodities is the means by which economic integration, and indeed convergence, will occur between states. States can consequently find common interests in multilateral cooperation. A hegemonic state can also mitigate geopolitical conflict by anchoring the world trading system and by wielding a 'soft' power of cultural, diplomatic and political practices alongside a 'hard' power of military might.

In the current context, liberal IPE is focused on the global diffusion of political and economic power. In particular, it is concerned with managing the decline of US hegemony in ways that extend liberal norms and rules while avoiding Great Power conflict. More specifically, it seeks to incorporate China and other emerging powers into US-led institutions.

Although liberalism broadens the scope of analysis, it too has several gaps and omissions. First, liberalism ignores the social relations of production that are the source of profit and class division in capitalist society. Second, liberal notions of global economic convergence fail the test of empirical verification. In fact, even after several decades of trade and investment liberalisation, divergent forms of wealth, income, and growth still stratify the world economy. The reason for this is that globalisation has occurred largely through transnational relations of class exploitation in production. Finally, liberal IPE disassociates the state from the social relations of capitalism and thus obscures the economic logic of war and militarism.

The argument of this chapter is that a third perspective – Marxism – offers a more accurate picture of IPE. Whereas realism isolates the state, and liberalism isolates the market, Marxism grasps the social relations that tie the two together. As Marx pointed out, the antagonistic social relations between the owners of the means of production and those who must work for wages form the basis of class divisions under capitalism. This relation also allows for the exploitation of labour without direct intervention by the state. In this context, the state assumes a 'relatively autonomous' form: it enforces private property and manages class relations and the accumulation process on behalf of capital. Regarding interstate relations, states tend to advance the political interests of globalising capital: securing investments, markets and resources, and disciplining any states or political movements that trouble this agenda.

In this paradigm, a state will be *imperialistic* to the extent that it participates in global modes of economic exploitation and political domination. However, because the world economy turns on national modes of state and class formation, inter-imperialist rivalries will occur, sparking hegemonic power transitions. The dialectical twist of Marxism, though, is that resistance from below will accompany the social relations of capitalism. For Marxist theory, these movements – from working class and peasant-based struggles to indigenous and anti-colonial movements – are the hope for peace, democracy and equality globally.

Marxism thus offers three propositions on IPE. First, the world economy is marked by cross-border ties of class exploitation and therefore generates combined and uneven development on a systematic basis. Second, war and militarism are indirect forms of market competition and class domination globally. And lastly, a range of resistances are bound to contest the social relations of capitalism. With this in mind, peace and global justice can only be achieved through mass movements for socialism on both national and international scales. Using these insights, the next section maps the strategies and tactics of US imperialism since the Second World War.

Hegemonic Liberalism: US Grand Strategy Since the Second World War

The *Pax Americana* can be traced to the end of the Second World War. In 1945, the US military occupied the major zones of global capitalism, commanded a monopoly on atomic weaponry, and operated hundreds of overseas bases. After the war, the US economy accounted for half of world economic activity, and was three times larger than the Soviet economy and five times larger than the British economy. The United States was consuming roughly 50 per cent of all critical raw materials in the world economy, and US manufacturing firms were beginning a wave of direct investment abroad, particularly in Europe, Canada and Latin America.

In this context, US elites found a vested interest in a twofold strategy of hegemonic liberalism (Klassen, 2014). First, the United States would pursue an 'open door' system of trade and investment in the world economy as well as new institutions of multilateral governance. This was the liberal vision of US planners at the time. Yet US elites also assumed that US capital would anchor the world economy, that multilateral institutions would incorporate US norms and principles, and that the United States would use such leverage to maintain its global dominance. This constituted the hegemonic vision of US grand strategy.

As the post-war period developed, the United States tried to apply this strategy universally. With regard to the world market, the Bretton Woods Agreement of 1944 established the International Monetary Fund (IMF) to resolve balance of payments crises, and the International Bank for Reconstruction and Development (now the World Bank) to facilitate long-term infrastructure projects. With de facto control of these institutions, the United States shaped the post-war economic order. The Bretton Woods Agreement also established a new monetary system of fixed exchange rates, pegging the US dollar to gold at $35 an ounce. The US dollar was considered as 'good as gold' and became the key currency of international payments.

In the interstate system, the US strategy of hegemonic liberalism was omnipresent. In Western Europe, the key objective was to integrate Germany into a regional bloc under US dominance. As US secretary of state Dean Acheson put it at the time, the task was to create a "well-knit larger grouping of Atlantic states within which [a] new [European] grouping can develop, thus ensuring unity of purpose of [the] entire group and precluding [the] possibility of [Europe] becoming [a] third force or opposing force' (Acheson, 1952). In 1949, NATO was established for precisely this reason – as well as for guarding against internal leftist movements, which were close to taking power in several European countries.

In Eastern Europe, US strategy was to 'foster the seeds of destruction in the Soviet system', as the National Security Council put it in a secret planning directive. In Asia, US policy was to position Japan at the centre of a regional trading bloc under US military protection. Towards the Third World, the United States supported decolonisation as a means of breaking down the European empires, while nonetheless fearing the radical edge of national liberation movements. As a result, the United States adopted an eclectic strategy of decolonisation in some countries and recolonisation in others by the British and French. At the same time, the United States developed new capacities for managing the class struggles of the Third World without resorting to colonialism. In 1950, it fought to prevent communist forces from coming to power in North and South Korea. In 1953, the Central Intelligence Agency (CIA) overthrew the democratic government of Mohammad Mossadegh in Iran, which had nationalised western oil companies. In 1954, the United States backed a military coup in Guatemala as part of reversing populist policies of a democratic government. In these ways, the United States developed new techniques of informal empire.

Despite these successes, US strategy hit a wall in the 1960s. First, in the geopolitical realm, US power was undercut by the military failures in Indochina as well as by its policy of backing dictators in Latin America, Africa and the Middle East. Second, the economic structures of the Bretton Woods Agreement began to break down as German and Japanese firms came to dominate world markets. In this context, the United States began to run balance of payments deficits with Germany and Japan in 1966 and trade deficits with the rest of the world in 1971. The US economy, then, could no longer anchor the world market as it had since the Second World War. Indeed, as European banks and investors began to dump the US dollar for gold, President Nixon suspended convertibility in 1971, raised tariffs on imports and imposed a new monetary system based on floating exchange rates. The United States also refused to cooperate in any regime to govern global finance, forced a revaluation of Japanese and German currencies, and abolished capital controls to further expand US capital's reach abroad. Through such moves, the United States reconfigured the global economy in ways that empowered US primacy.

In the neoliberal period, a new structure of production, accumulation, and class and state formation emerged. With the end of Bretton Woods, the United States was able to run systematic trade deficits with Europe and Asia, which were forced to recycle dollar payments into US Treasury bonds or Wall Street securities. In the process, the dollar was saved as world money, capital controls were weakened in rival states, and the United States was able to run trade and government deficits. At the same time, Wall Street became the centre of global finance, and US firms gained access to new investment funds. Through these new modes of financialisation, the world economy was reconstituted under US centrality. President Reagan's defeat of the US labour movement also paved the way for a new regime of 'flexible accumulation' in the US economy – one based on low wage, deskilled, racialised, gendered and part-time labour markets.

Alongside these economic shifts, the United States pursued an aggressive military policy. In Latin America, it backed military coups in Chile (1973) and Argentina (1986), and financed the Contras against the Sandinista government in Nicaragua. After the 1979 revolution in Iran, the United States established Rapid Deployment Forces in the Gulf, and supported Saddam Hussein's invasion of Iran the following year. After the Soviet Union occupied Afghanistan, the United States also financed the *mujahideen* resistance to the communist government in Kabul. At the same time, Reagan supported South Africa's invasion of Angola and labelled the African National Congress a terrorist organisation. Through these international proxy wars, the United States tried to weaken or defeat the anti-imperialist and anti-capitalist resistance of the 1970s and 1980s.

It is vital to recognise that, with the fall of the Soviet Union and the transition to capitalism in China, the last obstacles to US grand strategy fell by the wayside. Indeed, after 1990, the United States was able to achieve the fundamental goals of hegemonic liberalism: the globalisation of capital and preeminent power for the United States itself. As a sign of this project, the *Defense Planning Guidance* of the Bush I Administration called for a strategy to '[preclude] the emergence of any potential future global competitor'. To this end, the *Quadrennial Defense Review* of the Clinton Administration argued that the role of the US military is to 'sustain American global leadership', and to secure 'uninhibited access to key markets, energy supplies and strategic resources'. In line with this, the *National Security Strategy* of the Bush II Administration aimed to 'dissuade potential adversaries from pursuing a military build-up in hopes of surpassing, or equalling, the power of the United States'. Likewise, the *National Security Strategy* of the Obama

Administration posits that the United States should 'underwrite global security' by 'renewing American leadership' and reviving the national economy as 'the wellspring of American power'.

Across the governments of the post-Cold War period, then, a single strategy has been advanced – one of globalising capital and US primacy. To these ends, the United States has engaged in permanent war, intervening in countries such as Panama, Colombia, the former Yugoslavia, Iraq, Afghanistan, Pakistan, Haiti, Libya, Somalia, Yemen, Honduras, Venezuela and Syria. However, US strategy has been challenged, if not degraded, by new dynamics in the global political economy.

New Vectors of Crisis and Conflict: US Power in Decline?

The question of hegemonic transition is one of the most important in contemporary world politics. Various analysts have noted that, from the terrorist attacks of 9/11 to the financial crisis of 2008–09, the United States seems to have suffered multiple setbacks.

Consider, first, the economic crisis of the past several years. The neoliberal expansion of the US economy ended in the late 1990s, as the rate of profit for US industry began a steep descent. In this context, capital moved into the financial sector, which began tapping US workers for mortgages, consumer credit and student loans as new sources of returns (see McNally, Chapter 23 in this book). The bursting of the US debt bubble and the collapse of Wall Street in 2008–09, thus expressed the fundamental contradictions of capital accumulation and class formation in the neoliberal period. The crisis also exposed the high degree of economic integration between the United States and the rest of the world. Europe was hit particularly hard because of its banks' purchases of US mortgage-backed securities, whose value collapsed. The crisis then exacerbated the European Union's internal imbalances, specifically those between importing and exporting states, and hampered the European Union as a political force in world politics. As a result, EU attempts at challenging US global primacy are also in crisis. Although Germany has increasingly embraced a liberal defence of military interventions in failed or failing states since the mid-1990s, it has done so cooperatively through multilateral or NATO-led missions, as in Afghanistan and the former Yugoslavia. In this context, France seems to be the only Western European country with an independent military agenda, particularly in Africa.

The rise of China is a different matter altogether. With double-digit growth rates for much of the post-cold war period, China is expected to surpass the United States as the world's largest economy in next decade or so. Although Chinese growth is coupled to the foreign direct investments of transnational corporations, and to the import demand of the North American and European economies, China weathered the economic crisis with growth rates of 6 per cent or higher. In fact, over the past few years, China has become the largest manufacturing and exporting power in the world, and in 2010 imported more from Germany than the United States (Black, 2011). In addition, private Chinese firms now account for more than 30 per cent of all Chinese exports, up from less than 5 per cent in 2000 (*Financial Times*, 2012). Furthermore, hundreds of billions of dollars of Chinese investment have penetrated Africa, Central Asia and Latin America as part of securing land and resources for long-term development. Moreover, in several high-tech sectors – for example, in clean energy, military, and computer technology – Chinese capital is now competing with top producers in Western Europe and North America. For these reasons, China has become a major anchor of finance, production and trade in the global economy. Furthermore, with hundreds of millions of peasants yet to enter the urban labour market, China will remain a competitive space of production. To this end, China's bureaucratic and capitalist state will seek to manage the super-exploitation of Chinese workers.

The key question for this chapter, though, is how do these economic shifts bear on geopolitical dynamics? On the one hand, Chinese state doctrine articulates a policy of 'peaceful rise' through domestic development and non-confrontational foreign relations. More specifically, China has aimed to increase trust, reduce trouble, develop cooperation and refrain from confrontation in global politics. From China's standpoint, the country has become a first-class global power and deserves to be treated as such by the United States. With this in mind, China views the US 'pivot' to Asia as a means of reasserting a dominant but declining hegemony in a critical zone of global capitalism. In doing so, the United States is creating a tinderbox that could be ignited by several flashpoints, including a declaration of independence in Taiwan, rearmament of Japan, a forward positioning of missile defence batteries in the region, a war in Korea, and a closing of Chinese trade routes.

Facing these scenarios, China has begun a military modernisation programme, involving new spending for aircraft carriers, nuclear submarines, cruise and ballistic missiles, and stealth fighter jets. However, despite US fears of Chinese expansionism, the aims of China's military modernisation have been 'keyed to the defence of a continental power with growing maritime interests as well to Taiwan's unification and are largely conservative, not expansionist. China is developing internal control, peripheral denial, and limited force-projection capabilities consistent with these objectives' (Fravel, 2008: 126).

At the same time, Chinese strategists have begun to articulate a 'strategic distrust' of US foreign policy, and a zero-sum rivalry in the making (Lieberthal and Jisi, 2012). With this in mind, a growing current in China calls for a new alliance with Russia; for a more robust maritime strategy in the South China Sea; and for the Chinese state to use its economic powers more aggressively towards the United States. Others, however, have warned against antagonising China's largest trading partner, as any political or military conflict would only disrupt economic development – the core aim of Chinese grand strategy. It is clear, then, that the United States and China are locked in complex forms of rivalry and interdependence. The United States is still the dominant power globally, but the trajectory of Chinese development suggests that a 'unipolar exit' may occur in the future, if it has not already (Layne, 2012: 204).

The development of the BRICS bloc is another sign of realignment in the world system. The BRICS account for 40 per cent of world population, 25 per cent of world landmass and 25 per cent of world GDP. The BRICS are divided by distance, language, culture and status, but have forged a new political space for balancing the United States and NATO and for discussing new approaches to capitalist development. Although the BRICS have been cautious in challenging US imperialism, they have delineated a three-pronged vision of world politics moving forward, involving global financial reform, a new development agenda and multi-polar regionalism. In particular, the BRICS have called for a new international monetary regime, a reform of the IMF, the World Bank and the UN Security Council, a new round of multilateral trade negotiations, a new development bank of the BRICS themselves and a reinforcement of international law to counter US and NATO unilateralism.

As Vijay Prashad (2013: 15) points out, though, the BRICS platform is limited in several ways. First, 'the domestic policies of the BRICS states follow the general tenor of what one might consider Neoliberalism with Southern Characteristics', involving harsh labour exploitation. Second, 'the BRICS alliance has not been able to create a new *institutional* foundation for its emergent authority'. And finally, 'the BRICS project has no ability to sequester the *military* dominance of the United States and NATO'. As a result, the BRICS face a potential contradiction between the political vision of multi-polarity and the economic logic of neoliberal capitalism under US dominance.

The course of the 'global war on terror' has also signalled weaknesses in US militarism. In Afghanistan, the United States and NATO built a state in which political power is concentrated in the President's Office and in provincial networks of warlords and sectional leaders. In this context, the Taliban re-emerged as a nationalist Islamist insurgency, forcing an early retreat of US and NATO forces (Klassen, 2013). Similarly, in Iraq, the United States destroyed the old state and tried to impose a new one through neoliberal and sectarian strictures, precipitating a civil war as well as an armed insurgency against US military forces. Given the debacles of these military occupations, the United States has embraced more indirect methods of intervention elsewhere, including drone attacks and Special Forces operations in Pakistan, Yemen and Somalia. Israel's 2006 war on Lebanon was also coordinated with the United States, which repeatedly blocked any move toward an early ceasefire. The victory of the Lebanese Hezbollah was a major blow to US and Israeli designs for the region, and set an example of resistance for Iran, Syria and Russia.

To contain the Arab uprisings, the United States has utilised similar methods of indirect involvement. In Egypt, it worked to keep former President Mubarak in power until the revolution became too powerful to ignore or suppress. The United States then fortified ties between the Egyptian military and the Pentagon, and notwithstanding the popular movement, backed the military coup of July 2013. While the United States and NATO pursued regime change through air strikes in Libya, other methods were used elsewhere. In Bahrain, a Saudi-led invasion of the Gulf Cooperation Council (GCC) crushed the popular protests of 2011 (see Chapter 20). Likewise, in Yemen, former dictator Ali Abdullah Saleh agreed to cede power to his deputy, Abdrabbuh Mansour Hadi, in an agreement facilitated by the United States and the GCC. Finally, in Syria, the CIA was deployed to arm and train an insurgency against Bashar al-Assad's Ba'athist government. After gaining early victories, the insurgency suffered a series of defeats and became dominated by sectarian, al-Qaeda-linked forces. Following a chemical attack in Damascus in August 2013, the United States itself backed down from air strikes after Russian diplomacy averted a regional war from occurring, involving possibly Syria, Iran and Hezbollah on one side and the United States, Israel, Turkey, Jordan and the GCC states on the other. On the Syrian battleground, then, the reality of multi-polarity has asserted itself in stark terms.

Resistance Beyond Multi-Polarity

The United States is still the dominant power globally and seeks to maintain its position of hegemony in the capitalist world system. However, two dynamics are degrading US primacy. First, the internationalisation of capital has created new zones of production, exploitation and accumulation in the world economy. These new spaces of capital are linked to the political economy of US primacy, but also express an independent capacity for producing commodities, exploiting labour and exporting investment capital. China, in particular, is developing a fusion of state and class powers to rival the United States and other top economies in the contemporary world market.

Second, the US military has been unable to win any strategic battles since 9/11. Although the US military 'commands the commons' of the sea, sky and space, and is unrivalled in nearly every form of hard power, it has not been able to buttress or extend the 'unipolar moment'. Instead, the wars of the past two decades have drained the US Treasury, exhausted the population at home and generated new security threats for the United States itself. With budget cuts looming, and with the failures of Iraq and Afghanistan in mind, the military itself is wary of new interventions, as the Syrian conflict has demonstrated to date. But if US economic power recedes in the future, the military will likely be called upon for new wars and conflicts, perhaps involving China. As part of this, the US military is increasingly focused on Africa as an emergent zone of economic competition.

The shift toward multi-polar regionalism, then, does not in any way herald an end to neoliberal patterns of economic exploitation and political domination. To the extent that the BRICS can impede or arrest US and NATO unilateralism, a modicum of law and order might replace the permanent wars of the past two decades. But to the extent that neoliberalism is embraced by the BRICS at home and abroad, the social wars of capitalism are bound to move to the fore of global politics – and to challenge the BRICS themselves. On this note, it is worth recalling that, in the context of neoliberalism, massive protests have rocked Brazil; authoritarian tendencies have emerged in Russia; a Maoist insurgency has spread across one-third of India; economic exploitation and political repression have continued in China; and social inequalities have deepened in South Africa.

With this in mind, any project for peace and global justice will have to look beyond the BRICS agenda, and to ground itself in a different set of political agents: in transnational social movements of working class and oppressed peoples. Put differently, any politics of anti-imperialism must also involve a politics of social transformation. To this end, a new solidarity of working class and oppressed peoples' movements must be built on local and global scales.

Although such movements have been weakened significantly by neoliberal policies and internal difficulties, signs of recomposition are evident globally. In China, for example, the number of 'collective incidents,' including strikes and public protests, has risen dramatically in the past two decades. In Latin America, mass movements of peasants, workers and indigenous people have, over the past decade, reclaimed the public sphere, altered the balance of class forces, and taken power through elections in countries such as Bolivia, Venezuela and Ecuador. Throughout the Arab uprisings, working class forces have also been active, whether through organising strikes, forming unions, or contesting neoliberalism and western interventions in the region. Moments of resistance have also occurred in the United States itself, for example through Occupy Wall Street, various teachers' strikes, anti-war and global justice protests, and nationwide struggles of immigrant workers. To further build an anti-racist, feminist and working class angle on anti-imperialism, activists in North America have also networked with trade unions, women's organisations, and democratic and socialist currents in Iraq and Afghanistan. In Western Europe, the level of social contestation has been much greater, combining anti-war and pro-Palestinian activism, student-led university occupations, urban riots around policing, unemployment and racism, and anti-austerity strikes and demonstrations.

The key lesson is that the social relations of capitalism form a crucible for mass movements of working class politics – and that such movements hold hope for ending the neoliberal project and its related wars and conflicts. For this reason, social movements for peace and global justice must look beyond the politics of multi-polarity to a politics of social transformation informed by anti-capitalism.

Select Bibliography

Acheson, D. (1952) 'The Secretary of State to the Embassy in France', 19 September. *Foreign Relations of the United States, 1952–1954*, Vol. 5, Part 1, Western European

Security, Document 174. Available at http://history.state.gov/historicaldocuments/ frus1952-54v05p1/d174 (accessed 14 June 2014).

Black, J. (2011) 'Germany's future rising in East as exports to China eclipse U.S.' *Bloomberg News*, 6 April. Available at: www.bloomberg.com/news/2011-04-06/germany-s-future-rising-in-east-as-exports-to-china-eclipse-u-s-.html (accessed 2 June 2014).

Financial Times (2012) 'Chinese exports by type of enterprise', 10 September. http://blogs. ft.com/beyond-brics/2012/09/10/chart-of-the-week-who-is-making-chinas-exports/ chinese-exports-by-type-of-enterprise-sep-2012/ (accessed 2 June 2014).

Fravel, M. T. (2008) 'China's search for military power', *Washington Quarterly*, 31(1) (Summer): 125–41.

Klassen, J. (2013) 'Methods of empire: nation-building, development and war in Afghanistan', in J. Klassen and G. Albo (eds), *Empire's Ally: Canada and the War in Afghanistan*. Toronto: University of Toronto Press.

Klassen, J. (2014) *Joining Empire: The Political Economy of the New Canadian Foreign Policy*. Toronto: University of Toronto Press.

Layne, C. (2012) 'This time it's real: the end of unipolarity and the *Pax Americana*', *International Studies Quarterly*, 56: 203–13.

Lieberthal, K. and Wang, J. (2012) *Addressing US–China Strategic Distrust*. Washington DC: Brookings Institution.

Prashad, V. (2013) *Neoliberalism with Southern Characteristics: The Rise of the BRICS*. New York: Rosa Luxemburg Stiftung.

CHAPTER EIGHT

Neoliberalism, Crisis and International Migration

Pietro Basso

International migration is one of the most significant phenomena of modern times. Its roots lie in historical colonialism and the international division of labour created by it, characterised by the exploitation and oppression of non-white continents by the European powers, and subsequently also by the United States and Japan. Today's neoliberal industrial and financial globalisation has grafted itself onto this past (which is still present), resulting in three intertwined effects: it has swelled internal migration within newly capitalist countries, accelerated international migration, and increasingly driven the latter along the South–North axis.

The crisis since 2007 has neither reversed nor halted migratory movements globally, as their multiple underlying causes continue to operate. However, the crisis has slowed migratory movements towards the Organisation for Economic Co-operation and Development (OECD) countries, where 'economic migration' has not returned to pre-crisis levels. By contrast, migration has swelled towards the BRICs, the Gulf Arab states and Turkey, which are new centres of attraction for emigrants from non-white continents.

Restrictive and repressive neoliberal migration policies have placed immigrant populations as a whole in a subordinate legal, material, political and symbolic situation. At the same time, these policies have increased the number of undocumented immigrants, which have come to form a kind of 'zero-rights' immigration used by states and firms as weapons to push down wages and working conditions of the entire labour force. Immigrant workers have thus become the global prototype of the precarious, 'flexible', super-exploited worker of the neoliberal era.

This chapter first examines the root causes of international migration and the contradictory effects of the current crisis. It then argues that, despite the exploitation and institutional racism disseminated by state authorities in immigration countries, international migration continues to be a potent force for social change, laden with positive potential, as day after day migration grinds down national differences and prejudices within the global working class. The struggles of immigrant workers that have developed in recent years (from the United States to Europe, from China to the Gulf Arab states and South Africa)

have contributed greatly to this outcome. These struggles are also rich in significance for native workers in immigration countries, who increasingly experience
precarious working conditions and gradually begin to feel like immigrants in their
own land of birth. The growing interaction and eventual coming together of the
expectations, experiences and organised actions of proletarians of all nations and
colours, fostered by international migration, constitutes a social force capable of
mapping out an alternative to neoliberal capitalism: that is, an alternative social
system, not just a modification of economic policies.

A Global, Epoch-Making Phenomenon

'The Age of Migration' is the phrase chosen by Stephen Castles and Mark J.
Miller (2009), and it could not be more appropriate. It stands for the international dimension of migration, and refers to the post-war period from 1945 to
present. Indeed, this period is distinguished from an earlier period of still-sig-
nificant international migration – that of 1850 to 1914 – because migration
has become a truly global process. This global characteristic differentiates
contemporary migration from all other so-called voluntary or forced migrations
in the past. Migration today is a permanent and long-term phenomenon with
enormous economic, social, political, cultural and personal consequences for
both emigration and immigration countries. It is both a product of and a factor
in epoch-making changes.

A few basic figures help to underscore the size and development of the
phenomenon. From 1950 to 2005 world population more than doubled from 2.5
to over 6 billion. Over the same period the number of international emigrants
of all types ('economic migrants', asylum seekers, ecological migrants, internationally displaced persons and so on) more than tripled from 60 million to 200
million. The gap between these two processes is likely to widen over the next
30 to 40 years. According to projections by the International Organization for
Migration (IOM), the world population is likely to reach 9 billion in 2050 (30
per cent greater than now), while the number of international emigrants is set
to double reaching over 400 million. Migratory movements of enormous proportions are continuing *within* individual countries, notably within Asia, Africa and
Latin America. Intra-national migration has involved 740 million people to date
and, together with unprecedented urbanisation processes, is a main driver of
international migration (IOM, 2011).

While such colossal migratory movements predate the neoliberal era, they
have nonetheless accelerated under neoliberalism. In the so-called Golden Age
of capitalist development (1945–75) the number of worldwide emigrants/immi-
grants grew by 60–70 per cent. Under post 1980s neoliberalism their numbers
more than doubled, with particular intensity in the new millennium. Over
the same period (1980–2012), immigration accounted for 40 per cent of total
population growth (OECD, 2013: 13). International migration has also shifted

direction. Whereas South to South patterns predominated 50 years ago, today the trajectory is increasingly South to North.

Root Causes of International Migration

The root causes of international migration are multiple and intertwined. Its main, historical cause derives from the uneven and unequal form of development that arose with European colonialism. As Karl Marx wrote:

> The discovery of gold and silver in America, the extirpation, enslavement, and entombment in mines of the aboriginal population, the beginning of the conquest and looting of the East India, the turning of Africa into a warren for the commercial hunting of negroes, signalised the rosy dawn of the era of capitalist production. These idyllic proceedings are the chief factors of primitive accumulation.
>
> (Marx, 1952 [1867]: 372)

For the colonised peoples, the process of concentration of the commercial and usurious capitals that gave rise to industrial capital in Western Europe – the so-called original accumulation – represented a process of original disaccumulation. Industrial development in Western Europe, moreover, had even more devastating effects on colonised and subordinate countries. European colonialism stripped the lands of natural resources and forced indigenous peoples into genocidal working legions, literally squeezing the lifeblood out of them. Colonialism also destroyed local crafts, traditional industry and manufacturing (beginning with textiles). It ruined indigenous peoples' millennia-old agricultural infrastructures and dispossessed the colonised peoples of the technical and productive expertise accumulated over generations.

Colonialism systematically destroyed the treasures of their culture and sciences, starting with the burning of Mayan books in July 1562, as ordered by Diego De Landa. Colonialism took indigenous trade into its own clutches and bled their polities' coffers dry. Colonial leaders plotted the moral breakdown of the colonised peoples, enlisting and training indigenous elites, officials and foot soldiers to control and repress the populations. Colonial leaders worked skilfully to freeze the most archaic local traditions and systematically stirred up inter-ethnic and inter-religious rivalries. In this way, European colonialism profoundly subordinated the developmental trajectories of indigenous and other peoples of colour; as Rodney argued (1972), colonialism *brutally underdeveloped* them. In the resulting system of international division of labour, colonised countries were forced to provide the colonising countries with raw materials and workers. This erected a massive obstacle to any subsequent independent development.

Even after the achievement of political independence, the former colonies had to incur debts with their very dispossessors in order to pursue industrialisation, to modernise their agriculture, and to achieve an at least partially independent development. The so-called 1980s Third World debt crisis, which first exploded in Mexico in 1982, suggests that the earlier, formal types of colonialism have been replaced by a new type of imperialist colonialism: financial colonialism (Chesnais, 1997). Burdened by foreign debts, a long-term consequence of this original disaccumulation, many peripheral countries with colonial or semi-colonial histories (for example, the Central and Latin American, Northern African and South Asian societies) were forced into structurally entrenched patterns of debt-led development. Many of these societies have been unable to break the vicious circle of dependency set in motion since the 16th century, which is repro-duced in new ways. The reproduction of colonial dependency breeds poverty and inequality, which in turn fuels emigration from these countries. They are in debt because of their subordination to imperialist countries, which have grown rich from their dominant position in the capitalist international division of labour. Their condition of dependency forces workers in poor countries to perform a role of suppliers of low-cost labour-power to Western countries and their firms.

It is not possible here to explain all the mechanisms reproducing interna-tional inequality and poverty in the recent decades of neoliberal globalisation (see Pradella, Chapter 2 of this book). I shall limit myself to drawing attention to three processes that have had a major impact on migration.

- The capitalist transformation of Asian, Latin American and African agri-culture. Multinational corporations have taken control of large swaths of agricultural production and commerce, operating both upstream and down-stream of production. Currently about 35 per cent of the global labour force (over one billion people) are employed in agriculture, many as formally inde-pendent smallholders. International competition and various forms of peasant exploitation by multinational enterprises force many among this immense army of workers to abandon the countryside for the city in order merely to survive. The industrialisation of agricultural production and probable intro-duction of private land ownership in China threaten to make such migratory movement occur on a huge scale.
- A never-ending sequence of seemingly local wars such as, for example, the wars in Iraq, Yugoslavia and the Congo. These wars displace entire sectors of the population and force them to leave the country.
- Environmental disasters. According to an estimate by the IOM (considered to be conservative by some), ecological migration could affect between 200 and 250 million people by 2050.

International migration responds to the vital need of Western countries for immigrant workers. Immigration, and the increasing labour supply it allows for, is necessary for Western firms to maintain their competitiveness. It also enables Western states and households to offset the dismantling and restructuring of the welfare state, coping with the ageing of the population privately and relatively cheaply (in monetary terms). Increasingly restrictive immigration policies do not aim at stopping immigration (Basso and Perocco 2003: 8–22). Their core principle consists in granting a residence permit only to those immigrants who have an employment contract, and they attribute the right to apply for it not to the immigrants themselves but to their employers. This is one provision of Italy's 2002 Bossi–Fini law that has become a model for the rest of Europe and the United States. In this way, restrictive immigration policies aim at rendering immigrants hyper-precarious and blackmailed guest workers forced to make every sacrifice and to be, if possible, temporary immigrants. This condition of extreme precarity is particularly evident for those immigrant workers effectively blackmailed because of their illegal status. Restrictive immigration legislation – and this is a point of the highest importance – does not just produce precarity and 'illegal' employment for immigrant workers. Rather, by fostering the stratification of the labour market, restrictive legislation aims at expanding extreme precarity throughout the whole labour market.

In order to understand the acceleration of international migration in recent decades, we also need to consider another important source: the rising expectations for both socio-economic improvements and political freedom of working populations in the Global South. These aspirations have, for example, been a driving force in the recent uprisings in the Arab world. But if, as often happens, people's own country of birth is unable to offer dignified employment and a dignified existence, this possibility is sought wherever such conditions have historically accumulated.

This is particularly true for women from Eastern Europe, Latin America, Arab and black Africa, and Asia, who now constitute almost half of all international emigrants and a growing share of the more highly skilled workers. Here is another change of epochal importance. Today, frequently women, rather than men, start the migration process for the entire family or village, or emigrate alone as a result of the irrepressible, widespread aspiration towards a better life. On the one hand, women are forced to seek work outside their home and to cope with the afflictions of such work (especially if it is performed in other homes). On the other hand, whatever these afflictions are, many women intend to escape from their conditions of material hardship, the suffocating duties of domestic prisons, and unbearable personal relations. Emigrant women from the South and the East have come to perform strategic functions in the global economy, from agricultural and industrial production to domestic services. They provide low-cost domestic work and care for the wealthy globally and in countries rich in material resources. To be sure, this international transfer of care and love brings to mind the extraction of gold, ivory and rubber by classical colonialism (Ehrenreich and Hochschild, 2002). Emigrant women, however, are not passive and invisible subjects: they struggle by force of necessity to make themselves visible. Women emigrants are, no less than male emigrants, bearers of a profound need for social and personal emancipation.

This picture has become decidedly more complicated over the last 30 years.

Indeed, the South has expanded eastwards while new centres of accumulation have formed in the South, attracting millions of immigrants and thus fostering South–South migration. At the same time, in the North and particularly in Europe, a geographical and social polarisation has developed, leading to a new wave of South–North and East–West migration within its enlarging boundaries. Nevertheless, the core of Abdelmalek Sayad's analysis, in my view, remains sound:

> A specific bipolarity is characteristic of the contemporary world, which is divided into two unequal geopolitical ensembles—a rich, developed world, a world of immigration, and a poor, 'undeveloped' world, the world of emigration (real or only virtual). This bipolarity can be considered the condition which generates migratory movement and, even more certainly, the current form of immigration, the only true immigration (socially speaking), that is the one that comes from all of those countries, from those continents even, grouped together under the single name of Third World.
>
> (Sayad, 1999: 236; author's translation)

The Effects of the Crisis

While the global economic crisis has not reversed the process described above, it has led to some significant changes. So long as the underlying causes of global migration remain in effect, this phenomenon, far from drying up, will expand. Research conducted by Gallup in 135 countries between 2007 and 2009 found that '16 per cent of the global adult population wishes to leave their country. This means that 700 million people, more than the entire population of the American continent, would leave their country for ever if they had the means to do so' (Naim, 2010). Only 10 per cent of them were aged over 35, and 50 per cent of them already had a relative who had emigrated abroad with whom they were in contact. The crisis, in fact, does not affect only the West, and often has particularly harsh effects outside the West. Immigrants, moreover, are increasingly permanent. This is especially so if they have family back home who depend on their remittances. These immigrants often seek to avoid returning home, which would represent failure. It is thus unrealistic to imagine an en masse return to emigration countries. Although states and firms are trying to promote temporary labour migration, it is unlikely that we will witness in future decades a predominance of temporary over permanent labour migration; permanent migration today accounts for two-thirds of the total. A specific case, of course, is migration from neighbouring countries, as it allows workers to return home temporarily before emigrating again (circular migration).

The crisis, however, has led to three important changes. First, the crisis has worsened working conditions for immigrants, both in absolute terms and relative to home country workers. This starts with the rising unemployment rate, which increased in OECD countries by 5 per cent between 2008 and 2012.

For some nationalities of immigrants it is much, much worse. North Africans, for instance, suffer from unemployment rates near 27 per cent. While the crisis spreads extreme precarity to broader and broader sections of the working class, the intensification of state racism (a system of socio-economic, legal, political and ideological discrimination realised by the state) mystifies the causes of the crisis by blaming immigrants for its effects.

Second, according to OECD's *International Migration Outlook 2013*, the crisis has slowed economic migration to OECD countries. By 2011 pre-crisis levels had yet to be reached. For the OECD, 'the Great Recession, although it has put a break on movements overall to a certain extent, has ... not fundamentally changed the dynamic of international migration in most countries, which rely more and more on cross-border movements to maintain the size of their workforces' (OECD, 2013: 18). The number of asylum seekers continues to increase, as a result of processes of break-up, war and the explosion of social and ethnic conflicts under way in many areas of Africa, the Middle East and Asia.

Third, the slowdown in economic migration to OECD countries is paralleled by an increase in migration to the Gulf Arab states, the BRICS and Turkey. In the Gulf, especially, there is a large majority of immigrant workers. Russia, too, has seen increases with millions of immigrants entering from the former Soviet Central Asian Republics. China, historically a nation of emigration, has begun to receive sizeable contingents of Vietnamese immigrants. India attracts immigrants from Bangladesh and Brazil from Portugal. South Africa receives immigrants from the rest of sub-Saharan Africa. In some cases the immigrants are manual workers or women seeking domestic work. In other cases the immigrants are young people with a high or medium-to-high level of education. In all of these countries – countries both of emigration and immigration – public debate has emerged with regard to the causes, benefits, dangers and potentials of these processes. This debate has itself become global.

A Powerful Factor of Social Change

Contemporary international migration is ever more global, structural, larger in scale and permanent. There are clear indicators of the growing rootedness of immigrants from the South and East, even in those countries that became immigration countries only in the neoliberal period. This is the case, for example, in Italy, where the increasingly permanent nature of migration in recent decades is proved by the number of family reunifications, the reduction in time for reunifications, the increase in mixed marriages, the expansion of second and third generations, and of the school population consisting of the children of immigrants, the purchase of a home, the start-up of independent businesses, the opening of current bank accounts and so on.

A large number of male and female workers – despite not having entertained the possibility right from the beginning and despite continuing to dream of returning home – have been drawn into an experience which is increasingly marked by permanence. That is why the terms emigrants and immigrants are more appropriate than migrants to describe processes that are characterised by fewer and fewer individuals who are recurrently on the move – 'birds of passage', to use Piore's dreadful metaphor. The permanent character of the settlement of the new generations of immigrants in the United States and Europe has been well understood – *a contrario*, of course – by theorists of the 'clash of civilisations' following Huntington and the hacks of Islamophobia in the Caldwell vein. These have warned against the transformation of the West into multicultural societies and tried to create in the public a feeling of distance from and hostility to the immigrant populations.

This vast process of epoch-making significance is an extraordinary factor of social change. International migration profoundly transforms both emigration and immigration societies. On the one hand, it links emigration countries to the whole world on material, cultural and political levels. On the other hand, after having transformed the United States, it is also transforming European societies into multiracial, multinational, multicultural and multireligious societies. International migration permanently transforms workplaces (as the majority of immigrants are workers) as well as schools, neighbourhoods, apartment blocks, public places, services, associations, trade unions and literary production. International migration also transforms the emotional life of individuals and their relationships of friendship and love.

The speed of this change has been stunning. Thirty or 40 years ago only a few European metropolises could be considered global cities. None of them, excepting Marseilles, was situated in Southern Europe. Today the whole of Southern Europe is teeming with small and mid-sized cities populated by dozens of different nationalities and languages, all connected to the world by a thousand networks.

This extraordinary transformation of social and personal relationships, induced by international migration, is rich in positive potential, as were previous epochal transitions from the horde to the tribe, from nomadism to the establishment of the first cities, and so on through to the transition from feudalism to the modern bourgeois society – even though in each of these historical transitions, especially the most recent, great treasures of knowledge and civilisation have been lost. The greatest of these potentially positive effects, in my view, is the possible overcoming of the national and racial antagonisms that afflict the working classes and humanity. According to Saskia Sassen international migration has led to the emergence of a 'global class of disadvantaged workers', which is 'more global and hence indicative of the future, rather than of a backward past, than is usually assumed' (2007: 189). This class, or better this section of the working class, is indicative of the future insofar as its experience is directly global and is composed of both immigrant workers and of an increasing number of home country workers who feel insecure and like immigrants in their country of birth.

Two Opposing Prospects

State institutions in immigration countries are opposing this epoch-making march towards multiracial, multinational and multicultural societies through specific policies and discourses. They have produced a system of discriminations that merit the title of *state racism*, which creates inequalities based on ethnicity, nationality, religion, class and gender. State racism immerses large numbers of immigrant workers in circles of informal and hidden employment. State racism stirs up false antagonisms between long-settled and new immigrants as well as between white workers and workers of colour. State racism does everything to arouse and exacerbate popular racism. Official authorities behind state racism do not hesitate to proclaim war on immigrants by building walls and detention centres, issuing special laws and exercising special procedures against immigrants. If the global economic crisis worsens further, European democracies will undoubtedly move in this direction and further exacerbate state racism.

The epochal transformation that is under way, however, can take a completely opposing direction. It can lead not just to a conflict between immigrant populations and their direct exploiters, but also to a *general conflict* between the working class and the capitalist class. The class struggle will decide. Immigrant workers have always been an integral part – and often a very combative part – of the working class movements. In 1886 in the United States, for example, German, Italian and Polish immigrant workers played a crucial role in the historic international fight for an eight-hour working day. Immigrants were likewise protagonists in the workers' and social struggles of 1968–69 in France, Belgium and Italy (although in this case the immigrants in question came from the South of Italy). Immigrants, too, were at the forefront of battles for the 35-hour working week in Germany in the early 1980s.

More recently, millions of immigrants went on to the streets protesting against the proposed 'snare bill' on the great day of struggle on 1 May 2006 in the United States, campaigning instead for the legalisation of all undocumented workers. The movement had significance beyond these immigrants alone. The movement succeeded in an extraordinary manner in turning on its head the debate on immigration reform in the United States. It inspired a new generation of young activists, overcame existing barriers and revitalised the 'anti-globalisation' movement which had been in decline since 9/11. For the first time in decades in the United States, the idea of a general strike emerged, evidently not for immigrants alone, but for all workers. Thanks to the strength of this mobilisation, 'the first of May crossed the US border once again, without authorisation, and was reintroduced into the country' (Akers-Chacón, 2010: 88–9; author's translation). The struggles straddled the US–Mexican border, bringing together workers in ways that signalled encouragement, organisation and the possibility of struggle on a global scale.

Smaller-scale immigrant worker struggles are also significant for the working class as a whole, transcending national distinctions. Take the case of workers in the logistics sector in Italy. Their struggle, which started around Milan in 2008 and continues today, has come to involve thousands of workers. The geographical focal point is between Bologna and Piacenza, in the Centre-Nord of Italy. Involving both self-organisation and effective trade-union organisation by SI-Cobas in workplaces where 'illegal' employment, on-call work and semi-slavery conditions were prevailing, this struggle has imposed respect for the national employment contract and for workers' dignity on the employers. The mostly immigrant logistics workers have attacked a key neoliberal practice – the outsourcing by large companies (such as IKEA, UPS, GLS, TNT, Bartolini and the Coop) to cooperatives employing low-paid immigrants. This is one of the ways these companies reduce labour costs and thereby the cost of a number of essential services. Despite police intimidation, these workers are striking in order to have their demands introduced into the new national employment contract (which employers would like to be drawn up along concession bargaining lines), and to force the retraction of political layoffs and other repressive measures against them. These workers are mainly from North Africa and Asia. One of them, Mohammed Arafat, aged 29, from Egypt, summed up the general value of these struggles with these words:

> After the January 25 Revolution, at TNT [Piacenza] we would always say: 'this is Tahrir Square too'. Ours, in fact, has been a minor revolution. No one would have bet on it a few years ago. We have shown that united we win. So, I have just one message for workers struggling in my country: you are the union. You don't need to follow anyone, just yourselves and your needs. You have to take your future into your hands, never looking at your personal, immediate interests. It's all of your interests taken together that must guide you, as it's only with unity and solidarity that you can win.

In this case, too, this message of struggle has arrived from the South, from the vibrant Egyptian Intifada, before heading back South again, vindicated. And this message is not just about outsourcing, neoliberalism and the unions: it is about big and small revolutions.

The chain of examples could be much longer, including numerous strikes and revolts by Indian, Pakistani, Nepalese, Indonesian and Philippine immigrants in Kuwait or in Dubai; the struggle of the Bangladeshi labourers in Manolada (Greece); the role played by African immigrants in the magnificent struggle of the Marikana miners; the never-ending series of struggles by the *mingong* in China; the uprisings by second-generation immigrants in Paris, London and Stockholm .... Each struggle contains a message that does not concern only the immediate needs of their protagonists or the immigrant populations in general, but concerns the working class as a whole. It is no mere chance that all these struggles have all aroused – at different degrees – a sentiment of sympathy, and even imitation also in sectors of home country populations and workers.

Struggles against discrimination, against the laws which produce illegality, the denial of the most basic rights, starvation wages for appalling hours and workloads, the violations typical of subcontracted work, and against social marginalisation are directed against the *effects* of neoliberal policies. Yet each one of these struggles, especially if it is conducted with radicalism, raises the question of the causes generating these social pathologies. The struggles can lead to the questioning not only of the inequality between home country and immigrant workers in the national sphere, but also of the roots of these disparities and of international migration itself.

The causes are diverse, but include the unequal development between North and South, between imperialist and dominated countries, war, the brutal capitalist exploitation of the land and those who work the land, environmental disasters and so on. All these relations are not caused solely by specific policies, but rather by the capitalist system as such and its centre in the West. These relations do not involve only specific sections of the working class, but the entire international working class. Neoliberalism has made it clear that the destiny of the working class is indivisible. As Marx said, 'labour cannot emancipate itself in the white skin when in the black it is branded'.

Called by these struggles and those under way in the Global South against the effects of imperialist domination, 'labour in the white skin' cannot avoid answering. So far, large sectors of the working classes in Europe and the United States have tried, in some way, to resist neoliberalism dreaming of an impossible return to Keynesian policies. They will have to accept that neoliberalism is nothing but the best ideological-political form for the late, almost decrepit, capitalism of the early 21st century. In order to go beyond neoliberalism it is necessary to go beyond capitalism, its obsession for profit and labour exploitation, its discriminations, its growing inequalities, its organic racism, its inherent brutality, its chaos and its incurable dementia.

Select Bibliography

Akers-Chacón, J. (2010) 'La persecuzione degli undocumented e la lotta per i diritti degli immigrati negli Stati Uniti' ['The persecution of the undocumented and the struggle for the rights of immigrants in the United States'], in P. Basso (ed.), *Razzismo di stato: Stati Uniti, Europa, Italia [State racism: United States, Europe, Italy]*. Milan: FrancoAngeli.

Basso, P. and Perocco, F. (eds) (2003) *Gli immigrati in Europa. Disuguaglianze, razzismo, lotte [Immigrants in Europe: inequalities, racism, struggles]*. Milan: FrancoAngeli.

Castles, S. and Miller, M. J. (2009) *The Age of Migration: International Population Movements in the Modern World*. Basingstoke: Palgrave Macmillan.

Chesnais, F. (1997) *La mondialisation du capital [The Globalisation of Capital]*. Paris: Syros.

Ehrenreich, B. and Hochschild, A. R. (ed.) (2002) *Global Women: Nannies, Maids and Sex Workers in the New Economy*. New York: Henry Holt.

International Organization for Migration (IOM) (2011) *World Migration Report 2010 – The Future of Migration: Building Capacities for Change*. Geneva: IOM.

Marx, K. (1952) [1867] *Capital*. Chicago, Ill. and London: Encyclopaedia Britannica.

Naim, M. (2010) '700 milioni: la più grande migrazione del secolo' ['700 million: the biggest migration of the century'], *Il Sole 24 Ore*, 23 February.

Organisation for Economic Co-operation and Development (OECD) (2013) *International Migration Outlook 2013*. Paris: OECD.

Rodney, W. (1972) *How Europe Underdeveloped Africa*. London: Bogle-L'Ouverture.

Sassen, S. (2007) *A Sociology of Globalisation*. New York: W. W. Norton.

Sayad, A. (1999) *La double absence* [*The Double Absence*]. Paris: Editions du Seuil.

CHAPTER NINE

Neoliberalism, Social Reproduction and Women's Resistance: Lessons from Cambodia and Venezuela

Sarah Miraglia and Susan Spronk

The struggle for women's liberation has come a long way since the times of Marx and Engels. Women have won the right to vote, to run for political office, and to seek a profession of their choice. Countries as diverse as India, the United Kingdom, Germany, Brazil and Argentina have had female heads of state. Where it is accessible, technological advances in birth control allow women to control when they get pregnant and whether to carry the pregnancy to term. Spousal rape is now considered a crime in many jurisdictions. Article 7 of the UN International Covenant on Economic, Social and Cultural Rights stipulates that women should receive equal pay for equal work.

Despite this considerable progress, women are far from achieving equality with men. Worldwide, women continue to labour for wages that are much lower than men. As of 2010 women in the European Union still earn 84 cents to every dollar a man makes, and in the United States women earn 77 cents. The gender wage gap is even more extreme in countries of the Third World. In 2010, women with low levels of education in Zambia made 59 cents for every dollar made by men with similar levels of education. Such extreme inequalities are also found in advanced capitalist countries, particularly amongst racialised populations. In Canada, for example, as of 2011 racialised women made 48 cents for each dollar earned by their male counterparts. In short, poor women in the global South and from the global South bear the brunt of a racialised and patriarchal economic order.

The facts above suggest that the uneven development of capitalism produces a contradictory force for the liberation of women. While we see important advances in women's liberation for a privileged few, as women have been increasingly integrated into the labour market, these advances are far from being shared equally amongst women across global racialised and class divides. In this chapter, we argue that although inequality between men and women in the global North and South existed long before neoliberalism, poor women of the global South have been the hardest hit by the capitalist project of neoliberalism. We ground this analysis by examining the politics of production and reproduction in Cambodia and Venezuela, where women have responded to the pressures of this 'double burden' by struggling for land and water – the fundamentals of life.

Neoliberalism: Reprivatisation of Social Reproduction

Under neoliberalism, increased market participation, whether as a wage worker or a small entrepreneur hawking wares purchased with a micro-credit loan, has been billed as the path to women's emancipation. Far from empowering women, however, neoliberal policies have had deep and deleterious consequences for women's lives. Cuts in public expenditures and the privatisation of health, education and welfare services combined with women's increased participation in the paid economy have placed increased pressure on women's 'double burden', resulting in a 'squeeze on care'. That is, neoliberal policies shift the costs and labour associated with social reproduction from the public to the private/domestic sphere. This downloads the costs of adjustment onto women, a process that Isa Bakker (2003) describes as the reprivatisation of social reproduction. As feminist and socialist analyses as early as Marx and Engels have highlighted, alternatives to capitalism and neoliberalism must therefore seek to rectify the inequalities created by the sexual division of labour, under which women are primarily responsible for unpaid, 'reproductive' work in the household at the same time as they perform paid, 'productive' work for others.

Marx's co-author, Engels, was the pioneer of feminist and materialist Marxism. In his book *The Origin of the Family, Private Property and the State* (2004 [1884]), Engels analysed the way that the institution of private property transformed the family into its contemporary monogamous form. Engels argued that previous societies in which production took place communally had matrilineal family organisations, where women were equal to or had more power than men. With the institutionalisation of private property and bourgeois property laws that regulated the 'traditional' marriage, women became equal to slaves because they performed reproductive work for free and were owned by their husbands or fathers. Engels also observed, however, that capitalism creates the possibility for women's liberation from family-based patriarchy because it affords opportunities for women to become economically independent by working as wage labourers. Given the sexual division of labour, however, women will only be truly free, theorised Engels, if the unpaid work of childcare and household maintenance are provided in a socialised manner (for example, by the state as social services). Engels' work highlighted how women face what contemporary feminists call a 'double burden': women must sell their labour-power in order to earn wages for their 'productive' work, although they remain responsible for unpaid, 'reproductive' work at home.

The strain of the double burden is compounded by the fact that women are incorporated into the labour market under conditions of structural subordination. In a 1997 essay, 'Women workers and capitalist scripts: ideologies of

domination, common interests and the politics of solidarity', post-colonial and
Marxist feminist Chandra Mohanty investigates the way that patriarchal ideologies inform the gendered and racialised scripts that define 'women's work' in
order to justify paying women workers low wages. She compares the common
ways in which employers in three different cases draw on ideologies of women's
work as flexible, temporary, invisible and domestic to naturalise the categories of
work. Lacemakers in Naipur, India are viewed as temporary employees engaged
in leisure activity that they can do at home; immigrant women assembling electronics in Silicon Valley are viewed as performing tedious and 'unskilled' work,
their income as merely a supplement to the family wage; the work of the black
migrant women serving in small, family-owned businesses in Britain is viewed
as an extension of family loyalties. Despite their different experiences, Mohanty
emphasises that women's work is depicted as an extension of their natural
abilities and embodies their roles as wives and mothers. While the naturalisa-
tion of the gendered division of labour justifies the subordination of women's
work, the characterisation of women as a cheap, temporary and unskilled labour
force also creates a cross-class basis for demanding a collective political voice,
creating the possibilities for a transnational feminism which creates a demand
for women's political representation, developing the platform of women's human
rights as women and, crucially, as workers.

The Women and the Politics of Place (WPP) framework (Harcourt and Escobar,
2005) provides a framework to understand the way that neoliberalism has
impacted women's lives and a place to look for alternatives – in the concrete
struggles that women wage in their daily lives. The WPP framework works
to 'demystify theory that ignores women's experiences of their lived body, the
local economy and the environment in order to relocate their politics of place
as key to our understanding of globalization' (Harcourt and Escobar, 2005: 2).
Methodologically, WPP identifies globalisation as a material and embodied
practice, and privileges women's struggles as they emerge in relation to their
local politics of place. This method generates comparative analyses of women's
struggles across multiple sites, and points towards globalisation's structural
inequalities.

The 'politics of place' approach challenges the universalising and deterministic assumptions that animate much of the scholarship on globalisation by
demonstrating the synergistic relationships between the local and the global.
The interplay of the local and global is a mutually constitutive process negotiated
at multiple levels of social life. Bodies, households, states and nations are the
grounds upon which capitalist modes of production are shaped and reshaped.
The politics of place framework further disrupts the biological basis of racial
and ethnic differences by offering relational analyses of identities as constructed
through geopolitical, social and economic changes that shift over time and across
space. By deconstructing globalisation as an over-determining force, the politics
of place approach opens up space for developing alternatives.

The elements comprising the WPP framework culminate in comparative analyses of women's struggles across multiple sites. By identifying women's struggles and strategies of resistance through place-based politics and building a relational analysis of globalisation, WPP accumulates strategies of resistance that can be shared through transnational networks and used by social justice advocates and activists. The WPP framework also exposes globalisation's fault lines and highlights structural vulnerabilities.

The Struggles of Women Garment Workers in Cambodia

Cambodia is a small country in South-east Asia bordered by Viet Nam, Laos and Thailand, with a population of approximately 14 million ethnic Khmers. Once a French colony, the small nation has struggled through wars, genocide and political unrest since gaining independence in 1953. In the mid-1990s, Cambodia's prime minister (PM) set a course for economic modernisation, a process of transition from a closed, agricultural society to a 'free market' economy. Signalling his commitment to economic change, the PM initiated the process of acceding to the World Trade Organization (WTO) in 1994. In preparation for membership, Cambodian leaders adjusted their economic and social policies in compliance with the neoliberal agenda of the WTO. The adjustments included the usual prescriptions: trade liberalisation, tariff reductions, elimination or reduction of government subsidies to industry and agriculture, and the privatisation (that is, the transfer of public goods or services to a private entity) or commodification (in other words, the introduction of for-profit mechanisms into public systems) of public services and utilities. These policy adjustments have increased wealth at the national level, but the wealth has trickled down unevenly to the population.

Accession to the WTO culminates in the primitive accumulation of capital, which Marx defined as a process that separates labourers from their means of production and creates a class of people 'with nothing to sell except their own skins' (Marx, 1978 [1867]: 431). In the Cambodian context, trade liberalisation resulted in deleterious consequences for rural farmers whose livelihoods depended on subsistence farming and selling goods at the local markets. Trade liberalisation brought an influx of foreign goods sold at prices that Cambodian producers could not compete with. Land grabbing and forced evictions by the state on behalf of private developers compounded the losses incurred by rural families. Divorced from the traditional means of production and subsistence, large swathes of the population were made dependent on waged labour, but the availability of jobs is not without gendered consequences. In Cambodia, as elsewhere, the feminisation of labour has altered the structure of work and employment: flexible hours and short-term contracts, poverty wages and the deskilling of work processes represent an employment structure that favours women workers.

As Cambodian women entered into waged production in the garment factories, they were confronted by the material realities of trade liberalisation and the feminisation of labour. In the globalised garment industry, competition is a powerful force that drives working conditions downward, and Cambodian factories are no exception. Since the industry first began, garment workers have routinely faced exploitation in the workplace. They are compelled to work extra hours, paid an abysmal wage, prohibited from using the restroom, subjected to violence, exposed to toxic chemicals, denied maternity and sick leave and lack job security.

Women are responding to the exploitative labour conditions with practical acts of workplace resistance, but they are also responding with strategic acts of resistance aimed at knowledge and information sharing. The Worker Information Center (WIC), a community-based organisation (CBO), offers a case study into the strategic nature of women's resistance. WIC is a multifaceted CBO which not only provides support to workers for problems in the workplace, it offers workers English language classes, makes connections with activists outside of Cambodia and hosts information sessions that introduce workers to neoliberal economic structures. WIC documents clearly outline the neoliberal policies that shape women's struggles as workers, but they also begin to map the capitalist processes that link worker struggles to the struggles faced by rural communities.

The far-reaching effects of neoliberal policies politicise women across rural and urban divides. While garment workers are struggling in defence of their rights as workers, rural women struggle to defend their land and resources against encroachments. For some Cambodian leaders, economic development has provided opportunities to grant rewards or increase personal wealth. The land tenure struggle around Boeung Kak Lake is a telling example of this dynamic. Boeung Kak Lake, a Phnom Penh community, was home to approximately 4,000 landholding Khmers. In 2007, Phnom Penh municipal leaders leased the lake and surrounding villages to Shukaku, Inc., a private development firm co-owned by Senator Lao Meng Khim, a Phnom Penh representative and close ally of Cambodia's ruling party, the Cambodian People's Party (CPP). The protests that ensued offer a glimpse into the politics of place approach in the Cambodian context.

The Boeung Kak land grab precipitated the formation of the League of Women Struggling for Housing Rights. The group comprised women whose land rights had been revoked, and also included women with past experience organising campaigns against illegal land seizures by the state. Their efforts included tactics that drew inspiration from the local context and offered a representation of government authorities that resonated with sympathetic audiences. In one instance, the protesters burned effigies to symbolically display the removal of evil spirits from the leaders involved in the land deal. As a Buddhist society, ridding evil spirits references religious beliefs that are widely recognised and understood. In another instance, the protesters bared their breasts to signal the desperation of the situation. Khmer women are religiously and traditionally modest, and would be otherwise unlikely to engage in public displays of nudity. In the Cambodian context, this tactic conveyed a clear message. These strategies drew on local customs, values and beliefs to convey locally intelligible messages with impact. Beyond these locally based strategies, the protesters also made use of their insightful understanding of neoliberal capitalism by filing a complaint with the WTO regarding its support for Cambodian land use policies.

The protests were met with decisive state action and, in 2012 13 women, including a 72-year-old grandmother, were arrested during a peaceful protest. The women were each sentenced to up to two and half years in prison, but the case took a turn shortly after they were sentenced. A leading activist in the struggle over land tenure, Yorm Bopha, brought unwelcome international attention to the case when she caught the attention of US Secretary of State, Hillary Clinton, who took the issue directly to the PM. Yorm's actions resulted in the release of the 13 activists, but not long thereafter Yorm was arrested and imprisoned for charges that were unrelated to the Boeung Kak evictions. Yorm's arrest did not silence her or her allies; it emboldened them. Her arrest and imprisonment brought unwanted attention to the political favouritism shown by Cambodia's elites. Diverse actors including the WTO, Hillary Clinton and a vast array of international nongovernmental organisations (NGOs) have expressed their concern over the arrests. The case has also drawn international attention to the land struggles in Cambodia, and individuals worldwide are now looking at the situation with an eye to justice and equity for Cambodia's landless population.

Women, Water and Empowerment in Caracas, Venezuela

In Venezuela, the Bolivarian Revolution (1998 to present) is advancing the most radical alternative to neoliberalism in Latin America. Under former President Hugo Chávez, a self-proclaimed socialist and feminist, the government enacted many reforms that have advanced women's empowerment by providing public (state) support for programmes that aim to meet basic needs, such as housing, health, education, and water and sanitation. Women have been the primary beneficiaries of these public programmes and their principal protagonists. The participation of women has been at the centre of the revolutionary process, or 'el proceso' as it is known in Venezuela. Reforms in the urban water and sanitation sector serve as a powerful illustration of the transformative nature of the Bolivarian Revolution, which has improved women's lives by addressing the needs of reproduction.

There is no such thing as a universal experience of women in Caracas, Venezuela when it comes to the politics of water and sanitation. Like most cities in the world, Caracas is characterised by deep racial and class inequalities. The wealthy neighbourhoods are concentrated in the east, which has high-rise condominium buildings where women of lighter complexion cool off from the afternoon heat in their swimming pools, while women in the barrios (poor neighbourhoods) scattered throughout the city often have to borrow water from a neighbour or collect water from a broken pipe. The local water company in Caracas is publicly owned and operated, but throughout its history it has primarily served the upper and middle classes. High-quality water and sanitation infrastructure were constructed in the formal, planned city, while *barrio* residents resorted to constructing their own 'illegal' connections to the city system, or could access resources for infrastructure through clientelistic networks, depending on the party in power. This piecemeal development of services in the *barrios* has created incomplete, fractured water and sanitation networks, and highly uneven service access within neighbourhoods.

This uneven development of water infrastructure and service provision has the highest negative impact on the lives of poor women. Previous to the reforms affected by the Bolivarian Revolution, in some *barrios* water would only reach some households for a few hours every three weeks. To make matters worse, residents could not predict when the water would come. In the 1980s and early 1990s, poor residents would take to the streets in daily protests to try to pressure government authorities to fix the situation. Since household activities such as doing the laundry, bathing the children and cooking are considered women's work, it is not surprising that most of these protesters were women. The lack of adequate sanitary facilities is also a particularly feminist issue since women and girls who must use public spaces for carrying out their most personal and private body rituals experience sexual harassment, violent assault, rape, teasing and stalking when they go out and defecate in the open in bushes, fields and gutters on the road. Access to adequate water and sanitation has deep, gendered implications.

Under the management of a progressive mayor in the early 1990s, the municipal government established local forums to hear citizens' concerns about their problems with water and sanitation, which became the forerunners of something more substantial. When Chávez was elected president in 1998, a city-wide communal water council was created in Caracas, comprising representatives of the water company, municipal government and *barrio* residents. The entities, known as the technical water tables, have improved services, as well as the relationships between *barrio* residents and the local water company. Established at the national level in 2000, there are now over 9,000 technical water tables nationwide. As of 2011, they had initiated 1,500 community-managed infrastructure projects. In Caracas, the coverage of drinking water service rose from 82 per cent in 1998 to 89 per cent in 2003, and sewerage from 64 per cent to 72 per cent. Through participation in the technical water tables, *barrio* residents now have more control over the distribution practices and the design and location of water and sanitation infrastructure. While the problem of water and sanitation delivery has not been solved in Caracas, the technical tables have made service more predictable by improving the lines of communication between the *barrio* residents and the local water company. Now residents are given a schedule for when water will arrive at their household and provided with tanks to store water between cycles.

The successful experience of the technical water tables has been scaled up to a broader range of services at the neighbourhood level in institutions known as communal councils. In January 2007, Chávez proposed that such councils be created in all realms of society in order to create a new form of communal state, which would not only deal with questions of reproduction, such as the provision of food, water, education and healthcare services, but also the production of these goods and services. According to the *National Plan for Economic and Social Development 2007–2013*, 'since sovereignty resides absolutely in the people, the people can itself direct the state, without needing to delegate its sovereignty as it does in indirect or representative democracy'. The technical water tables have thus prefigured Venezuela's radical experiment in participatory democracy, which aims to create a new form of self-administered state based on community councils.

The participants in these bottom-up institutions of self-administration are predominantly women. As Sujatha Fernandes (2007) has pointed out in her study of *barrio* women's organising in Caracas, many women are involved in public community-level politics and committees because of their domestic responsibilities in the home. Women's participation thus helps to render public those problems that are experienced in the private sphere, putting into action the feminist adage, 'The personal is political.' Fernandes claims that despite the fact that men still dominate the informal and formal political arena in Venezuela (only 18 per cent of parliamentarians are women) an increase in women's involvement in community-level programmes 'has created forms of popular participation that challenge gender roles, collectivise private tasks, and create alternatives to male-centric politics' (2007: 98). For these reasons, the Bolivarian Revolution has also been a women's revolution, and *barrio* women are among the process's most ardent supporters.

It may be a stretch to label the Bolivarian Revolution in Venezuela a 'socialist-feminist' alternative. Women activists, particularly in the *barrio*, often identify as 'socialists' but not 'feminists' since this term that tends to be used by upper and middle-class women connected to the NGO technocracy. Nonetheless, the list of gains for women since Chávez was first elected in 1998 is a long one. With general poverty halved and extreme poverty quartered, women have been the main beneficiaries of most social programmes, including education, health, housing and pensions for the elderly. There has been a doubling of women's participation in the workforce – from 43.3 per cent of women employed in 1996 to 81.2 per cent in 2002, and it has increased steadily since then. The government has established a women's ministry, a women's bank that extends low-interest loans to women's cooperatives, and tribunals that deal specifically with violent crimes against women. Maternity leave has increased to 26 weeks (the longest after Norway and Canada) and paternity leave has been created as well. The new labour law announced in May 2013 also recognised non-salaried work traditionally done by women (housework), supporting the rights of housewives to receive pensions. As a result of such changes, Venezuela has transformed from being one of the most unequal societies in the region to the most equal, thus reversing the class polarisation experienced under neoliberalism, and improving the lives of women in particular, since they are the poorest of the poor.

Socialist-Feminist Alternatives

Marx's ideas are fundamental to women's liberation. A feminist reading of Marx's body of work enables us to think through the illusory distinctions between the private and public spheres, and opens up space for recognising the ways that the capitalist system has benefited from women's unpaid labour through the exploitation of difference. Since women are the lowest earners in society as a result of the devaluing of their labour-power at the same time that they remain responsible for unpaid reproductive work, socialist feminists highlight the need for a dual struggle. Women need to address and confront the unjust economic order that is expressed in class societies, at the same time as they address and confront the constantly regenerated patterns of gender inequality and subordination that are expressed not just in economic terms but also socially, culturally and politically. Overcoming the inequalities exacerbated by the neoliberal form of capitalism thus requires struggles to improve access to the basic means needed to reproduce life.

The case studies from Cambodia and Venezuela highlight how the politics of production and reproduction intersect in women's lives. In the case of Cambodia's garment workers, we find that while their labour is devalued by ideologies that regard sewing as an unskilled task enabled by women's natural inclinations in domesticating the sphere, the actual value of their labour facilitates the reproduction of Cambodian life at the level of the household, the community and the national budget. Women's resistance strategies aim to expand women's access to the most fundamental means to reproduce life, such as land. In Venezuela, women's activism around the politics of reproduction – the provision of household water – inspired early experiments in the co-delivery of services which are now being scaled up to create a different kind of state and to experiment with forms of collectivised production. While the radical transformation of the communal state remains an unrealised dream, reforms that socialise the provision of basic services such as water, education and health have been fundamental in reducing poverty and inequality, transforming the lives of poor women in particular.

Select Bibliography

Bakker, I. and Gill, S. (2003) 'Global political economy and social reproduction', in I. Bakker and S. Gill (eds), *Power, Production and Social Reproduction*. New York: Palgrave Macmillan.

Engels, F. (2004) [1884] *The Origin of the Family, Private Property, and the State*. London: Resistance Books.

Fernandes, S. (2007) 'Barrio women and popular politics in Chávez's Venezuela', *Latin American Politics and Society*, 49(3): 97–127.

Harcourt, W. and Escobar, A. (eds) (2005) *Women and the Politics of Place*. Bloomfield, Conn.: Kumarian.

Marx, K. (1978) [1867] *Capital, Vol. I*, in R. C. Tucker (ed.), *The Marx-Engels Reader*, 2nd edn. New York: W.W. Norton.

Mohanty, C. T. (1997) 'Women workers and capitalist scripts: ideologies of domination, common interests and the politics of solidarity', in M. J. Alexander and C. T. Mohanty (eds), *Feminist Genealogies, Colonial Legacies, Democratic Futures*. New York: Routledge.

CHAPTER TEN

Exploding in the Air: Beyond the Carbon Trail of Neoliberal Globalisation

Andreas Malm

In late 2008, as the waves of the financial crisis rolled over the globe, General Motors announced the closure of a minor plant in its bulging portfolio: the SAAB factory in Trollhättan, western Sweden. For the town and the broader region, which had revolved around the axis of car production since the 1950s, it was a death sentence. Over the following months, the debate over another lingering threat, mortal to a far larger entity – the habitable biosphere – incidentally flared again: the world community prepared itself for some decisive decisions at the COP-15 (Conference of the Parties) summit in Copenhagen. A small town hanging in the balance, and a whole planet – with unusual flagrancy, the crises of capitalism and climate change crossed paths.

At this conjuncture, a bold proposition was floated. Why not kill two birds with one stone? Why not save the jobs in Trollhättan by converting the plant to the production of something other than cars, something that contributes to the urgent departure from the fossil economy – think windmills, solar panels, vehicles for public transportation? Tellingly, the idea was advanced by a small circle of activists around an individual militant, Lars Henriksson, a veteran auto worker and tireless proponent of alternative forms of unionism. The official union leadership never warmed to the idea and the right-wing government would not even consider interfering with the creative destruction of the market: its inclination was to let matters run their course.

And so the SAAB factory finally ceased production in 2011, but the tools and the conveyor belts were not yet ready for the scrap heap. Instead, they ended up in China. With exactly the same equipment, Chinese workers now build exactly the same SAAB models, but at a considerably lower price. Trollhättan struggles with some of the highest unemployment rates in Sweden. No decisions were taken in Copenhagen, of course; in 2010 Swedish emissions of greenhouse gases rose by a record 11 per cent. Over the longer term, it might seem as if Swedish emissions are on the decline, but this is a mirage generated by the relocation of industrial production to other parts of the world – notably

China – from which ever-growing mountains of goods, including SAAB cars, are imported. And the jobs keep on haemorrhaging from Swedish to Chinese industry, and the Chinese emissions continue to increase by leap and bounds.

The incident of the abortive proposition for converting the SAAB factory points to several general patterns, in the recent past and in the likely near future. First, industrial capital is gradually, seemingly irresistibly, leaving the traditional core and setting up shop in newer territories such as China. Second, emissions of carbon dioxide inexorably rise as long as global accumulation proceeds apace. Third, alternatives to this insanely destructive business-as-usual will have to come from below: no United Nations or governments, or least of all companies, can be trusted to promote them by their own will. In Henriksson's words, 'if we want reason to prevail, we have to arm it, equipping it with enough social muscle so that it can challenge the powers that be'. But – fourth, and most crucially – such muscle is as yet badly lacking. This chapter explores the links between the first two patterns and concludes by returning to the question of an alternative path. What would it take to break with business as usual?

Fossil Capital Descends on China

In the early 19th century, British manufacturers took the momentous step of replacing their water wheels with steam engines. Instead of abundant, cheap, carbon-free water, they chose to fire their production of commodities with the far dearer fuel of coal. One major reason for the shift was the quest for cheap and disciplined labour. 'Natural falls of water', said the most authoritative steam-engine manual of the time, 'are mostly found on rivers in the open country; but steam-engines can be placed in the centres of populous towns, where labourers are easily procured'. According to a prominent bourgeois economist, steam had the invaluable advantage of allowing factories to assemble 'in the centre of a population trained to industrious habits' (see Malm, 2013). With the transition to steam, coal became the general lever of surplus-value extraction, and ever since, the prime mover of business-as-usual has been a compound we might label 'fossil capital': a relentless accumulation of capital *through* the combustion of growing quantities of fossil fuels.

In the late 1960s and early 1970s, labour in the advanced capitalist countries seemed to turn ever more expensive and undisciplined, as strikes and unrest engulfed the old industrial centres, pushing up wages and subverting managers' authority on the shop floor. This was one of the components of the crisis of capitalism erupting in those years and lingering in the form of persistent stagnation for another two decades. Part of the solution was the relocation of manufacturing industries. In a truly global economy such as the one evolving since the 1970s, customers can be reached from practically anywhere, sites of production can be dissociated from sites of consumption, and capital can choose between export platforms on the merits of their labour-power.[1]

From the 1980s onwards, foreign direct investment (FDI) flows grew faster than cross-border trade; from 1990 to 2009, they quintupled, reaching a historic peak just before the financial crisis. By that time, 'emerging markets' had decisively surpassed developed countries as receivers of FDI, and among them, China outshone all others. It was this inflow of capital that impelled the development of the Chinese economy at such breakneck speed. From 1990 to 2008, industrial output increased by a factor of 26; that of foreign-invested enterprises (FIEs) – joint ventures and companies wholly owned by foreigners – by a factor of 332. The same engine drove the Chinese export boom. In 2001, when the People's Republic of China (PRC) conclusively committed itself to global neoliberalism by entering the World Trade Organization (WTO), easing restrictions on foreign ownership, relaxing requirements on local cooperation, and in general throwing the doors of the Chinese economy wide open, the share of goods exported that were produced by FIEs exceeded 50 per cent, up from 0.1 per cent in the early 1980s.

The secret behind this surge in foreign-financed, export-oriented production was never very well kept. The *Economist* affirmed that the ascent of China was safeguarded by its 'almost unlimited supply of cheap labour. By some estimates, there are almost 200m under-employed workers in rural areas that could move into industry.' In the words of two other surveys, employers became 'accustomed to having a seemingly unlimited supply of very cheap labor, and being able to insist on certain qualities in their workers', such as 'a compliant and flexible personality, and the willingness to work very long hours' (Yongding, 2006; Banister and Cook, 2011). They were easy to procure, and trained to industrious habits.

A necessary condition for labour-power to be cheap and disciplined is, as intimated by the *Economist*, the presence of a reserve army of labour. But the physical presence of propertyless workers eager for a wage can never be a sufficient condition for attracting investment. They will only be practically accessible for surplus-value extraction if there is a basic infrastructure in place – first and foremost, power plants and electricity grids capable of delivering the requisite energy. In countries that do not have extensive facilities for the combustion of fossil fuels from the beginning, these facilities have to be built: relocation of production requires expansion of energy infrastructure, the rise of chimneys where none stood before. Another condition for a transnational corporation (TNC) to arrive is a reliable power supply upheld and bolstered by the host country's government; no capital would come if it had to establish a power supply from scratch or ensure its maintenance. The lever must be in place.

There was a spike in fossil energy combustion in China at the turn of the millennium. After a fall in the second half of the 1990s, the consumption of coal

---

1   The following sections draw on Malm (2012). Full sourcing can be found there.

– by far the most important fuel in the Chinese mix – doubled over the next seven years. Manufacturing industry was the most voracious sector. Having lost some appetite in the late 1990s, it took swelling volumes again, absorbing more than 90 per cent of all coal in 2002, mainly for the generation of power and heat. The spike coincided not only with entry into the WTO, but also with the coming to fruition of governmental plans to attract foreign capital; banking on FDI as the recipe for national development, Beijing expanded energy infrastructure to cater for the incomers. Their needs were, however, greater than the PRC could satisfy on its own: in 2007 it became a net importer of coal. The black stone was shipped from mines in (among other countries) Australia and Viet Nam to feed the Chinese plants.

But energy infrastructure is, again, not a sufficient condition for realising the promise of inexpensive, submissive workers. If they are disconnected from major arteries of transportation, the commodities will not reach the world market smoothly, and perhaps not at all. There have to be rails; highways; warehouses; ports and airports to ferry raw materials, components, finished goods, managers and CEOs between affiliates and markets, factories and headquarters. Given that modern transport systems are almost completely reliant on oil – accounting for 61.4 per cent of all petroleum consumed in 2008 – globalisation of production translates into larger emissions of CO_2 in this sphere as well: the more fragmented and integrated the production chains, the more fuel will be burned.

To pave the way for FDI, Beijing launched an enormous expansion of transport infrastructure in the 1990s. It was most conspicuous in the cities along the south-eastern littoral, the traditional, now rejuvenated gateway for incoming capital. The shipping of goods from China to the world left growing traces of CO_2 in the sky; for every relocation of export-oriented production to the PRC, the distances to be travelled were stretched out, causing a rise in emissions per product. In the year 2000, inputs – raw materials, parts and components – accounted for a stunning 85 per cent of global CO_2 emitted in the cross-border transport of commodities, with finished goods only taking the remaining 15 per cent. Such emissions from within globalised production chains gravitated markedly towards China.

In the 1990s, total CO_2 emissions grew at a global average rate of 1 per cent per year, jumping to 3.4 per cent between 2000 and 2008. Most of this explosion happened in China. Between 2000 and 2006, 55 per cent of total emissions growth originated in its territory; by 2007, the share had risen to two-thirds, and China had eclipsed the United States as the top emitter on Earth. The key that ignited the Chinese explosion was export. Other drivers, such as population growth, changing lifestyles, government expenditure and household consumption, were insignificant or puny by comparison. The conclusion seems unavoidable: to reach the centres of its populous towns, where labourers were easily procured and trained to industrious habits, capital deployed fossil energy as its vehicle. Or, put differently: China became the chimney of the world because it was seized upon by globally mobile capital as its workshop.

Where Capital Goes, Emissions Follow

A Swede or a Brit does not emit CO_2 through wearing a T-shirt from Bangladesh or China: it has already been emitted, from the factory where the T-shirt was sewn, from the power plant that supplied the factory with electricity, and further back along the supply chain. A sequence of emissions running all the way from the extraction of the fossil fuels through to assembly can be seen as embodied in the T-shirt. Who should count as responsible for such emissions embodied in trade? The country where the goods are consumed, not where they are produced, says a choir of researchers and policy makers – including from China – whose voices have grown loud in recent years. The argument from governments in the producing countries appears to make sense: you Westerners enjoy wearing our T-shirts, driving our cars, talking in our smartphones, listening to music in our iPods, and just because the manufacturing happens to be done by 'us', you cannot shirk responsibility for the emissions. In fact, you only benefit from having relocated the manufacturing to us, since it makes all these comforts cheaper to you.

In the discourse on 'consumption-based emissions accounting' – now widely seen as the more sensible alternative to the established production-based statistics – the blame for the Chinese explosion tends to be transferred to the Western consumer. The implications are sometimes stated explicitly. Studying the embodied emissions in US–Chinese trade, one team of researchers argues that 'workers making goods in the developed world enjoy comparatively lavish lifestyles versus their counterparts in the developing world, a lifestyle which in many cases *induces substantial environmental impact*'. Chinese emissions are 'dominated by the manufacturing of products consumed by *workers*'. Representing a majority of US consumers, they – the workers – should assume responsibility; their lifestyles are the source of the problem (Xu, Williams and Allenby, 2010).

US or other Western workers, however, never initiated the outsourcing of production to China. In fact, if anyone ever resisted such moves, it was precisely the Western – including the US – labour movements, who, in a sense, were the intended targets. The relocations were aimed at outflanking their bargaining power, reversing their previous victories, freeing capital from the straitjackets of high wages and comparatively decent working conditions. Capital moved to China not on the request of, *but against the fundamental interests of* workers in the West. The agent behind the emissions explosion were not consumers in the West responding to Chinese bargain offers, but the *owners of firms* chasing the lowest production costs and seeking to increase their profits.

No one has better analysed the immediate class dimension of this logic than Beverly Silver in her *Forces of Labor: Worker's Movements and Globalization since 1870*. Silver identifies a recurring 'spatial fix' in the modern history of capital: 'each time a strong labor movement emerged, capitalists relocated production to sites with cheaper and presumably more docile labor, weakening labor movements in the sites of disinvestment but strengthening labor in the new sites of expansion'. Capitalists used their mobility in space to escape the problem of strong labour, only to create it anew in what was supposed to be their sanctuary. As a corollary, Silver proposes the theorem 'where capital goes, labor-capital conflict shortly follows'. We can now add another dimension to her law: where capital goes, emissions immediately follow.

The social and ecological dimensions are here indissolubly united: 'fossil capital' denotes a unity of energy and exploitation, realised through the process of accumulation, in motion since the early 19th century and now, in the decades of the still unbroken grip of neoliberalism, proceeding on an arrantly global scale. Can it be stopped?

Mitigation With Muscles

Needless to say, the dynamics of fossil capital under neoliberal globalisation is not the sole force driving our new business-as-usual – not in the world as a whole, and not in China. But it is a major one. Any meaningful attempt at reducing emissions would have to tackle it. Any ambitions to stabilise climate would, in all likelihood, have to extinguish it. As things currently stand, there is no room within the process of climate negotiations for confronting fossil capital as a global phenomenon. With the possible exception of the Bolivarian states of Latin America and some other governments of peripheral countries, radicalised by sheer necessity in their struggle for survival, all negotiators showing up at the annual UN summits – from China as much as from the United States – owe their principal allegiance to capital. They do not congregate to even consider the idea of questioning it.

While the Chinese state follows the protocol of paying lip service to climate change mitigation – sometimes even posing as a pioneer in sustainable energy – realities on the ground tell a sordid story. Consider only the case of coal. In response to extreme levels of air pollution, unbearable smog enshrouding entire cities for weeks on end and threatening to trigger mass protests, the central government has embarked on a partial switch from the main culprit – coal – to less intrusive fuel. The choice has fallen on gas, more specifically on synthetic natural gas (SNG), produced in plants where ordinary coal undergoes gasificiation. As of 2013, nine such facilities had been approved and another 30 proposed, amounting to the greatest SNG programme in history. Burning SNG leaves the air deceptively clear. But it emits seven times more CO_2 than conventional natural gas, up to 80 per cent more than common coal, twice as much as gasoline when fuelling vehicles (Yang and Jackson, 2013). If the SNG 'solution' is pursued further, the state would be throwing the country from the ashes of the urban air into a fire of truly epochal proportions.

On a global scale, the CO_2 explosion is running its course towards biospheric meltdown. The post-2000 business-as-usual of more than 3 per cent annual emissions growth puts us on track for a rise in mean temperatures of 4 °C within the next 50 years – a warming that would, in the matter-of-fact words of leading climate researcher Kevin Anderson, be 'incompatible with any reasonable characterisation of an organised, equitable and civilised global community. A 4 degrees future is also beyond what many people think we can reasonably adapt to.' To have any chance of maintaining some orderly civilisation, we have to stay below 2 °C. What would that require? According to Anderson, to secure as little as a 50 per cent chance of avoiding more than 2 °C warming:

> global energy-related CO_2 emissions have to decrease by 10–20 per cent per year, hitting zero between 2035 and 2045'. Flying, driving, heating our homes, using our appliances, basically everything we do, would need to be zero carbon – and note, zero carbon means zero carbon.
>
> (Anderson, 2012: 29, 25)

Cuts of this magnitude have no historical precedent.

Then what could possibly be done to accomplish this last-ditch effort? Anderson has to acknowledge the obvious: the market cannot do it. What is the alternative? Planning. In another article, Anderson and his colleage Alice Bows used the term 'planned economic recession'. They do not say it loudly, but 'planned economic recession' does, of course, objectively constitute a war against capital. The stubbornness of fossil capital and its allies pushes us towards the necessity of highly centralised planning. The same logic informs a fresh paper in *Energy Policy*, in which Australian researchers Laurence Delina and Mark Diesendorf ask, 'Is wartime mobilization a suitable model for rapid national climate mitigation?' Their answer is a roaring yes. Only by centralising powers under 'a special Ministry for Transition to a Low-Carbon Future', Delina and Diesendorf argue, can energy consumption be restricted, funds raised, labour redirected, renewable energy technologies rolled out at the necessary speed. A more absolute antithesis to neoliberalism is hard to imagine.

In the absence of a mighty mass movement, however, 'it seems unlikely that governments will undertake emergency mitigation, *even when life-threatening climate disasters occur*' (Delina and Diesendorf, 2013: 377; emphasis added). Someone would have to compel them to abandon neoliberal dogma and defy some of the most entrenched material interests on Earth. What social force could have the muscles for that? In his agitation in a little corner of industrial Sweden, Lars Henriksson has dared to suggest the unthinkable: the organised working class just might be the one. Auto workers, for instance, are positioned in the centre of a giant 'system for mass production of advanced, high-quality technical goods' – exactly what is needed for a mega-switch away from fossil fuels (Henriksson, 2013: 80).

Indeed, only through mass production can the components of a fossil-free society – in electricity, transport, housing, every sphere of economic life – be churned out fast enough to avoid the worst-case scenarios. Delina and Diesendorf estimate that a transition to zero consumption of fossil fuels and

100 per cent utilisation of renewable energy could be achieved in 25–30 years for individual countries and 40 years for the world, if productive apparatuses were geared to that end. This is also the main reason to oppose nuclear power and carbon capture and storage. Neither technology can be mass-produced; both require enormous constructions that take years if not decades to complete. But a rebooted car factory can pour out wind and solar farms in almost no time. Ironically, then, industrial plants are assets for a transition. This is one reason why environmentalists who laud the closure of car factories are so terribly wrong. This would also apply to China. Foreign capital has assisted in the establishment of what may now be the world's greatest capacity for mass production – exactly what the PRC will need once it embarks on the eradication of its overgrown emissions. Fossil capital has assembled the spades with which its grave could potentially be dug.

And the gravediggers are there, if only as a ghostly presence: workers have a *material interest* in converting production to social ends. This is Henriksson's major point. Jobs would no longer fly away in the quest for profit. They would be designed for the tasks needed to place the local economy on a sustainable footing, within the framework of a comprehensive plan, in a web of thousands of links to the rest of society. Here is an unlikely but unassailable logic: industrial workers are the most strategically placed agents of the transition. The problem is, of course, they have so far evinced little appetite for the idea. As the globalisation of production has whittled away their material bases or cornered them with the constant threat of relocation, their bargaining power has been severely undermined.

The Struggle for Climate Jobs

In some countries, however, this idea has begun to fly. In Britain and South Africa, it goes under the name 'One million climate jobs'; in Norway, a more modest 100,000. In China itself, despite the increasing labour unrest in the country (see Pringle, Chapter 17 of this book), there is no known equivalent; it appears to presuppose an independent trade union movement and freedom of speech, two conditions absent in the PRC. After yet another failed UN summit on climate change, numbered COP-17 (Conference of the Parties), held in Durban in late 2011, the South African campaign was launched through the publication of a booklet radiating possibilities. It begins by decrying how unemployment continues to ravage the fabric of South African society. Indeed, the starting-point must be the immediate class interest: 'Almost half the working population in our country don't have work, and many will never find work during the rest of their lives' (Bahadur et al., 2011: 16, 5). Officially, the unemployment rate hovers around 25 per cent; in reality it is closer to 40 per cent. Indubitably, five years of economic crisis have exacerbated the generalised predicament of casual, precarious, insecure jobs. At the same time, climate change is already putting serious pressure on some of the poorest communities in South Africa, particularly in the key area of water access. Some of the emitting sources are close to home: the country is responsible for nearly half of Africa's emissions and ranks 12th globally, because of the peculiarly fuel-guzzling, coal-burning minerals-energy complex dominating its economy. So what is to be done?

Switch electricity to wind and solar power. Cut energy use through higher efficiency in industries and retrofitted houses; shift from private cars to public transport; phase out oil-based agriculture and localise food production: shut down one emissions source after another, by means of dearly needed labour. Some jobs would have to be sacrificed – in coal mines and coal-fired power plants, most obviously – but the researchers involved in the campaign estimate that no fewer than 3 million new 'climate jobs' could easily be created, making a deep dent in unemployment statistics, with innumerable positive feedbacks.

If manufacturing and installation are fast-tracked, all electricity in South Africa could be produced from renewable sources by 2040. Feeding into the goals of the campaign, the National Union of Metalworkers has called for 'a publicly-owned and community-controlled renewable energy sector', harvesting the abundant wind and sun; to convert half of all electricity to such sources in ten years, 150,000 full-time workers would have to be summoned (Bahadur et al., 2011: 23–4). Zero waste would generate another 400,000 jobs; expansion of the rail network, redesign of cities and manufacturing of buses and bicycles hundreds of thousands more; restoration of polluted rivers to secure precious water resources, establishment of farms catering to local demand, renovation and building of carbon-neutral housing ... an entire society has to be reconstructed. Note that the spur to such a transformation does not spring from the lunatic left dreaming up another scheme for a planned economy, but from the transgression of biospheric boundaries, which – so the science tells us, like it or not – simply mandates it. And it requires work to be done.

The South African 'One million climate jobs' campaign has garnered support from some 40 organisations, including trade unions – COSATU, National Union of Mineworkers, the transport, municipal, metal workers – environmental movements, universities and faith groups with varying degrees of active involvement. But it is not one great family open to everyone who wants a win–win world. 'We face the opposition of powerful vested interests who make super-profits from the existing mining- and energy-intensive system in South Africa – this is the foundation upon which the capitalist economy in South Africa was built and continues to develop' (Bahadur et al., 2011: 6). Hence the need to mobilise all social forces that do not profit from the circuit of fossil capital. Reflecting the shifting composition of the working class, campaigns for climate jobs are not based on a narrow segment of industrial workers. Rather, they have the potential beauty of uniting the entire class and its social allies, in a project whose ultimate rationale is, of course, human survival.

But the antagonism will always be there. It is a matter not only of temporary emergency measures clashing with the interests of capital: on the other side of the transition, things would be changed forever. The means of production would, for a start, be anchored in renewable energy. Coal can be sent from mines in Australia, Viet Nam or South Africa to whatever place capital currently favours for production. So can oil and natural gas, from Alberta or Alaska, Gaza or Ghana, but energy from sun, wind and water can only travel over limited distances: sunshine from Algeria cannot be dispatched to Bangladesh. Nor is it likely that constantly growing volumes of transportation can ever be powered by renewable energy – certainly not biofuel, lest humanity be starved. The premise of the spatial mobility of capital is the burning of fossil fuels; conversely, *the effect of a transition away from them would be to tie down the means of production in communities*. Fossil-free economies would, it seems, have to be localised, running counter to the innermost logic of globalised capital – but not, again, to the interests of labour. Workers would have little to lose from chaining their economies to local supplies of sun, wind and water, and they would have if not a world, than at least a say over their future to win.

So far, no campaign for climate jobs has approached anything like a critical mass. The proposals might still come across as hopelessly starry-eyed science fiction. Perhaps it would require some ultra-extreme weather event, or an outright economic collapse, or a combination of both, to really get things moving. We could hope that reason would amass sufficient muscles for the transition to begin under less disastrous and disorderly conditions. But because of the overall weakness of the forces of labour and our general political predicament, summed up in the saying 'it is easier to imagine the end of the world than the end of capitalism', the idea sounds far too good to possibly come true. Workers and their associates spearheading a break-out from the fossil economy, centrally planned in dialogue with local communities, reaching zero emissions within a few decades? It is a dizzying idea, light-years from any current trajectory. It might also be the very best chance we have.

Select Bibliography

Anderson, K. (2012) 'Climate change going beyond dangerous: brutal numbers and tenuous hope', *Development Dialogue*, 61: 16–40.

Bahadur, A. et al. (2011) *One Million Climate Jobs: A Just Transition to a Low Carbon Economy to Combat Unemployment and Climate Change*. Available at: www.climatejobs.org.za

Banister, J. and Cook, G. (2011) 'China's employment and compensation costs in manufacturing through 2008', *Monthly Labor Review*, March: 39–52.

Delina, L. L. and Diesendorf, M. (2013) 'Is wartime mobilisation a suitable policy model for rapid national climate mitigation?' *Energy Policy*, 58: 371–80.

Henriksson, L. (2013) 'Cars, crisis, climate change and class struggle', in N. Rathzel and D. Uzzel (eds), *Trade Unions in the Green Economy: Working for the Environment*. Abingdon: Routledge.

Malm, A. (2012) 'China as chimney of the world: the fossil capital hypothesis', *Organization and Environment*, 25(2): 146–77.

Malm, A. (2013) 'The origins of fossil capital: from water to steam in the British cotton industry', *Historical Materialism*, 21(1): 1–54.

Silver, B. (2003) *Forces of Labor: Workers' Movements and Globalization since 1870.* Cambridge: Cambridge University Press.

Yang, C.-J. and Jackson, R. B. (2013) 'China's synthetic natural gas revolution', *Nature Climate Change*, 3: 852–4.

Yongding, Y. (2006) 'The experience of FDI recipients: the case of China', in S. Urata, C. Siow Yue and F. Kimura (eds), *Multinationals and Economic Growth in East Asia: Foreign Direct Investment, Corporate Strategies and National Economic Development.* London: Routledge.

Xu, M., Williams, E. and Allenby, B. (2010) 'Assessing environmental impacts embodied in manufacturing and labor input for the China–U.S. trade', *Environmental Science & Technology*, 44(2): 567–73.

CHAPTER ELEVEN

Defend, Militate and Alternate: Public Options in a Privatised World

David A. McDonald

The privatisation of public services such as water, electricity and health care has been at the centre of neoliberal transformation for the past three decades. Starting with outright divestitures of such essential services as water and sanitation under Margaret Thatcher in the United Kingdom and Augusto Pinochet in Chile, privatisation has since spread to include virtually every service sector imaginable (from education to prisons) and almost every country in the world. It has also morphed into a more complex array of institutional and ideological formats, most notably the emphasis on public–private partnerships (PPPs), which reduce the risk for the private sector but have the same basic effect of transforming essential services into commercial, profit-oriented enterprises.

The effects of privatisation have been rising costs, lowered wages, increased environmental problems, substandard services and a host of corruption-related mishaps, to name but a few of the far-reaching concerns documented by a growing mass of literature on the topic. It is typically low-income, marginal-ised groups – women in particular – that are most negatively impacted by this commercialisation, largely in countries in the South, but increasingly in the North as well, as evidenced by the truly global anti-privatisation movement.

Opposing privatisation is one thing. Presenting alternatives is another, and critics of privatisation are often confronted with the objection that they present no substitutes. To some extent this is true, with the vast majority of literature critiquing privatisation having little to say about what should replace it (beyond the status quo, which is not always desirable). The literature that does exist tends to suffer from a lack of conceptual and methodological rigour, making it difficult to compare alternative models across time and place.

In practice, there is no shortage of actually existing examples of alternatives to privatisation. Throughout the world governments have been reclaiming public services and/or reworking existing public systems, in part because of the failures of privatisation and in part because of the need to democratise and (re)energise state bureaucracies. There are also entirely new and innovative forms of public services taking shape.

This chapter explores these public service trends and examines an emerging literature that attempts to build better definitions of what constitutes an 'alternative to privatisation'. We look at how such models might be conceptualised theoretically, and how we might measure their 'success'. In contrast to neoliberal models of analysis, the attempt is not to build a blueprint for an 'ideal' public service, but rather to offer broad parameters for what might be considered acceptable 'norms' in the delivery of core amenities such as water and health care, while at the same time allowing for political, cultural and environmental differences depending on context.

What Is an Alternative to Privatisation?

For many, the most obvious alternative to privatisation is state provision. Be it municipal, regional, national – or some combination thereof – state-owned and state-operated services dominated the services scene for much of the 20th century. This was not always the case, however. Most modern networked services (at least in Europe and its colonies) started as private enterprises in the 1800s, only to be municipalised and nationalised in the 1900s in an effort to create more 'rational' and 'efficient' public monopolies that could ensure reliable services to industry and an emerging mass-consumption society. There was broad consensus from the 1940s onwards – in both market and socialist countries – that the state had a responsibility to guarantee base provision of essential goods and services in areas where markets on their own had failed. In this respect, efforts to return services to the public sector today are not entirely new, with the history of the 19th century offering some interesting lessons for contemporary change.

But it is equally true that state provision has had its flaws, with welfare governments in the West often seen as paternalistic and exclusionary, creating vastly unequal pockets of public provision along race, class and gender lines – problems that were often reproduced by post-colonial regimes. Socialist states, though sometimes much better at distribution, also suffered from top-down, undemocratic decision making, resulting in supply-side services that ignored needs on the ground and ran roughshod over environmental constraints with their emphasis on large, technology-driven projects.

As a result, contemporary demands for alternatives to privatisation are as much about questioning and reconfiguring the state as they are about bringing the state back in. Community groups, labour unions, social movements, faith-based establishments, non-governmental organisations (NGOs) and other non-state actors are demanding a bigger role and a bigger say in what public services should look like today. Moreover, the number and range of these groups has mushroomed over the years – demographically and ideologically – making it difficult to lump together actors as diverse as worker co-ops and autonomous peasant associations.

The push towards decentralisation by neoliberal technocrats, state authorities and financial institutions has also complicated matters, as has the growing number of neoliberal-minded global public bodies such as the World Bank and the United Nations. 'Public' provision can involve a complex network of different levels of government, sometimes working together (or at odds) with one another, and increasingly in partnership with some form of non-state partner. As noted previously, PPPs have become the most prevalent form of privatisation over the past two decades, but state partnerships with NGOs, community groups and other not-for-profit agencies are on the rise as well. Some are profit-oriented but many represent a trend away from privatisation, increasingly referred to as public–public partnerships (PUPs).

The extent to which these PUPs can be considered positive alternatives to privatisation is a matter of ongoing debate. The participation of non-state players has moved discussions about alternatives to privatisation beyond the stale position of state versus the private sector, but any meaningful conversation about effective public services must be grounded in a deeper evaluation of objectives and performance. Just because a service is owned/operated by a public and/or not-for-profit agency does not mean it is a 'successful' public service provider. Faith-based agencies might only cater to their own kind. NGOs might not have the resources necessary to provide adequate levels of services. Community-driven services might rely on self-exploitation, and so on.

There are also concerns with the growing emphasis on 'corporatised' services – that is, state-owned and state-operated entities at arm's length from the state, and increasingly run on commercial principles that mimic the private sector. They might not operate on a for-profit basis, but they often function using market doctrines, valorising the exchange rate of a service over its use value, prioritising financial cost–benefit analysis in decision making, and employing private sector management techniques such as performance-based salaries. These 'public' entities often see their service delivery mandates framed in market terms of maximising efficiency, promoting free enterprise and serving individual consumer sovereignty.

But no one ever said that public was simple. Any serious engagement with public service provision involves messy organisational, spatial, ideological and economic tensions. And what might be considered a successful public service provider in one place or sector might be very problematic in another. There is no *a priori* way of determining if a public service model is going to work. Analysts, activists and practitioners must be prepared for careful, lengthy and tension-ridden processes of (never-ending) change, and should be open to a wide range of possibilities. Participatory budgeting, for example, might be effective in one place at one time, but it might not work in other locations, and it might not prove sustainable as communities become weary of regular meetings or distrustful of the process. Sharing successes and failures of this sort across time and place will need to be part of the learning process.

In other words, there are no hard definitions for what constitutes an 'alternative to privatisation'. Rather than lying along a linear trajectory of state ownership at one end and private ownership at the other, there are other forms of publicness that splinter off this straight line or combine actors and responsibilities in very unconventional ways. The degree of state or non-state ownership and control is neither a singular nor an exclusive marker of 'publicness'. It is a matter of who is served and how. And while we can argue for a definition of alternatives that is as free of private sector influence as possible, it is conceptually and politically mistaken to assume that a simple public–private binary exists.

Identifying Alternatives by Objectives

It is also useful to discuss alternatives to privatisation by their intended objectives. I have broken these into five broad categories here. The first refers to alternatives in which the primary objective is simply 'defending the status quo'. In the fight against privatisation we often forget that the vast majority of services that exist are still provided by the public sector (an estimated 90–95 per cent of the world's water services, for example). There is much that can be improved (even rejected) about these public sector service delivery models, but much of it is still done reasonably well, and we should not fall victim to the negative rhetoric of neoliberal public sector bashing that has become part and parcel of today's marketised mantra.

Having said that, there are few, if any, public services in the world that cannot be improved, and there are many places where public services are extremely weak or nonexistent. It is therefore incumbent upon us to pay attention to efforts aimed at 'revising the status quo'. Defending poor public services does little to advance a political or intellectual agenda on alternatives to privatisation. It is essential that we explore efforts that have gone into making public services more democratic, more participatory, more equitable, more transparent, more environmentally sound and so on. It is also essential that we understand both the successes and failures of such efforts. Examples range from the well-known – but imperfect – participatory budgeting models of Latin America to lesser known initiatives such as community-based monitoring of public health services in rural India and worker co-ops delivering water in Bangladesh. In some cases reforms leave institutional structures intact, while in others they dismantle old forms of the state with a broader set of actors and innovative forms of governance, opening up new vistas of reform.

A third category of objectives is that of 'reclaiming public services'. After the privatisation euphoria of the 1980s and 1990s many national and municipal governments are finding themselves once again in control of essential services, either as a result of a political struggle to remove a private firm (such as the 'Water Wars' of Cochabamba, Bolivia), or because the private sector provider fled an unprofitable situation, leaving the state/community to pick up the pieces (as with water services in Buenos Aires in the early 2000s). Whatever the cause (an understanding of which is essential to assessing the outcomes), there is a large and growing list of previously privatised services that are now back in public hands – sometimes with dramatically reconfigured governance structures and operating ethos, but not always. The remunicipalisation of water in Paris, France, in 2010 is an excellent example of a reversal of privatisation that has improved service delivery, lowered prices and expanded the social mission of the new public entity, Eau de Paris. By contrast, efforts to remunicipalise water in Dar es Salaam, Tanzania, have been driven largely by the World Bank and have been largely focused on creating a more market-oriented ideology within the public administration.

Fourth, there are what we might call 'utopian models' of service delivery. These are proposed or theorised systems that do not yet exist in practice but which can animate academic and popular debate. There is value in utopian thinking for several reasons. First, much policy scholarship originates from narrow-minded thinking based on what advocates believe will be acceptable to powerful interest groups and state bureaucrats. In these cases the horizons of thought are often predetermined by the dead weight of the present. Utopian thinking, by contrast, can allow us to start with probing questions about the ethical principles and necessity of change, rather than its feasibility as shaped by existing power relations and the balance of (capitalist) forces. Utopian thinking might also allow us to ask fundamental questions about the social creation of needs in contemporary society and what kind of ecological footprint we might want to leave, focusing our minds on alternative social forms, alliances, politics of scale and processes of how we might get there. Some of the literature on 'the commons' falls into this category, spanning a wide range of (sometimes problematic) possibilities.

A final category is 'historical models' of non-private service delivery. As noted previously, the public/private debate is not new, having swung back and forth at several times over the past 150 years. And yet previous experiences tend to be ignored in current debates, with little reflection on the experiences and lessons of places such as the Soviet bloc, early communist China, 19th-century municipal socialisms and 'African socialisms'. Even unlikely places such as the American West showed fervent anti-corporate attitudes to service provision in the early 1900s, leading to the creation of some of the most famous public service networks in the world today, such as California's state water supplies. Much of the research done on these previous models was caught up in the particular politics of the time (Cold War tensions, and so on) and could benefit from a revised assessment and evaluation, but instead of reinventing the wheel – or remaking the same mistakes – there may be advantages to re-examining models of past public services to see what traction they may have today.

Looking at historical models is also a useful way to remind ourselves that the fight against for-profit, segregated, commodified service provision can be won – at least in part. But it also reveals some of the less salubrious aims of a 'developmental state'. Keynesian interventionism, for example, was typically introduced to recalibrate and resuscitate the conditions of capital accumulation and market dominance, rather than to undermine them. It thus laid the economic and political foundations for reintroducing monetarist and neoliberal policies in the 1980s, as was the case with many examples of developmental states in the

South at that time, such as Ghana, Bolivia and Malaysia. In other words, state ownership can sometimes be little more than a temporary way of stabilising market conditions in preparation for future privatisations, with (neo)liberalism and (neo)Keynesianism often representing little more than points on a relatively narrow pendulum swing.

Evaluating 'Success'

Another challenge in the search for alternatives to privatisation is the ways in which we evaluate actually existing examples. Unless we can say with some degree of confidence that this or that public service is something worth fighting for, and that it appears to work better than privatised options, we are left with little more than a rhetorical shouting match, with proponents of a particular public service left to defend systems in ways that are difficult to support, let alone advocate for adoption elsewhere.

It is also critical that alternative evaluation systems go beyond the narrow financial data employed by neoliberal institutions such as the World Bank and international consulting firms such as KPMG. One trend in this regard has been to develop normative criteria that offer a core of universal principles while at the same time broadening out from marketised parameters and allowing for contextual differences.

One way to approach this is to extrapolate from debates over privatisation, reinterpreting criteria used by organisations such as the World Bank (including efficiency and accountability) and moving them beyond their thin neoliberal tropes. It is also important to include criteria unique to public services, such as 'public ethos' and 'solidarity', and to have benchmarks (such as equity) with suffi-cient elasticity of meaning to allow for variations in interpretation. The aim here is to challenge or rule out overly narrow neoliberal interpretations of success, which can limit discussions of performance to narrow financial grounds, while at the same time adding additional factors such as gender discrimination and affordability, which are often ignored by mainstream analysts.

A set of proposed criteria is summarised in Table 11.1 (overleaf). Not every measure can be examined in depth in every case, but these criteria can act as basic reference points and an alternative measuring stick for comparative use across place and sectors.

It is also important to note that there are no 'perfect' models of public service delivery. No single service provider can realistically meet all of the normative criteria outlined here, and what might be deemed important in one place at one time (for example, community participation in decision making) might be less important in another context. There is no one blueprint for success.

The neoliberal methodological approach to evaluation is very different, by contrast, arguing that all human behaviour is ultimately based on self-interest that responds to signals from the market. There might be differences in the way people produce and consume a service, but self-maximisation is seen to be central to all service behaviours, with concepts of marginal utility serving as a universal indicator to explain everything from 'willingness to pay' to the creation of 'social capital'. Using this rationale, neoliberal researchers see individualised behaviour behind every action, allowing them to argue that deviations from marketised behaviour are aberrations not worth appraising.

At the other extreme, some analysts reject any notion of universal norms, seeing them as an imperialising (and largely Eurocentric) force. Social perceptions of water, historical practices of medicine and localised forms of energy production are seen to be too different from place to place to allow for consistent forms of assessment, or reproducibility, and should not be subject to imposed globalised standards. In other words, some analysts believe that all universal evaluative criteria should be rejected.

I would argue that it is possible to navigate a path between these polar extremes, one that allows for the use of broadly acknowledged universal goals (such as equity and accountability) while at the same time recognising that generalisations are fraught with cultural and political tensions that may be irreconcilable at times. The normative criteria in Table 11.1 are therefore intended as a relatively fluid reference point for research, not a fixed anchor. The aim is to allow for context-based evaluations that acknowledge local norms but do not fetishise difference. Spiritual interpretations of water are diverse, for example, but the notion of equitable and affordable access to water can be interpreted more universally, and seen as a non-negotiable right, forcing open a debate about the mechanisms by which these 'norms' are achieved and the extent to which they have been 'successful'.

Such normative criteria also allow us to better compare experiences with public services in locations as diverse as France and Uruguay, while also allowing us to take into account the varied circumstances that have allowed some public service entities to become relatively progressive in an otherwise deeply uneven and heavily marketised world. We can also see why good public service experiences are not as easily transferable from one place to another (or one sector to another) as organisations such as the World Bank would like us to believe, and why a neoliberal template can never fully shape human behaviour.

Conclusion

In the end, there are no magic bullets for good public services, and the wildly diverse range of 'alternatives to privatisation' in the literature can be frustrating. But I take this diversity as a healthy sign. It represents a dynamic range of actually existing realities in an emerging field of study and practice. Despite what the mainstream press has to say, anti-privatisation debate and practice is happening, it is robust, and there are myriads of positive examples of public service delivery around the world.

Table 11.1 Criteria used to evaluate alternatives to privatisation

Equity	Is availability of the service equitable for different social groups?
	Is the quality and quantity of the service equitable?
	Are prices equitable?
	Is equity formalised, legalised or institutionalised in some way?
Participation in decision making	Is the depth and scope of participation adequate?
	Is participation equitable?
	Is participation formalised, legalised or institutionalised in some way?
	Is the model of participation sustainable?
Efficiency	Is the service delivered in a financially efficient manner?
	Are adequate investments being made in long-term maintenance?
	Do efficiency gains undermine other potentially positive outcomes?
	Do efficiency gains take into account other services and/or levels of government?
Quality of service	Is the overall quality of the service good?
	Is quality improving?
Accountability	Are service providers accountable to end users?
	Is accountability formalised, legalised or institutionalised in some way?
Transparency	Does the general public understand the operating mandates of the service provider?
	Are decisions about service delivery regularly communicated to the public?
	Is transparency formalised, legalised or institutionalised in some way?
Quality of the workplace	Do frontline workers participate in policy making for the service?
	Are workers paid a fair salary and benefits?
	Are there adequate numbers of workers to ensure quality, safety and sustainability?
	Are there good relations between frontline workers, managers and end users of the service?
	Is there equity among workers?

Sustainability	Are there sufficient financial resources available to ensure successful continuity of the service? Is there sufficient political support at different levels of government? Is the service using natural resources in a sustainable way?
Solidarity	Does the service help build solidarity between workers, community, bureaucrats, politicians, NGOs and end users? Does the service help to build solidarity between different service sectors (e.g. with public health officials)? Does the service help to build solidarity with other levels of state?
Public ethos	Does the model help to create/build a stronger 'public ethos' around service delivery? Does the model promote thinking and dialogue about concepts of public ownership and control? Does the service model explicitly oppose privatisation and commercialisation?
Transferability	Is the model transferable to other places (in whole or in part)?

The water sector is arguably the most vibrant in this regard. This might be because it has been one of the services most affected and politicised by privatisation. It is also the only truly non-substitutable service in the world, making alternatives essential. Water services are also relatively simple, technologically speaking, and easier to reimagine than more complex services such as health care and education. There are also effective and well-coordinated national and international groups that have opposed water privatisation for over two decades, and are now proposing and operating real alternatives on the ground.

Electricity, by contrast, is an example of a service that has seen relatively little action in the way of alternatives, largely for the exact opposite reasons to those given for water: multiple forms of energy exist; it is technical and capital intensive (though it need not be); there has been relatively little understanding of the complex nature of unbundling that has taken place in the sector; and it is typically operated at a scale that makes local organising more difficult. As a result, few regional – and no international – fora exist that are working on alternatives to privatisation in electricity. Positive examples of alternatives are emerging – and several national electricity systems have been renationalised over the past few years – but they are fewer in number and more isolated than for water.

Geographically, the largest number of interesting alternatives is to be found in Latin America. This will come as little surprise to readers familiar with that region's larger experimentation with socialism, and alternatives to neoliberalism more generally, as well as its long history of anti-corporate struggle. Africa, by contrast, is arguably the weakest region in terms of 'successful' alternatives, constrained in large part by the ongoing stranglehold of international financial institutions such as the World Bank, the relatively conservative/neoliberal regimes in power, and limited state capacities. There is civil society and labour resistance to privatisation on the continent, but this has not often transferred into effective mobilisation for public alternatives.

It is also important to reiterate the point that there are no 'ideal' alternatives. No single service provider will excel at all of the criteria for 'success' listed above, and few can be neatly typologised. Alternatives to privatisation need not fit into tidy little boxes and need not be replicable elsewhere. Ideological milieux, institutional histories, state capacities, the availability of capital and environmental conditions are but a few of the factors that can make or break an alternative, and a model that works in one place might prove a failure in another. Pittsburgh is not Phnom Penh is not Pretoria.

And yet we should not abandon a commitment to universal norms and expectations, such as equity, sustainability and transparency, as long as they are made to be contextually meaningful and practical. Research methods must be equally elastic, with sufficiently flexible conceptual frameworks to take into account particularities while at the same time allowing for meaningful comparisons across regions and sectors. There might be no single model that works for every sector in every place, but there must be some way of deciding whether an alternative to privatisation can be considered successful or not.

Scale is another factor to keep in mind. There are successful alternatives at local, regional, national and even transnational levels; from water provision systems in small rural areas that service several hundred people, to national health systems that service millions. The scale of a public service is not, a priori, a determinant of its success. Being large can be beneficial in some ways (economies of scale, national standards) but detrimental in others (public participation, cultural appropriateness). Ditto for being small, where we must be particularly watchful of the sometimes blind celebration of 'community involvement', and the fetishisation of the local, often resulting in extra work for women and girls, and creating low-quality service standards for the poor. Small might be beautiful at times, and large might be efficient at others, but there is nothing axiomatic about size or scale when it comes to alternatives to privatisation.

A related point is the question of technology. While much of the scalar debate takes place with reference to politics (participation, democratic oversight and so on) the kinds of technology employed can have equally important influences on the success or failure of an alternative service delivery system. Most electricity systems, for example, are national or regional high-voltage grids that require coordination on a large political scale, with massive amounts of capital and considerable technical knowledge. Creating localised, democratised non-commercial alternatives can be hindered by these technological structures.

Water production, by contrast, is still artisan in places, and even where it is fully industrialised tends to be locally sourced and managed because of transport constraints. Water treatment and distribution involves relatively simple technology, as can some healthcare provision, with localised health systems able to use relatively simple techniques such as oral rehydration that can be provided with minimal training (very different, of course, from high-end tertiary health care which has tended to use technology as a way of insulating itself from public accountability). As a result, some service sectors lend themselves more easily to technological innovations that are appropriate for descaled applications with community control and ownership. These technologically determined scenarios need not be the case, but it is critical to see the roles that technology can play in shaping alternatives to privatisation.

There is also a need to better understand the gendered dimensions of publicness. There is a sizeable literature on the negative effects of privatisation on women, but relatively little research has been conducted on what a more positive public service might look like from a gendered perspective. Some theoretical and methodological work is emerging in this regard, but future research and action on alternatives to privatisation must take gender more seriously.

Finally, there is a need for better connections across sectors. Research on public services tends to be done in sectoral silos, as does much of the activism on this topic. While it is true that health care is very different from transportation, education or electricity, there is much to be learned about the successes and failures in these different fields, and even more to be gained from a united public sector front.

Acknowledgement

This chapter draws on Chapters 1 and 2 of my co-authored and co-edited book *Alternatives to Privatization: Public Options for Essential Services in the Global South* (McDonald and Ruiters, 2012). The book explores theoretical and methodological debates about the meaning and practice of 'successful' public services, drawing on empirical evidence from over 40 countries in Asia, Africa and Latin America.

Select Bibliography

Bakker, K. (2013) 'Neoliberal versus postneoliberal water: geographies of privatisation and resistance', *Annals of the Association of American Geographers*, 103(2): 253–60.

Cumbers, A. (2012) *Reclaiming Public Ownership: Making Space for Economic Democracy*. London: Zed.

McDonald, D. A. and Ruiters, G. (2012) *Alternatives to Privatization: Public Options for Essential Services in the Global South*. New York: Routledge.

People's Health Movement (2012) *Global Health Watch 3*. Available at: www.ghwatch.org/ghw3

Sclar, E. (2000) *You Don't Always Get What You Pay For: The Economics of Privatisation*. Ithaca, N.Y.: Cornell University Press.

Sultana, F. C., Mohanty, T. and Miraglia, S. (2013) 'Gender justice and public water for all: insights from Dhaka, Bangladesh', Occasional Paper, No. 18, Municipal Services Project, Cape Town. Available at: www.municipalservicesproject.org/publication/gender-justice-and-public-water-all-insights-dhaka-bangladesh (accessed 4 June 2014).

CHAPTER TWELVE

Utopian Socialism and Marx's Capital: Envisioning Alternatives

Hugo Radice

Socialists have for the most part been reluctant to advocate any specific form of society as the outcome of their critical analyses of capitalism. The immediate reason for this may well be the historical inadequacies of 'actually existing socialisms', of whatever variety. It is also a simple consequence of the overall pre-eminence of capitalism during the last 200 years or so, since its institutions and practices have shaped people's political common sense. While precapitalist orders were ruled by an élite or class constituted by tradition, religion or simply force, the ideology of capitalism has usually proclaimed the 'voluntary' adherence of its members through some form of democracy. As a result, arguments for socialism have usually begun from a presumption of democracy, coupled with a commitment to challenging capitalism's economic and social inequalities.

I suggest that the absence of an explicit utopian dimension in socialist debates has seriously weakened our ability to respond to the resurgence of (neo)liberal capitalism since the 1970s. I begin with a brief definition of a socialist utopia in Part I of Marx's *Capital Vol. I*, and then set out four key issues that arise in elaborating this definition, focusing on work, production, distribution and education. I then suggest that Marx's critique of capitalism helps us to find the seeds of a future utopia in the day-to-day functioning of capitalist society: this can be the starting-point for building a more effective movement for democratic egalitarianism.

The Free Association of Producers: Four Key Issues

Very near the start of his most comprehensive analysis of capitalism, Marx gives us a snapshot of a possible socialist utopia:

> Let us now picture to ourselves, by way of change, a community of free individuals, carrying on the work with the means of production in common, in which the labour-power of all the different individuals is consciously applied as the combined labour-power of the community.
>
> (Marx, 1965 [1867]: 78)

This, in essence, is the idea of a free association of producers (hereafter FAP).

A would-be FAP evidently faces a daunting task in establishing and repro-ducing a social order that can meet humanity's needs. The failures of socialism as it actually existed in the 20th century (Radice, 2010) are often attributed by socialists to the determined opposition of capitalist ruling classes to any encroachment on their powers and privileges. A better socialism, however, has proved very hard to figure out, both in academic studies and in utopian fiction. In this section I explore the issues by examining four propositions which, taken together, may provide a starting-point for discussion.

*a) Production Should Be Seen as Embracing Both the Physical
Transformation of Nature into Means of Subsistence, and
the Political Administration of These Activities*

The fragmented character of mainstream social thought is particularly acute in regard to the relation between 'economics' and 'politics', because their ideolog-ical separation forms a crucial step in legitimising unequal access to the means of production under capitalism. In all liberal conceptions of the state, the most important liberty is that relating to individual property rights: the freedom of a property-owning citizen to alienate their property through exchange. The corollary, reflecting the political context of absolutism in which capitalism first emerged, is that as far as possible the state's role should be restricted to ensuring that freedom. Neoclassical economists have put forward different views on how this can be done, but a central mainstream tenet today is the 'efficient markets hypothesis', that is, the view that markets provide the most efficient means of allocating resources. Underpinning this view is the anthropological premise of 'economic (wo)man', who comes to the market equipped with given tastes and motivated by the desire for individual advantage. Socialists have found it difficult to challenge the mainstream's understanding of both the state and the individual, which have by default become part of our 'common sense'.

On the one hand, *market socialist* models have accepted the idea that consump-tion is the primary purpose of production, and that it takes place in privately constituted households which determine their own patterns of expenditure. Recognising that capitalist economies are characterised by gross inequalities of wealth and power, they mainly argue for these to be challenged *politically* through the redistributive taxation of income and capital by the state, or through public ownership of certain spheres of production (notably 'utilities' such as gas and water). This standpoint lay at the heart of 20th-century social democracy, but it has been politically marginalised by the rise of neoliberalism since the 1980s.

The alternative socialist model of *central planning* rejects the efficiency of markets and argues instead that the direct allocation of resources to the produc-tion of an agreed variety of goods and services is more efficient. However, in the literature it remains commonly assumed that responsibility for planning is held by a state constituted over and apart from its citizens, and historically 'actually existing' communism collapsed as soon as its own ruling élite began to question the effectiveness and legitimacy of state planning.

An FAP can challenge this historical failure through the collective democratic planning of production. In the early 1940s the Austrian politician and philosopher Otto Neurath challenged Hayek's classic rejection of socialist planning on grounds of informational efficiency, arguing that the scientific community organised extremely complex networks of activity without recourse to markets (O'Neill, 2006). Earlier, guild socialism had offered an approach to economic democracy based on the political determination of resource allocation through enterprise-based and sector-based public deliberation. Yugoslav self-management offered an alternative in principle from the 1950s to the 1970s, although its functioning was continually undermined by market forces, including foreign competition, and by an all-powerful one-party state able to intervene at will. The key step is to integrate 'economic' and 'political' decision making into a public structure for arriving at agreed collective decisions. As LeGuin (1974) illustrates, this is messy, cumbersome, often frustrating, and requiring above all the wholehearted commitment of the great majority of citizens to that public structure. Furthermore, extending the collective process of democratic economic decision making internationally adds a further set of political challenges.

The primary objection by liberals to collective democratic planning concerns freedom of choice, which has been at the forefront of recent neoliberal assaults on the public sector. This can only be challenged by rejecting the modern consumerism that demands always not only 'more' but 'different', and the manipulation of tastes and desires by private producer interests.

A second common objection concerns technological innovation, where mainstream economists argue that central planning eliminates the financial incentive that a market economy offers to producers who can reduce their own cost of production below the prevailing level. To socialists, innovators are motivated not only by personal financial gain, but also by the wider social benefits of their work.

b) Work Is Understood as Useful Labour that Meets the Human Need for Creativity as Well as Subsistence

By useful labour, I mean first labour that provides goods or services that meet social needs. These needs can be expressed directly, rather than through the presentation of money or credit in payment. Many needs have historically been met in capitalist economies through the provision of what even mainstream economics used to recognise as 'public' goods, especially where economies of scale justify having only a single supplier; where provision is necessarily universal regardless of any individual expression of need, as in the case of defence; or where substantial 'external' effects exist, as with immunisation programmes or the control of pollution. Especially in conditions of natural resource limits and the threat of climate change, such public good considerations may apply to a very large proportion of production.

But what motivates us to work? Under present-day neoliberalism, it is generally assumed that work is a bad, not a good, and that we only undertake it when offered the promise of a carrot (money) or the threat of a stick (dismissal). While this is primarily applied at the individual level, it is reinforced by the promotion of economic nationalism, in which workers are urged collectively to work harder in order to compete with the workers of other countries. But in an FAP, we do not consider exclusively the benefit that we ourselves receive from our work: we also regard the benefits of others as a benefit to ourselves. Given the fundamental importance of material subsistence, it is in relation to work that the general moral critique of individualism has its most important application. Furthermore, there is no intrinsic limit to the scale and scope of this application, short of humanity as a whole.

The question of creativity, already raised in relation to innovation, applies to work in general. Marx himself criticised the dehumanising consequences of modern industry, visible in the monotony of endlessly repeated actions, and in the appropriation by owners of skills now embodied in machinery (or today also in information systems and their operation). He also recognised that the growing application of science and technology increased the use of skilled workers, technicians and managers. Today even the most skilled, as well as professionals in fields such as law, medicine and education, are themselves subject to deskilling and coercive control. Yet it is absurd to imagine that people only 'perform' under the promise of extra reward or the threat of punishment, and even the most routine of work activities usually offers some intrinsic satisfaction.

This is especially true of that huge range of activities, outside of places of employment, that provide a large part of our necessary subsistence, as well as leisure activities. Unpaid work in the household or in the wider community has been regarded by many socialists as an unrecognised subsidy to the wages of employment (see Spronk and Miraglia, as well as Ozmen in this book). If all that work was rewarded at the going rate for waged employment, the measured value of labour-power (the cost of reproducing wage labour) would be substantially higher. However, such unpaid work takes place in contexts radically different from the workplace; typically its planning and execution of activities does not entail monetary calculation, and is infused instead with intrinsic values of mutual support and service to others. The corollary of this is that such values also remain at some irreducible level in paid work, as has always been recognised in humanistic critiques of so-called scientific management (for example time and motion studies) by sociologists and social psychologists.

Whether creativity is a real human need remains a disputed question. Many have argued that while the 'young' Marx passionately espoused an anthropological standpoint of historical progress as the realisation of a human essence, the 'mature' Marx saw history as the outcome of social structures (or modes of production) developing in a clear sequence through the actions of individuals and groups (see Fleischer, 1973). In those varieties of socialist thought that come closest to our FAP, such as council communism and syndicalism, the structuralist view is rejected in favour of a humanism that comes from social practice, rather than being innate in the human mind. From such a standpoint, creativity exercised in production for social need is itself a need for all of us.

c) An Association Can Only Be 'Free' If There Is General Acceptance of Substantive Material Equality as the Basis for Equal Participation in Production and Reproduction

George Orwell wrote in *Homage to Catalonia*:

> The thing that attracts ordinary men to Socialism and makes them willing to risk their skins for it, the 'mystique' of Socialism, is the idea of equality; to the vast majority of people Socialism means a classless society, or it means nothing.
>
> (Orwell, 1938: 104)

In a time like the present, in which inequality of wealth and income is once again reaching staggering levels, this view appears hopelessly idealistic and outdated. Instead we are invited not only to envy the rich and seek to emulate them, but to be grateful to them because of the jobs they create and their 'charitable' donations. Recently there has been a modest backlash, with critics like Wilkinson and Pickett (2009) arguing from empirical data the harmful consequences of inequality for the health and well-being of all. But I suggest that our FAP will be doomed to failure if it is not founded upon a positive case for equality, rather than upon the critique of (extreme) inequality.

Part of the problem is simply that, outside of relatively small units such as extended families, cooperatives and subsistence communities, the available evidence on the effects of inequality is restricted by the absence of any proper benchmark of real equality. Czechoslovakia during the high period of communism (1956 to 1968) recorded the lowest degree of income differentiation, of around 1:3, with the Scandinavian countries achieving ratios of 1:5 or 6 in their heyday. Czechoslovakia registered in 1948 the highest electoral support ever achieved by a communist party in Europe, while Scandinavia pioneered social partnership and the welfare state in responding to the Great Depression of the early 1930s: in both cases, we can infer a high level of commitment to social solidarity. In addition, although there is certainly scope for oppression and inequality in family businesses or cooperatives, the available evidence suggests that they function most effectively on the basis of relative equality and mutual respect.

A key problem is the extent to which rewards are believed to be differentiated with some degree of fairness according to the type of job. Surveys have often suggested that people want jobs that are dirty and dangerous, or that require very high levels of attention or affect, to be more highly rewarded; yet such rankings typically contradict the other two main arguments about pay relativity in capitalist societies. These are first that pay over a career should reflect the relative cost of acquiring the necessary skills (or in modern parlance, 'investment in human capital'), and second, that pay should (like the price of commodities in general) reflect the 'scarcity value' of the workers in question. High-paying professions often conveniently combine these two arguments, while many of the jobs that are highly ranked because of the needs that they meet are nevertheless badly paid because they rank low on the other criteria (for example nursing). Further confusion arises from the intentional substitution of 'equality of opportunity' as a goal, in preference to substantive equality. But this substitution entails a retreat from the pursuit of equality through redistribution, as well as the demotivation of those who lose in the competitive struggle for inclusion in the elite.

However, debate on the relative rewards for different jobs typically takes as given the way in which society's labour is divided into specific individual jobs. The division of labour, first systematically studied in relation to capitalism more than 200 years ago by Adam Smith, is not preordained but socially constructed. There are three interwoven elements that shape this division of labour. First, there is the *social division of labour* into particular sectors on the basis of what they produce: this is represented in official UK statistics by the SIC (Standard Industrial Classification). Second, there is the *detailed or technical division of labour* within the workplace (for example Smith's famous pin factory case study): this entails the division of the overall production process into specific tasks. While these two strands constitute what mainstream economics calls the demand for labour, the third one is the *occupational* classification, in essence a subjective self-classification by would-be employees based on formal qualifications, experience or simply inclination. Despite the evident complexity, modern industrial societies have increasingly similar divisions of labour; this reflects an increasing global homogenisation of production technologies and consumer tastes, driven in large measure by the rise of transnational corporations and standardised structures of state regulation and delivery.

But as such, this standard model has deeper origins in the social relations of production. The workplace division of labour owes more to the exigencies of employer control that any imperatives arising from specific production technologies. Occupational differentiation reflects the long-term processes in which those who must sell their labour shape what they offer to the available demand. In short, what we face as workers is a set of occupational choices established by a capitalist labour market, to which people have necessarily adapted down the generations.

In an FAP there is no reason why we should simply accept this. As utopian writers have often suggested, doing the same set of tasks year after year eventually offers little in the way of challenge; as Marx put it, ' constant labour of one uniform kind disturbs the intensity and flow of a man's animal spirits, which find recreation and delight in mere change of activity' (1965 [1867]: 341). The idea of sharing especially disagreeable but necessary tasks among everyone is evident in utopian fiction, for example Huxley (1962) and LeGuin (1974). In recent years the concept of a portfolio career – either simultaneously or sequentially undertaking different types of work – has been much touted, usually among those with the resources and security to risk such a radical departure from the norm. But the most important dimension of the capitalist division of labour that the FAP can dissolve is the *vertical* division of labour, between labour of conception and control and labour of execution, or more generally between manual and mental labour. This directly confronts what some analysts of industrial societies (both capitalist and Soviet-communist) have identified as a new ruling class, namely those who have expert knowledge, which leads to our final issue.

d) Education Is Based on Ensuring That All Are Capable of Participating in Useful Labour and in Its Direction

The critical literature on education is enormous, but a key common thread is the idea that it has been organised in capitalism, whether by private interests or by the state, primarily to make people employable by equipping them with the skills needed to find a role in the spectrum of jobs offered under the capitalist division of labour. Against this stands the progressive ideal of education as emancipation: the provision of knowledge and values for understanding the world and participating fully in society.

At this point in the evolution of neoliberal capitalism in Britain, for example, workers have been subjected to a particularly pure version of the employability objective, enforced through the techniques of new public management and the twin mantras of choice and equality of opportunity. The array of opportunities is taken as given by the existing offers of employment, generated under competitive market conditions; thus schooling in practice sorts out children by age 16 or 18 into a hierarchy of given skills and capabilities, which largely determines their future life chances in terms of income and social standing.

In this system, the current view that work is bad (see (b) above) means that teachers are incentivised through punishments and rewards based on their success in raising the level of the job hierarchy which their pupils are able to reach. Teachers at every level therefore, from pre-school to university, compete for the brightest entrants because they are more likely to reach higher levels, with the teachers' success then evaluated through league tables of achievement (supposedly adjusted to allow for pupil background). Head teachers become chief executives driving forward the struggle for competitive advantage in the educational marketplace.

An FAP could instead transform education away from this relentless competition for access to privilege, towards the principle of equipping everyone to participate in society on an equal footing. Instead of particular schools, teachers and individual pupils being rewarded with income and status for their competitive success, their purpose would be to provide all pupils with the skills and capabilities that enabled them to undertake tasks across a *vertical* spectrum, from the execution of necessary routine physical and mental work, to the supposedly higher tasks of agreeing goals, designing production and organising social labour. Resources would be allocated for this purpose on the basis of continual evaluation of needs across individuals and communities, undertaken by those communities with appropriate transfers during the transition period.

Education for equality would have profound consequences for social cohesion and inclusion. Imagine a world in which everyone knew they were able to participate fully in deciding social objectives, and shaping the political processes through which they are achieved. This would be, in terms of recent political slogans in Britain, both a 'big' and a 'good' society.

Making Connexions to the Present: The Relevance of Marx's Capital

For many socialists, the works of Karl Marx and Friedrich Engels remain an important source of ideas. In the Communist Manifesto of 1848, they strongly criticised the utopian socialists of the early 19th century, and it became conventional to see this as a rejection of any form of utopian thinking. But their criticism was really that the utopian socialists did not ground their visions in the social transformations taking place as industrial capitalism developed. Geoghegan (1987) argues that there are many ideas about a possible socialism in the writings of Marx and Engels, and on through the Marxist tradition as a whole. Returning to the quotation from Marx earlier, the remainder of Capital Vol. I is focused on analysing capitalism, but I think that it is also possible to infer from it a more detailed agenda for socialism.

Part I of Capital Vol I presents a world in which production is regulated predominantly by the market, that is, the exchange of commodities and the circulation of money. By analysing in depth the concept of value, Marx suggests that a fundamental tension exists between value in use and value in exchange, which underlies the mysterious role of money, the ubiquitous alienation of the producer from the product and the phenomenon of commodity fetishism. The alternative suggested by Marx's utopian snapshot is one of collective planning of production through the agreed allocation of resources. Value in use and value in exchange are thereby reconciled in purposive action aimed at meeting social needs; but this raises the obvious question of how in practice that purposive action is to be undertaken.

In Part II, he draws out the concept of capital as a social relation, based upon the separation of workers from the means of production, and shows how capital can extract and accumulate surplus-value behind the appearance of a free and equal exchange of labour-power for wages. Without this social relation, an FAP has to decide how resources are to be distributed, and what connection made, if any, between the distribution of productive labour and the allocation of the resulting products for consumption.

Part III then examines the capitalist labour process, showing how the capital advanced to finance production is divided between material inputs, whose value is transferred to the product, and labour-power, which creates additional (surplus) value, as long as its duration is extended beyond the time required to produce the commodities required for the worker's sustenance. Marx thereby identifies the length of the working day as a key terrain of social conflict under capitalism, and one which, contrary to the classical claim that economic life is regulated by an invisible hand, can only be resolved by the very visible hand of the state. The inference for the FAP is that its members would have to reach agreement on the duration of working time, and the distribution of that time between meeting their consumption needs, and building up the material means of production.

In Part IV Marx argues that capitalism can overcome the physical limits that the length of the working day places upon exploitation, by transforming the material and social organisation of production. In the evolution from simple cooperation to manufacture to modern industry, workers are stripped of the skills and capacities that characterise artisanal production, subjected to a more and more detailed division of labour within the workplace, and finally transformed tendentially into a 'mere appendage' of the machine system in modern industry. Once again, the struggles over these transformations of production entail the continuous intervention of the state, not only in relation to the consequences within production (deriving from the owners' exercise of property rights, and the conflict between those rights and the moral and material condition of workers) but also in the spheres of education, health and culture. In an FAP, technological advances that reduce the amount of labour needed to produce goods and services will unequivocally benefit the associated producers, who can decide how to make use of the labour time that they have saved.

Parts V to VII return from the sphere of production to the visible sphere of exchange and accumulation of capital, or in modern mainstream parlance, the macro-economic functioning of capitalism. Marx analyses in Part V the interrelations between 'absolute' surplus-value, arising from the extension of the working day beyond that needed simply to reproduce the capacity for work, and 'relative' surplus-value, arising from the transformations of productive technique that reduce the time needed for this purpose. In Part VI he examines a topic dear to the heart of all workers, the level of wages and the forms that wages take. In Part VII, he turns to the accumulation of capital: its source in the expropriation of surplus labour, its normal processes of simple and expanded reproduction, its relation to population growth, and above all the potential for interruption, breakdown and economic crisis.

Throughout these sections, Marx continues to point out the ever-present role of the state in ensuring the conditions of reproduction and accumulation, as well as popular struggles of resistance and political contestation. For example, he explains how the living standard of workers depends not only on money wages, but on the prices of the goods they buy; how political economists justify the wealth of capitalists by claiming that it is their natural reward for investing, while blaming poverty on the profligacy of the poor; and how accumulation raises the productivity of labour, but also creates a reserve army of unemployed workers. While an FAP would no longer reproduce an ever-deepening division between propertied capitalists and propertyless workers, many of the issues discussed in these chapters would recur in the form of complex decisions facing the collective producers.

Finally, Part VIII of *Capital Vol. I* forms an epilogue which, unusually, is in chronological terms a prologue: the historical origins of the capitalist social order. These eight short chapters set out the agenda for generations of subsequent historical scholarship on what is usually termed the transition from feudalism to capitalism, and also what Marx defined as the historical tendency of capitalist accumulation and the modern theory of colonisation. As such, they constitute for a would-be FAP a sort of cautionary tale: one of social struggles over centuries and continents, that in fits and starts and through many unpredictable contingencies leads to the emergence of a social order that, while deeply divided and crisis-ridden, nevertheless generates remarkable advances in humanity's potentialities. For all the certainty that Marx expresses in his famous depiction in Chapter 32 of the growing revolt of the working class, the transformation of capitalism into socialism is no historical necessity. Rather, the possibility of socialism gives purpose and meaning to our struggles for a better way.

Conclusions

It is important to restore a utopian component to contemporary socialist thinking. I explored discursively some of the issues that typically arise in attempts to elaborate the model of a free association of producers. I then rejected the widely held view that Marxism's founders set aside utopianism in 1848 as part of a general break with the humanism of their youth. I argued instead that the analysis that they developed in the years after 1848, with of course all its own faults and fancies, does nevertheless display the contours of a new society in a way that should be seen as reshaping utopian socialism in response to actual historical developments. The lesson that may be drawn is that the effective development of a socialist society depends on recognising the seeds of material interdependence, creativity and self-government hidden within the private and public institutions that currently mediate human encounters. If *Capital Vol. I* remains the most compelling general account of how capitalism works, then it may help in providing an analytical framework within which a strategy of change can be shaped.

Select Bibliography

Fleischer, H. (1973) *Marxism and History*. New York: Harper & Row.
Geoghegan, V. (1987) *Utopianism and Marxism*. London: Methuen.
Huxley. A. (1962) *Island*. London: Chatto & Windus.
LeGuin, U. (1974) *The Dispossessed*. London: Gollancz.
Marx, K. (1965) [1867] *Capital: A Critique of Political Economy, Vol. I*. London: Lawrence & Wishart.

O'Neill, J. (2006) 'Knowledge, planning and markets: a missing chapter in the socialist calculation debates', *Economics and Philosophy*, 22: 55–78.

Orwell, G. (1938) *Homage to Catalonia*. London: Secker & Warburg.

Radice, H. (2010) 'The idea of socialism: from 1968 to the present-day crisis', *Antipode*, 41(S1): 27–49.

Wilkinson, R. and Pickett, K. (2009) *The Spirit Level: Why Equality is Better for Everyone*. London: Allen Lane.

Part II
Alternative Cases

Beyond Neoliberalism and New Developmentalism in Latin America: Towards an Anti-Capitalist Agenda

Abelardo Mariña-Flores

Neoliberal economic policies implemented in Latin America since the mid-1970s have shown national specificities. They have been shaped by the articulation of specific nations in the world market, by their relation with the imperialist centres, and by internal social and political struggles. The heterogeneity of national trajectories was reinforced during the 2000s since the 'progressive' governments that took office in most Latin American countries (the so-called 'pink tide') implemented a wide range of alternative policy programmes. Some programmes have been shyly social democratic, as in Chile (2000 to 2010), Honduras (2006 to 2009), Guatemala and Paraguay (2008 to 2012), El Salvador (since 2009) and Peru (since 2011). Others are allegedly anti-neoliberal, as in Brazil and Argentina (since 2003), Uruguay (since 2005) and Nicaragua (since 2006). Finally, some programmes are intentionally anti-imperialist and pro-socialist, as in Venezuela (since 1999), Bolivia (since 2006) and Ecuador (since 2007), thus joining Cuba's socialist trajectory started in the 1960s.

The relatively strong economic dynamics across most of Latin America since 2004 and the relatively mild impact of the continuing global crisis since 2008 have been due partly to the alternative policies implemented. This has raised two specific, but interrelated, debates. The first refers to the possibility of long-term national capitalist development, with a particular focus on new developmentalism as a proposed alternative to neoliberalism. The second refers to the conditions required for constructing an alternative to capitalism, that is, a new type of (post-soviet) socialism.

This chapter contributes to these debates by adopting a Marxist approach based on three premises:

1 Capitalism is, since its historical genesis, a world system of wage-labour exploitation geared towards capital valorisation and accumulation. The world capitalist market articulates nation-states in a hierarchical and asymmetrical structure: centres and peripheries, regional subcentres and subperipheries.

Therefore, intrinsically contradictory imperialist and inter-imperialist relations
of dominance–dependence and confrontation rule its dynamics.
2 Capital valorisation and accumulation are social processes based on the
general antagonism between capital and wage-labour. Upon this fundamental
antagonism, capitalism presents two intrinsic contradictions that cause its
recurrent crises: the tendential fall of general capital profitability, and the
opposition between productive and financial-speculative mechanisms of capital
valorisation.
3 Economic policies, beyond their instrumental dimensions, are the synthetic
result of economic and political force correlations, at the state and inter-state
levels, among classes and class fractions that engage in the local, national and
world spaces of valorisation and accumulation.

The first section of this chapter analyses the post-war boom of Latin American
developmentalism and its crisis in the 1970s. The second section presents an
overview of the region's trajectory during the 1980s and 1990s which focuses first
on the contradictory outcomes of neoliberalism that propitiated the emergence
of the 'pink tide' in the 2000s, and, second, on the achievements and shortcomings of the progressive policies implemented in the 2000s. The third section then
examines the limits of new developmentalism and of classical developmentalism
as social and national development strategies, putting forward the need for a
radical alternative agenda. This has to be both anti-neoliberal and anti-capitalist.
The final section discusses the central issues involved in the construction of an
anti-capitalist agenda in the light of Latin American progressive experiences of
the last decade.

Boom and Crisis of Post-War Developmentalism

The post-war world boom unfolded in Latin America through accumulation
regimes grounded on import substitution industrialisation (ISI) processes
focused on the expansion of wage-labour and internal markets. National development programmes, based on extensive industrial, commercial and social
policies, were considered as a requirement to overcome the structural asymmetries between industrialised centres and underdeveloped peripheries, to diminish
social inequalities and to improve general living conditions. Latin American
developmentalism was based on the theory of dependence that flourished within
the Economic Commission for Latin America and the Caribbean (ECLAC). Raul
Prebisch's understanding of the world economy, which played a decisive role
in the Commission, rested on the notion of unequal and exploitative centre–
periphery relations. The anti-imperialist implication of this approach is still a
reference for scholars, policy makers, and social and political movements in Latin
America.

During the 1950s and 1960s Latin American industrialisation involved widespread processes of proletarian urbanisation and the expansion of the 'middle classes', increasing per-capita income, real wages and social benefits, and partial construction of public education and health systems. It also modified the region's articulation with the world market. Because of the slow growth of imports and exports, both in absolute terms and relative to gross domestic product (GDP), Latin America's share in world trade continuously diminished. In the 1960s international trade diversified: the United States lost its place as main commercial partner at the expense of Western Europe, and intraregional trade strengthened.

The actual results of developmentalism in the region were deeply contradictory. Despite the consolidation of ISI processes, local accumulation increasingly relied on foreign direct investment (FDI) (as a financing mechanism given the shortage of credit to the region) and on imports of machinery and equipment (as a means for technological innovation). Besides generating negative pressures on the balance of payments accounts, FDI and fixed capital goods imports reinforced the region's dependency on the developed centres. Despite the expansion of internal markets and consumption, sustained unequal distribution patterns among sectors, subregions, and between the urban and rural areas generated permanent social and political unrest.

Repression of social movements, leftist parties and revolutionary organisations was carried out systematically by the anti-communist military regimes imposed by the United States and backed up by local powers since the 1930s (in El Salvador, Nicaragua, Paraguay, Guatemala and Haiti). Counterinsurgency strategies were reinforced after the triumph of the Cuban revolution in 1959, extending military dictatorships to Honduras, Brazil, Bolivia and Argentina in the 1960s. Ultimately, national accumulation processes, despite their dynamism, could not disengage from the general tendencies of world capital accumulation. It was the structural profitability crisis that unfolded worldwide since the end of the 1960s and during the 1970s that imposed objective limits to Latin American developmentalism.

Falling profitability was the central cause of stagnation tendencies. It also determined pressures on the structure of relative prices caused by increased competition, which, in the context of expansive Keynesian-oriented anti-cyclical policies, manifested through inflation. Increasing fiscal and external deficits were the consequence of the attempts to offset diminishing private productive investment and increasing economic instability. The accentuated social and political unrest in the 1970s, which impelled and/or reinforced electoral and armed revolutionary projects (in Chile, Colombia, Guatemala, Nicaragua and El Salvador), was bloodily confronted by the existing dictatorships, by a new wave of coups d'état, and by dirty wars carried out even by civilian regimes such as Colombia and Mexico.

From 1973 in Chile and Uruguay, 1975 in Peru and 1976 in Argentina, Latin America became a laboratory of radical liberal adjustment policies (the 'monetarist experiment'). These were the first manifestations of the economic, social and political strategy of world capital against workers and peasants intended to recover general profitability (Mariña, in Kotz, 2012: 13–14). Continued accumulation and economic growth during the last part of the 1970s was sustained by the boom of external debt impelled by the massive recycling of petro-dollars to the region by the international financial system, one of the initial manifestations of the financialisation tendencies of world capital valorisation. The debt crisis in the 1980s, driven by skyrocketing interest rates in the United States (the Volcker shock) provoked an acute decay of economic systems (even with the destruction of local currencies caused by hyperinflation). This provided the material basis for neoliberal transformation aimed at reconfiguring legal and institutional structures through privatisations, anti-labour measures and external liberalisation policies.

Neoliberalism and the Search for New Developmental Paths

From the violent beginnings of neoliberalism in Latin America, neoliberal advocates attacked state-led development programmes, particularly ISI policies, arguing that state intervention was the ultimate cause of the recurring balance of payments crises. Allegedly, by hindering competition, such programmes generated inefficiencies that induced the weakening of private productive investment and stagnation, fiscal and external deficits, and increasing debt and inflation.

Besides misinterpreting the real causes of crises, the neoliberal critique of Latin American developmentalism overestimates the protectionist nature of ISI policies and also the extent to which governments were responsible for their actual anti-competitive features. During the 1950s and 1960s, in fact, these policies, although restricting a wide range of imports (especially of final goods), were quite liberal toward fixed capital goods imports and FDI. Protectionism, moreover, was not a unilateral policy decision, but the result of the confluence of the interests of local capitalist groups and of their foreign partners – both benefited from oligopolistic profits generated in the relatively protected internal markets. Above all, the neoliberal discourse conceals its real objective: through the free operation of markets, neoliberalism does not aim to achieve the efficient technical and social allocation of productive resources, sustainable growth and increased employment and welfare. Rather, neoliberalism is a class strategy aimed at boosting capital profitability and accumulation through regressive income distribution; the crushing of organised labour; the expropriation of state, social and communal property; sectoral and geographical reallocation of multinational corporations, and the extension of spaces of wage-labour exploitation.

The gradual return to civilian regimes in Latin America in the 1980s and 1990s was linked to negotiations with local and imperialist hegemonic forces that imposed the prevalence of neoliberal restructuring programmes. The progression of such programmes had extensive general outcomes. Deindustrialisation processes and labour reforms led to the weakening of the industrial proletariat and trade unions, resulting in the increasing precarity of labour, informal employment (especially in the service sector), and migration movements within the region and towards the United States and Western Europe. Slow economic growth, precarity of labour and state retreat from its productive and social functions caused general impoverishment. The massive entrance of FDI during the 1990s, along with the restructuring of local economic groups (particularly in their relations with transnational capital and imperialist centres), resulted in new forms of articulation of the region in the world market. This too was part of the recomposition of the international division of labour carried out through the worldwide liberalisation of all types of capital international flows (commercial, productive and financial-speculative). After stagnating in the 1980s, international trade expanded vigorously in the 1990s. In these two decades the United States recovered its dominant position as Latin America's major trading partner to the detriment of Western Europe, while intraregional trade moved up slightly.

Beyond these overall trends, the specificities of national economic policies resulted in the unfolding of different paths, particularly in the case of the three biggest economies of the region. As liberalisation in Brazil involved a certain degree of state management, it allowed for the relative protection of endogenous industrial poles of accumulation that greatly increased their intraregional relations. Brazil thus consolidated its position as the dominant regional subcentral power. In contrast, the radical and indiscriminate liberalisation in Mexico resulted in extensive deindustrialisation and the consequent externalisation of accumulation dynamics through an enhanced subordinate integration to the United States. In Argentina, radical neoliberal policies also propelled a widespread deindustrialisation and, prominently, accelerated integration with Brazil.

Because of its globalising, pro-financial, anti-labour and anti-ecological features, neoliberalism had contradictory effects on international, social and interclass relations. The successful geographical relocation strategies of multinational corporations radically modified productive and commercial capital international flows. This sparked the emergence of new dynamic poles of productive accumulation in the peripheries (the 'BRICS'). In the 2000s the periphery relatively displaced traditional capitalist hegemonic centres (the United States, Western Europe and Japan) as the global economic engine. Yet the spread of financial and speculative mechanisms of capital valorisation also determined the recurrent inflation and burst of speculative bubbles. Since the 1990s financial crises have been deeper and more extended. The economic, social and ecological devastation generated by neoliberalism helps to account for the waves of anti-neoliberal and growingly anti-systemic movements. These movements, however, are diverse: even though they all oppose the neoliberal disaster and demand the resumption of any type of development path, they still lack a common vision of an alternative future.

In Latin America diverse social and political movements have flourished since the 1990s: the Bolivarian movement in Venezuela, indigenous nationalities in Ecuador, coca growers in Bolivia, Zapatistas in Mexico, landless rural workers in Brazil, piqueteros in Argentina, and human rights and student movements in Chile. Each manifested itself in a context where the objective contradictions of neoliberalism had increased and notably exploded through financial crises: in Mexico in 1994–95, Argentina in 1995, Brazil in 1998–99, and Argentina again in 2001–02 (Burbach, Fox and Fuentes, 2013: 19–25). These crises gave rise to deep recessive tendencies which culminated in the US 'dot.com' crisis in 1999–2001.

In the 2000s, resistance movements propelled the electoral triumph of left and centre-left governments in most Latin American countries (with the exceptions of Colombia, Costa Rica, Mexico, Panama, the Dominican Republic and Haiti). This 'pink tide' has been the outcome of two, sometimes combined, paths. In the first, it resulted from the condensation of social struggles, not necessarily class oriented or with strong national organisational bases, such as in Venezuela, Argentina, Bolivia and Ecuador. In the second, the 'pink tide' resulted from the advance of workers and/or progressive political organisations (parties, party fractions and/or coalitions) that were linked in various ways with social movements, as was the case in Chile, Argentina, Brazil, Uruguay, Nicaragua, Honduras, Guatemala, Paraguay, El Salvador and Peru.

The progressive policies implemented by these governments in the 2000s, aimed at relaunching economic growth and social development, have shown positive achievements. The consolidation of formal democracy has been complemented in some cases with broader forms of popular representation (including the new constitutions of Venezuela, Bolivia and Ecuador) and innovative forms of participative democracy, especially at the local levels (Bolivia's and Ecuador's indigenous communities, Venezuela's communal councils, and Brazil's participatory budgets). Progressive income redistribution and reduction of extreme poverty have been achieved through expansionary real wages, employment policies and social programmes. The renegotiation of relations with international economic institutions and multinational corporations has liberated resources for social programmes and local accumulation. The promotion of new types of regional institutional schemes has opposed the US-led Organization of American States and the failed Free Trade Area for the Americas. The Bolivarian Alternative for the Peoples of Our Americas (ALBA), the Unitary System for Regional Compensation (Sucre), the Bank of Alba, the Community of Latin American and Caribbean States (CELAC), the Union of South American Nations (UNASUR) and the Bank of the South, among others, have reinforced intra-regional economic, educational, health and political cooperation. This has helped to enhance both the unfolding of progressive programmes and resistance against imperialist aggressions.

Stronger economic growth, employment and relative stability, however, have rested on some conjunctural positive effects of the unfolding of neo-extractivist and financialised tendencies in the region. The primary commodities price boom (agricultural, mineral and fuels) stimulated an increase of exports and production in which multinational firms are significantly involved. The resulting expansion of export revenues – which was reinforced in some countries (mostly Central

American) by increasing exports of manufactured goods and by an improvement of the terms of international trade for South American countries – accounts for the improvement of trade balances (with merchandise trade surpluses in Venezuela, Brazil, Argentina, Chile, Bolivia and Peru).

The sustained expansion of the region's international trade in the 2000s rested on the diversification of its trade partners: the United States sharply reduced its weight (from half to one third of total merchandise trade), and the region benefited from flows with China (from 3 to 12 per cent), from intra-regional trade (which reached 20 per cent), and from flows with other countries excluding Western Europe (9 to 14 per cent). Overvalued national currencies and high real interest rates have attracted capital inflows (foreign direct and portfolio investments) which, by financing current account deficits and increasing foreign reserves (which have doubled relative to GDP), have been a condition for the financial stability in the region that has helped to sustain accumulation.

The successful continuity of these programmes is nevertheless somewhat uncertain. First, their implementation faces the permanent opposition, with different degrees of virulence, of national dominant classes and of imperialist formal and informal powers. Second, the social and political support for these programmes tends to erode. This depends on the fact that, on the one hand, social movements that are not class-oriented – because of the hegemony of reformist positions among parties and trade union leaders – tend to demobilise whenever their limited political and economic demands are fulfilled. Class-oriented movements, on the other side, tend to become alienated when their more radical and comprehensive objectives are not or only insufficiently achieved. Third, the positive external conjuncture on which these programmes have relied, namely the high prices of primary products and the vigorous foreign financial inflows, can prove to be temporary. The reversal of these conjunctural factors – which is not unlikely, given the continuation of the world crisis – would trigger and/or reinforce economic vulnerabilities, and this would surely strengthen internal and external opposition. The coup d'état attempts in Venezuela (2002) and Bolivia (2008), the overthrow of the mildly progressive presidents of Honduras (2009) and Paraguay (2012), the rightist electoral triumphs in Chile in 2010 and Guatemala in 2012, the strengthened opposition in the Venezuelan elections in 2013, all are clear reminders of the difference between seizing governmental power and state power. These examples show the permanent necessity to build up economic, social and political strength to protect and reinforce progressive trajectories.

The Limits of Developmental Strategies (Classical and New)

There is much debate about the characterisation of the progressive policies imple-mented in Latin America. Their retrieval of the role of the state in the promotion of economic and social development would involve a positive leap forward from neoliberalism (Féliz, 2012: 2). But these policies' reliance on the globalising and financialised trends of world capital accumulation also has negative elements of continuity with some of the central features of neoliberalism (Gambina, 2013: 100–1). The active state policies implemented have certainly broken, to various degrees in each country, with the hegemony of the radical anti-statism of the original neoliberal programme synthesised in the Washington consensus (Williamson, 1990). Since these policies generally assume state intervention only as complementary to markets, however, they tend to converge both with the updated neoliberal programme (the so-called post-Washington consensus) and with the new developmental discourse.

The post-Washington consensus, derived from the World Bank's 1997 annual report (World Bank, 1997), accepts the necessity of neutral state intervention as complementary to the operation of markets to mitigate inequalities, provided it is based on the protection of existing property rights. The new developmental discourse – which emerged in the 2000s as a critique of the Washington consensus and allegedly of the post-Washington consensus – sustains the possibility of overcoming the contradictions of neoliberalism through renovated state-led programmes. New developmentalism also, however, sustains the centrality of the market as a means that can (and should) be harnessed in order to allow low and medium-income nations to 'catch up' with developed ones (Khan and Christiansen, 2011).

Characterising all progressive policies implemented in Latin America as new developmental is unfair. There are cases where policies incorporate programmatic and practical objectives aimed at advancing towards a post-capitalist society (for example in Venezuela, Bolivia, Ecuador and of course Cuba). Above all, the relevant issue is to inquire about the objective and programmatic causes of their shortcomings in order to overcome them. Their neo-extractivist and financialised inclinations are the result of the augmented structural subordination of economic and social reproduction processes to globalised local and multinational industrial and financial corporations after almost 40 years of neoliberal hegemony. Such progressive governments, incapable of integrally surmounting such structural tendencies, have ended reinforcing them in the 2000s because of their conjunctural functionality in terms of economic growth and stability.

Programmatically, the long-term organisational and political weakness of socialist left organisations in Latin America, rooted in their violent defeats in the 1970s and 1980s, was reinforced by the worldwide debacle of socialist movements caused by the collapse of the Soviet bloc and the consolidation of pro-market reforms in China in the 1990s. The abandonment by many of the remaining left organisations of notions of class struggle, imperialism and socialism as analytical and programmatic frameworks was a universal tendency. In general, anti-capitalism turned into anti-neoliberalism and associated claims that nationalist states which ensure the good operation of markets can in turn lead to a new era of development.

New developmentalism retrieves and purportedly updates the central objectives of classical developmentalism. Vindicating ideas that an active state can create the conditions for national development, new developmentalism emphasises the need for efficient governance capacities compared with the insufficient institutional design of classical developmentalism. In contrast with the endogenous orientation of classical developmentalism, new developmentalism sustains the replicability of successful industrialisation experiences based on efficient articulations within the world market, and it presents ISI and export promotion as complementary. New developmental advocates offer a reformist alternative which, in opposition to radical class-based social transformation approaches, does not question the foundations of capitalism.

The new developmental discourse, however, has serious theoretical and practical limitations. Its neutral and seemingly technical notion of the state, which is very similar to that found in the post-Washington consensus, ignores economic and political contradictions among classes and class fractions. New developmentalism thus reduces the essential issues of development to a matter of 'good governance' which depends on the subjective ethics of economic bureaucracies, instrumental training and coercive evaluation. Its idealist view of the possibility of taming markets, sometimes leading and sometimes following them, ignores the complex and contradictory nature of competition and the power of multinational corporations. Disregarding the hierarchical relations among nation-states in the world market, new developmentalism overlooks the asymmetries of economic and political international relations.

Both classical developmental and new developmental strategies sustain the possibility of achieving national development within the capitalist system, the former by relatively decoupling from, and the later by efficiently engaging with the world market. The first one underestimates and the second one dismisses the fact that capitalist development involves a continuous reproduction of imperialist relations of dominance and dependence, which impede simultaneous national developments. Both developmental strategies, moreover, disregard the nature of capitalism as a system of class exploitation which impedes general social development.

Any policy programme that promotes productive investment and formal employment, improvements of general living conditions and poverty reduction via higher wages, benefits and social programmes, involves a desirable shift away from neoliberalism. Hence, any anti-neoliberal agenda has to be socially developmental. But a radical anti-neoliberal agenda capable of promoting universal social and national development has to be critical of both the classical and the new developmental projects. A genuinely alternative agenda has to be anti-capitalist.

Towards an Anti-Capitalist Agenda

In the last decade Latin America has been a progressive space of theoretical, political and practical debate. The debate has centred around whether to

administer class and international contradictions within a reformist developmental capitalist trajectory, or to push openly for an anti-capitalist project. The
recovery of socialist ideals, first in Venezuela ('21st-century socialism') followed
later in Bolivia (communitarian) and Ecuador (good living), is based on critical
analyses of the collapse of the 20th-century 'real socialism' and of preceding
regional socialist experiences (Cuba since 1959, Chile 1970 to 1973, and the
Nicaraguan Sandinistas 1979 to 1989) (Burbach et al., 2013: 2–8). A discussion
of the main issues involved in the age-old dialectical relation between reform and
revolution is necessary to advance a worldwide anti-capitalist agenda.

The first issue is that *state-led* development programmes implemented by
progressive governments – however socially, economically and politically radical
– tend to be overpowered by the strength of hegemonic economic groups. These
groups seek to impose their own long-term interests and objectives. In the process,
these social forces tend to mute such policy progressiveness by subordinating it to
market forces. Latin America's neo-extractivist-inclined policies are a clear example
of this tendency. By renegotiating the operating conditions of multinational
and local firms, restructuring state-owned enterprises, and even expropriating
some other firms from local and foreign capital, the governments of Venezuela,
Bolivia, Ecuador, Brazil and Argentina have taken control of larger portions of
primary export revenues. These governments have then channelled their increased
resources towards social programmes and to the strengthening of internal markets.
Despite some beneficial effects, however, the subordination of these developmental
policies to world market competitive imperatives weakens their socially progressive
prospects. Besides maintaining reproductive reliance on the world market, these
policies disincentivise the expansion of less profitable activities, hindering the
necessary long-term diversification of productive structures.

A stronger alternative trajectory is that of *state-controlled* development
programmes. By weakening capitalist economic groups, this trajectory can help
to limit the short-term negative effects of capitalist competition. In the long term,
it can erode the centrality of market competition in the process of social reproduction. The progressive governments of Venezuela, Bolivia and Ecuador have
used greater direct state control over strategic sectors alongside alternative forms
of governance as a response to the political challenges and/or economic insuffi-
ciencies of private capital groups. But the seizure of state power and creation of
state-owned enterprises, although necessary, are insufficient for the long-term
fulfilment of a radical alternative developmental project (see Marois, Chapter 3).
State-controlled programmes can be subordinated to the economic and political
agendas of existing and emergent bureaucratic and capitalist groups. These social
forces, by defending their particular interests, generate economic inefficiencies,
and through their subordination of popular social movements they inhibit the
radicalisation of social transformations. Many of the debates and confrontations
found within Latin America's progressive governments are an expression both of
the prevalence of pro-capitalist positions in the state and of the plainly clientelist
and corrupt practices that sustain the power of bureaucratic groups.

The necessary antidote to the bureaucratisation of state-controlled programmes is the expansion of forms of *social control and ownership* from below. This is necessary in order to collectively supervise economic and ecological efficiency, in order to promote radical transformations of legal, ideological, educational and institutional frameworks, and ultimately in order to institute non-capitalist relations of property, production, distribution, exchange and consumption. The issue of substantive versus formal democracy is central in this matter. The concrete experiences of progressive social and political movements, parties and governments have to be the starting point for articulating in a new way representative and participative structures, horizontal and vertical lines of power and government, and mechanisms of deliberation, decision making, execution and evaluation at all levels. In Venezuela, for example, the promotion of social missions for education and healthcare, of cooperatives in the agricultural and industrial sectors, and of direct workers' control and co-management in state companies has faced the opposition not only of anti-government forces but also of corrupt and bureaucratised officials and leaders within the Bolivarian movement.

The construction of substantive democratic forms and mechanisms of social control involves a permanent process of definition, impulse and appraisal of the objectives and priorities of alternative programmes. When such processes are based on the interests of the citizens (diversified along economic, ethical, gender, religious and cultural lines), social control, however legitimate and rightful, tends to become limited in its goals and conflictive in its operation. Therefore, social control should be based on the common general existence of human beings, not as citizens, but as members of the social working force that collectively produces to satisfy social needs and to accomplish social reproduction. Consequently, social control should be *working class-led*. That is, social control and ownership must be based on the general interests and objectives of worker-consumers who can effectively accomplish their individual and collective rights, preferences and desires provided they articulate them to the fulfilment of general social needs. Therefore, the development of an independent and anti-vertical class-based political and economic consciousness and organisation is crucial for the construction of an anti-capitalist agenda.

Anti-neoliberal and anti-capitalist programmes require strong national economic, social and political foundations not only to confront domestic capitalist economic and political power but also to resist imperialist pressures. As the long-term success of isolated national development projects is unlikely, these national foundations have to be transcended in the direction of constructing internationalist and anti-imperialist programmes that require solidarity and support from workers in the imperialist countries (see Pradella, Chapter 2). Coordination of national struggles and development programmes through solidarity and common actions has been the objective of the processes of supranational institutional construction carried out in the last decade in Latin America. Strengthening of regional sovereignty and self-determination is of central importance to help regain control over domestic natural resources and strategic industries. Upon these material and institutional bases progressive social forces can better organise cooperative and fair international economic and political relations. Strengthening regional sovereignty and building a new international order are indispensable measures for overcoming the powers of capitalist states and multinational corporations, and for confronting imperialism as a whole.

The continuity of progressive projects in Latin America depends on their capacity to deepen and extend their social and political support, and their international economic and political links within the region and worldwide. This requires a permanent critique of national developmental strategies, and the elaboration and coordination of an anti-capitalist agenda based on the strengths and creativity of progressive movements all over the world. The propagation of working class-led and socially controlled state programmes is a condition for creating a real socialist alternative to world capitalism.

Select Bibliography

Burbach, R., Fox, M. and Fuentes, F. (2013) *Latin America's Turbulent Transitions: The Future of Twenty-First-Century Socialism*. Winnipeg, Canada, and New York: Fernwood and Zed Books.

Féliz, M. (2012) 'Neo-developmentalism: beyond neoliberalism? Capitalist crisis and Argentina's development since the 1990s', *Historical Materialism*, 20(2): 1–19.

Gambina, J. (2013) *Crisis del capital (2007/2013) La crisis capitalista contemporánea y el debate sobre las alternativas* [*A Crisis of Capital (2007/2013): The Contemporary Capitalist Crisis and the Debate on Alternatives*]. Buenos Aires: Fundación de Investigaciones Sociales y Políticas.

Kahn, S. R. and Christiansen, J. (eds) (2011) *Towards New Developmentalism: Market as Means Rather Than Master*. Abingdon and New York: Routledge.

Kotz, D. et al. (2012) 'Sur la crise du capitalisme neoliberal' ['On the crisis of neoliberal capitalism'], *Actuel Marx*, 1(51): 11–26.

UNCTADstat: http://unctadstat.unctad.org

Williamson, J. (1990) *Latin American Adjustment: How Much Has Happened?* Washington DC: Institute for International Economics.

World Bank (1997) *World Development Report 1997: The State in a Changing World*. New York: World Bank/Oxford University Press.

CHAPTER FOURTEEN

Crisis and Class, Advance and Retreat: The Political Economy of the New Latin American Left

Jeffery R. Webber

This chapter assesses the political and economic dynamics of the Latin American left in the lead up to, and fallout from, the ongoing global economic crisis that began in 2007. A leading Argentine Marxist, Claudio Katz, argues persuasively that for anyone interested in making sense of the modern Latin American left in any period over the last century or so, it is necessary to establish some measure of the balance and movement in power relations (ideological, social, economic, political and military) between at least three social forces with distinct interests and capacities: the rural and urban popular classes and oppressed groups, the domestic ruling classes, and imperialism – particularly, but not exclusively, of the United States (Katz, 2007). The strength of the left – understood in all its complex social movement, party and regime modalities – simultaneously flows out of and reinforces dialectically the objective organisational strengths of the popular classes and oppressed groups within this overarching balance of forces at any given time (Webber and Carr, 2013).

In tracing the trajectory of the left within this wider balance of forces, the chapter is divided into five parts. It begins by exploring the parameters of the left's weakness in the 1990s and the associated consolidation of the neoliberal economic model. It then turns to an analysis of how neoliberal consolidation turned into neoliberal crisis through the vector of the 1998–2002 regional recession. Third, it charts the rise of extra-parliamentary and parliamentary left rearticulation out of the wake of the neoliberal crisis at the turn of the century. Fourth, it explains how the initial radicalism associated with the extra-parliamentary left was increasingly moderated through a combination of the structural stresses of electoral participation and a worldwide commodity boom driven by China's dynamic accumulation within the world market over this period. Fifth, there is a brief portrait of both the aggregate economic fallout in Latin America from the global crisis beginning in 2007, and the heterogeneity of its effects across different subregions and countries. The concluding section then points toward the early political repercussions of the dynamics of the global crisis and world political conjuncture throughout Latin America, and possible directions into the near future.

The Nadir of the Left in the 1990s

The Latin American left reached its lowest point in living memory in the early 1990s. From that vantage point, it would have been very difficult to foresee that in less than a decade the region would transform itself into the leading edge of anti-neoliberal resistance in the world. There had been a fierce physical and military annihilation of large swathes of the organised left and the leadership of its associated social and trade union organisations in the preceding decades. In Brazil, Paraguay and the Southern Cone of South America – Argentina, Chile and Uruguay – a series of right-wing military dictatorships established over the 1960s, 1970s and 1980s targeted leading individuals and rank-and-file activists in the organised left, trade union and peasant movements, and human rights organisations. A trail of death was left in the wake of these regimes, and the socio-political – not to mention psychological – destruction wrought on these societies as a result meant that the rearticulation of the left in its various forms would be halting and hesitant in the decades to follow.

In Central America, a not dissimilar military attack was launched against the left in the 1970s and 1980s, this time in the form of counter-revolutionary authoritarian regimes facing off against mass guerrilla organisations such as the *Frente Farabundo Martí para la Liberación Nacional* (Farabundo Martí National Liberation Front, FMLN) in El Salvador, and the *Unidad Revolucionaria Nacional Guatemalteca* (Guatemalan National Revolutionary Unity, URNG) in Guatemala. The peace processes and accords that closed those civil wars in the 1990s were hardly a compromise between two equal sides. Rather, they left behind them hundreds of thousands killed at the hands of military and paramilitary forces and an utterly routed left. Of course, both the military dictatorships of the Southern Cone and the right-wing regimes and death squads of Central America were systematically supported by the US empire. These levels of sheer violence on the part of the domestic ruling classes and imperialism are absolutely central to the subsequent rolling-out of neoliberal economic restructuring in the 1980s and 1990s. In order for that political project to come to fruition, the organised capacities of the popular classes and oppressed first had to be defeated (Grandin, 2011).

If that was the political and military balance of forces in the early 1990s, the ideological scene likewise showed little remorse to the left. The Soviet Union and its client states in Eastern Europe had collapsed. Cuba's regime, so inextricably bound up in the bipolarity of the cold war by that point, entered into immediate economic crisis as its principal sugar exports to the Soviet Union plummeted, while the economic embargo from the United States continued in place. A 'special period' of austerity was introduced on the island at the same time as the rest of the region was moving toward a full embrace of the market. In Nicaragua the revolutionary regime of the *Frente Sandinista de Liberación Nacional* (Sandinista National Liberation Front, FSLN), first established in 1979, was defeated in elections in 1990 by a conservative candidate after a decade of violent destabilisation on the part of the *Contras*, a right-wing paramilitary force backed by the United States.

Even for those sections of the Latin American left that had never been enamoured with the bureaucratic authoritarianism of the Stalinist model, the collapse of the Soviet Union marked a turning point, after which great confusion and fatalism entered the ideological landscape with a vengeance. Left and centre-left parties moved dramatically to the right, as the whole political spectrum narrowed. Electoral debates between the mainstream political parties in the 1990s turned on technical issues regarding how fast to roll out austerity, privatisation and liberalisation, with very few significant forces calling into question the logic of the neoliberal model of accumulation in its entirety. Social movements retreated in large numbers to localised, community-based projects, where their reliance on internationally financed non-governmental organisations (NGOs) tended to increase, a context which fed into their already accelerating depoliticisation. Strategic aims of power at the level of the state began to recede from the left's purview.

Economically, this was the season of neoliberal ascent. Behind an ideological guise of the free market, strong and coercive states throughout the region rammed through policy agendas of free trade, austerity, financial liberalisation, privatisation of state-owned enterprises, and the retrenchment of welfare and developmental programmes. Disarticulated organisations of the social and political left were unable to mount much of a defensive struggle. In the 1990s, the major exceptions to the trends of weakening social movements in the region were the Landless Rural Workers Movement (MST) in Brazil, the *Zapatistas* in Southern Mexico, and the indigenous movement in Ecuador.

The uneven international process of neoliberalisation led to a series of worsening social conditions in Latin America, and a difficult terrain for left recomposition. The old organisations and associational forms of urban working classes were decomposing as trade union power declined. In most countries, there was a dramatic informalisation of the world of work, with insecure environments and no contracts. In the countryside, peasants and indigenous communities were dispossessed of their land through processes of liberalisation in the agrarian economies. Their numbers swelled the ranks of the urban informal proletariat now populating the shantytowns on the edges of major cities. Growing social inequality and poverty marked the condition of the region as a whole by the end of the 1990s, after the 20-year experiment with orthodox neoliberalism. While the military hand of US imperialism was perhaps less evident in the 1990s than it had been in previous decades in the region, its economic might was exercised without precedent through the mediating channels of the World Bank, International Monetary Fund and Inter-American Development Bank.

The Crisis of Neoliberalism in Latin America

The ideological promise of neoliberal advocates in Latin America, as elsewhere, hinged on the promise of a rising tide that would lift all boats. The pain of austerity in the short term would be transcended over the medium and long run, as private investment flooded the market and sparked job growth, and as bloated state-owned enterprises were displaced by free competition and the dynamism of the market. Rising rates of employment would also lower rates of poverty, even as the system allowed the rich to get richer as an incentive mechanism. By the close of the 1990s, however, it was all too evident that even this minimal justification for the immediate social devastation of neoliberal structural adjustment could not hold up under scrutiny.

Economic growth over the course of the 1980s and 1990s – the core neoliberal epoch of Latin America's 'silent revolution' – included a modest boom (1991–97), positioned between 'the lost decade' of the 1980s and the 'lost half-decade' between 1997 and 2002. The neoliberal policy era in Latin America progressed through the 'deep recession' of 1982–83, the 'false dawn' of a temporary and meagre recovery in positive per capita growth from 1984–87, the increasing depth and breadth of neoliberal policy implementation between 1988–91, and a thorough attempt to consolidate the model throughout the 1990s and early 2000s in the midst of increasing contradictions and crises – the Mexican peso crisis in 1994, Brazil's financial breakdown in 1998 in the wake of the Asian and Russian crises, and, most dramatically, the Argentine collapse which reached its apogee in December 2001 (Green, 2003: 72–118). Following 20 years of debt rescheduling, the region's total debt was approximately US$725 billion by 2002, twice the figure at the onset of the debt crisis in the early 1980s. Poverty rates between 1980 and 2002 increased from 40.5 per cent of the population in 1980 to 44 per cent in 2002 (Damián and Boltvinik, 2006: 145). In absolute figures, this translated into an increase of 84 million poor people across the region, from 136 million in 1980 to 220 million in 2002. Latin America continued to be the most unequal part of the world, such that, in 2003, the top 10 per cent of the population earned 48 per cent of all income (Reygadas, 2006: 122).

The recession between 1998 and 2002 was the worst to have struck Latin America since the early years of the debt crisis. Poverty and inequality shot up across the region, after 20 years of declining social conditions and empty promises. The chasm between the ideology of neoliberalism and the material reality facing the rural and urban popular classes became unsustainable. The answer from the great bulk of the conservative regimes in power at that time, however, was simply an acceleration of neoliberal policies. The problem, as they assessed it, was one of consistent and widespread bureaucratic failure to fully implement initial structural adjustment programmes, rather than an issue inherent to the neoliberal paradigm itself. But if this agenda had been possible to sell to significant parts of the Latin American public at the outset of the debt crisis, in a period of left defeat, debt crisis and panic over hyperinflation, after two decades of failed experimentation, ending in a massive recession, the bitter pill became increasingly difficult to swallow.

Latin America's Left Resurgence

A new recomposition of the social and political left emerged out of this conjuncture. Its first expression was perhaps the election of Hugo Chávez on a moderately left ticket in the 1998 presidential elections in Venezuela. But the larger part of this story in the early 21st century was an explosion of extraparliamentary forms of social struggle – road blockades, strikes, land occupations, worker takeovers of abandoned factories, protests and even quasi-insurrectionary waves of mass action that toppled neoliberal governments in Argentina, Bolivia and Ecuador. A diversity of social subjects were involved in this rearticulation of popular movements, with unemployed workers leading unrest in Argentina, indigenous urban informal proletarians and peasants at the helm in Bolivia, and the Confederation of Indigenous Nationalities of Ecuador (CONAIE) playing a vanguard role in Ecuador. The demands of these movements between 2000 and 2003 shifted increasingly from defensive struggles against neoliberal continuation in a context of recession toward offensive anti-capitalist struggles that sought a strategy of socialist transition in the novel setting of the 21st century.

However, a recovery in growth levels across South America by 2003, and a concomitant turn away from extraparliamentary revolt and toward electoral politics, witnessed a moderation of strategic horizons and the rise to office of left and centre-left governments throughout most of South America and parts of Central America in the mid to late 2000s. If these areas had been controlled almost exclusively by parties committed to neoliberal orthodoxy in the 1980s and 1990s, it was by the mid-2000s impossible to run openly on a neoliberal ticket and succeed in electoral politics in most of Latin America. The ideological sea change ushered forth by the recession of 1998–2002 and the rearticulation of the militant social left in the early years of the century was remarkable. Argentina, Bolivia, Brazil, Chile, Ecuador, El Salvador, Guatemala, Nicaragua, Paraguay, Peru, Uruguay and Venezuela were among the countries in the region that witnessed electoral victories of self-described left or centre-left parties in the first decade of the 21st century. This political reorientation of the Latin American scenario was occurring, of course, alongside shifts in the region's political economy and its relationship to the world market.

Latin America's Commodities Boom and the Compensatory State

A set of unique regional dynamics in South America over the last decade, related to patterns of accumulation elsewhere in the world market (notably high rates of growth in China), kicked off a concerted shift towards the acceleration of mining, oil and gas extraction, and agro-industrial monocrop cultivation throughout the continent. Similar to the period normally described as 'neoliberal,' massive multinational corporations are deeply embroiled in the extension of extraction at the heart of this primary-commodity-led growth everywhere in the region. Those cases in which centre-left regimes have entered into joint contracts between state-owned enterprises and multinationals, and negotiated relatively higher royalties and taxes on these extractive activities, are no exception.

Skimming from the rent generated, many South American governments have established what Uruguayan political economist Eduardo Gudynas (2012) terms 'compensatory states', whose legitimacy rests on the modest redistribution achieved through the priming of often already existing cash-transfer programmes to the extremely poor, without touching the underlying class structure of society. Other political economists prefer the term 'neo-developmental' states, but this conceptualisation sometimes exaggerates the heightened role of the state and the weakened role of multinational capital in the most recent period of Latin American development. Indeed, the very reproduction of these political economies depends upon states prioritising the maintenance and security of private property rights and juridical environments in which multinationals can profit. But there are a set of contradictions that impede the easy reproduction of South American compensatory states, even in a period of booming commodity prices.

Because the legitimacy function of relatively petty handouts runs on the blood of extraction, the compensatory state increasingly becomes a repressive state, on behalf of capital, as the expansion of extraction necessarily accelerates what David Harvey calls accumulation by dispossession, and the variegated forms of resistance it regularly spawns (Harvey, 2003: 144). In the representative and ongoing case of the TIPNIS in Bolivia, the steamrolling of the rights to self-governance of indigenous communities resisting highway construction through their territory illustrates the coercive wing of the compensatory state in action. Indigenous self-government in Bolivia is to be defended by President Evo Morales, it would seem, only when the claims are to territories marginal to the state's development project.

The compensatory state in Latin America co-opts and coerces in response to such signs of opposition, and builds an accompanying ideological apparatus to defend multinationals – an ideology in which communities of resistance are vilified as internal enemies acting in concert with the interests, or even in the pay of, various instruments of imperialism. The discursive gestures of state officials, of course, safely set to one side the obvious imperial character of the dispossessing activities of multinational corporations – now called 'partners' rather than 'bosses' in development – within the matrix of the new extractivism. Whatever the ecological and social contradictions of this development strategy over time, however, its fairly impressive capacities for reproduction in the short term are demonstrated in the Bolivian case.

In the midst of the commodities boom driven by China's dynamism, aggregate economic growth has been steady in Bolivia, averaging 4.8 per cent between 2006 and 2012, with an apex of 6.1 in 2008, and a low of 3.4 in 2009, in the immediate fallout from the world crisis. The first semesters of 2013 have witnessed 6 per cent growth, with above-average projections for the year as a whole from the likes of the International Monetary Fund (IMF). Growth has been maintained in spite of a general and accelerating decline in mining mineral prices at the international level since April 2011, with prices of lead dropping 10 per cent, tin 14 per cent, and silver 28 per cent in 2013 alone (Webber, 2013).

Bolivian growth has not suffered thus far because natural gas prices and regional demand for gas have been moving in the opposite direction. The export of natural gas to Brazilian and Argentine markets continues to outpace all other national exports. Between January and May 2013, the value of external sales of natural gas reached US$5 billion, up 15.6 per cent relative to the same period in 2012. According to figures from the National Statistics Institute of Bolivia, gas exports constituted 52.8 per cent of total exports in the first trimester of 2014, followed by industrial manufacturing (24.2), mining (17.2), and agriculture (4.5). In 2013 the country logged a record peak of foreign direct investment (FDI), again mostly in gas. The Morales era has witnessed an unprecedented accumulation of international reserves, and inflation rates have been clamped at levels that keep Milton Friedman satisfied from the grave.

The general development strategy, according to Marianela Prada Tejada, executive of the cabinet that runs the Ministry of Finance, is to 'take advantage of the possibility of growth through the exploitation of natural resources, with the state capturing the surplus and redistributing it to social programmes and to other economic sectors that generate employment' (personal interview, 28 June 2013, La Paz, Bolivia). Indeed, Morales has been able to capture a bigger share of the rent generated from this commodities boom than did orthodox neoliberal regimes of the past due to moderate increases in the taxes and royalties exacted from multinational petroleum companies, even if this does not warrant the label 'nationalisation'. As a result, there have been notable declines in poverty and extreme poverty, and improvements in health and education.

One redistributive channel of rent to the poorest sectors has been a series of targeted cash-transfer programmes, which now reach roughly 33 per cent of the population – Bono Juancito Pinto (funds to encourage children to attend school), Renta Dignidad (a small monthly payment to the elderly poor), and Bono Juana Azurduy (funds to improve health care for expecting mothers, as well as medical care afterwards). Official government figures suggest an impressive fall in poverty from 60.6 per cent of the population in 2005 to 45 per cent in 2011, and in extreme poverty from 38.2 per cent to 20.9 per cent over the same period. Rural areas have been most affected, with extreme poverty falling from 62.9 per cent in 2005 to 41.3 per cent in 2011.

Unsurprisingly in this context, the government is popular. In a poll of the major cities conducted in June of this year, the administration's nationwide approval rating was 54 per cent. In El Alto, the indigenous shantytown that borders the capital city of La Paz, support for the government sits at 66 per cent. And, for the first time, just under half the population of Santa Cruz – historically the national heartland of reaction and white supremacy – approves of the government, even though it is led by the country's first indigenous president. Indeed, Morales as a personal figure is more popular than the government as a whole, enjoying an extraordinary 73 per cent approval rating in El Alto, and 51 per cent in Santa Cruz.

In Venezuela too, high rates of growth and redistribution efforts have helped to secure a high level of popularity for Chávez, and his successor, Nicolás Maduro (Spronk and Webber, 2014). After recovering from the steep collapse in gross domestic product (GDP) in 2002 and 2003 – which hit -8.9 and -7.8 per cent respectively as a consequence of political crisis spurred by an unsuccessful coup attempt and business-led oil lockout – growth in GDP soared on high petroleum prices to 18.3, 10.3, 9.9 and 8.2 per cent in the years 2004–07. There was a drop to 4.8 per cent in 2008 as the international oil price took a fourth-quarter plunge from US$118 to US$58 a barrel as centrifugal waves of the global crisis spread out from its epicentres in the United States and the Eurozone. Within six months, however, world oil prices recovered, and counter-cyclical spending brought the Venezuelan economy up to 4.2 per cent growth in 2011 and 5.6 per cent in 2012.

A significant cut of the oil revenue captured by the state over this period was directed toward social programmes – known as missions – in health, education and housing. According to official national statistics, the cash income poverty level fell 37.6 per cent under Chávez, from 42.8 per cent of households in 1999 to 26.7 per cent in 2012. Extreme poverty dropped 57.8 per cent, from 16.6 per cent to 7 per cent between 1999 and 2011. If these income poverty measures are expanded to include welfare improvements from the doubling in college enrolment since 2004, access to free health care for millions of new users, and extensive housing subsidies for the poor, it is easy to see how there have been very real material reasons for the popular classes to continue supporting the government.

An Attenuated Crisis of Capitalism in Latin America

The impact of the ongoing global crisis of capitalism since 2007–08 has been relatively muted thus far in the region. Aggregate growth in Latin America and the Caribbean as a whole was comparatively high at 4.8 per cent in 2008. The delayed fallout of the crisis struck by way of momentary deceleration to -1.9 per cent in 2009, but this was followed by rates of 5.9 per cent and 4.3 per cent growth in 2010 and 2011 respectively. Relatively steady commodity prices on the international market, sustained by the still only modest slowdown in China, are crucial in explaining these trends. In addition, there has been an increase in FDI in the region, and counter-cyclical spending on the part of most governments since 2009, drawing on an unprecedented accumulation of foreign reserves as a result of the commodities boom since 2003.

But this overarching picture conceals considerable heterogeneity across different subregions and particular countries. Notably, South America, with the exception of Venezuela, has been the least affected, mostly because trade patterns in South America have shifted in the last decade dramatically toward the Chinese market, and to a lesser extent Europe. Mexico, Central America and the Caribbean were struck much more severely early on by the crisis, given their deep integration with the US economy. The crisis in the United States meant for these areas the collapse of their principal export market, in one direction, and, in the other, a slowdown in remittances returning from migrant labourers based in the United States, as well as the temporary or permanent return of many labourers from the United States as they lost their jobs, applying added pressure to labour markets at home.

The Politics of Crisis

The political repercussions of the current world conjuncture in Latin America are proving to be as diverse as the economic dynamics. At the level of governmental forms, there has been a consolidation of the centre-left regimes in South America, with electoral continuity of moderately reformist parties in power in Brazil, Argentina, Uruguay and Paraguay, among other cases. These regimes have benefited from being able to manage modest redistribution policies in a context of high commodity prices while appeasing, and in many cases further enriching, their domestic capitalist classes. The geopolitical pull of these regimes in South America in this setting, particularly that of Brazil under Luiz Inácio Lula da Silva ('Lula') and now Dilma Rousseff, has been a factor in attracting the regimes that have typically been considered to be more radical in character – Bolivia under Evo Morales, Venezuela under Hugo Chávez (and now Nicolás Maduro) and Ecuador under Rafael Correa – increasingly into the centre-left orbit. The fact that the language of 'neo-developmentalism' promoted by centre-left regimes has considerably more cachet in the region as a whole in 2013 than that of 21st century socialism is one basic indication of the ideological shifts underway since the decline of the extraparliamentary radicalism of the early 2000s.

Meanwhile, orthodox neoliberalism has consolidated itself at the government level in Mexico under the new government of Enrique Peña Nieto, in Chile under Sebastián Piñera (the most right-wing government in Chile since the dictatorship of Augusto Pinochet), in Guatemala under Otto Pérez Molina (linked to scorched earth campaigns and other human rights abuses during his time as a military commander under the dictatorship of Efraín Ríos Montt), and the conservative legacy of Álvaro Uribe in Colombia fundamentally lives on under his successor Juan Manuel Santos.

In extraparliamentary terms, the far right has been equally active, seeking to counter the leftward trajectory of politics in the region in the last 15 years. Successful coups d'état have been carried out in Honduras in 2009, against democratically elected centre-leftist Manuel Zelaya, and in Paraguay in 2012, against the reformist priest Fernando Lugo. A failed coup attempt, mimicking in some ways the one of April 2002 in Venezuela, was carried out in Bolivia in 2008. Paramilitary goons and private security companies operate in the interests of extractive multinational capital in the mining and oil and natural gas industries throughout much of the region, intimidating and assassinating social movement activists who get in the way.

The extraparliamentary left, meanwhile, is taking on distinct forms in different country contexts. In ostensibly conservative Chile, the incredible student-worker uprisings of 2011–13 have shaken to the core the stability of the Piñera government. In Colombia, a nationwide rural strike in August and September 2013 crippled the Santos government, and sparked major sympathy demonstrations by students and workers in the major cities. In Mexico, a defensive strike by teachers against the restructuring of public education in 2013 was the biggest workers' demonstration in the country for several decades. In Brazil, June and July 2013 witnessed massive demonstrations, sparked by an increase in public transit tariffs in major cities, that brought to the fore some of the basic contradictions of the development model introduced by Lula and continued under Rousseff. And in Honduras, a national movement of resistance has risen up in impressive unity against the consolidation of the coup regime under President Porfirio 'Pepe' Lobo.

At the same time, self-styled radical regimes rooted in the accumulation model of extractive capitalism have also been facing increasing opposition from the social left. In Bolivia, protesters have engaged in demonstrations and strikes against the end of subsidies to domestic natural gas consumption, and the extension of a highway through the TIPNIS, among other major conflicts since the second administration of Morales began in January 2010. In Ecuador, anti-mining activism has pitted a new left opposition against Correa's government, with CONAIE playing a leading role. In Venezuela, finally, far-left forces within *chavismo* are struggling against conservative, bureaucratic layers within their own movement at the same time as they face off against imperialism and the recalcitrant Venezuelan right in the wake of Chávez's death.

While there are no simple roadmaps – tactical or strategic – for building anti-capitalist alternatives in contemporary Latin America, the historical record since the early 1990s suggests that building capacities for organisation and activity of the popular classes and oppressed as against ruling classes and imperialism are required first steps in what will necessarily be an extended struggle. Recognising the structural limitations of the developmental strategies of compensatory states to facilitate the further development of such capacities is a prerequisite for building both country-specific and region-wide movements oriented toward a more profound, structural transformation of extant forms of domination and exploitation.

Conclusion

As this chapter has tried to show, since 1998 the Latin American social and political left has experienced a dramatic rearticulation relative to its nadir of the early 1990s. Out of the crisis of neoliberal legitimacy during the recession of 1998–2002, extraparliamentary movements rose up in a series of defensive actions that eventually shifted to offensive anti-capitalist struggles in a number of cases. The recovery of economic growth across much of South America in the context of an extraordinary China-led commodities boom, however, provided the material context for the consolidation of centre-left regimes through electoral victories and the advance of the compensatory state in several countries. This relatively easy international environment for the reproduction of the compensatory state was confronted with a rougher terrain as aggregate growth in the region stumbled in 2009. However, as this chapter has shown, the global crisis has been relatively attenuated in the Latin American scene by the relative continuity in commodity prices, FDI, and the capacity for counter-cyclical spending through the tapping of unprecedented foreign reserves accumulated by many states since 2003.

Nonetheless, if we consider past commodity cycles in the region, and the structural tendency of global capitalism toward crisis, the smooth reproduction of centre-left regimes is unlikely to continue indefinitely into the future. Already, signs are evident of a hard-right shift in certain countries at both the extraparliamentary and parliamentary levels, as well as incipient left oppositions to self-styled radical regimes that rely on alliances with multinational capital in order to perpetuate a model of accumulation rooted in the extraction of primary materials. If commodity prices begin to fall, and there were already signs of this in mining minerals over the course of 2013, the financial lubricant of compensatory states which has in recent years minimised the overt character of class conflict through relatively petty handouts to the urban and rural poor will no longer be available, and a sharpening of political forces, with a harder left and a harder right, is likely to cause problems for centre-left compensatory states.

Select Bibliography

Damián, A. and Boltvinik, J. (2006) 'A table to eat on: the meaning and measurement of poverty in Latin America', in E. Hersberg and F. Rosen (eds), *Latin America after Neoliberalism: Turning the Tide in the 21st Century?* New York: New Press.

Grandin, G. (2011) *The Last Colonial Massacre: Latin America in the Cold War*, 2nd edn. Chicago, Ill.: University of Chicago Press.

Green, D. (2003) *Silent Revolution: The Rise and Crisis of Market Economics in Latin America*, 2nd edn. New York: Monthly Review Press.

Gudynas, E. (2012) 'Estado compensador y nuevos extractivismos: las ambivalencias del progresismo sudamericano' ['Compensatory state and new extractivism: the ambivalences of South American progressivism'], *Nueva Sociedad*, 237 (Jan.–Feb.): 128–46.

Harvey, D. (2003) *The New Imperialism*. Oxford: Oxford University Press.

Katz, C. (2007) 'Socialist strategies in Latin America', *Monthly Review*, 59(4): September.

Reygadas, L. (2006) 'Latin America: persistent inequality and recent transformations', in E. Hersberg and F. Rosen (eds), *Latin America after Neoliberalism: Turning the Tide in the 21st Century?* New York: New Press.

Spronk, S. and Webber, J. R. (2014) 'Sabaneta to Miraflores: afterlives of Hugo Chávez in Venezuela', *New Politics*, 14(4): Whole Number 55 (Summer).

Webber, J. R. (2013) 'Managing Bolivian capitalism', *Jacobin*, 13.

Webber, J. R. and Carr, B. (2013) 'Introduction: the Latin American left in theory and practice', in J. R. Webber and B. Carr (eds), *The New Latin American Left: Cracks in the Empire*. Lanham, Md.: Rowman & Littlefield.

CHAPTER FIFTEEN

Taking Control: Decommodification and Peasant Alternatives to Neoliberalism in Mexico and Brazil

Leandro Vergara-Camus

This chapter analyses the alternatives to neoliberalism of the Zapatista Army of National Liberation (EZLN) in Chiapas, Mexico, and the Movement of Landless Rural Workers (MST) in Brazil. Despite important differences these two movements have been generating autonomous rural communities with their own power structures that have managed to defy and partially replace the state as well as mitigate the negative effects of market imperatives.

These development alternatives have been made possible because these movements have achieved and maintained a territorial control. In turn, territorial control has enabled their members to have access to non-commodified land and produce a variety of food crops for self-consumption. To a certain extent, access to land has also allowed for the decoupling of social reproduction from the logic of the market, and enabled people partly to protect themselves from the growing need for money accentuated by neoliberalism. Because they are based on popular class power and are opposed to the alienation inherent to capitalism, these development alternatives are clearly anti-neoliberal and contain elements of anti-capitalism. However, these communities' non-capitalist practices are not in themselves sufficient, and as with all social subjects, the members of these movements are faced with the imperative of having to engage in market relations in order to find paid work or sell their products. To this end, both movements have tried several strategies that have achieved limited results. The EZLN and the MST by themselves do not have the capacity to transform the social relations of reproduction and production beyond the spaces they control. The chapter ends by assessing these movements' political strategies and the challenges they are currently facing.

Going Back to Marx to Assess Peasant Alternatives to Neoliberalism

In order to assess peasant alternatives to neoliberalism, we ought to turn our attention more to the issue of whether (and to what extent) these alternatives change the social relations of production and reproduction between human beings and their environment, rather than whether they serve as models and can be scaled up to the global level. In other words, any assessment needs to examine the achievements, limitations and contradictions of these alternatives for the concrete human beings involved in them.

As has been theorised by Karl Marx, Robert Brenner and Ellen Wood, capitalism is based on the contradictory combination of a set of social relations characterised by:

- the separation of workers from their means of production
- market dependence of producers
- the dominance of absolute private property
- the imperative of competition among producers
- production for capital accumulation
- the separation of the economic from the political
- commodity fetishism
- the predominance of exchange value over use value.

Marx used the term the 'so-called primitive accumulation' to refer to the historical process that encompassed the early development of all these features in England, and pointed to the importance of the imposition of a set of laws, policies and institutions that radically changed the social conditions in which people lived, worked, interacted and even made sense of their world. He also highlighted that all these laws, policies and institutions had a common objective: the expropriation of the means of production from the labourers, because it is only by cutting access to land, which provides the ability to obtain their own food, that labourers become obliged to enter the market to secure their livelihood and social reproduction. As was shown by Marx himself, this process takes centuries to unfold and is resisted by labouring classes in a variety of ways. Indeed, the slow establishment of absolute private property was resisted in Brazil and Mexico for over 160 years (Vergara-Camus 2012). In this chapter, I propose a theoretical framework to help assess the potentialities of the peasant alternatives of the MST and the EZLN.

As Marx wrote in his *Economic and Philosophical Manuscripts of 1844*, the establishment of private ownership of the means of production is the beginning of a process of alienation of human beings. This is because private ownership prevents labourers from fully realising their creative potentialities for transforming nature and the social environment. We can fully enjoy this ability only when we maintain control of our work, the labour process and the product of our labour. However, the imposition of private ownership of the means of production forces men and women without property to sell their labour power, and so alienate themselves from their creative potentialities in exchange for a wage.

Through this process, human beings under capitalism are alienated from their individual and collective nature in four ways (see also Radice, Chapter 12). First, people are alienated from their labour as it is controlled by the owner of the means of production. Second, people are alienated from the product of their labour, which becomes an object with intrinsic value that presents itself as something external to them and their labour. Third, people are alienated from their nature of creative and social beings, because the labour process is turned into an individual and atomised activity. Fourth, people are alienated from other human beings, who as capitalists are responsible for this alienation or as workers become competitors in the labour market.

Building on his concept of alienation, in *Capital Vol.* 1 Marx argued that the process of labour exploitation was mediated by and wrapped around a mystification that he called 'commodity fetishism', through which social relationships between human beings are suppressed and transformed, by human beings themselves, into relationships between objects that take on a life of their own (Marx, 1990 [1867]: 165). Thus social relations between human beings become mediated through commodities, money and exchange value. The labour that enters into the production of value seemingly disappears. In capitalism, land, like any other 'object', is transformed into a commodity with seemingly intrinsic value and appreciated for that alone.

Neoliberal globalisation, having at its core the expansion of absolute private property and market competition, should be understood as the latest phase of primitive accumulation in the Global South. That is, it should be seen as the most recent expansion of the process of alienation of producers and dominance of exchange value over use value in the countryside. Correspondingly, the land struggles of the MST and the EZLN are resisting the latest phase of primitive accumulation in their respective countries.

Territorial Control and the Control of the Means of Production and Reproduction

The form taken by the land struggles of the EZLN and the MST confronts neoliberal globalisation. The struggles do so by claiming the primacy of use value, which re-establishes moral and political limits on the functioning of the economy against the threat posed by the dominance of absolute private property over land. The first step in these struggles has been to uncover the political and class nature of neoliberalism and to tackle the struggle for land collectively, by recovering and forming a people's power capable of claiming autonomy against the state and the market. Participation in these movements, just as participation in a communist party did for Antonio Gramsci, functions as schools of self-government for the popular classes. The struggle for land is thus a struggle not simply for the means of production and reproduction, but also for control over a specific geographic area upon which other types of social and political relations can develop.

In the case of the EZLN, this process of developing autonomy occurred as the guerrilla organisation managed to convince indigenous communities to adhere to its radical political project. This led communities to fuse their traditional indigenous forms of organising communal life with those of the guerrillas. Through this process indigenous communities and guerrillas created an organisational structure which replaced state institutions in Zapatista indigenous communities. Since then, the Zapatista movement has generated an accelerated process of indigenous people's power, with its own institutions, service provisioning (education, health, conflict resolution and justice), political practices and counter-hegemonic culture.

In the case of the MST, the territories that the movement controls correspond to different phases of the struggle for land in Brazil. The first type of MST territory has been the encampment: where families prepare to occupy a property, and once the occupation begins, this becomes the space from which MST squatters consolidate their people's power to confront the landowner or the state. The second type of territory controlled by MST has been the settlement: the rural community constituted once the land has been won by squatters and granted by the state.

The MST encampment is a specific space that can be reconstituted in different locations, including by the fringes of a road, on a section of public or private property, or on another property after expulsion from a previous one. Usually the squatters live for several years in precarious conditions under a black canvas tent, with rudimentary sanitation and under constant threat of repression or expulsion. In contrast to the Zapatistas, these territories are discontinuous and often geographically distant from one another. However, the similarity rests in the fact that the occupied territories represent the spaces in which members of the organisation are politicised. In these spaces members acquire an identity and a collective political cohesion through participation in a number of decision-making institutions – cells, sectors, the coordinating committee and the assembly – as well as at different levels of the organisation (from the encampment, to the region, to the state or the country as a whole) (Fernandes, 2005).

The squatting families combine several strategies to ensure survival. During the first waves of occupation in the 1980s, families subsisted on the solidarity of their civil society allies (churches, trade unions, social movements, non-governmental organisations (NGOs) and academics), the support of their extended families, and by working as wage labourers in nearby farms. Since the 1990s, squatters have also put pressure on local authorities to provide a basic food basket. In an encampment, since the main goal is the conquest of the land and since everyday life is organised around a large number of meetings and discussions, the political dimension of the struggle tends to impose itself over economic preoccupations. But once land is conquered this politicisation decreases and the arduous battle to remain on the land begins, as does mobilisation to gain access to services and infrastructure.

Linking Land to Use Value, Labour and Life

In the discourse of the Zapatistas and the Landless struggles, the desire not to be at the mercy of another person's will in order to meet their families' needs is one of their primary motivations. Peasants contrast the advantage of having access to land in order to feed their families with the obligation of having to rely on money to achieve the same basic objective when landless. The desire to control the pace of work is also among both the Zapatista and MST members' motivations. Urban unemployment and marginalisation are often presented as disempowering experiences, which members want to transcend. It follows that gaining and protecting access to land as a means of production, regaining or maintaining control over their work, and the freedom to make decisions on matters of agricultural production – all objectives that prioritise use value over exchange value – characterise the EZLN and the MST struggles for land. Land, as it allows for the production of food, is represented more as the basic foundation of life than as a mere means to a end. Land is understood as a way to ensure self-sufficiency and well-being rather than as a source of wealth, monetary accumulation or capital.

However, the need to engage in market relations to satisfy a significant amount of basic needs (such as complementing basic nutrition, purchasing consumption goods, accessing healthcare and so on) also turns the products derived from the use of land and labour, which are loaded with exchange value, into a potential source of money. Hence two interpretations of land coexist in the social practices of MST and EZLN peasants. In the first case, land is use value because it allows people to produce food for self-consumption, and in the second, land produces exchange value which can be used to buy products on the market. Moreover, in parallel to these two conceptions of land, a third one develops from the struggle for the land itself. The conquest of land is seen as the result of a collective political struggle, which valorises land beyond both its use and exchange values. This political meaning of land often leads MST and EZLN members to resist the commodification of land even more than for survival reasons. Finally, the rituals, ceremonies, and festivities that are fundamental expressions of indigenous identity and culture speak of a deeper relationship with land, which is added to these three meanings in the case of the Zapatista indigenous peasants.

The ethnolinguistic Carlos Lenkersdorf (1996) has argued that with regard to the relationship between humans and land, the Mayan worldview establishes fundamental limits, as land cannot be 'owned'. This is in contrast to understanding the fruits of human labour (for example, maize, beans or a house), as belonging to the labourer. However, this conception of land transcends the idea of use value because the importance of land goes beyond its use to meet the needs of a family. It represents the source of life itself (Lenkersdorf 1996: 110), and it has to be treated as a subject, not as an object. Even though this fourth meaning often contradicts other meanings, it still influences the Zapatista struggle.

In line with these conceptions of land that emphasise its use value, both movements have promoted a form of land tenure that favours its decommodification. The Zapatistas have returned to the original meaning of article 27 of Mexico's Revolutionary Constitution of 1917 by reducing the maximum extension of the possession of land to 50 hectares and preventing the sale of *ejido* land. The MST does not have the ability to determine under what form its members will receive their actual titles. However, in order to prevent members from losing their land should they be unable to pay their debts, the MST has recommended that its members do not change the title of possession to one assigning private property, as is their prerogative after ten years. However, this relationship with land is not fixed in time. Land relationships are constantly being modified by members of the EZLN and the MST themselves as well as by the imperatives of market competition, which can also be triggered by a deep crisis of the peasant economy.

Self-Sufficiency and Non-Capitalist Relations of Production in Chiapas and Brazil

In Chiapas, despite the apparent widespread commercial activities in areas formerly considered to be dominated by subsistence farming, it cannot be said that the forms and relations of production are strictly capitalist in the sense defined above. First, land in indigenous regions is not directly subject to competitive market imperatives because people's access to land is not strictly mediated through private property. Rather, access occurs through an institution called the *ejido*, in which land is held collectively by the community. Families have usufructuary rights and cannot in principle sell their plot. Second, because of the severity of the crisis of peasant production, the prime objective for indigenous peasants remains production (mostly of maize and beans) for self-consumption rather than for the market. Third, in many cases 'commercial production' (of coffee, cattle and chilli) does not displace subsistence production because it takes place in a small section of the plot. Fourth, the sale of this production or of any surplus of the food production is not for accumulation purposes but simply geared to acquiring monetary income to cover additional basic needs, such as the acquisition of sugar, salt, soap, lime, cloths, and instruments to till the soil. Fifth, exchange relations do not have strictly speaking capitalist characteristics. They are not always mediated through money, but instead often go through relationships based on family or community reciprocity, solidarity or barter involving actual products, exchange of food for future work, and so on. Therefore, the logic that governs the practices of local actors in the indigenous regions of Chiapas suggests that the logic of use value still coexists with the logic of exchange value.

However, the Zapatista peasants do not stand outside of capitalist relations. They have been directly affected by the global neoliberal restructuring of agriculture. The vast majority of Zapatistas have had numerous experiences of wage labour on surrounding farms and cities, as well as of temporary migration to other parts of Mexico and the United States. As with the vast majority of rural households in Mexico, EZLN families combine several occupations and economic activities to secure their livelihoods and social reproduction. However, these strategies are mostly subordinated to retaining the peasant character of the family, because their otherwise alienating market experiences have made them appreciate how access to land allows them greater control over their lives. Zapatista families and the EZLN as an organisation have therefore made a conscious decision favouring self-sufficiency in their productive objectives and the development projects that have been launched since 1994. Many projects, such as community cooperatives, green manure production and the dissemination and exchange of agroecological knowledge about soil management, have been designed to increase food production and their autonomy from the market.

In other projects, such as the collective production of cloths and of honey or participation in weavers' cooperatives, the goal has been to provide an additional source of cash income for families or to pay the travelling costs of their community representatives, without disrupting food production. Yet many Zapatista families remain subject to competitive market imperatives because of the scarcity of land, albeit under less dramatic circumstances than if they held land under private property. Although they are not at risk of losing their land, population pressure and the low price of agricultural products compel members to look for alternative sources of income.

The social bases of the MST are much more heterogeneous than those of the EZLN. In the 1980s, a large proportion of the landless families had not experienced total dependency on the market. Like the current Zapatistas, many resorted to commercial exchange only to buy the products that they could not produce themselves, and exchange was often through the barter of products. These relationships often involved their subordination to a traditional landlord. Since the 1990s, the militants have increasingly been rural workers without personal histories of access to land, and poor urban families surviving in the informal sector. This generation of landless people has been fully integrated into capitalist relations. The struggle of this generation to become peasants and partly self-sufficient should thus be interpreted as a disconnection from the mechanisms of capitalist exploitation instead of a reconnection with a lost peasant past.

Although capitalist relations are more pervasive in the Brazilian countryside, self-sufficiency is also the first goal of landless families and the core development alternative offered by the MST. This goal is achieved by prioritising production of the food that makes up the basic diet of peasant families, the diversification of commercial production, and the use of unpaid family labour. In addition to growing vegetables for self-consumption, the vast majority of the settlers also raise chickens and pigs. In some cases, members have created cooperatives around these activities in order to provide families with a constant supply of meat for self-consumption and to sell the surplus on the local market. Settler families also combine several survival strategies, where one or several family members work temporarily in the city or in agriculture, or migrate to other regions of the country in order to contribute to household income. Hence, the social relations within rural families that involve some non-capitalist mechanisms play an important role in resisting neoliberalism. However, self-sufficiency is not the main goal on the horizon of MST members.

In parallel with self-reliance, the MST has sought to help its members find ways to secure the monetary income needed for peasant family survival. In Southern and South-Central Brazil, the vast majority of MST settlers have chosen to secure a monthly cash income by purchasing dairy cows with government loans. But aside from milk production, after a few years most families also resume the cultivation of soybeans, maize, wheat or sugar (Wright and Wolford, 2003: 152–76). Over the years, these agribusiness-controlled crops gain in importance because government credits reinsert the settlers' families into the circuit of capital (accumulation in the market), as families are faced with the imperative of finding the monetary income required to repay loans (that is, they face the discipline of debt).

To further augment monetary income, almost from its inception the MST has promoted the creation of producer groups or cooperatives of different types. However, this strategy has been largely unsuccessful, and only local and regional conventional cooperatives have persisted. Thus, after several years of having won rights to their plots of land, MST peasant families reinsert and subordinate themselves to capitalist agriculture, but this time with the advantage of being able to rely on their access to land as a fallback survival strategy in times of crisis. Their degree of autonomy and ability to delink from the market, however, exceed those of any other type of rural or urban worker.

Scope, Limits and Challenges of the Alternatives Presented by the MST and the EZLN

The main achievement of the EZLN and the MST is to have defended the right of access to land for poor rural families and to have established the social and political conditions that allowed over 60,000 families in Chiapas and from 800,000 to 1.3 million families in Brazil to gain access to land through several organisations. A second achievement has been to politicise thousands of peasant families in ways that led to the establishing of political control over specific territories, on which experiences of self-government have been carried out. The different logic that governs the social relations upon which these alternatives to neoliberalism are based has allowed peasant families to feed themselves, take control of their labour, and substantially improve their welfare.

Here lies the most radical (and anti-capitalist) potential of these alternatives. Although use value and non-capitalist relations predominate in certain aspects of peasant production, one of the main limitations of these alternatives is the difficulty of transcending the limits of the extended family or community and establishing exchange relations based on use value and relationships of reciprocity at the regional, national and international levels. This is extremely difficult when the national economy is organised under a completely different (capitalist) logic.

In this context and in the case of MST, not a single cooperative – not even the ones that focus on transforming relations of production and privilege use value internally – has been able to put these principles at the centre of their exchange relations with other producers. In their relationships with the 'outside', the logic of the market and competition prevail.

The same has happened with the Zapatistas, even though many relations of production can be said to be non-capitalist in indigenous regions. For the Zapatistas, cooperatives represent more a way of improving integration into the market than a way of developing a parallel system of exchange. In all fairness, such a challenge far exceeds the organisational capacities of these movements, and also depends on the willingness or ability of other allies to engage in these types of relationship.

The MST's strategy for improving the integration of its members into the market has been basically political. It has been based on the premise that the expansion of market space for peasant production and the improvement of the conditions of their market integration would only be possible through the support of the state. In turn, state support would only be achieved through political class power by 'massifying the struggle': that is, by increasing the number and size of encampments and victorious occupations, and by participating in the coordination of the national struggle against neoliberalism.

Internationally, the MST accompanied this strategy by taking a leading role in the creation of Via Campesina and the coordination of its international campaigns, such as the global campaign for agrarian reform. Throughout its existence, the MST was able to maintain a pragmatic policy towards the state and institutional power. It has opposed neoliberal policies through demonstrations, marches and occupations of public buildings. At the same time, the MST has depended on the state for the expropriation of land and financial resources for the development of settlements. The MST has also pressured the state for credits, technical support, and programmes for settler families. Therefore, different forms of mobilisation were able to unify the landless (squatters) with the landed (settlers) of the movement.

However, ever since Lula da Silva assumed power in 2003, the increasing but still limited support for peasant families and the accelerated development of the anti-poverty programme, *Bolsa Família*, which provides monetary income to families living under extreme poverty, have changed the economic and social conditions on which the strategy of MST was based. According to critics like Arruda and Fernandes, between 2003 and 2010 Lula distributed land to only 211,000 families, which is less than neoliberal President Cardoso. The current President Dilma Rousseff has expropriated only 28 properties since she began her mandate in 2012. These two measures have made landless people less willing to join an encampment, and the number of land occupations are falling. According to the *Comissão Pastoral da Terra* (CPT) occupations fell from 285 in 2003 to 30 in 2011 and a mere 13 in 2012. The main source of attracting new activists and traditional basis of MST political strength is thus fading away.

The EZLN, although it has taken a totally different strategy in its relationship with the state and institutional politics, also privileged a political strategy. The EZLN has failed to establish the foundations for a national political strategy that would allow it to develop a broader economic strategy revolving around control over natural resources in indigenous territories. Although the EZLN had the support of the indigenous movement in its negotiations on indigenous autonomy with the federal government, it could not prevent the state from, first, negotiating the issue of land occupations separately with indigenous peasant organisations of Chiapas, and second, withdrawing from the negotiations on indigenous rights and refusing to honour the agreements signed in San Andrés (de Grammont and Mackinlay, 2009). Ever since, the Zapatista strategy has been to strengthen the process of building political autonomy in indigenous regions of Chiapas.

Finally, despite having significant support in various sectors of civil society, neither organisation has been able to lead a coalition of anti-neoliberal resistance movements, or at least to force its national government to implement substantial reforms in favour of peasants and other popular sectors. As I have argued elsewhere (Vergara-Camus, 2012), the great majority of social movements in Mexico and Brazil have opted for supporting electoral politics and collaborating with the state, often seeking to develop clientelist ties rather than oppose neoliberal policies. Given this it is far from certain that the spontaneous mass protests in Brazil in June and July 2013 will provide a new opportunity for the MST to change this situation as they were still geared towards placing demands on the state.

The difficulties experienced by the MST and the EZLN demonstrate the extent to which struggles for land and the development alternatives of these movements are specific responses to the conditions of indigenous peasants in Chiapas and landless peasants in Brazil. It would be erroneous to attempt to extract a 'model' from these particular experiences. The struggles of peasant movements in Latin America, and elsewhere in the Global South, show that models do not and should not exist. There are lessons that should be highlighted from these experiences, nonetheless.

The EZLN and MST victories have been achieved through the collective construction of a specific type of people's power. This constructed power has been strong enough to partly replace the state and to allow the control of a territory in which members have set limits on the commodification of land (as a means of production) and on the monetisation of the relations of reproduction and production. In other words, in the face of the commodification of all spheres of life by advocates of neoliberal globalisation, these movements and their members have opposed neoliberalisation via a process of relative decommodification. For each movement, the anchoring point of the whole process has been a class-specific and context-specific form of collective control over the means of production by labourers.

Select Bibliography

De Grammont, C. H. and Mackinlay, H. (2009) 'Campesino and indigenous social organizations facing democratic transition in Mexico, 1938–2006', *Latin American Perspectives*, 36(4): 21–40.

Fernandes, B. (2005) 'The occupation as a form of access to land in Brazil: a theoretical and methodological contribution', in S. Moyo and P. Yeros (eds), *Reclaiming the Land: The Resurgence of Rural Movements in Africa, Asia, and Latin America*. London: Zed Books.

Lenkersdorf, C. (1996) *Los Hombres Verdaderos. Voces y Testimonios Tojolabales* [*The real men: Tojobales voices and testimonies*]. Mexico City: Siglo XXI.

Marx, K. (1990) [1867] *Capital. A Critique of Political Economy. Vol. I*. London: Penguin.

Vergara-Camus, L. (2012) 'The legacy of social conflicts over property rights in rural Brazil and Mexico: current land struggles in historical perspective', *Journal of Peasant Studies*, 39(5): 1133–58.

Wood, E. M. (2009) 'Peasants and market imperative: the origins of capitalism', in H. Akram-Lodhi and C. Kay (eds), *Peasants and Globalisation: Political Economy, Rural Transformation and the Agrarian Question*. London: Routledge.

Wright, A. and Wolford, W. (2003) *To Inherit the Earth: The Landless Movement and the Struggle for a New Brazil*. Oakland, Calif.: Food First Books.

CHAPTER SIXTEEN

The Rise of East Asia: A Slippery Floor for the Left

Dae-oup Chang

Over the last few decades, East Asia has truly become a global factory. It produces more than a third of global manufacturing export value while attracting more direct investment and growing more than twice as fast as other developing regions (and seven times faster than developed economies). Naturally, our understanding of East Asia has also changed. Traditional analyses of East Asian development focused on how Western capitalism has been diffused to East Asian nations, with East Asian countries merely emulating the West. Contrary to this, the more recent literature on the 'resurgence' of East Asia tries to put the region back into the history of global development and recognises its dynamic nature. However, in its understanding of East Asia as external to the development of global capitalism and characterisation of East Asia as too much of a wishful alternative, this literature turns a blind eye to the many problems of East Asian development.

This chapter questions the validity of East Asian developmental enthusiasm. It locates East Asia as an integral to global capitalism and East Asian development as full of contradictions. It argues that in order to find democratic alternatives to neoliberal capitalism, progressive and pro-democratic academics, activists and students must not look to fast economic growth, the strong state or cultural heritage, but to the continuous struggles of the ordinary labouring population of the global factory.

The rise of East Asia: Reality or Myth?

Since the 1980s East Asia has become a growth engine of the world and a central feature, if not 'the' central feature, in global capitalism. Experts argue that East Asia will soon outpace traditional advanced economies, and this argument has a firm material basis. A World Bank report predicts that East Asia will account for about 40 per cent of the world economy by 2025 (Gill et al., 2007: 2). This claim is based on its remarkable growth drive, which seems unstoppable in the near future. As of 2007, the share of global gross domestic product (GDP) (in purchasing power parity terms)[1] of East Asian countries (including the ten member countries of the Association of Southeast Asian Nations (ASEAN) plus China, Japan, South Korea, Mongolia, Hong Kong SAR and Taiwan) was 24.75 per cent, exceeding that of the United States (21.3 per cent) and the European Union (22.7 per cent). Behind this increasing share of the global wealth is East Asia's increasing contribution to global manufacturing exports, which reached one-third of the global total by 2008.

Evidence suggests that this remarkable growth was not just due to favourable external conditions such as consumerism in advanced economies, but to many native dynamics. During the contemporary rise of East Asia, intra-regional trade has become much more important than before, doubling between 1995 and 2004 to reach US$1,296 million (ADB, 2008: 87) – about half of the total value of trade to and from East Asian economies. Likewise, it was East Asian investment, rather than capital input from the West, that drove its remarkable growth. The majority of foreign direct investment (FDI) stock to East Asia has originated from the newly industrialising countries (NICs) of Hong Kong, South Korea, Singapore and Taiwan, and from Japan. This has been the case for the FDI-driven export boom in Southeast Asia since the 1990s. China's export drive relies on the same investment flow but on a much larger scale. In 2010, according to Chinese official statistics, China alone attracted a total of US$105.735 billion in FDI. About US$88.18 billion was from ten East Asian countries and regions.

The current recession in advanced economies caused troubles for the export-oriented East Asian economies. Many experienced a severe downturn, with negative or near to zero growth in 2009. Obviously, the global recession had a negative impact even on the engine of the growth in the region, China. China's manufacturing sector fell to minus 4.2 per cent in 2007 and hit bottom in 2009 with minus 16 per cent growth. This does not reverse East Asia's importance in the global economy. Rather, the recession seems to have made the region more important to global recovery. East Asia outperformed all other economies and contributed about half of global GDP growth in 2008. The region contributed about 40 per cent of global growth in 2012. During the recession its contribution to global GDP became bigger, increasing from 25.3 per cent in 2008 to 28.32 per cent in 2012, according to the International Monetary Fund (IMF). It also shows that East Asia became by far the biggest economic region, exceeding the European Union (19.35 per cent) and the United States (18.87 per cent) by 2012. These developments also had an effect on extreme poverty reduction, giving rise to expectations that East Asia will play a more important role in lifting less developed countries *within and beyond* East Asia out of poverty.

Such expectations have changed traditional perceptions of East Asia and given birth to literature on 'the rise of (East) Asia'. This new literature differs dramatically from earlier analyses; it predicts an 'era of the East', and presents East Asian development as a model alternative to global neoliberalism.

---

1   GDP adjusted according to the relative value of local currencies.

This post-economic development literature, including some important works from the 'left', does not try to locate East Asian development in Western emulation. Rather, East Asian development is seen to have its own innovative, distinctive, authentic and positive characteristics. In doing so, this literature partly overcomes the traditional Orientalist and linear understanding of development as East Asia is put back into world history as an active participant. The view of internal dynamism replaces the former static accounts where motivations to change needed to be injected from outside. The literature still tries to find something authentic, but 'nicely' authentic, that has allowed the region's distinctive capitalist development. Some go even further, to argue East Asia is authentic enough to present an alternative to global capitalism itself.

However, Orientalism prevails. Occupied by too much wishful thinking in the search for alternatives, and with an obsession for finding authentic features, this literature turns a blind eye to the many capitalist contradictions inherent in East Asian development. In so doing, this new literature:

- presents East Asian development as a less exploitative or even class-conflict free process
- describes the East Asian capitalist state as an independent and neutral agent defending national interest and pursuing national development
- understands the rise of East Asia as a result of a harmonious process of East Asian integration and a peaceful rise
- looks for the origins of East Asian development in something authentically East Asian or from East Asia's internal dynamics.

Misleading Theories of East Asian Alternatives

'Developmental state theory' was the first theory to present East Asia as an alternative model, by turning once negative 19th-century East Asian characteristics into positively 'authentic' ones promoting alternative development. While state-led development fell victim to the 1980s debts crises in the Third World and the Keynesian welfare state in advanced countries neared exhaustion, social scientists such as Alice Amsden, Peter Evans, Stephen Haggard, Chalmers Johnson and Robert Wade discovered a different developmental story unfolding in East Asia. Chalmers Johnson's 1982 book on Japanese industrialisation and the role of the state in it launched the concept of the 'developmental state'. These East Asian states tend to intervene in the economy, with a strong capacity to devise and implement industrial policies. They have the power to mobilise private players for planned goals, and display organisational coherence and autonomy. East Asia came under the spotlight not because it was the only region pursuing state-led development but because it was doing relatively better, with remarkable economic growth.

By the 1970s it had became increasingly apparent that the western Keynesian state could not prevent or reverse the mounting economic downturn. Unprofitable productive forces had been created during the boom (the overaccumulation of capital). Consequently, profitability began to fall in the industrialised countries by the late 1960s. The 1970s oil shocks dramatically increased cost pressures on capital. In short, the end of the post-war boom offered a golden opportunity for neoliberalism to replace statism as the leading ideology of development. State-led development in the Third World also could not overcome the 'structural constraints' of capitalist development. First, hidden imperialist interests still overshadowed many attempts to develop independent economies, even in the post-colonial era. Corporations from former colonies exercised significant influence over Third World natural resource and primary commodity markets. Developing countries suffered from inherited debts to former colonial masters. State-led industrialisation, moreover, relied on imported means of production, which led to recurrent balance of payment problems. Despite economic growth, foreign debts continued to increase.

In addition, recession in the advanced economies cut away at the prices of primary commodities. This reduced foreign currency income for developing countries. Worse still, overgrown state apparatuses came to exercise too much power over the people, cultivating ripe conditions for authoritarian regimes. Wealth distribution did not improve much. Otherwise radical plans to transfer sovereignty from past colonial masters to the people of independent countries succumbed to the increasing participation of private capital in nationalist development projects.

In this context East Asian state-led development became the last stance of the post-war development dream. Academics looked to the East and found that Japan and the first-generation NICs commonly had an 'effective state that repaid debts, successfully climbed the ladder of industrialisation, educated their workers, reformed their agricultures – in short developed' (Radice, 2008: 1166). The Japanese economy achieved a remarkable 10 per cent annual average growth in the 1960s, and became the second biggest economy of the world by the late 1960s. South Korea and Taiwan showed an average growth rate of 9.2 and 9.5 per cent respectively between 1961 and 1980. These economies successfully launched export-oriented industrialisation and transformed from agrarian to industrial societies by the 1980s. Importantly, this development seemed to be led not by private actors but by highly effective states (Öniş, 1991). Inspired by the institutionalist school in political science and the classic late-developmental works of Gerschenkron and List, advocates of the developmental state suggested that the state could have roles far beyond that of perfecting the market. Indeed, the state could maintain the economic and political relationships conducive to fast industrialisation in favour of national development goals.

Developmental state theory transformed the East Asian states from unimportant spectators to privileged actors of world history. However, the theory also severely misrepresents East Asia. First, it underestimates the contradictory world-historical context of the actually existing developmental states.

In fact, all successful developmental states in the 20th century were semi-sovereign states. They surrendered half of their sovereignty to the United States and became an integral part of US-led cold war development in order to secure aid, resources, and market access for capital accumulation. The development of Japan and the NICs was not a result of independent states pursuing independent development under the brilliant leadership of state bureaucrats, but a result of being a node of the US-driven cold war capitalism. Contrary to the image of the developmental state being a defender of some dubious national interest as a closed unit, these states connected the labour of the capitalist core to the periphery. What was peculiar was that they actually benefited from being truly integral to the global system of uneven development rather than suffering from it.

Worse still, developmental state theory focused on a wrong kind of internal characteristics in order to fit them into to a fabricated ideal-type state. The class characteristics of particular states were downplayed. The sovereignty retained by developmental states was used to squeeze its working population in the export industry, which produced goods for US and European Fordist workers. Autonomy from the dominant powers of global capitalism and capital was the least visible feature of these states. The theory is also *reactionary* in terms of its theoretical foundation and its practical implication for people on whom this model of development could be imposed. The theory reduces the complex social relations of development to relations between two institutions – the market and the state (echoing neoliberal approaches).

In explaining development by looking at the interaction between the market and the state, both of which are presented 'class neutral', developmental state advocates are as uncritical as neoliberals about the ways in which these categories present unequal capitalist class relations. The market presents class relations as technical relations between owners of different sources of revenue whose functions are naturally given by the particular commodities they happen to own – this is what capitalists and mainstream economists make major efforts to do. On the other hand, the state translates class relations into relations between individual citizens or different interest groups – that is what our politicians try to do particularly during the elections – without regard to their position in the class structure. Both are mystifying unequal social relations and appear to be class-neutral institutions. And these are the concepts of market and the state in developmental state theory.

Rather than questioning the fundamental nature of social relations behind the two institutions, the theory is only concerned with how the state as a legitimate representative of individual citizens intervenes in these relations, effectively allocating or mobilising different sources of revenue. In this sense, developmental state theory is a theory for 'eternal capitalism' – an ultimate bourgeois social theory that aims to eternalise and naturalise capitalism as given. This reactionary nature is reflected in the theory's development model, in which ordinary working populations have no roles but to work hard until the gains of capitalist development trickle down to them. In this sense, the theory is a mirror image of neoliberalism and presents no alternative.

There is another theory of alternative development emerging from the East Asian experience: the theory of harmonious regional development (HRDT). In this theory every participant appears to take the fruit of their development back home. This scenario is based on a modified version of the 'flying geese theory' (originally developed by Kaname Akamatsu in the 1930s to show how Japan industrialised by emulating advanced economies).[2] HRDT applies this model to understand the consecutive catching-up industrialisation processes for a specific geographical group in East Asia (Kasahara, 2004: 10). First, the more advanced economies in East Asia transfer their old technologies, labour-intensive industries and capital to less developed countries so they can recycle old productive capacity. Second, once less developed countries manage to emulate the more advanced ones, they too repeat the same pattern with their less developed neighbours. Third, the more advanced countries also function as export markets for the less developed ones by allowing 'reverse imports'. Regional cooperation is thus seen as an important underlying reason for the subsequent rise of East Asian countries. HRDT goes further in trying to export this model to other developing parts of the world. Advocates argue that East Asia can set up integrated production networks elsewhere to create other development miracles while producing goods for price-sensitive East Asian consumers (ADB, 2011: 41–2).

The actual existing East Asian integration process is not as rosy as the process presented by HRDT, but much more uneven and unequal. The extent to which Japan and the first generation NICs can offer alternative export markets to the United States and European Union is rather limited. In other words, reverse import is a myth. The increasing intraregional trade does appear to show that strong economies in East Asia became an important market for developing countries, as we saw above. However, a closer look reveals that this is driven by the increasing flow of components and parts through vertically integrated production networks across East Asia, whose end-products are still consumed in the advanced economies such as the United States and European Union.

The Asian Development Bank (ADB) estimates about 67.5 per cent of exports, either parts or final products, still end up in the United States and European Union (2008: 71). If anything, reverse import is done by transnational corporations (TNCs) from the first-generation NICs. These firms did not exit from markets, but rather expanded their operations to developing countries through FDI. Therefore, the earnings of less-developed countries exporting low-end final products and components are easily offset by the increasing import of high-end products and

---

2   The theory was named after 'the graphic presentation of three time-series curves' of import, import-substitution production, and export 'for a particular product, with time dimension on the horizontal axis' (Kasahara, 2004: 2). It has a three-step scenario: 1) A late industrialising country has to import manufactured goods produced in more developed countries at the initial stage of industrialisation; 2) Once local firms gain productive capacity, they then produce goods to substitute for imported ones; and 3) Then they export goods to advanced economies.

sophisticated core components from the advanced economies. This also hampers smooth technological transfer to local firms in less-developed countries, as the core technology remains firmly in the hands of advanced countries. The consequence is 'the continued dependence of foreign subsidies on capital as well as technology and component inputs from abroad, without developing linkage with local suppliers' (Kasahara, 2004: 16). Because of this, the degree of import substitution in the second-generation NICs is significantly lower than the level Japan and the first generation NICs enjoyed. Consequently, more often than not, the integration of developing countries (except China) into the regional division of labour resulted in greater trade deficits (Kasahara, 2004: 21).

Contemporary East Asian integration is based on trade and investment relations resembling North–South relations. It is a highly uneven process with clear winners and losers. Winners include Japan and the first-generation NICs which own both the capital and the technology. Most of the Southeast Asian countries are accumulating trade deficits. The least-developed countries suffer from increasing trade deficits against middle-income countries as well. For them, integration is not a blessing but a harsh developmental environment they have to cope with. Regional integration is a double-edged sword, creating both a more tightly connected stronger East Asia and more uneven development within East Asia.

The theories outlined above fail to properly theorise and understand East Asian development mostly because they miss the internal nature of the relations between the global whole and East Asia. East Asian development needs to be understood as internal, rather than external, to global capitalism throughout history, forming the totality of global capitalism from colonial to the cold war and to neoliberal development. Only if we take this perspective can we realise where to begin looking for emerging alternatives to neoliberal capitalism.

China as an Alternative?

The China-driven rise of East Asia in recent years is an integral part of global neoliberal capitalism rather than a result of authentic alternative development in China. Yet for some, China's ascent is an alternative to neoliberalism. Giovanni Arrighi, for example, in his *Adam Smith in Beijing* (2007) maintains that China's ascent is qualitatively different from the European or US ascent. He argues that unlike the West, the Chinese world of the East (from the Song all the way to the Qing dynasty) had no commercial and territorial empires competing for colonies through wars. This difference is based not simply on Chinese culture but on China's Smithian market economy, featuring labour-intensive, non-capital-dominant and environmentally sustainable characteristics. Arrighi believes that China has been maintaining this non-capitalist market-based development throughout its history. This distinctive development enabled China to introduce neoliberalism only as far as it served national interests, and to pursue inward rather than expansionist development. On the ground level, China is not yet a capitalist society mainly for two reasons. First, the state is not dominated by capitalists but insulated from them, and second, China develops through accumulation without dispossession, as the Chinese population effectively own the land as well as the means of production through township and village enterprises (TVEs).

There are two major interrelated problems in this: the misinterpretation of the transformation of social relations in China and the failure to see contemporary Chinese development as internal to global capitalism. Arrighi describes private firms and their rural–urban migrant (apparently waged) workers producing goods in export processing zones as if they are a minority in the Chinese economy. However, according to official statistics, the number of China's internal migrant workers employed outside their home towns reached 153 million by 2010. An absolute majority of them work for private capital. Capitalist wage workers are no longer a supplementary workforce but the backbone of the economy, accounting for more than half the urban workforce in China today. Many TVEs and urban collective enterprises have either collapsed or been privatised, and the remainder now employ less than 5 per cent of the total workforce. Even workers in state-owned enterprises (SOEs) (which employ only one in ten workers in manufacturing) have become indistinguishable from other ordinary, although relatively well-off, wage workers. Second, dispossession is a major feature of Chinese development. Between 1999 and 2005, there were about 1 million cases of land dispossession reported to the Ministry of Land and Resources, and some 40 million farmers lost their land.

This transformation did not merely have internal causes, but was co-related to neoliberal capitalism on a world scale. China's export bonanza was an essential part of the short boom of neoliberal capitalism after the 1997–98 Asian economic crisis. China was equally essential to the making of the current crisis of neoliberalism. The global recession was triggered by a debt-driven housing boom in the United States. During the short boom, credit was offered at historically low interest rates to some of the poorer US population through subprime mortgages, which were securitised and sold by financial institutions blindly pursuing profits. Meanwhile, US working-class consumers could afford imported Chinese consumer goods. This market, and the high rate of labour exploitation, meant that entrepreneurs in China kept making profits despite the overaccumulation of capital. Therefore, the quasi-boom created by the creation of fictitious capital (which is created whenever credit is given based on a claim against future labour) underpinned and was supported by the rise of China, creating a temporary 'win–win scenario' for East Asian capital and US consumers.

Having failed to see China as a part of the integrated totality of global capitalism, Arrighi reaches the strange conclusion that it is neither capitalist nor neoliberal for China to supply a huge capitalist workforce to manufacturers from all over the world, produce commodities for the world market and in doing so to contribute greatly to the neoliberal accumulation of capital at global scale. Similarly theories that claim to understand East Asia as external to global capitalism conclude that East Asia, as the most important continent of labour during the heydays of neoliberalism, is not neoliberal East Asia. Yet if Chinese workers are working for a global neoliberal economy, China is surely both neoliberal and capitalist. If East Asia functions as an engine of neoliberal capitalism, East Asia is neoliberal.

Arrighi's theorisation of China demonstrates very well the difficulties involved in theorising both East Asian development and alternatives emerging from it. He removes the capital–labour contradiction from China by calling it a non-capitalist market economy. He describes China-driven regional development as a peaceful process by arguing that China would pursue foreign policies free from its capitalist motivation. He describes the Chinese state as an independent and neutral agent of national development. Finally, he tries to find the origin of the Chinese ascent not in China's inseparable relation to global capitalism but in something authentically Chinese. In our view none of these arguments hold up, so alternatives to neoliberalism must be sought elsewhere.

Locating Alternatives in East Asian Workers

Now, if we admit that East Asia is a core continent providing global capitalism with labour, and that by doing so it is an integral part of that capitalism, East Asia also needs to be considered as being at the centre of labour struggles in and against global neoliberalism. Alternatives to global capitalism and neoliberalism do not emerge from somewhere external to them. The contradictions of capitalism and the potential social forces dreaming, practising and realising new alternatives beyond capitalism are emerging from *within* capitalism. If East Asia offers any alternative to global capitalism and neoliberalism, it is not the authentic interventionist state, or Confucian entrepreneurship, or some mysterious 'oriental' propensity toward harmonious development, or the quasi-socialist state of China. Our quest for alternatives in East Asia needs to start by looking at the long-term struggles of ordinary East Asians working for global capitalism. East Asian development is as full of capitalist contradictions as any other part of global capitalist development, and it is the ordinary working population who have been challenging these contradictions and thereby offering alternatives. Their struggles for alternatives to global capitalism have a long and often heroic history.

East Asian workers have fought brutal imperialist powers, which have integrated East Asia into world capitalism. In almost all East Asian communities, anti-imperialist trade unions and peasant organisations emerged in the search for alternatives to peripheral capitalist development. Many removed colonial regimes and achieved independence. Their struggles were targeting not only the peripheral nature of development but also capitalism itself. Therefore not all states voluntarily joined global capitalism after independence.

Many new East Asian states sought alternatives by joining together in Bandung, Indonesia in 1955. At the Bandung conference, 29 new independent nations (including eight East Asian states) tried to turn their individual efforts to find alternatives into a collective initiative for democratic, inclusive and independent development. It is true that the principles outlined at Bandung did not materialise in the end. Mass movements for alternatives in East Asia at that time could not build solidarity strong enough to force the rulers of nation states to continue the journey without surrender to the cold war superpowers in pursuit of narrow national interests. It was nationalism and the growing national bourgeoisies that overshadowed the internationalist spirit of Bandung.

However, the experience of collaborating for a collective alternative to global capitalism is an important one and can be built on. Indeed, the contemporary integration of East Asia creates a material basis for regional solidarity, widening direct contact and cooperation between social movements across East Asia. As we saw above, economic development occurred first in *the US allies in the Far East,* with half-sovereign states. They achieved economic growth under the auspices of the United States and by taking advantage of a disciplined workforce. Hundreds of thousands lost their lives in this pursuit of development. However, again these workers were not just workers. They were *democratisers* too. In Korea and Taiwan, ordinary working people have become the underlying force of the democratisation movement since the 1970s. Trade unions emerged despite the heavy and violent suppression of the state. In the 1980s unions strived for not only political but also economic democracy (Chang, 2013: 97–107), gradually disman- tling two of most brutal dictatorships in the world. The unions proved that there is no authentically anti-democratic characteristic in East Asia, and created an alternative to authoritarian development supported by cold war capitalism.

In addition to these alternatives in the past, there are alternatives emerging from East Asia in the present. Neoliberal development brought many setbacks to people's pursuit of alternatives. Most of all, it shackled economic democratisa- tion by turning the economy into a so-called 'politics-free' zone. The neoliberal expansion of East Asia created a large population who have to rely on selling their labour-power in a capitalist system, one way or another, for their survival. Meanwhile, substantive democratisation has stagnated in all East Asian countries, as democratisation at best meant electoral democracy but without any scope for the fundamental democratic transformation of society. The new democracies allow 'democratic' states to intervene in markets in favour of economic elites while they discourage people's political aspirations for economic democratisation.

The East Asian states quickly became neoliberal states whose prime goal is to secure the best market conditions for capital accumulation at any cost. They offered an opportunity to economic elites to restore their power over labour by assisting the market to fragment the working class into many different segments. Informal and insecure forms of labour then became a driving force of neolib- eral development in the region. This results in a complex condition for social movements of labouring people pursuing more democratic development in East Asia. However, despite difficulties we see emerging struggles of people to challenge this development across East Asia.

These struggles for the future of East Asia may not follow the usual model of working-class mobilisation, as neoliberal development offered no conditions for a coherent industrial working class to emerge (Chang, 2013). Instead, working-class struggles are everywhere. They are not only in factories, in export processing zones (EPZs), and in industrialised cities, but also outside the immediate places of production. Struggles exist across sectors and communities as well as in workplaces and homes.

The Anti-Dam movement of the rural poor in Thailand and the vehement protests against land grabs in Cambodia and China demonstrate the desperate struggles of the marginal classes for democratic control over their means of production. Struggles also involve factory and domestic workers. Despite the setbacks caused by neoliberal development, the labour movement of industrial workers found new dynamics in the emerging struggles of workers against extremely insecure forms of employment. The determination to create a fair society that Korea's so-called irregular workers' struggles demonstrate reminds us of the uncompromising struggles of industrial workers for political and economic democratisation in the earlier period of industrialisation. Even the workers previously regarded as the most docile – Chinese internal migrant workers – have begun to turn themselves into a political force. The wave of strikes in 2010, mostly organised and participated in by migrant workers, demonstrated accumulating discontents among migrant workers as well as the transformative power of this new class of young-generation migrant workers.

At the periphery of East Asia, in countries such as Cambodia, workers in the informal economy form a majority of the working population. Their attempts to challenge the extreme forms of poverty and inequality precipitated by neoliberalism present a new hope for social transformation.

Conclusion

These diverse struggles give us some important lessons to consider in our quest for alternatives. First, neoliberal development not only undermines social movements but also creates new subjectivities of social movements. This is evidenced by the active participation of the unprivileged, who include informal economy workers, migrant workers and the rural poor, in struggles for alternatives. This offers a starting point for our journey to alternatives. Second, it is increasingly clear that the labour movement model based on the concept of a solid/fixed/coherent working class is difficult to apply under these conditions, and the old alternatives such as the social contract between organised industrial workers, big capital and interventionist states are no longer as promising as they used to be. More importantly it shows us that the formal democratisation of the state that is, the production of an electoral democracy – does not guarantee a more democratic society in which the social production of wealth is based not on exploitation but on solidarity and cooperation.

These struggles also establish concrete alternatives to neoliberal capitalism. Migrant workers' movements in East Asia's financial and industrial hubs reaffirm the most important principles for alternative development, such as non-discrimination against people on the basis of their race, gender, nationality and property, while irregular workers' struggles highlight the principle of equal reward for equal work. Continued struggles of the dispossessed in rural and urban East Asia demonstrate people's untamed aspiration for more democratic control over the means of production and environment against corporate interests. Transnational solidarity movements push for more accountability of TNCs and strengthened public surveillance over the speculative activities of financial capital. Women's movements strive to bring more democracy into the supposedly private sphere of 'domestic' social relations. From the efforts made for a collective alternative to colonialism and cold war capitalism, to their struggles presenting concrete alternatives to neoliberal policies and principles, to the formation of new subjectivities and ubiquitous forms of class struggles, East Asian development offers us a rich basis for democratic alternatives to neoliberal capitalism.

Acknowledgement

This work is based on research organised by the Institute for Social Sciences at Gyeongsang National University, which is supported by a National Research Foundation of Korea Grant (NRF-2013S1A5B8A01055117).

Select Bibliography

Asian Development Bank (ADB) (2008) *Emerging Asian Regionalism: Partnership for Shared Prosperity*. Manila: ADB.

ADB (2011) *Asian Development Outlook 2011: South-South Economic Links*. Manila: ADB.

Arrighi, G. (2007) *Adam Smith in Beijing: Lineages of the Twenty-First Century*. London: Verso.

Chang, D.-O. (2012) 'The neoliberal rise of East Asia and social movements of labour: four moments and a challenge', *Interface*, 4(2): 22–51.

Chang, D.-O. (2013) 'Labour and the "developmental state": a critique of the developmental theory of labour', in B. Fine, D. Tavasci and J. Saraswati (eds), *Beyond The Development State: Industrial Policy into the Twenty-First Century*. London: Pluto.

Gill, I., Kharas, H. J. and Bhattasali, D. (2007) *An East Asian Renaissance*. Washington DC: International Bank for Reconstruction and Development, and World Bank.

Kasahara, S. (2004) 'The flying geese paradigm: a critical study of its application to East Asian regional development', UNCTAD discussion paper. Available at: http://unctad. org/en/docs/osgdp20043_en.pdf (accessed 10 June 2014).

Öniş, Z. (1991) 'The logic of the developmental state', *Comparative Politics*, 24(1): 109–26.

Radice, H. (2008) 'The developmental state under global neoliberalism', *Third World Quarterly*, 29(6): 1153–74.

CHAPTER SEVENTEEN

Labour as an Agent of Change: The Case of China

Tim Pringle

Does China's development pathway represent a 'new developmentalist' alternative to neoliberal policies? Or does the fact that over 250 million Chinese people have been lifted out of poverty at the same time as the country has integrated into the global capitalist system render the country a poster child for neoliberalism itself? By focusing on the central question of labour relations, this chapter argues that in fact neither interpretation can help us understand China's transition from a centrally planned command economy to a decentralised market economy. Instead, the emerging new labour movement opens up the space to think about alternatives beyond the inequalities of neoliberalism and the top-down structural impositions and constraints on labour generally associated with new developmentalism. Furthermore, thinking about Chinese development from a labour movement perspective reminds us of a core aspect of Marx's thinking – the relationship between class struggle and change.

The structure of the chapter is straightforward. First, I take an historical approach to examining the principal features of China's transition from a labour perspective. Then I look at the response of workers. Finally, I take up the question of the alternatives that are emerging in the demands of a working class that, as we shall see, has undergone both an unmaking and a remaking. The chapter broadly addresses the question of building a labour movement which, by virtue of the sheer size of the working class in China, has the potential to generate alternatives to global capitalism.

China in Transition

Although there was significant continuity between pre and post liberation China, most of the literature dates the birth of 'new' China to the Communist Party of China's (CPC) victory over the Guomindang. The Guomindang was initially founded by the anti-imperialist nationalist Sun Yat-sen and later led by the fanatical anti-communist Chiang Kai-shek; the CPC's victory over his party concluded more than two decades of intermittent civil war. The People's

Republic of China was formally established in October 1949 when Mao Zedong famously announced that the 'people of China have stood up', ending centuries of imperialist incursions by the West and Japan and dispatching the Guomindang to Taiwan.

For most of the decade that followed, China emulated the Soviet model, as thousands of technicians and millions of roubles arrived from the USSR as part of an aid programme designed in part to offset the US policy of containment of the new republic. However, tensions between Mao and Stalin developed throughout the 1950s, culminating in the withdrawal of Soviet technicians – with the blue-prints of various large-scale development projects – as the two 'socialist' states teetered on the brink of war. China was left in a state of semi-isolation that continued right up to the eve of the reform era in 1978. From an international perspective, China was contained by the post-war policies of the United States and its concomitant determination to control, or least influence, the outcome of decolonisation around the world. China nonetheless contributed towards processes of post-colonial state building with aid and support for infrastructure projects, notably in Africa.

Prior to 1978, Chinese labour relations centred on the construction of the urban *danwei* (or work unit) into which state-owned and collectively owned enterprises were organised. The *danwei* was understood not as a set of means of production but as a unit of labour, comprising all employees from the general director down to the cleaner, who were all equally employees of the state and organised into the same trade union (Pringle and Clarke, 2011: 6). Industrial workers enjoyed higher standards of living than peasants in China, who were mostly excluded from the *danwei* by a system of household registration (*hukou zhidu*) that divided the population into urban and rural categories. The household registration system formed part of an overall development strategy that prioritised heavy industry over rural development, and required a degree of administrative state coercion to prevent migration to the towns.

As politics polarised during the late 1950s, any inherent stability that this state-led, redistributive and repressive model of development might contain was continually rocked by political campaigns. Following the successful implemen-tation of China's First Five-Year Plan (1953–57), which nationalised the entire economy, Mao and his supporters in the CPC embarked on a series of campaigns that included wildly ambitious production targets (the Great Leap Forward, 1958–59) and an all-out attack on the party-state bureaucracy – the Cultural Revolution (1966–69), which only just stopped short of civil war. Indeed, the consequent fear of a return to the chaos and economic stagnation of the Cultural Revolution years at least partly informed the CPC's decision to introduce a major agricultural reform known as the Household Responsibility System (HRS) in 1978 (Pringle, 2013). The HRS heralded the return to household-based farming and the dismantling of collective people's communes that had been set up during the collectivisation of agriculture in the late 1950s. Even more dramatically, it paved the way for a new industrial strategy that was to break, via privatisation, the 'iron rice bowl' of permanent employment and relative welfare security that the urban working class had secured under the *danwei* system. The journey back to capitalist labour relations, which pitched the interests of labour against those of private capital while the state withdrew from the micromanagement of industry, had begun. What did this mean for labour? More importantly, what were the demands raised by labour?

'Crossing the River by Feeling for the Stones': The Triumph of Gradualism

Profoundly conscious of the potential power of China's now much larger working class, the CPC approached industrial reform with caution, as epitomised by Deng Xiaoping's phrase cited above. Fixed-time contracts gradually replaced permanent employment for new hires after 1986 and state-owned enterprise (SOE) managers were given powers over hiring, firing and profit retention. The 1989 Democracy Movement, which culminated in a bloody crackdown on students and workers who had formed autonomous organisations, slowed the pace of SOE reform as the state, fearful of reigniting further national-scale protests, pulled back from implementing widespread redundancies. However, increasing competition from township and village enterprises that had emerged out of the disbanded rural communes and an expanding private sector fuelled by foreign direct investment (FDI) increased the economic pressure on the large loss-making state sector. As China moved to the centre of the global capitalist economy during the 1990s, the case for restructuring gradually took on the mantle of political timing rather than political choice as the influence of competitive capitalist accumulation came to dominate the CPC's economic policy.

The Fifteenth Party Congress in 1997 was a key event in the transition to an economy dominated by capitalist labour relations integrated into global production networks via China's engagement with globalisation. Having recovered from the trauma of the massacre in and near Tiananmen Square, the CPC formally announced the policy of 'holding on to the large and letting go of the small and medium-sized enterprises'. Despite the continuing emphasis on caution, this announcement was interpreted as a green light for the privatisation of many SOEs and consequent laying-off of up to 50 million urban workers (though the numbers vary). Laid-off SOE workers were exhorted to 'liberate thinking' (*jiefang sixiang*) and 'jump into the sea'(*xia hai*) of self-employment – effectively the informal economy. The state attempted to cushion the impact of mass lay-offs via a policy of phased redundancy (*xiagang*), stipulating that SOEs should provide retraining to laid-off workers and keep them on the books for three years with a monthly livelihood stipend. Phasing redundancy in this way did not head off resistance, but the sequencing, 'spin' – the term 'privatisation' was carefully avoided in official discourse – and the multiple categories of redundancy all helped to divide workers and moderate the resistance discussed in the next section.

As employment in the state sector shrank, the private sector grew, with increased diversity of ownership and the expansion of special economic zones.

Export-oriented private companies did not carry the welfare responsibilities and employment guarantees associated with SOE employment. Moreover, their adoption of flexible employment practices that frequently violated legally backed labour standards on wages, working hours, health and safety and reproductive rights, facilitated integration into global markets via ever-decreasing lead times for orders from international brands outsourcing production to China. Suppliers became one node in global production chains which transferred risk down the chain and eventually on to the young shoulders of the millions of people moving into off-farm employment for the first time. Restrictions on residence remain in place as a form of social control rather than a demographic policy instrument, but they have been considerably relaxed to ensure the release of what Marx called a reserve army of labour (that is, new swathes of unemployed workers) from the countryside who serve to discipline the 'new' workforce and keep wages down.

The consequence was that Chinese workers employed in these new spaces of accumulation were subject to harsh and sometimes violent labour regimes (Chan, 2001) influenced by the forces of neoliberal globalisation. Suppliers to global brands indulged in hyper-exploitation to meet lead times and local governments frequently ignored China's first national Labour Law (1995) in an effort to maintain investor-friendly environments. However, the state did not leave the ensuing class conflict to the mercies of unregulated market forces, as many neoliberals might have wished. The Party has certainly withdrawn from the day-to-day management of industrial relations via the dismantling of the *danwei* in what could be construed as a neoliberal rolling-back of the state. However it has deployed administrative (*hukou*) and legal institutions (the construction of a regulatory labour relations framework) as conduits for direct state intervention in labour relations and evolving labour markets. Above all, the state has limited legal labour organisation to the CPC-led All China Federation of Trade Unions (ACFTU).

Underlying these interventions has been a determination to uphold social stability and maintain CPC rule, as the Party has adopted aspects of both neoliberal and state-led prescriptions in pursuit of economic growth. For example, while the deregulation of labour markets has been a key aspect of neoliberal policies globally, China's labour markets have remained subject to sometimes contradictory regulatory and institutional influence. The fragmentary impact of *hukou* restrictions continues to hinder the integration of urban and rural labour markets as well as weaken workers' ability to defend collective rights and interests. Labour markets are further segmented by spatially influenced variations, as different types of enterprise ownership collide with different local political economies at different stages of transition.

In 2008, the state appeared to move against the global tide of employment informalisation that has been such a distinguishing feature of neoliberal globalisation. The introduction of the Labour Contract Law (LCL) in the face of organised opposition from the forces of domestic and international capital appeared to be an attempt to slow the rate of informalisation by providing workers with stronger and standardised contractual rights. The LCL carries an entire chapter on collective contracts, suggesting a move to encourage the collectivisation of labour relations and even promote – albeit very cautiously – collective bargaining as an instrument of class compromise. Also in 2008, the Labour Mediation and Arbitration Law attempted to render juridical channels of dispute resolution more user-friendly to workers. While these laws and policies do little to change the fact that labour power has become a commodity in China, they nevertheless do not entirely conform to the global trend of informalisation and the removal of constraints on the commodification of labour.

Despite the weak position of labour in the transition period, the CPC has not relaxed the ban on independent working-class organisation. The Trade Union Law grants an organisational monopoly to the ACFTU, which remains obliged by its own constitution to accept the leadership of the CPC. Attempts by workers to organise outside these restrictions are severely punished with prison terms. At the same time, the ACFTU has come under considerable pressure from the CPC itself to improve its credibility among workers, especially migrant workers in the private sector, where the institution remains weak and largely ineffective. The source of this pressure has been China's nascent labour movement, to which we now turn our attention.

The Forces of Labour in China

As a central plank of CPC policy following the Fifteenth Party Congress, the restructuring of SOEs left the traditional urban working class with very little room to manoeuvre. Although the ACFTU stood to lose from the demise of its power base in the state sector – principally as a labour welfare bureaucracy, rather than a representative organisation of workers – it was never likely to put the interests of workers before party policy. Nevertheless workers themselves did not simply roll over and there was widespread but geographically scattered resistance to redundancies (Cai, 2002). The resistance climaxed in a six-week protest by as many as 80,000 laid-off oil workers in the city of Daqing in 2002, during which the state deployed army units on the outskirts of town and riot police in the squares occupied by the workers.

Yet from a strategic perspective, the fact that most protests against restructuring were organised *after* workers had been laid off – including in Daqing – meant that local authorities were faced with issues of crowd control rather than having to break strikes and restart production. To this end, the Ministry of Public Security issued guidelines to local police forces not to exacerbate the tension by resorting to blanket repression as protests by laid-off workers were coming to a head. The most effective repression involved the arrest of workers' leaders combined with an immediate 'goodwill' subsidy to workers to meet their most urgent financial needs, such as food bills, a child's school textbook or medical expenses. In general the process of breaking the 'iron rice bowl' was skilfully managed by the Party, preventing laid-off workers from making common cause with those still in employment – and thereby transforming protests into strikes. This is significant because strikes have the inherent capacity to disrupt or even stop production. If the protests by laid-off oil workers had spread to those still in work, the immense power of energy sector workers in particular would have been felt at different nodes of the global production chains that FDI and the Chinese state had carefully constructed.

The situation in the private sector presents a different set of conditions. The 'unmaking' of China's traditional urban working class has been accompanied by the 'making' of a new proletariat as millions of people moved into non-agricultural employment. Current official figures put the number of migrant workers at approximately 250 million, in effect the largest rural–urban migration in human history. As *xiagang* proved an effective policy instrument to administer restructuring, so *hukou* has demonstrated its capacity to supply and discipline a young workforce employed in the manufacturing, construction and service sectors.

In the early to mid-1980s, the first generation of migrants found themselves in a straitjacket of exploitation as they left the land in search of a way out of poverty. Capital provided the main body of the garment (employment) while the state fastened the straps with various legal and political constraints on resistance (*hukou*) and organisation (denial of the right to organise). Most acts of resistance were short-lived and fragmented by place-of-origin loyalties as class consciousness remained undeveloped among young people encountering the factory system for the first time. These protests were often met with local state-sponsored or employer-organised violence. Demands were generally directed at local government officials via demonstrations outside local labour bureaux as migrant workers attempted to induce the local state to enforce the minimum labour standards stipulated in China's first national Labour Law (1995).

Class Consciousness

Scholars have contrasted the scattered, street-based 'protests of desperation' of SOE workers in 'rustbelt' industries with the 'protests against discrimination' of migrant workers denied the same rights as urban workers. Lee (2007) argues that migrant workers are more likely to use the law in their attempts to uphold employment rights, a process that forms part of a wider struggle for full citizenship denied by *hukou*. This approach is critiqued by Anita Chan (2008) on the grounds that the situation of migrant workers is often just as desperate as that of laid-off state workers and that the former also resort to extralegal 'militant' forms of protests on the streets. Chan seems to suggest the difference is one of 'consciousness' but does not clarify whether this is a class consciousness or some form of 'citizen' consciousness: '[T]he day when migrant workers demand abolition of the *hukou* system will mark the maturation of their consciousness'.

Recent empirical reality allows us to cut through this debate. Since the turn of the century, a number of factors have combined to produce conditions in which migrant workers have been able to move from defensive protests targeting government officials to strikes aimed directly at employers, reflecting the emergence of class consciousness as expressed through collective strike action (compare Basso, Chapter 8). These include the onset of structural labour shortages beginning in 2003; the arrival of second and third generations of migrants whose connection to the land is much weaker than that of their parents; and an accumulation of knowledge of both the factory system and the law. Widespread access to information and communications technology has helped the current generation of migrant workers to understand their stronger bargaining position in global production chains and also to organise labour actions more effectively. At the same time, the generalised alarm in government regarding the political risks of maintaining high levels of inequality that have emerged as a result of the reforms has also encouraged local officials to implement labour laws that at least restrain the worst excesses of employers.

Lee is certainly correct to argue that migrant workers have made use of the juridical channels of dispute resolution through which the state has tried – and failed – to individualise and fragment labour struggles. But these tactics have not ruled out street protests, short work stoppages and even the occasional battle with the police. In Guangdong province, the growth in legal activism has not prevented other forms of resistance. For example, long struggles for diagnosis, medical care and financial compensation from employers for occupational disease, such as the campaigns by Gold Peak battery workers and Lucky Gem jewellery workers, demonstrate a nonlinear mix of tactics. These include pursuing suppliers through legal channels, shaming multinational companies in the media, disrupting shareholder meetings outside China, strikes, protests and even occupations of government offices.[1] Indeed it is rare for disputes to follow a 'common sense' linear progression from juridical channels to some form of collective disruption of capital accumulation, as 'militancy' rarely follows set patterns and formulae.

A more reliable framework for interpreting the growth of migrant worker labour disputes distinguishes between individual labour rights and collective class interests. This approach is used by Chan and Pun, who suggest that 'the making of a new working class is increasingly conscious of and participating in interest-based or class-orientated labour protests' (2009: 287). I would add that this approach to understanding growing labour militancy in China should not be based on an assumption that there is a clear line dividing struggles over individually defined labour *rights* and labour *interests* collectivised by workers' autonomous agency.

One indication of the transition from rights to interests in authoritarian post-state-socialist countries such as China is the emergence of demands that go beyond the minimum standards stipulated by the law. These can be both economic and political, and can elicit state intervention and compromises

---

1   See Globalization Monitor: www.globalmon.org.hk/tags/cadmium-poisoning

from capital – or not. For example, a wave of strikes across six Southern ports in Guangdong between March and May 2007 climaxed in a 33-hour stoppage at the Yantian International Container Terminals (YICT), which is part of the Singapore-listed Hutchinson Port Holdings Trust and the fourth largest port in the world. The strike by well-paid gantry and tower crane operators had an immediate and potentially disastrous impact on exports to Western markets. It was launched in pursuit of three basic demands: lowering of pay differentials with white collar workers; an increase in basic pay including a paid lunch break; the replacement of the management-sponsored staff association with an effective trade union funded by the workers themselves.

In 2010 in another example, the demand for an effective plant-level trade union was echoed in a watershed 19-day strike by workers at Honda's Ben Tian car-parts plant in Foshan, Guangdong province. As at the port, the demands were political and economic: a pay rise and the 'reorganisation' of the trade union at the plant via the recall of the existing trade union representatives and the election of a new committee. With their operations in China heading towards a complete halt, Honda's management had little choice but to participate in collective bargaining with 30 elected worker representatives who had obtained advice from China's best-known labour scholar, Professor Chang Kai. The dispute triggered a wave of strikes that spread beyond Guangdong and beyond the auto industry, again highlighting the strong bargaining position of workers in sectors that are thoroughly integrated into global markets. In my view, these events provide the key to consolidating and expanding the emerging labour movement as the strikes seek to constrain globalised capital.

Both strikes ended with management making significant concessions to the economic demands of the workers. Equally important was the role of the ACFTU in these disputes. One result of the rise in workers' confidence to pursue their grievances through strike action has been significant pressure on the state union to improve its capacity to represent workers. In part this reflects the CPC's determination to head off independent worker organisations that could threaten the regime itself – the example of the Solidarity trade union in Poland was not lost on the CPC leadership. Thus at Yantian, the deputy chair of the Shenzhen Federation of Trade Unions (SFTU) rushed to the scene of the strike at 2 a.m., arriving to find a rowdy and tense situation. The SFTU told workers it supported their pay demands but that the establishment of a union branch at the port must be in accordance with the Trade Union Law. The workers' more radical demand for an organisation of representatives directly funded by the workers themselves would constitute an illegal organisation. In the negotiations, the SFTU played a mediating role using its political connections with the CPC to extract guarantees from management not to take revenge on strike leaders after the dispute was settled.

During the Honda strike, the official trade union at provincial level (Guangdong) and city level (Guangzhou) went beyond the level of mediation and provided passive support to the workers' demands for a substantial pay rise. In contrast, the local township trade union's response was to organise a physical picket-line attack on militant workers, for which it was instructed to issue an unprecedented public apology after pictures of the incident were widely publicised. The attack reignited worker solidarity, and the apology served as an indication to the strikers that they had the support of the higher-level unions.

Both strikes produced at least partly elected trade union committees mostly made up of frontline workers. The strikes also represent the impact of shop floor militancy on a Party-led institution that had traditionally relied on appointed officials usually selected from the ranks of management. It is here that a second key strategy for building the labour movement comes into the spotlight. The demand for direct trade union elections so that workers can choose their own representatives has become an increasingly common feature of strikes. This strategy reduces the impact of the absence of freedom of association and has the potential to build a layer of enterprise-level trade union representatives closely connected to the lives and demands of ordinary workers. Although the unions operate under the legal constraints of the Trade Union Law, there is the potential for sector-level networks to cohere over collective bargaining issues – as indeed has been the case in the auto industry and even in some Walmart retail stores.

Two key factors render the growing class consciousness of China's expanding working class particularly important for forcing changes to production relations. First, the state's policy of tying economic development to integration in global markets has provided workers with an important source of structural power: the capacity to disrupt global trade flows and production chains as demonstrated by the Yantian port workers and Honda auto workers respectively. Imagine the potential (class) power generated by workers in these two sectors coming together in joint action! Second, the sheer size of the Chinese working class renders it a central player in determining the future of global capitalism and potential alternatives. According to the National Bureau of Statistics, there were 770 million employed people in China at the end of 2013. While it is important to avoid indulging in any kind of deterministic optimism on the basis of these figures, it is nevertheless difficult to overestimate how central the Chinese working class has become to neoliberal globalisation – and its possible demise.

Alternatives to Development: State-Led or Worker-Led?

The CPC has certainly implemented – some would argue pioneered – a number of policies associated with new developmentalism. A national minimum wage set by local city governments and based, according to the regulations, on 'actual existing conditions'; cash transfers to the urban poor in the form of a means-tested minimum income subsidy; and employment creation – but not full employment – have been at the heart of the CPC's entire reform-era strategy. However Deng Xiaoping's famous slogan for the reforms – 'let some get rich first, so that others can get rich later' – appears to be an embodiment of the class-based neoliberal 'trickle-down' prescription for economic growth. And yet, as Harvey notes, the market can do 'little to transform an economy without a parallel shift in class relations, private property and all the other institutional arrangements that typically ground a thriving capitalist economy' (2005: 122).

The transformation of China's class relations has been guided by the CPC's concerns to retain its status as the ruling party in a one-party state presiding over a system which was once described as a mixed economy structured around state-led initiatives by the former chief economist at the World Bank, Joseph Stiglitz.[2] Property rights have been gradually broadened – though hardly clarified in the neoliberal sense – to allow a full range of enterprise ownership. This has in turn led to the rise of a capitalist class with close and often corrupt ties to the CPC.

In 2002, the CPC announced that it would allow business owners to join the Party, in what the *Economist* (2007) termed 'a massive networking opportunity for bosses'. In 2004, the Constitution was amended to recognise and protect a 'citizen's lawful private property [as] inviolable', and in 2007 the Private Property Law of China was passed despite considerable opposition from leftists within the Party. On the other hand, all land remains the property of the state. Agricultural land is allocated for up to 30 years via tradeable land use rights overseen by village committees on the basis of (in theory) family requirements – an institution broadly supported by a majority of farmers.

The system has not excluded land grabs chiefly carried out by property developers working closely with party committees at the county level. Such activity has provoked widespread protests in the countryside, and left approximately 60 million people affected with little option but to seek non-farm work even as their *hukou* status as farmers denied them access to permanent urban residence. We might be reminded of the period of primitive accumulation that cleared the commons and heralded the growth of capitalism in England.

The central government has proved incapable of preventing such digressions and unwilling to curb the repression that accompanies them. The experience of China's rapidly expanding working class in the reform era has demonstrated (yet again) that state-led development requires a heavily repressive hand over labour. Indeed, the Chinese state's capacity to 'pick winners' and use the banking system to support selected SOEs at the same time as implementing widespread privatisation in the state sector and developing investor-friendly special economic zones to attract FDI has rested on the institutionalised repression of the Chinese working class.

The reforms have not been some kind of grand neoliberal shock programme of full-blown privatisation inspired by the Chicago school, as in much of Latin America or following the collapse of the Soviet Union. However Chinese development hardly fits into a programme of 'full employment as a primary goal' as stated by the Sao Paolo structuralist school.[3]

---

2   See http://mises.org/daily/2960.

3   See www.tenthesesonnewdevelopmentalism.org

State and capital in China have demonstrated willingness to work together to ensure that emerging capitalist social relations are shored up by existing fragmentations rooted in geographic, spatial, gendered and cultural-linguistic divisions. And they have not hesitated to conspire in the repression of militant workers and activists organising in the workplace in order to prevent China's 'class against capital' from becoming a 'class for itself' – to use the language employed by Marx to explain how unified labour movements emerge. But in spite of the constraints, the process of conscious class cohesion that is unfolding in China carries the potential for autonomous working-class organisation(s) based in workplaces that can act as both an entry point for militants and an institutional class memory that draws on lessons from defeats and develops strategy and tactics for future struggles. If we accept – as contributors to this book do – that such capacities lie at the heart of a genuine break with neoliberalism, and potentially capitalism itself, then the unparalleled size and global reach of the Chinese working class renders its struggles of profound relevance to making another world possible.

Select Bibliography

Cai, Y. (2002) 'The resistance of Chinese laid-off workers in the reform period', *China Quarterly*, 170: 327–44.

Chan, A. (2001) *Workers under Assault: The Exploitation of Labor in a Globalizing Economy.* New York: M.E. Sharpe.

Chan, A. (2008) Review of *Against the Law: Labor Protests in China's Rustbelt and Sunbelt. China Perspectives* (1): 114–55.

Chan, C. and Pun, N. (2009) 'The making of a new working class? A study of collective actions of migrant workers in South China', *China Quarterly*, 198: 287–303.

China Perspectives 2008 (1), available at: http://chinaperspectives.revues.org/3503 (accessed 29 January 2014).

Economist (2007) 'Property rights in China', 8 March.

Harvey, D (2005) *A Brief History of Neoliberalism.* Oxford: Oxford University Press.

Lee, C. K. (2007) *Against the Law: Labor Protests in China's Rustbelt and Sunbelt.* Berkeley, Calif.: University of California Press.

Pringle, T. (2013) *Chinese Trade Unions: The Challenge of Labour Unrest.* Abingdon: Routledge.

Pringle, T. and Clarke, S. (2011) *The Challenge of Transition: Trade Unions in Russia, China and Vietnam.* Basingstoke: Palgrave Macmillan.

CHAPTER EIGHTEEN

Alternatives to Neoliberalism in India

Rohini Hensman

Modern India's relationship with the capitalist world economy has been through three broad phases. First, British colonialism ruined a flourishing textile industry in India and converted the country into a source of raw materials for its own manufacturing industry, forcing India into the position of a colony subordinate to an imperial power. Second, the post-independence Indian National Congress (hereafter Congress) government embarked on a process of industrialisation in an economy that was heavily protected though not completely cut off from global capital. The third period, globalisation and neoliberalism, is usually traced to the economic liberalisation of 1991, when India began a process of reintegration into the world economy.

This chapter sketches an outline for each of these three periods, introducing the social forces and struggles that could constitute the basis for moving forward from neoliberalism to an economy where production is for need, not profit, and working people control their lives and work.

The Colonial Period

Between 1850 and 1900 the British rulers over India built more than 25,000 miles of railways for their own purposes. In doing so they introduced the industrial processes necessary to maintain the network and hired tens of millions of workers, mainly through Indian contractors resembling Marx's description of petty capitalists. Larger capitalists and more stable workforces developed in various industries, resulting in the formation of a capitalist class and a proletariat, both of which were relatively well developed by the time of Independence in 1947 (Hensman, 2011: 32–3, 36–7). Partly in response to workers' struggles over wages and working hours and partly in response to English textile manufacturers who feared competition from an unregulated Indian textile industry, the British colonial government introduced the first Indian Factories Act in 1881. The act was amended and strengthened in response to continuing struggles. Other labour legislation was also passed, including the Trade Unions Act (1926) and the Industrial Disputes (ID) Act (1947) (Hensman, 2011: 95–7).

This legislation provided protection to a section of the labour force but

discouraged collective bargaining. The Trade Unions Act allowed for the registration of unions; however it neither required employers to recognise and negotiate
with them, nor prohibited the victimisation of members by employers. The ID Act
made it mandatory for unions to give strike notice two weeks before embarking
on industrial action, during which period compulsory arbitration could be
imposed. The legislation also created a sharply segmented labour market. For
example the Factories Act (revised in 1948) – which provided for registration
of employers and employees, and covered working conditions, working hours,
the prohibition of child labour and so on – did not apply to workplaces with
electric power that had fewer than ten workers, or those without power that
had fewer than 20. Most other labour laws likewise omitted these workers as
well as agricultural labourers, who thus constituted an informal labour force,
deprived of legal recognition as workers and denied protective legislation.
Although the Trade Unions Act did apply to them, in practice it proved almost
impossible for them to form or join a union without losing their jobs (Hensman,
2011: 97–100).

Colonialism created a large proletariat, but it was internally divided by
gender, caste, ethnicity and religion. During the 19th century, there emerged
Indian social reformers such as Jyotirao and Savitribai Phule, who were influenced by radicals like Thomas Paine, and fought against the extreme oppression
of women, girls, lower castes and 'untouchable' castes (now known officially as
'scheduled castes' and self-identified as Dalits) in India. These reformers inspired
a younger generation, the most famous of whom is B. R. Ambedkar, himself a
Dalit, who chaired the Drafting Committee of the Constituent Assembly after
Independence. Dakshayani Velayudhan, the only Dalit woman in the Constituent
Assembly, fought for the rights of Dalits, women and workers.

While British rule allowed the emergence of movements for the emancipation of women and Dalits, it also saw the emergence of extreme right-wing
organisations, both Hindu and Muslim, which in the 1920s and 1930s drew
inspiration from Italian and German fascism. Their unchecked growth and
activities resulted in the catastrophe of Partition (1947), in which an estimated
1 million people were killed and 15 million were displaced. Its toxic legacy
remains today, with right-wing Hindu organisations persecuting Muslims and
other minorities in India, right-wing Islamist organisations in Pakistan and
Bangladesh persecuting Hindu and other minorities, a continuing hot–cold
war between India and Pakistan, and Kashmir claimed by both. The right-
wing Hindu nationalist organisation Rashtriya Swayamsevak Sangh (RSS)
was banned temporarily after Gandhi was assassinated by Hindu extremists
in 1948, but survived and later spawned a large and growing 'family' of organisations (known as the *Sangh Parivar*). Their goal is a *Hindu rashtra* (Hindu
nation-state), and the political ideology that inspires them is known as
Hindutva (not to be confused with the Hindu religion). One of the main rivals
to the Congress Party, the Bharatiya Janata Party (BJP), is a member of this
family.

The Indian Developmental State

For the post-Independence Congress government, the main task was state-planned industrialisation, including electrification and the development of heavy industry. In pursuit of this goal, state authorities employed a variety of means to encourage foreign investment in technologically advanced sectors such as oil refining, electrical engineering and pharmaceuticals, and Indian private sector investment in less capital-intensive manufacturing industries. Protective tariffs, import restrictions and currency control led to a withdrawal of British capital and an Indian takeover of their concerns. With the Second Plan (1956), the state began to build up heavy industry despite US opposition, obtaining collaborations with German and British private capital, the Soviet Union and East European countries. After drastic import controls were imposed during a foreign-exchange crisis in 1957–58, foreign companies in technologically advanced sectors formed joint ventures with Indian companies to gain access to the protected market. By the 1960s the state had partially taken over many services formerly provided by foreign capital, including electric power, transport, banking and life insurance, and production of key industrial inputs such as coal, and the trend continued (Hensman, 2011: 36–8).

The Congress vision of development included a measure of social justice, and for the Congress left this meant strong union rights. An upsurge in the labour movement after the Second World War strengthened this section, but as the upsurge subsided the Congress right, which supported domestic business, gained in strength. In 1950, there was an attempt to pass a new Trade Union Act requiring compulsory recognition of representative unions by employers, collective bargaining, and protection from victimisation for trade union activities, along with a comprehensive Labour Relations Bill to replace the ID Act. But the bills were opposed by the ministries in charge of railways, defence establishments, and posts and telegraphs, and lapsed in 1951. Former trade unionist V. V. Giri became labour minister in 1952 and tried to reintroduce the bills, but again encountered opposition.

Millions of informal workers continued to work for the public sector as well as private enterprises. Policies encouraging informalisation were enacted by the Janata Party when it won the elections in 1977, and were continued by Indira Gandhi when she came to power again in 1980 (Hensman, 2011: 101–4). Agricultural workers too were overwhelmingly unorganised. Together with marginal farmers, who could not survive unless family members engaged in wage-labour, they constituted a large and growing majority in the countryside. Rural class conflict was exacerbated by the fact that most agricultural labourers were Dalits. Their attempts to organise and claim their rights challenged the caste hierarchy, and were therefore met with the utmost brutality: rape, massacres, and the torching of entire villages.

By contrast, permanent employees in the public sector enjoyed employment security, which was extended to large enterprises in the private sector by the introduction of Chapter VB of the ID Act in 1976, stipulating that permission had to be obtained from the government before employers could close down establishments or dismiss workers. Job security enabled these workers to form strong unions, bargain collectively, and win benefits such as healthcare, paid leave and retirement benefits. Affirmative action in the form of job reservations in the public sector enabled a small section of Dalits and Adivasis (tribals or indigenous people) to share these benefits.

Meanwhile, the provision of social security and welfare for vast numbers of working people outside these sections remained abysmal. Vastly overcrowded public hospitals in cities offered in-patient and out-patient services, but even these were unavailable in most parts of the country. State schools left out millions of children, many of whom were engaged in child labour. Loss of employment could throw workers into destitution. The only universal welfare measure was the Public Distribution System (PDS), which provided rice, wheat, sugar and kerosene at subsidised rates. Although migrant workers and the homeless were excluded by the requirement for an address, and corruption was widespread, it provided a safety net for many who might otherwise have starved.

The worst victims of this model of development were the tens of millions displaced by large dams, mines and infrastructure projects. The 2012 report of the Working Group on Human Rights in India and the United Nations estimates that 60–65 million have been displaced since Independence, over 40 per cent of them Adivasis and another 40 per cent Dalits and other rural poor. The colonial Land Acquisition Act (1894) was used by the post-colonial state to dispossess these people of their homes and livelihoods, supposedly in the interests of 'public purpose'. Even where compensation was considered, it was only for the owners of land; the vast majority, who were landless, received no compensation. Despite sporadic resistance, a development agenda resting on large-scale involuntary dispossession continued in full force.

In Bombay (now Mumbai), the most industrialised city in India, with a strong presence of women in its workforce and unions, a case against the 'marriage bar' (dismissal of women workers when they marry) was taken up and pursued to the Supreme Court level, where it was finally won in 1965. Struggles for equal wages, maternity leave and childcare were fought and won in the formal sector, but unions had no counter-strategy when employers retaliated by ceasing to recruit women (Hensman, 2011: 214–17). This revealed a more general failure to fight against discrimination, which also affected Muslims, Dalits and Adivasis, and for equal opportunities legislation (Hensman, 2011: 132–7). In 1979, a Supreme Court verdict acquitting two policemen who had raped a tribal girl, Mathura, sparked a huge upsurge of protests from women and the birth of the autonomous women's movement in India. A partial overhaul of the obsolete rape laws inherited from British rule was one result of the movement, which also branched out to tackle other forms of violence and discrimination against women and girls.

While the performance of the Indian economy from Independence to 1991, with its absence of major famines and average growth rate of around 3.5 per cent per annum, was incomparably better than the zero to negative growth rate and famines that killed millions during British rule (Drèze and Sen, 2013: 2–3), informal labourers and the displaced, who constituted the overwhelming majority, continued to be disempowered in significant ways. Permanent workers in the formal sector were able to form powerful unions, but were increasingly under attack by employers from the late 1970s. The 1980 industrial policy encouraged subcontracting and offered incentives to companies to relocate production from unionised workforces in cities to non-unionised workers on greenfield sites, thus helping employers to smash some of the strongest unions.

Globalisation and Neoliberalism in India

The most significant changes came after 1991 with the liberalisation of international trade and capital flows, which intensified with India's accession to the World Trade Organization (WTO) in 1995. The Indian capitalist class was split between sections who had mismanaged their businesses for decades and could not survive in a more competitive environment, who opposed liberalisation, and more aggressive corporate groups, like the Ambanis, who realised that the future of Indian capital lay in its ability to operate with global economies of scale and access global capital markets. The latter backed neoliberalism, not least because it brought about a wave of privatisations (in oil, telecoms, financial services and so on), of which they were the main beneficiaries. Indian GDP growth accelerated after 1991, crossing 9 per cent per annum between 2005 and 2008 before declining after the global crisis, and even then remaining second only to China among major economies (Drèze and Sen, 2013: 4, 19). The income of the wealthy and the new consumerist urban and rural middle classes (the top 20 per cent) increased considerably after 1991. However, for the rest of the population there was little improvement in income levels (Drèze and Sen, 2013: 29–32). Consequently, inequality increased massively.

Liberalisation unleashed a wave of corporate restructuring. Industrialists complained that India's 'rigid' labour laws obstructed this process and needed to be 'reformed'. They campaigned against laws and regulations that provided job security to permanent workers and prohibited the employment of contract workers to do permanent jobs that were considered part of the core activities of an establishment. Their excuse was that these provisions interfered with 'flexibility'. Yet the way in which industrialists used informalised labour suggested that their real reason was to deprive workers of their union rights by removing obstacles to dismissing them if workers tried to organise. The industrialists' campaign reached its peak when the National Democratic Alliance led by the BJP was in power from 1998 to 2004, and came to a halt after the Congress-led United Progressive Alliance (UPA) came to power. Under the UPA other policies were explored, such as the provision of generous subsidies to businesses in special economic zones (SEZs) (Hensman, 2011: 110–12).

Although India's labour laws were not changed, the changed industrial relations climate, in which state institutions and the judiciary were overtly pro-employer, allowed informalisation and the denial of union rights to proceed. The case of the Manesar automobile plant of Maruti Suzuki India Limited in Haryana, where 75 per cent of the workforce consisted of precarious workers paid roughly a quarter of the wages of permanent workers, illustrates this. The first attempt by workers to form an independent union in 2011 failed because the labour commissioner refused to register it and management forced union leaders to sign letters of resignation under threat of imprisonment and torture. A second attempt in 2012 succeeded, according to leaders of the Maruti Suzuki Workers Union (MSWU), because deputy general manager for human resources Avanish Dev helped them with the registration. The MSWU submitted a charter including the demand that contract workers should get the same pay and benefits as regular workers. On 18 July, while union leaders were arguing against the suspension of a Dalit worker who had protested when a supervisor abused him in casteist terms, there was fighting in the factory, a fire broke out, and Avanish Dev was later found dead. Some 147 activists – many of whom were not in the plant at the time – were accused of murder, arrested and jailed. Another 546 permanent workers and 1,800 contract workers were dismissed. A year later, as the International Commission for Labor Rights reported in *Merchants of Menace: Repressing Workers in India's New Industrial Belt*, neither the criminal investigation nor the labour dispute had made any progress.

The use of contract workers for permanent jobs and victimisation of union activists in such a large plant are prohibited by law, yet the state government not only colluded with management, it went further, and arrested and jailed workers on false criminal charges. Haryana is only an extreme example of generalised state collusion with informalisation and union-busting in the post-1991 period. It is not surprising that wages stagnated while workers fought to retain at least minimal control over their work and employment conditions.

Sexual harassment of women at work, always rampant in the informal sector, was taken up by women's groups in a sustained manner in 1992 after a social worker in Rajasthan, Bhanwari Devi, was gang-raped for opposing child marriage and the rapists were acquitted. By 1997, the Supreme Court had issued guidelines for tackling sexual harassment at work. The Sexual Harassment at Workplace Act became law in 2013. Bhanwari's struggle for justice had emboldened other women and girls to fight against forced marriage, sexual assault and domestic violence, but it also illustrated the backlash that struggles against the oppression of women and girls could provoke. The caste equation in the countryside changed, with upper castes moving out and backward castes becoming the main perpetrators of atrocities against Dalits (Teltumbde, 2007). Several cases of so-called honour killings demonstrated the brutal backlash against young people whose marriages defied traditional caste norms.

The universal PDS became a targeted one in 1997, with a higher subsidy for below poverty line (BPL) recipients than for those considered above the poverty line, who were effectively eased out of the system by 2001. This resulted in even greater exclusion errors than before. The scandal of starvation deaths in 2001 while granaries were overflowing inspired the Right to Food campaign. It scored several victories, including the National Rural Employment Guarantee Act (NREGA) (2005), which promised 100 days of employment per year building public works for each rural household at minimum wages. If the state was unable to supply work, it was obliged to provide unemployment benefit. Implementation proved enormously difficult because of the hostility of local vested interests. Wherever it was made to work, the recipients (a large proportion of whom were women) benefited, and local agricultural wages went up (Hensman, 2011: 246–50). The Food Security Bill (2013) pulled together and expanded existing government schemes, promising subsidised grain to 75 per cent of the population, food for pregnant and lactating women and children aged 6 months to 6 years, maternity benefits, and midday meals for schoolchildren aged 6 to 14 years.

At 1.2 per cent of GDP, India's public expenditure on health is among the lowest in the world, with public health facilities extremely limited and often very badly run. The National Rural Health Mission, launched in 2005–06, is a promising initiative, and in 2011 the High Level Expert Group on Universal Health Coverage recommended free health care for all, yet funding for public healthcare continues to be grossly inadequate. Instead, the trend is towards schemes like the Rashtriya Swasthya Bhima Yojana, in which the government pays the insurance premium for BPL families to enrol with private insurance companies that cover the cost of their treatment in government and private hospitals (Drèze and Sen, 2013: 148–52). Apart from the exclusion of many who cannot pay for private healthcare, such schemes also result in several distortions. For example, by privileging high-cost surgical procedures, they neglect prevention and treatment of the widespread diseases that account for more than 98 per cent of illnesses; patients are burdened with out-of-pocket expenses; post-operative complications are not treated; and unnecessary procedures including hysterectomies are common. Such 'public–private partnerships' result in public money going into private rather than public health provision, thus moving away from universal health care.

The 21st century has seen much more emphasis on education as a right, starting with the Sarva Shiksha Abhiyan (Education for All Movement) and culminating with the Right to Education Act (2009), which promises free compulsory education to all children between the ages of 6 and 14. Some activists saw this as a significant step forward. However, there were also criticisms of the legislation, which did not pledge to provide good-quality elementary state education to all. Rather, the authorities required private schools to take 25 per cent of 'disadvantaged' students, whose expenses would be paid by the government. These steps resulted in a much higher proportion of children having access to schools, yet the quality of schooling remained poor. Even where standards were higher, the emphasis on rote learning discouraged critical thinking. Apart from a tiny minority of elite institutions, these drawbacks afflicted private schools almost as much as state schools (Drèze and Sen, 2013: 120–6).

Thus welfare provision remained stunted, partly because of a narrow income-tax base and widespread tax evasion. Given that liberalisation was supposed to end the corruption of the 'licence-permit raj', it is an irony that the black economy continued to flourish and corruption was rampant during this period, especially in sectors such as real estate, infrastructure projects, mining and telecoms. However, the fight-back was also more vigorous, scoring a major victory in the passage of the Right to Information Act (2005).

The anomaly in the Land Acquisition Act (1894), whereby 'public purpose' was supposedly secured by massive displacement of the poor, became even more glaringly obvious when the beneficiaries of land acquisition were private busi-nesses and the threat to the environment from deforestation and large dams was better understood. Here too there was increasing resistance, resulting in the passage of the Forest Rights Act (2006). This Act gave Adivasis and other forest dwellers much stronger rights over their habitats. In addition, the new Land Acquisition, Rehabilitation and Resettlement Act (2013), while still allowing for forcible acquisition, put much greater emphasis on consent, compensation and environmental protection than its 1894 predecessor.

All this adds up to a picture that is more complex than pure neoliberalism. Paradoxically, 'it is precisely during the period of high globalization that civil society campaigns and judicial interventions have placed the right to work, the right to food, the right to education, the right to health and the right to informa-tion firmly onto the agenda' (Chandoke, 2013: 155–6). All these initiatives were watered down by opposition, yet their impact has been significant.

To find a straightforward example of pro-corporate policies, we need to turn to Narendra Modi, the former BJP chief minister of Gujarat who became prime minister in 2014, who offered massive handouts to corporate groups, facilitated the displacement and pauperisation of rural working people, led opposition to welfare legislation, and opposed, at considerable public expense, the appointment of an independent anti-corruption watchdog. In Modi's Gujarat unfettered neolib-eralism could triumph because he created a mass base for it through virulent Hindu nationalism and brutal persecution of minorities (Gopalakrishnan, 2008). Conversely, sections of the top 20 per cent who were not necessarily Hindu nationalists backed him because he supported their sense of entitlement to the privileges they enjoyed and resentment against subsidies for the poor.

Alternatives in India

No viable alternative can emerge without an all-out fight against caste and gender oppression in India. The backlash against any progress made in the struggle for women's rights has been ferocious, and concerted opposition to a deeply misog-ynist culture needs to be taken up within the working class (see also Chapters

9 and 21). The backlash against Dalit struggles to improve their lives has been equally ferocious. The failure of Dalit leaders to respond adequately has led a leading activist to suggest that Dalits should turn to class politics (Teltumbde, 2007). The enthusiasm with which the Maruti union took up the victimisation of a Dalit worker suggests that the time could be ripe for such a turn.

An alternative would have to combat the persecution of ethnic and religious minorities without pandering to minority ethnic supremacism or religious fundamentalism. Protection of the environment must also be on its agenda. Finally, it would have to emphasise Marxist understandings that capitalism is inherently global, and can only be defeated by a global movement. The debate in India over a workers' rights clause in WTO agreements revealed that the left parties and sections of the non-party left believe that resisting integration into the world economy is an adequate form of opposition to globalised capital (Hensman, 2011: 304–17). In such a context, it is important to reiterate that concrete steps to build international solidarity among workers are essential to an effective fight against global capitalism.

The Communist Party of India (CPI) and Communist Party of India (Marxist) (CPI(M), the largest party in the Left Front) were in power in West Bengal from 1977 to 2011, but failed to offer any alternative to neoliberal development. Their land reforms helped to consolidate a stable majority, yet the redistribution was neither as extensive as they claimed nor was it consolidated by forming cooperatives. Consequently, landlessness increased from 39.6 per cent in 1987–88 to 49.8 per cent in 2000. Poverty, malnutrition, homelessness, unemployment, healthcare and education were worse than in many other states. The death blow to the CPI(M)'s popularity was dealt by its violent attempts to displace thousands of farmers and rural workers in Singur in 2006 (to hand over fertile land at concessional rates for a Tata car plant) and in Nandigram in 2007 (for a chemical hub and SEZ) (Banerjee, 2007). The Left Front was voted out of power in the 2011 state assembly elections.

The strategy of the CPI (Maoist) is 'protracted people's war' to capture state power, and their main support base has been among Adivasis suffering state neglect and violence. Their programmatic document entitled 'Strategy and tactics of the Indian revolution' proclaims that their goal is a 'new democratic revolution' against imperialism, comprador bureaucrat capitalism and feudalism. The 'motive forces' named in it include the proletariat, landless, poor and middle peasants, semi-proletariat and petty bourgeoisie, with rich peasants seen as vacillating allies and the national bourgeoisie as a revolutionary force requiring protection. Theirs is not, therefore, an anti-capitalist revolution, and this has practical consequences. In a report entitled 'Mining companies are arming the Maoists', the Asian Centre for Human Rights showed how the alliance with the 'national bourgeoisie' includes providing protection to legal and illegal mining companies, which are displacing Adivasis and destroying the environment, in exchange for money and explosives. Contractors illegally siphoning off funds from NREGA's guaranteed work at minimum wages scheme are also protected.

The CPI (Maoist), by its own admission, murdered social activist Niyamat Ansari, who was fighting for these funds to reach their intended beneficiaries in Jharkhand. This alliance with rapacious capitalist interests precludes the possibility of building an alternative to neoliberalism.

By contrast, self-organised struggles against displacement have had some impressive victories and could contribute to building an alternative. In an uncanny echo of the film *Avatar* (2009), the Dongria Khond and other tribal and non-tribal forest-dwellers scored a spectacular success against the mining company Vedanta Resources, which had already received state approval to mine the bauxite under their Niyamgiri hills. They fought the incursion by appealing for their rights under Indian law and for international support for the rights of indigenous people. The legal battle resulted in a Supreme Court verdict requiring village assemblies to make the final decision. In all twelve villages selected by the state government of Odisha for the referendum, the mining proposal was rejected, unanimously and eloquently, by the villagers. This does not mean that Adivasis wish to remain segregated from the rest of society. As activist Dayamani Barla from Jharkhand explained, 'We should also be part of this development process by getting access to health, education, jobs, etc. .... We want the polluted rivers to be pollution free. We want wastelands to be turned green .... This is our model of development' (Basu, 2013).

Such struggles against mines, dams (the most famous being the Narmada Bachao Andolan), nuclear power plants (at Koodankulam, Jaitapur and elsewhere), and so on by local communities which are incompletely proletarian-ised, with some members self-employed at least part of the time, raise a crucial issue for Marxists: can these struggles become part of a socialist revolution?

In one sense the struggles capture the essence of that revolution, being struggles of working people against capitalism and for control over their lives and work. But do they seek to go forward to socialism, or backward to a pre-cap-italist era? This is where Barla's clarification is important. She makes it clear that while people are fighting against dispossession and environmental destruction, they do not wish to remain stuck in the past. It is worth considering whether Marx's remarks on Russian rural communes in his 1881 letter to Vera Zasulich might be adapted to find ways in which these forms of production can, through voluntary formation of cooperatives, 'turn over a new leaf without beginning by committing suicide' (see also Chapter 12).

In India the trade union movement has survived despite a very hostile envi-ronment, but it is disadvantaged by extreme fragmentation and lack of union democracy. A different model is offered by the New Trade Union Initiative (NTUI), a federation formed in 2006 by the coming together of independent unions reacting against the domination of unions by political parties or outside leaders. The NTUI thus represents an aspiration for trade union democracy, but also, by contrast with mainstream unions, its charter expresses the determina-tion to fight against all forms of oppression (class, gender, caste, race) and for social security, secularism, and democratisation of the state and society. Bringing together urban, rural, industrial, agricultural, domestic and forest workers as well as formal and informal employees, the NTUI attempts to bridge divisions in the working class and has an explicitly internationalist agenda. An important element in the emergence of the NTUI was the attempt to form workers' co-operatives, and this remains one of its goals (Hensman, 2011: 118–61).

In thousands of struggles across India, goals are set and organisations built by working people in consultation with middle-class activists who contribute their knowledge of English, legal and other skills, and contacts. It would be impossible to bring these groups under a single organisation, and this would in any case destroy their autonomy – the source of their strength. However, creating a shared (broadly Marxist) critical understanding of capitalism and the importance of working towards an alternative system is a realistic goal. Recognising the need for internationalism would enable Indian workers and activists to see their struggles in a global perspective.

Select Bibliography

Asian Centre for Human Rights (2010) 'Mining companies are arming the Maoists'. New Delhi: ACHR. Available at: www.achrweb.org/press/2010/IND20-2010.html (accessed 23 June 2014).

Bannerjee, S. (2007) 'Moral betrayal of leftist dream', *Economic and Political Weekly*, 42(14): 1240–42.

Basu, M. (2013) 'The voice of Jharkhand', *Economic and Political Weekly*, 48(23), available at: www.epw.in/web-exclusives/voice-jharkhand.html (accessed 18 June 2014).

Chandoke, N. (2013) 'Globalization and democracy: the equivocality of a relationship', in K. Stokke and O. Törnquist (eds), *Democratization in the Global South: The Importance of Transformative Politics*. Basingstoke: Palgrave Macmillan.

Drèze, J. and Sen, A. (2013) *An Uncertain Glory: India and its Contradictions*. London: Allen Lane.

Gopalakrishnan, S. (2008) 'Hindutva and neoliberalism: fascism, free markets and the restructuring of Indian capitalism', *Radical Notes*, October, available at: http://radical-notes.com/2008/10/ (accessed 11 June 2014).

Hensman, R. (2011) *Workers, Unions and Global Capitalism: Lessons from India*. New York: Columbia University Press.

International Commission for Labor Rights (ICLR) (2013) *Merchants of Menace: Repressing Workers in India's New Industrial Belt*, New York: ICLR. Available at: http://www.laborcommission.org/files/uploads/2FINAL_Merchants_of_Menace_lo_res.pdf (accessed 23 June 2014).

Teltumbde, A. (2007) 'Khairlanji and its aftermath: exploding some myths', *Economic and Political Weekly*, 42(12): 1019–25.

CHAPTER NINETEEN

Musical Chairs on the Sidelines: the Challenges of Social Transformation in Neocolonial Africa

Baba Aye

On 25 May 2013 African heads of governments gathered at the Chinese-built headquarters of the African Union to commemorate the 50th anniversary of the formation of the Organisation of African Unity. The theme was 'Pan-Africanism and the African Renaissance'; the attending leaders called for greater regional integration and celebrated Africa's re-emergence as a global power. Yet while the ruling elite of the continent celebrate, the majority of workers and poor people have little but angst to show for Africa's half-century of independence, which has been filled with economic, social and political tales of woe.

The 1960s, Africa's decade of 'postcolonial' independence marked by the twilight of the 'Golden Age' of capitalism, had heralded high hopes for social transformation to the benefit of the masses. The 1980s, however, ushered in transformation of a different kind, that of neoliberalism, via market-oriented structural adjustment programmes (SAPs). This transformation gave rise to the African tragedy. As much as the popular quest for alternatives to oppressive social structures marked Africa's decolonisation process, however, so too do popular aspirations for alternatives to neoliberalism mark the new millennium and a real 'African Renaissance'.

Utilising the Marxist theory of uneven and combined development (UCD), this chapter provides an assessment of the problems and prospects for emancipatory development in Africa. It explores the complexities of Africa's historical transformation and the main trends of struggles for alternatives. These processes are not simply interpreted as the peculiarities of Africa, but as within the wider totality of global capitalism and social resistances. The chapter concludes by stressing the centrality of popular struggle for Africa's transformative development beyond neoliberal capitalism and towards working masses' self-emancipation. This gives rise to a conceptualisation of permanent revolution, which encompasses political revolutions and the achievement of reforms within countries as part of a wider international socialist revolution.

Framing the Forces Shaping Africa's Pursuit of Development

Africa has been on the sidelines of world development since the dawn of capitalism. In the 1960s decolonisation appeared to promise a reversal of this situation, but to no avail. State leaders and intellectuals have responded with various theoretical and practical alternatives to address the challenges of development over the last half century. Their responses have been shaped by two interconnected factors: the overarching structures of uneven and combined development, and popular movements from below.

According to the theory of UCD, social formations are totalities which can be understood only in relation to their parts which themselves become intelligible only with reference to the whole. In this sense, all development is combined. But development emerges in an uneven manner. The evolution of capitalism into its imperialist stage deepened uneven development globally. This process, as Trotsky explains, leads to specific combinations of different stages within 'economically backward' countries, with their overall development acquiring a complex and combined character. Africa offers a striking picture of such a complexity. Industrialisation exists, but it is largely underdeveloped and spread unevenly across the continent. Nodes of industrialisation exist alongside localities with poor productive capacities. Africa's prevailing agrarian economies are directly integrated into the world economy through associated processes of urbanisation and international trade. These processes have led to the development of a small but influential working class alongside a weak comprador bourgeoisie (a domestic capitalist class that benefits from integration with imperialism), which has proven incapable of carrying out the thoroughgoing destruction of feudalism, the achievement of real national independence, and political democracy.

Social movement is the field where contestation between and within classes occurs over hegemony in shaping the pathways of development. As Colin Barker argues (2013: 432), conceptually and historically class struggle precedes concrete class formation and consciousness. Class struggle takes place within historically specific national and international social, economic and political contexts that can enable and constrain the alternatives proposed and pursued by different classes and class factions. What emerges as development grows out of such contestations, becoming institutionalised novel forms within states and institutions. Development is never simply and foremost a matter of economics. In Africa, politics and ideology have played crucial roles in the quest for transformative development. These have been central for the popular movements fighting against both the established social groups and the prevailing worldview, as well as different factions of the ruling class.

Africa sits at the bottom of the global 'hierarchy of backwardness' in relation to development. Over the last half-century, however, this condition has given rise to 'an epoch of uprisings' spread over four protest cycles which we explore in this chapter: the post-war period of anti-colonial struggles; different waves of resistance to the economic crisis between 1970–90 and 1990–98; a period of increased social and anti-capitalist activism since the late 1990s, and today's processes of social radicalisation on the continent (Dwyer and Zeilig, 2012). The sections that follow largely mirror such a periodisation.

The Legacy of Anti-Colonial Struggles

The African anti-colonial movement took the form of 'national liberation' movements and was therefore inadvertently nationalist. This movement emerged in the wake of the organic crisis of world capitalism that stretched from the Great Depression to the end of the Second World War. It united virtually all classes and political groups of 'natives' in struggles for independence. As the movement emerged, it asserted the rights of Africans to liberty, equality, democracy and self-determination as embodied in the Atlantic Charter and the Universal Declaration of Human Rights. The movement was also inspired by possibilities of a more egalitarian society and economic development, which the Soviet Union appeared to provide. At the time, domestic capitalist classes were almost nonexistent as European colonialists had systematically blocked their formation. The colonialists basically saw Africa as a source of raw materials and as a market for European goods. Colonialist forces violently pacified local landlords and chiefs. Where local landlords survived, as in parts of North Africa, they eventually became commercial farmers. In other instances, colonial taxation forced poor subsistence farmers to become rural petty commodity producers of cash crops for the market.

The basic extractive function of colonial capitalism begat a working class of migrants from the countryside organised mainly around mines, docks, railways and the civil service. The workers came to form the anti-colonial movement's heart and soul, serving as its unifying and liberating force. It was however a budding petty bourgeois class of intellectuals that established the pro-independence parties. The budding petty bourgeoisie also took up arms, and provided leadership, when the movement faced repression in settler colonies.

Radical scholar Frantz Fanon described the African nationalist project as 'false decolonisation'. This is because the emergent domestic ruling classes both maintained and were sustained by the underlying capitalist structure of colonialism. This is most clearly so where the elites chose to integrate into global capitalism. Despite otherwise radical rhetoric, it was also the case in those countries where the bureaucratic elite appeared committed to delinking from imperialism. International trade, development aid and subsequently debt peonage integrated these new sovereign states on a dependent basis. In practice, the domestic elites focused on consolidating their material and political bases of power. Indigenisation and nationalisation policies became instruments for local capital accumulation, laced with corruption as a means of primitive accumulation in perpetuity.

As the material base of the nascent bourgeoisie expanded, competition between its different factions spurred political mobilisations of ethnic and religious divisions, leading, for example, to civil wars in Nigeria, Chad and Mali. Politically, popular mobilisations from below – once central to nationalist struggles – were no longer tolerated by the new rulers. Trade unions were initially incorporated, then when they tried to assert their independence, repressed by the state. The elites also crushed any peasant agitation for a greater share of the wealth they generated. The political norm became one-party states and military dictatorships, supposedly essential for 'nation-building'. This state of affairs was deemed justified by incremental, albeit minimal, improvements in the lives of the working masses recorded in the immediate postcolonial years.

Restructuring and Contesting African Capitalism in the 1980s and 1990s

Things took a downturn as the pace of growth slackened in the early 1970s and with the global recession in the mid-1970s. The rising global crisis dealt death blows to the burgeoning import substitution strategies of the new African states. Mounting balance of payment problems sowed economic crises nationally. Disenchantment turned into despair, triggering new mass uprisings. By the end of the 1970s and amidst crisis, Africa's social movement organisations had gained a better understanding of their countries' limited sovereignty in the global market (Dwyer and Zeilig, 2012: 37). Their strategies increasingly promoted the deepening of internationalist collaborations with workers' organisations and other anti-establishment forces in the advanced capitalist countries. The movement was not homogenous, however, evolving from strong radical Marxist–Leninist influences to new 'civil society' demands. Yet through the 1980s anti-SAP riots, it reawakened anti-imperialist discourses and politics from below, while spawning a new generation of middle class intelligentsia organised as NGOists.

These challenges also gave rise to new formal institutional responses. The Lagos Plan of Action (LPA: OAU, 1980) was one such response, comprising Africa's first regional development framework. The LPA was formulated at the crossroads of hope and despondency as the ruling class's attempt to arrest widening unrest, with anticipated support from the international community. But this was also the period when the neoliberal globalist project was being unveiled by the developed countries and international financial institutions, from which LPA proponents envisaged receiving supportive aid. The LPA's stress on exogenous factors, including the legacy of colonialism, for understanding and transcending Africa's continued state of underdevelopment did not draw tears of guilt from Western elites. However, this does make the LPA an ongoing inspiration for a diverse array of nationalistic alternatives on the continent.

By contrast, the Berg Report (World Bank 1981), written in response to the LPA, put the causes of Africa's underdevelopment squarely at the doorstep of its 'political class'. Rampant corruption, state dirigisme, rent-seeking and poor governance were cited. New loan and development aid conditionalities demanded the rolling-back of the state and new market reforms supportive of private-sector-driven economies. The report positioned neoliberal SAPs as the sole panacea for African development.

In practice, though, neoliberal SAPs deepened the crisis situation rather than ameliorating it. The implementation of SAPs led to a second wave of struggles for independence: 'Africa exploded in a convulsion of pro-democracy revolts that saw eighty-six major protest movements across thirty countries in 1991 alone' (Dwyer and Zeilig, 2012: 52). The failure of structural adjustment and mounting popular resistance gave rise to the 1990 African Alternative Framework to SAP (AAF-SAP) – the United Nations Economic Commission for Africa's proposal for a new trajectory of socio-economic development. Notably, the LPA core policy objectives comprised its point of departure. However, given the global consolidation of neoliberalism by this time, the AAF-SAP offered only a defensive agenda. The proposal rejected the underlying assumption of perfect market competitiveness underpinning neoliberal SAPs, but shied away from directly attacking, let alone rejecting, neoliberalism altogether. This middle-of-the-road concession sought a pragmatic balance between the public and private sectors, between capital and labour. As a watered-down version of the LPA, the AAF-SAP had no socially progressive or transformative impact whatsoever.

Through the 1990s the World Bank oscillated between continued dismissal of any developmental role for states in Africa (1994 and 1995) and 'bringing back the state' to address recurrent market failures (1994 and 1997). Such vacillations reflected wider debates on East Asia and views on whether the economic 'miracle' there could be replicated in Africa. Mkandawire's 'Thinking about developmental states in Africa' (2001) was an effort to refute these 'impossibility' theses (lack of ideology and of autonomy, and dependence syndrome). Mkandawire stressed the importance of the 'external conjuncture' for the collapse of earlier postcolonial growth successes. He also went on to challenge the developmental benefits of the international financial institutions' (IFI) market-oriented policies, which instead 'maladjusted' the African states. His influential article contends that developmental states are not unknown to Africa, offering a Keynesian, developmentalist thesis that a restructured state apparatus that can also create and tame a national bourgeoisie will deliver Africa from the ravages of poverty and underdevelopment. Mauritius and particularly Botswana were presented as successful examples of this model. Indeed, these societies became high to middle-income countries from the 1960s, also thanks to state intervention. Structurally, however, these societies remain backward, with a sharp gap between impressive rates of growth in gross domestic product (GDP) and Human Development Index (HDI) rankings. It is also crucial to note that these are thinly populated states, and their arguable trajectory of success can hardly be generalised.

NEPAD and Neoliberal Consolidation in 21st-Century Africa

The much-vaunted New Partnership for Africa's Development (NEPAD), formulated in 2000, is best characterised as a self-imposed SAP for the continent. As a model, the NEPAD seeks to deepen partnerships with the advanced capitalist states and BRIC countries (Brazil, Russia, India and particularly China). The underlying basis remains the hegemonic neoliberal 'commonsense' of the post-Washington consensus as institutionalised with the World Trade Organization's and other IFIs' conventions. At the international level, NEPAD represents an attempt at a trade-off with the advanced capitalist countries with 'good (neoliberal) governance' on the part of African leaders in exchange for foreign aid, debt relief and foreign direct investment (FDI). Domestically, NEPAD promotes private-sector-driven growth and increasing 'social dialogue' with non-governmental organisations (NGOs). However, within six years of NEPAD's adoption, President Abdoulaye Wade of Senegal, one of its key advocates, declared it a failure. This failure was partly because Western funding pledges were left unfulfilled and partly because promised economic developments did not materialise. On top of this, promised political improvements fell through, notably the 'African Peer Review Mechanism' meant to instil liberal-democratic values in Africa's ruling elites.

Perhaps the most unintended consequence of NEPAD was that China has emerged as a key partner of the African states. While Africa's place in global trade remains marginal, FDI from China has increased from about US$2.5 billion in the 1990s to $31 billion by the mid-2000s. China's trade with Africa grew by some 700 per cent in the 1990s, and by 2010 China was Africa's second-largest trading partner, making significant inroads into sub-Saharan Africa. To help institutionalise this emerging relationship, the Forum on China–Africa Cooperation (FOCAC) was instituted in 2000. Six years later the China–Africa Development Fund followed. China has subsequently become an important alternative source of credit to the World Bank and the International Monetary Fund, providing soft loans and generous aid packages. China's apparent policy of 'non-interference' in domestic issues of governance also makes Chinese sources of capital attractive to dictatorial regimes.

While there remains debate over the underlying driving forces, many agree that the new China–Africa relationship constitutes a major change in post-cold-war international relations. Trade unions on the continent have questioned the benefits to the working class of Africa's patterns of trade with China, the associated working conditions, and the labour relations found in Chinese companies (Baah and Jauch, 2009). China's imports from Africa are mainly oil, raw materials and timber, while Chinese manufacturers flood the African market with cheap products. As just one consequence local textile factories have collapsed, throwing hundreds of thousands of workers into unemployment. Low wages and abysmal working conditions – a problem magnified by the systematic repression of trade union rights – have become hallmarks of Chinese companies on the continent. Many African governments, however, tend to support the Chinese employers against the workers' unions.

China's economic expansion into Africa forms part of a third scramble for Africa. Unlike the first scramble between European powers in the 1880s, and the second between the United States and the USSR in the 1960s and 1970s, this third scramble includes developing countries, chiefly China, in stiff competition for resources. The form China's role has taken is informed by the form of US and Western European imperialism within and outside Africa.

The new and refurbished partnerships of the African ruling classes with the West and China alike do not offer any real hope for the qualitative transformation of the continent and the emancipation of its working people.

Africa's New Millennium: Between Reform and Revolution

African history has not just been concerned with the economic needs of global capital. The 21st century unfurled in Africa with a rebirth of popular resistance from below, driven by social forces coming from the church, the informal sector, human rights movements, grassroots ecology movements and development NGOs. These popular agents of change were each committed to articulating alternative visions of survival and democracy. They advanced the idea of development as a human right, and demanded popular participation in governance. While these movements have deepened in the wake of the 2008–09 global crisis, they nonetheless represent both continuity and rupture with the African protest cycles through the 20th century. These popular movements also embody contradictory unities of reformist and revolutionary trajectories.

During the 1990s the pro-democracy movement expanded democratic space in Africa, providing niches for sustained activism to flourish. Its 'failure' radicalised ideas of alternatives. The trade unions became notably emboldened, and mass strikes were more frequent as the threat of banning unions subsided. In North Africa, new independent unions emerged and challenged practices of labour incorporation. For their part, petty bourgeois radicals (many of whom had been Marxist–Leninists before the fall of the USSR) and careerists alike spawned myriad NGOs, expanding the scope of development issues to include environmental degradation, climate change and gender mainstreaming. The rise of the Social Forum movement and the post-Seattle 'another world is possible' called activists to develop closer reciprocal linkages and internationalist perspectives of struggles within and beyond Africa.

The unions, popular organisations and coalitions, and social networks comprising this heterogeneous movement crafted a new repository of communiqués, resolutions, memorandums (to states) and proposed alternative national and pan-African development agendas. Most of these alternative proposals aspire to reform the capitalist system. This is not surprising, since the dominant ideology in society tends to be that of the ruling class. Furthermore, NGO funding and technical support derived mainly from social-democratic (and even liberal) donors in the West promote proposal-driven activism. Similarly, the reformist programmes of Global Union Federations and allied 'solidarity support organisations' can heavily constrain trade unions' perspectives in 'normal' times.

Strikes, processions, rallies, leafleting and other forms of mass mobilisation, however, have challenged from below the limitations of quasi-liberal democracy. Where revolutionary openings have burst out from these, they have started with demands for reforms or redress that 'the people want'. Where the confrontation between the state and the people has intensified, this has led to more radical demands for regime change, as in North Africa. The decisive element of victory for the popular movement is self-activity of the working class.

Working class revolutionary potentials do not just materialise on the eve of revolutionary moments, as labour militancy develops capacity over the years. The trajectory of and struggle for social transformation involves and is reinforced by the transformation of the actors in pursuit of change. Within the working class, and other social groups that constitute these actors, there are tensions between their rank and file and their institutional expressions, as well as between moderate and radical factions. These take many forms, such as increasing wildcat strikes, splits and the formation of new radical unions, organisations, parties, alliances and coalitions, and the possible foisting of more radical agendas onto reluctant leaderships. Combinations of these lead to momentous turning points that deepen the process of the revolutionary movement's self-awareness and actions. When these occur in the leading countries within subregions they could kick off conflagrations of popular movements, as in the Egyptian revolution for the Middle East and North Africa region (see Chapter 20).

The 2012 massacre of 34 striking miners in Marakana was such a moment in South Africa. The miners had formed a new union (the Association of Mineworkers and Construction Union, AMCU), breaking from the National Union of Mineworkers which had ties to the ANC government, and had become increasingly militant. In the wake of the Marakana massacre, the Economic Freedom Fighters party of Julius Malema found greater resonance for its radical rhetoric of nationalisation and economic justice. More significantly for revolutionary-transformative politics, however, might be the withdrawal of support from the ANC by the 340,000 member-strong National Union of Mineworkers of South Africa (NUMSA). The united front the Union is forging via protest marches and strikes can expand radical frontiers from below. This is especially so in a country that has witnessed the largest number of strikes and protests in the world over the last six years.

South Africa is not alone. The January 2012 uprising in Nigeria was a fleeting revolutionary moment, but one that has left lasting impressions. The movement's demand from below was becoming one for regime change. This frightened the trade union bureaucracy into calling off a massive general strike on its eighth day. The consequent seething anger was palpable on the streets and in the workplaces, sparking a subsequent spread of strikes across virtually all sectors. Inspired by the new mood of resistance after the January 2012 revolts, the Joint Action Front (the civil society component of the Labour Civil Society Coalition which includes the two trade union centres) adopted socialism as its core aim during its Third Congress in March 2013.

The challenge remains how to handle the trade-offs between the relative priorities of plausible short-term reform and the necessary claims of long-term structural transformation in understanding what is 'radically possible'. This handling has everything to do with what is considered the long-term goal. Before the Soviet Bloc's collapse and the fall of dictatorial nationalist parties and military juntas claiming to be Marxist–Leninist in Africa, the idea was fairly popular that socialism would be the long-term manifestation of social transformation. The verdict of a 1987 national debate in Nigeria, for example, was that the mass of the population favoured socialism as the system best able to ensure socio-economic and political development. The military government suppressed the report on the debate. Likewise, the anti-apartheid struggle in South Africa popularised the slogan 'Socialism is the future, fight for it now.'

Reform and revolution remain a constant tension in Africa. Moderate NGOs continue to pursue reformist projects and goals much like the Millennium Development Goals. More radical and long-term strategies nonetheless emanate from other civil society organisations (CSOs) and the working class. At the moment, however, the dominant tendency remains nationalist-reformist. One of the best-articulated national-reformist alternative views, which is winning growing support as a possible model beyond Southern Africa, is the South African Trade Union Coordination Council's 'Alternatives to Neoliberalism in Southern Africa' (ANSA) founded in 2003. This model materialised as a subregional project and found support from some social democratic foundations in Western Europe as an extension of the Zimbabwean unions' project on alternatives to SAP.

ANSA is conceived of as a self-determination project. Ideologically, it draws from a range of sources and experiences, including classic theories of under-development, comparative developmental lessons (including from China), and recent mainstream ideas including institutional economics, poverty analysis and new growth theory. ANSA perceives globalisation as an imperialist project precluding a future to most Africans. It argues that it cannot be known whether the alternative will be socialism or some other system. In this context the ANSA model is meant to provide a 'people-led' strategy for autocentric development which aims to foster grassroots-led regional integration, active popular mobilisation, sustainable development, women's empowerment, wealth redistribution, and new job opportunities in the formal sector. To achieve this model of holistic development, ANSA proposes the strategic and selective delinking of Africa from processes of neoliberal globalisation in order to negotiate a relinking, but under fundamentally different global production and distribution conditions.

Interestingly, although ANSA is conceptualised by trade union intellectuals, it disagrees with Marxian approaches that situate the working class as the vanguard force against capitalism. Reasons given include the decline of working class organisation and strength and the negative experiences of the Chiluba administration in Zambia. Chiluba's social base came from the unions and workers, but his administration aggressively pursued privatisation and was deeply corrupt. Furthermore, ANSA argues that the North–South contradiction in Africa likely overshadows classic capital–labour antagonisms. Consequently, the nation-state emerges as the most practical and strategic social unit for the advancement of the people's self-determination (Kanyenze, Kondo and Martens, 2006: 463–4).

These state-centric perspectives flounder in the face of facts. For one, the North–South contradiction is sustained within the context of a world capitalist market. For another, many anti-imperialist revolutions from below have been waged within nation-states in order to challenge local elites and domestic capital, including those who claim to have anti-imperialist credentials. Working class agency has been a key lever of change in these, as illustrated in the recent revolutions in Tunisia and Egypt (Aye, 2012: 59–68). Finally, the lack of a strategy beyond capitalism means accepting the confines of capitalism.

While ANSA makes an important contribution to the discourse of building alternatives, socialism must figure centrally in a non-capitalistic pathway for Africa's transformation. While reformist agendas recognise and promote mass mobilisation, they hold firmly to ideas that the state, not the struggling working class, must be the central agent of change and motive force of development. This is conceived of in a technical way, as if development itself would erase the 'backwardness' of the African people (Mamdani, 1995: 253). These agendas also lose sight of an important lesson from earlier nationalist-reformist experiments in Africa: that state power 'reflects not only, or even mainly, the national economic base on which it rises, but the supra-national character of the world economy today' (Cliff, 1963).

To be sure, reforms to capitalism can benefit the working majority by increasing their power and influence. Consequently Marxists, radicals and revolutionaries fight for and defend reforms that curtail poverty, increase equality and promote democratisation in all social spheres. Yet this should not blind activists to the dangers of reformism, or as Rosa Luxemburg warned against, the implicit or explicit view that socialism can be realised through social reforms. The capitalist classes have never willingly surrendered their power to working classes simply because the development of productive forces has outstripped the socio-economic relations they represent. In this sense, socialism is not merely an 'option' among alternatives; rather it can be established only through social revolution. In this, Trotsky's perspective on permanent revolution provides an appropriate theoretical and political strategy for oppressed peoples in Africa and the Global South. In this conceptualisation, socialist revolution can only triumph at an international scale. The deepening of capitalism's systemic crisis in Africa and globally, while not automatically determining the emergence of anti-systemic social forces, may open new horizons of struggle for revolutionary transformations to unfold.

Conclusion

The high hopes for social transformation with formal African independence have been frittered away for the immense majority of Africans. While resource-rich countries have witnessed significant growth in the past half-century, poverty and inequality are rising as intra-elite competition has furthered wars and political instability. There are both exogenous and endogenous factors behind this pitiable state. Imperialism still holds sway in a neocolonial form, using capital flight, structural adjustment, unequal terms of trade and at times direct military presence to subordinate African societies. In this context, the idea of a democratic developmental state has gained popularity as the centrepiece of most alternatives for structural change beyond neoliberalism. But these remain locked in illusory national-reformist propositions of delinking from globalist neoliberalism. These reformist proposals lose sight of the combined nature of Africa's underdevelopment within the overarching structures of global capitalist development. Through it all, the ruling elites in Africa enjoy wealth and the fullest fruits of capitalist 'development'.

It is critical to signal, finally, that the 'state' must always be understood in the light of underlying social class and power relationships. Working people cannot simply accept the capitalist state as is, and restructure it for emancipatory development. Rather, social struggles must create a new form of state that entails the utmost popular democracy from below. A new democratised state would be characterised by placing the production and distribution of goods and services under the control of working people's collectives, in both the urban centres and rural areas.

It is absolutely central to build social movements that fight not for renewal of the 'nation' or for 'real' independence, delinked from the capitalist world, but for revolutionary change rooted in an international struggle for socialist transformation. On the continent, the seeds of such movements are germinating in the three largest political economies: Egypt, in the grip of a revolution; Nigeria, with the rebirth of mass socialist politics; and South Africa, against the ex-national liberation movement. Their successes would have ripple effects across Africa and indeed the world.

Select Bibliography

Aye, B. (2012) *Era of Crises and Revolts*. Ibadan, Nigeria: Solaf.

Baah, A. Y. and Jauch, H. (eds) (2009), *Chinese Investments in Africa: A Labour Perspective*. Windhoek: African Labour Research Network.

Barker, C., Cox, L., Krinsky, J. and Nilsen, A. G. (eds) (2013) *Marxism and Social Movements*. Leiden: Brill.

Cliff, T. (1963), 'Permanent revolution', *International Socialism*, 12, available at: www. marxists.org

Dwyer, P. and Zeilig, L. (2012) *African Struggles Today: Social Movements since Independence*. Chicago, Ill.: Haymarket.

Kanyenze, G. Kondo, T. and Martens, J. (eds) (2006) *The Search for Sustainable Human Development in Southern Africa*. Harare: ANSA.

Mamdani, M. (1995) *Citizen and Subject: Contemporary Africa and the Legacy of Late Colonialism*. Princeton, N.J.: Princeton University Press.

Mkandawire, T. (2001) 'Thinking about developmental states in Africa', *Cambridge Journal of Economics*, 25(3): 289–314.

Organization for African Unity (OAU) (1980) *Lagos Plan of Action for the Economic Development of Africa 1980–2000*, Addis Ababa: OAU. Available at: http://labordoc.ilo.org/record/210754 (accessed 23 June 2014).

Trotsky, L. (1906) *Results and Prospects*, available at www.marxists.org

Trotsky, L. (1930) *Permanent Revolution*, available at www.marxists.org

World Bank (1981) 'Accelerated development in sub-Saharan Africa: a plan for action.' Washington DC: World Bank.

Zeilig, L. (ed.) (2009) *Class Struggle and Resistance in Africa*. Chicago, Ill.: Haymarket.

CHAPTER TWENTY

Challenging Neoliberalism
in the Arab World

Adam Hanieh

From the vantage point of late 2013, the clash of revolutionary and counter-revolutionary processes is perhaps nowhere more sharply posed than in the Arab world. Beginning with the revolts of 2011, which led to the overthrow of the Ben Ali and Mubarak regimes in Tunisia and Egypt, struggles against authoritarian governments have spread rapidly across the region. All countries have been profoundly affected by these movements, which not only threatened pro-Western rulers but also shook the stability of the state system established in the Middle East throughout the second half of the 20th century. At the time of writing, the immediate prospects of these revolts are unclear. Egypt is reeling from a bloody military coup that has brought a new wave of anti-democratic and anti-worker policies in its wake. In Syria at least 100,000 people have been killed by the Assad regime, with millions more displaced. Elsewhere across the Arab world, the demand for 'bread, freedom and social justice' remains largely unfulfilled, as governments continue to face deep-seated popular opposition.

According to the standard picture painted by many Western commentators and government spokespeople, the problems of the Arab world are a result of the stifling of capitalism by authoritarian regimes. The solution is a reorientation towards free markets and Western-style democracy. This chapter argues that, rather than too little capitalism, the reasons behind the uprisings need to be sought in the very nature of capitalist development in the Middle East. Of course, at the outset, the demonstrations were centrally united around demands to end years of nepotistic and dictatorial regimes, and they encompassed a very wide variety of social layers (including, in some cases, elements of the upper classes). But to concentrate on the surface appearances of these uprisings misses their real content. Factors such as imperialism, the nature of neoliberal transformation in the Arab world, and the pervasiveness of autocracy are all interdependent features of the way that capitalism has developed in the region. These factors are integral and essential parts of a totality, and exist through their interrelationship with the whole. It is not possible to separate or divide them from one another as discrete factors. Without confronting and overcoming this totality – capitalism itself –there can be no long-term solutions to the region's problems.

An important implication of this approach is that capitalism in the Arab world should be approached as a regional structure, not simply through examining what goes on within the borders of individual nation-states. There is a need to overcome methodological nationalist approaches, which, as Marcel van der Linden has remarked (2008), take the nation state as the basic, self-evident analytical unit for analysis. Cross-border or border-subverting processes are thus perceived as distractions from the 'pure' model. Understanding the specificity of capitalist development in the Middle East requires us to move beyond a focus on the national scale, to theorise the relationship between the national, regional and world scales. We need to map the ways these three scales are connected, and how this connection has structured state and class formation at the national level.

The chapter begins by tracing the development of neoliberalism in the Middle East, and its effect on various social groups and state structures. It then turns to look at the implications of the continuing global economic crisis that began in 2008, and the differential impact that the collapse of world markets has had on the region. The chapter concludes with a discussion of the challenges facing the left in building alternatives to neoliberal capitalism. It should be emphasised at the outset that this chapter does not purport to discuss the detail of individual countries or the experiences of specific revolts. The aim is to provide an overview of the way that capitalism has developed in the region, and possible paths beyond this social system.

Imperialism, the Middle East and Neoliberal Development

The most important feature of the Middle East is the region's absolute centrality to global capitalism. While the region has long formed a significant crossroads of trade and strategic influence, the discovery of the Middle East's vast supplies of hydrocarbons in the early 20th century positioned it at the centre of world politics. In the period following the Second World War, the region's rich resources of hydrocarbons became of immense concern to Western states (Mitchell, 2011). Principal among these countries was the United States, which had taken on the mantle of the leading power in the Middle East as rivals of Western Europe reeled from the aftermath of the war itself.

The modern state system in the Middle East largely originated from the machinations of British and French colonial rule throughout the 19th and 20th centuries. These European powers had essentially divided the region between themselves as 'spheres of influence' – graphically encapsulated in the secret 1916 Sykes–Picot agreement. Following the Second World War, the United States inherited this state system and took ultimate responsibility for ensuring Western dominance in the region. This took place with the support of the former colonial powers, particularly in the Arabian Peninsula where a close British relationship with the Gulf Arab monarchies continued to persist up until the 1970s. From the late 1960s onwards, US power also came to rest primarily on an alliance with the state of Israel – established in 1947–48 with the expulsion of the majority of its Palestinian inhabitants.

It was in this context that Arab nationalist and left-wing movements developed through the immediate post-war period. Many of these movements took their lead from Egypt's Gamal Abdul Nasser, who came to power in a 1952 coup and inspired similar 'Nasserist' movements across the Arab world. Other prominent examples were found in Yemen, Algeria, Syria and Iraq, where nationalist governments took power and attempted to wrest control of their territories from regimes that had been closely allied with colonialism. A central feature of the economic model implemented by these nationalist governments was a form of statist development that prioritised domestic control of industry, the provision of employment and food subsidies for the population, and state ownership of land and other resources. These governments were able to improve living conditions, but were also marked by authoritarian patterns of rule that attempted to repress political movements that displayed any independence from the state itself.

This development strategy was still very much capitalist in nature, despite the nomenclature of 'Arab socialism' used by many governments of the time. It was made possible because of the particular configuration of the international system – notably the rivalries between the Soviet bloc and the US-led capitalist world – and was simultaneously a response to an upsurge in radical movements across the region. Arab nationalist thought and practice, however, rested on a contradictory ideology that consciously downplayed the reality of different class interests in the project for Arab unity (Amin, 2010). In its dominant forms, this orientation actually prioritised the development of national capitalist classes through state support and protection.

By the early 1970s, this development strategy ran into clear difficulties. The increase in oil prices for oil-importing countries following the 1973 global economic slump, the cost of maintaining subsidised foods, rising debt levels, and the prodigious military expenditure associated with continuing conflicts in the region (notably the successive wars with Israel) placed considerable pressures on Arab governments. This period of crisis, by no means unique to the Arab world, ushered in the opening phases of neoliberalism. Backed by promises of financial support from Western states, the World Bank, the International Monetary Fund (IMF) and the Gulf Arab countries, Arab governments began to turn away from state-led economic models and embrace policies such as privatisation, deregulation of labour markets, and opening up to foreign trade and financial flows.

The experience of the Arab world confirms that neoliberalism is not simply a set of economic policies, but rather an attempt to reconstitute and strengthen the power of ruling classes through the defeat and fragmentation of labour and other social forces. For this reason, the turn towards neoliberalism was carried out under the heavy-hand of authoritarianism, which targeted repeated waves of popular protest against the new policy measures, including large-scale demonstrations, labour and student strikes. Indeed, several of the regimes that were to be overthrown in 2011 had their origins in this period as architects of structural adjustment programmes. In Tunisia, for example, the coming to power of Ben Ali in a 1987 coup marked the real commencement of neoliberalism. Likewise Egypt's Hosni Mubarak, who became president in 1981 following the assassination of his predecessor Anwar Sadat, was warmly endorsed by the IMF and World Bank, and eventually signed a structural adjustment plan in 1991. In Morocco and Jordan, repressive monarchies led the implementation of neoliberal measures, authorising violent crackdowns on those protesting about the onset of liberalisation in the 1980s. Authoritarianism was the midwife of neoliberalism.

The Contours of Neoliberal Reform

The main features of neoliberal reform in the Arab world closely resemble those found in other parts of the globe. Key among these policies were the liberalisation of ownership laws, particularly in the real estate, financial and telecommunication sectors; opening up to foreign investment flows; privatisation of state-owned industries; restructuring of tax regimes; labour market deregulation; and the relaxation of trade barriers. The changes that ensued as a result of these policies had a deeply transformative effect on the nature of class and state. They have also propelled a realignment of accumulation patterns within the region, and the linkages between the region and the world market.

One highly significant consequence of these policies was a change in the characteristics of rural life – notably land ownership patterns and the nature of agricultural production (Hanieh, 2013). This is particularly true in the North African countries of Morocco, Tunisia and Egypt, where a key focus of neoliberal reform has been the commodification of land – dismantling systems of tribal or collective property rights, removing any ceilings on rent or rights to tenancy, and turning state land into a privately owned commodity that can easily be bought and sold. Alongside the new laws that governed this commodification, price caps on agricultural inputs such as fertilisers, pesticides and water were lifted, and production was to be increasingly aimed at export markets. These policies meant that it became increasingly difficult for farmers to survive on the land, and led to a growing concentration of land ownership as farmers sold their properties to richer landowners or agribusiness companies. By 2004, the Middle East and North Africa (MENA) region was the second most unequal region for land ownership in the world, just behind Latin America and the Caribbean (for a more detailed analysis, see Hanieh, 2013, ch. 4).

The severe pressure placed on rural livelihoods as a consequence of these changes has been a crucial contributing factor to internal and international migration flows. Egypt and Morocco stand out in this regard, as the first and third-largest recipients of remittances from overseas workers of all countries in the Middle East between 1970 and 2008. As families lost the ability to sustain themselves on the land, many also migrated to nearby urban conurbations. In Morocco and Tunisia, the proportion of the population living in rural areas dropped by close to 20 per cent from 1970 to 2010. One of the outcomes of this rural to urban migration has been the growth of sprawling urban slums, located at the edges of cities and populated by millions of individuals engaged in informal work and day-to-day attempts at survival. These slums carry major political significance, altering the geography of urban spaces and pushing questions of housing, infrastructure and informal work to the front of debates around the nature of city life.

Other neoliberal policies were aimed at the privatisation of state-owned enterprises and the deregulation of labour markets (making it easier to fire workers and employ people on short-term contracts). These further contributed to a general deterioration in living conditions, which is reflected in consistently high unemployment figures. The official unemployment rates in Egypt, Jordan, Lebanon, Morocco, Syria and Tunisia averaged 11 per cent in 2008, the highest rate of any region worldwide. Moreover, these figures are highly misleading as they exclude the large number of individuals who are not seeking work. Young people represent a very large share of the total unemployed, exceeding 40 per cent in each of these five countries and reaching around 60 per cent in Egypt and Syria. Prior to the recent global economic crisis, this figure was among the largest of any region in the world. With regard to poverty levels, the proportion of the population without the means to acquire basic nutrition and essential non-food items (the 'upper poverty line') averaged close to 40 per cent across Jordan, Morocco, Syria, Tunisia, Mauritania, Lebanon, Egypt and Yemen (Achcar, 2013: 31; based on data collected from 2000 to 2006).

Alongside rural to urban migration, labour market policies have further reinforced the growth of the informal sector. In Egypt, Morocco and Tunisia, between 40 and 50 per cent of all non-agricultural employment is in the informal sector, a figure that is among the fastest-growing of any place on the planet. Three-quarters of new labour market entrants in Egypt from 2000–05 joined the informal sector, up from only one-fifth in the early 1970s (Hanieh, 2013).

But neoliberal policies have not had a uniformly negative affect on all layers of the Arab world. Accompanying the spread of poverty, these policies simultaneously led to a growing concentration of wealth in the hands of large business conglomerates, which benefited from privatisation efforts, liberalisation of capital inflows, and policies aimed at private-sector growth. One indication of this private accumulation can be seen in the growth of stock markets. In Egypt, for example, the average size of a company listed on the country's stock exchange grew more than 1,100 per cent from 2001 to 2007. Total market capitalisation rose by 700 per cent to reach 86 per cent of gross domestic product (GDP), up from 30 per cent in 2001. Companies controlled by just seven families represented more than 20 per cent of the country's entire stock exchange capitalisation in 2008. In Jordan and Morocco, the sizes of the stock markets increased by 600 and 500 per cent respectively, and also demonstrated pronounced concentration. In Syria, the private sector represented around 60.5 per cent of GDP by 2007, up from 52.3 per cent in 2000. Two major holding companies dominated this private sector, both fed through state contracts and close links to the Assad regime. The pattern is repeated across the region.

At the same time as the concentration of wealth proceeded within individual countries, the neoliberal period also witnessed the growing power of capital groups connected to the Gulf Arab states. This is an extremely important trend, and confirms that an understanding of capitalism in the Middle East must take into account the increasing significance of the regional scale, particularly the Gulf, to processes of national class and state formation. Flush with accumulated surpluses from the oil price rise of the 2000s, Gulf investors have been major purchasers of privatised assets throughout the region. Indeed, the number of foreign investment projects in the Middle East announced by investors from the Gulf Arab states was greater than any other source from 2003 to 2009. Most of these investments targeted countries in the Mediterranean area, Jordan, Lebanon, Egypt, Palestine and Syria. For these five countries, Gulf investments were more than three times those of the European Union and twelve times those of North America. From 2008 to 2010, the Gulf as a whole was the top-ranked source of total FDI for Egypt, Jordan, Lebanon, Libya, Palestine and Tunisia – surpassing investment flows from the United States, United Kingdom, China and any other European country. This internationalisation of Gulf capital is one factor behind the Gulf's increasingly prominent role in the aftermath of the Arab uprisings.

The Impact of the Global Crisis

With the eruption of the global financial crisis in 2008–09, many commentators were initially fairly sanguine about its possible impact on the Middle East. The source of this optimism was the region's relatively high GDP growth rates, which persisted in the immediate wake of the crisis. Following a visit to Egypt in February 2010, for example, the IMF claimed that the country had been 'resilient to the crisis' because of sustained and wide-ranging reforms since 2004. Of course, exactly one year later, the country would witness the largest and most significant protest movement for generations, in large part a direct consequence of the same 'sustained and wide-ranging reforms'.

What the IMF ignored were the highly polarised outcomes of neoliberalism itself. In reality, much of the region's population were enduring a state of prolonged and permanent crisis prior to the global collapse – high levels of poverty (particularly in rural areas); a lack of decent, stable work; widespread labour informality; and a lack of any real social support mechanisms. These multiple and pre-existing social crises are the context in which the effects of the global slump should be mapped.

An important aspect of these pre-existing crises was the growing cost of food. Food prices had been on a general upward trend from the early part of the 2000s, but 2007 and the first half of 2008 saw a sharp rise in global prices. In the Middle East, where reliance on food imports has long been a striking feature of economic development, this rise in food prices had severe consequences. Inflation in the MENA region rose at a rate greater than double that of world inflation in

2007–08. Although global prices dropped in mid-2008 as the world crisis began, prices in MENA continued their upward trend, with the food consumer price index increasing 53 per cent in Tunisia, 47 per cent in Egypt, 42 per cent in Syria, 22 per cent in Morocco and 20 per cent in Jordan (figures from July 2007 to July 2009). Governments were placed under severe financial strain in their attempts to maintain already reduced subsidy levels, while for poor families, who tend to spend much of their income on food, escalating costs had major effects pushing more and more people into poverty.

The region's reliance on food imports was very much connected to neoliberal policies in agriculture, which had shifted production away from local markets towards export-oriented agriculture. Policies such as these also shaped the different ways in which the crisis was transmitted to the region. Three important aspects of this can be highlighted (drawn from Hanieh, 2013, ch. 7):

• The drop in global demand from many key markets (particularly those in the European Union) meant that much of the region's exports plummeted following the onset of the crisis.
• The drop in remittances from overseas workers, upon which many families are dependent, was also a very significant factor. Much of this overseas workforce was concentrated in sectors that were to be hard hit by the crisis, such as agriculture, construction and low-skilled manufacturing.
• Financial liberalisation during the 2000s had exposed many Arab countries to fluctuations in foreign capital inflows. The global crisis reduced these inflows significantly, notably for tourist spending and FDI.

But the impact of the crisis was not felt evenly across the region. Most important in this regard was the experience of the Gulf Arab states (Saudi Arabia, Kuwait, Qatar, the United Arab Emirates, Bahrain and Oman). These countries are largely incorporated into the world market on the basis of their hydrocarbon exports, and possess sharply different social structures from those found in other Arab states. Current account surpluses initially plummeted in the Gulf states as a consequence of the drop in global oil prices from July to December 2008, and a fall in foreign capital inflows led to a puncturing of asset bubbles (particularly in real estate) as investors moved capital back to their home countries. The most graphic example of this was the collapse of the Dubai real estate boom in 2008–09. Accumulated surpluses from the oil price rise from 2000 to 2008, however, permitted these states to extend support to large Gulf companies that were threatened by the crisis. Billions of dollars were pumped into real estate projects and the financial sector in order to avert a potential collapse of the large conglomerates that dominate the Gulf's economies (and are very often owned or closely tied to the state and ruling families). At the same time, the Gulf monarchies were also able to use their heavy reliance on temporary migrant workers to avert the most serious ramifications of the crisis.

In all these states, migrant workers constitute at least half of the total labour force. These workers are frequently low-paid and lack all political and social rights associated with citizenship, which is restricted to a small layer of the population. As a result of this social structure, the Gulf states could reduce the sizes of their workforce (and slow the hiring of new workers), without fear of the impact of unemployment. Migrant workers who lost their jobs had little choice but to return home, as residency rights are linked to employment. One impact of this was the drop in remittances to Yemen (by 17.7 per cent) and Jordan (5.2 per cent) during 2009. These two countries were highly dependent on Gulf labour markets.

In short, the overriding characteristic of the way that the global crisis was experienced in the Arab world was an increasing differentiation of economic and political power through the region. The Gulf states were able to emerge relatively unscathed from the worst impact of the crisis, while neighbouring countries faced deepening problems. This unevenness was accentuated through 2010, as oil prices resumed their upward trajectory. Syria, Morocco, Jordan, Lebanon and Tunisia all saw their oil expenditure bills rise between 21 and 63 per cent over the 2009–10 period. Coupled with continuing stagnation in tourism and remittance receipts, these trends put severe strain on many government balance sheets. The Gulf's dominant position in the region as a whole was thus greatly magnified in the wake of the crisis.

Alternatives to Neoliberal Development

Struggles against neoliberalism in the Arab world were present long before 2011, and the varied paths of the Arab uprisings confirm how important these pre-existing experiences were to constructing the social and political movements that underpinned the uprisings. In Tunisia, for example, rank-and-file committees had previously brought together workers, unemployed and students in the infamous 2008 revolt in the Gafsa mining basin. Although eventually crushed by the regime, the Gafsa revolt was a key moment of popular contestation, lending a much more radical character to the Tunisian workers' movement (relative to neighbouring countries) and helping to lay the basis for the 2010–11 overthrow of Ben Ali. Similarly in Egypt, strike waves through 2006–08 in the country's textile factories, as well as earlier attempts by workers to establish unions independent of the regime, are important parts of the explanation for the continuing centrality of the Egyptian labour movement to the post-Mubarak social battles. In countries where earlier experiences of struggle have been less prominent or more brutally repressed (such as Syria, Libya and Yemen), or where regimes have used sectarian divisions to strengthen their rule (such as Bahrain), the course of the uprisings has been much more difficult and more prone to Western intervention.

New forms and organisations of social struggle have continued to develop over the last few years. Following the overthrow of Mubarak in Egypt, independent trade unions emerged that challenged the state-backed labour organisations of the Mubarak era. Strikes across the country demanded increases in wages and restoration of public ownership, and also took up the slogan of *tathir* – the 'cleansing' of owners and officials connected with the previous regime. Through 2011, there were more workers' strikes and labour protests than at any other point during the last 60 years.

These labour struggles have continued even in the wake of the 2013 military coup, compelling the new government to make harsh anti-strike laws a centrepiece of its legislative initiatives. Alongside the labour struggles other social movements have also grown in the post-2011 context. Perhaps most significant are women's movements in Tunisia, Egypt, Morocco and Yemen, which have formed a key point of contestation with ruling elites and challenged repressive measures that attempt to remove women from the public sphere and political mobilisation (see also Chapters 9 and 21). Popular campaigns against IMF and World Bank loans have also emerged, helping to shift the public debate around the direction of economic policy.

One key lesson that can be drawn from the experience of the last three years is that there are no alternatives to neoliberalism that remain within the framework of capitalist development and the continuing reality of Western control of the region. A fundamental break with the logic of neoliberalism requires a challenge to both imperialism and the position of local elites who have benefited from the preceding decades. This necessarily means taking hold of the immense resources held by the handful of families and corporations that dominate the economies of the Middle East. This is not simply a moral question of reclaiming ill-begotten wealth, but is a necessary requirement for reorienting economic development along socially useful lines, and most importantly, for breaking the fusion of political and economic power that characterises all states in the region.

A lack of clarity on this point is a major weakness of the left and radical forces in the Middle East. In the name of Nasserism and Arab nationalism, significant parts of the left continue to advocate alliances with a so-called 'patriotic bourgeoisie' (*ras al-mal al-watani*) and the military–security forces that remain at the core of the state apparatus. The starkest example is Hamdeen Sabahi, a prominent Nasserist leader in Egypt who came third in the 2012 presidential elections with a highly respectable 20.72 per cent of the vote. Sabahi's electoral platform called on 'national capitalism to achieve its social duty' and he promised to support this through investment incentives and other initiatives. More recently, he openly supported the military coup of July 2013, which has led to the deaths of thousands following a crackdown on supporters of the ousted Muslim Brotherhood government. The repressive powers seized by the Egyptian military in this instance will undoubtedly be used against any future popular movements that attempt to reclaim the revolution's slogan of 'Bread, freedom and social justice'.

At the same time, the political forces associated with the Muslim Brotherhood (and similar Islamist movements across the region) should not be seen as representing any coherent alternative to neoliberal capitalism. Despite support from poorer classes, these forces are frequently headed by large business groups which have little interest in bringing about a real change to the status quo. Indeed, as the experience of the Muslim Brotherhood government in Egypt confirmed so sharply, these movements have promoted a continuation of neoliberal policies and accommodation with Western powers. The repression of worker strikes and other popular movements, the rush to accept further loans from international financial institutions, and the close alliance with pro-Western Arab regimes in the Gulf (most notably Qatar), are all indicative of the orientation of the leadership of these Islamist movements.

Building an alternative to either of these two poles is neither a straightforward task nor simply a matter of putting forward political demands. For a variety of reasons the left remains very weak in the Arab world, and opposition movements over the last 20 years have often taken the form of political Islam. A reversal of the neoliberal models of development requires a renewal of the left, built upon independent mass political organisations that are rooted in the urban labour movement, including informal sectors, as well as the rural areas. For the left to grow in this way it must address all the key social questions, most particularly issues such as religious sectarianism, attacks against women's social and political rights, and the pervasive racism often shown towards migrant workers.

Essential to this rebuilding of the left is the recognition that the regional scale has assumed immense importance to the way that capitalism has developed in the Arab world. Most notably, the internationalisation of Gulf capital has brought with it a qualitative increase in the Gulf's political and economic power. Although this process is marked by rivalries between the Gulf states – notably Qatar and Saudi Arabia – the Gulf as a whole retains a principal interest in the unevenness of capitalist development which has typified the neoliberal period. For this reason, struggles to reverse neoliberalism will inevitably come up against the power of the Gulf states. (Again, this was powerfully indicated by Saudi and other Gulf support for Egypt's military coup in July 2013.) Developing a political expression to oppose this regional dimension will be critical to any renewal of the left in the Arab world.

The Arab revolts were very much shaped by the reality of the global economic crisis, and there is a distinct possibility of a further downturn in the global economy. Such an eventuality will have a deep impact on the Middle East given its close linkages with the world market. For these reasons, the continuing attempts by the people of the region to reverse the political and economic outcomes of neoliberal development are an essential part of the global struggle for a different, and better, future.

Select Bibliography

Achcar, G. (2013) *The People Want*. London: Saqi.
Amin, S. (2010) *Fi Naqd al-Khitab al-Arabi al-Rahen* [*A Critique of the Current Arab Discourse*]. Cairo: el-Ain.

Hanieh, A. (2013) *Lineages of Revolt: Issues of Contemporary Capitalism in the Middle East.* Chicago, Ill.: Haymarket.

Mitchell, T. (2011) *Carbon Democracy: Political Power in the Age of Oil.* London and New York: Verso.

Van der Linden, M. (2008) *Workers of the World: Essays in Global Labor History.* Leiden, Netherlands: Brill.

CHAPTER TWENTY-ONE

Socialist Feminist Alternatives to Neoliberalism in Turkey

Demet Özmen Yilmaz

Despite increasingly prevalent discourses emphasising gender equality and support for women, the subordination and exploitation of women prevails within neoliberalism. Remarkably, as Eisenstein (2005) and Fraser (2009) argued, some feminist initiatives with the ostensible purpose of empowering women are not far removed from neoliberalism itself. By contrast, a socialist feminist project is an alternative to mainstream gender approaches (Holmstrom, 2003). Socialist feminism differs from other feminist perspectives because it emphasises the centrality of the social reproduction process in capitalism while making a radical criticism of patriarchal capitalism and neoliberalism, focusing on both paid and unpaid labour. This perspective gives prominence to and prioritises current political and social struggles against neoliberal and patriarchal capitalism.

In Turkey women have collectively organised around socialist feminist ideals, and against neoliberal and patriarchal capitalism. One such organisation, the Socialist Feminist Collective, aims to develop alternative policies and activities that contest and weaken the overall domination of capital and patriarchy. Socialist feminists' struggles are often realised on the basis of the principle 'we want our due back from men, state, and bosses!'

Focusing on the Socialist Feminist Collective, this chapter seeks to evaluate the policies affecting women in Turkey and to discuss possible alternatives. The first part of the chapter looks at some recent policies framed under the rubric of 'women in neoliberal development' covering both paid and unpaid labour. The second part explores the development, activities, political and social demands for alternatives by feminist movements in Turkey, notably the Collective, which have accelerated in the neoliberal period. The Collective's demands focus on an alternative family structure, an alternative retirement programme, and an alternative system for the division of domestic labour and care. By way of conclusion I discuss the centrality of women in the 2013 Gezi resistance.

Women in Neoliberal Development in Turkey

Despite its own internal nuances, a socialist feminist perspective understands patriarchy as an oppressive system of social relations between men and women, and argues that there is a strong bond between patriarchy and capitalism (see Hartman, 1981). 'Patriarchal capitalism' depends on the unpaid labour of women, and is the structure within which female labour is trapped (Acar Savran, 2013). This remains so under neoliberalism and the associated discourse of 'placing women at the centre of development' – the new market-oriented version of former 'women in development' approaches (see Boserup, 1970). Indeed, it is more apt to refer to this discourse as 'women in neoliberal development', where gender equality is considered just one of a number of rational economic inputs for capitalist development (World Bank, 2012). The case of Turkey is illustrative.

In Turkey, neoliberalism emerged in the 1980s following a serious economic crisis, and took root as a process of class struggle. As is the case in many countries, neoliberal transformation was not a democratic process but was initiated under military rule (1980–83), which oversaw a process of dramatic social, economic, political and institutional transformation. Neoliberal transformation aimed to roll back the gains of workers, and this process has had negative consequences for women.

Neoliberal transformation in Turkey meant the institutionalisation of anti-labour policies. These included the repression of real wages, cracking down on workers' social rights and political organisation, setting new limitations on union rights, and the fragmenting of the production process. In consequence, emerging 'flexible' working, subcontracting and unemployment conditions have impacted women especially hard. Yet at the same time neoliberal processes have increased the participation of women in certain sectors of the labour force, notably the service sector and home-based work. At a broad comparative level, nonetheless, Turkey ranks last among the OECD countries in terms of women's participation in paid employment, at 27.8 per cent in 2012.

Far from providing any substantive workplace gains, the sectors where women are employed are those where they are the majority of employees, and their work is low-waged, precarious and informal. What is more, in Turkey as elsewhere, neoliberal policies concerning women's work do not consider as a problem pre-existing and continuing unpaid domestic work and the structurally unequal sexual division of labour in the home. Women's 'productive' potential is valorised while their very real reproductive contribution is ignored.

In the first 20 years of Turkey's neoliberal transformation, substantive policies intended to support women's work were practically nonexistent. Only since the mid-2000s has there been any emphasis on gender equality and women's work. The limited efforts made have had little positive impact on the persistent unequal division of domestic labour or on women's paid employment. Still, neoliberal advocates emphasise that gender equality will serve to enhance the economy and reduce poverty. Key policies include promoting 'entrepreneurship', flexible working modes and more active female participation in the labour force.

Such neoliberal policies are mediated by the cultural, religious and patriarchal values and practices in Turkey. In this nexus we can see the contradictory aspects of the symbiotic coexistence of capitalism and patriarchy. As it tends to extend the commodification of labour, capital aims to draw women into the labour market as one strategy to reduce the cost of labour power while social reproduction continues to rely on the unpaid labour of women in the home (Acar Savran, 2013). Patriarchy, for its part, tends to keep women primarily in the home. To sustain patriarchal capitalism, then, the tension between capitalism and patriarchy has to be transformed in such a way as to reconcile the family with flexible and precarious work.

In Turkey, the discourse on 'placing women at the centre of development' represents the efforts of capital and state actors to overcome this tension by integrating women into the market while keeping them at home. Such neoliberal policy responses present women as 'entrepreneurs' who must individually assume the risks of market integration. This transpires in the context of already flexible and precarious employment and as an extension of women's unpaid housework. The neoliberal entrepreneurial woman in Turkey must simultaneously reproduce her conservative role as mother and wife. Contrary to the gender-blind promises of neoliberal idealism, placing women in development in Turkey intensifies pre-existing patterns of highly exploitative paid and unpaid labour for women in ways that reinforce their subordinate position inside and outside the home. Indeed, the employment policies introduced in Turkey to help eliminate the subordinate position of women are inadequate because the policies focus only on paid labour, on the basis of an abstract notion of equality, which rests on a presumed male subject. A closer look at the data on women in Turkey will help illustrate how this dominant discourse and policy response reinforces the unequal sexual division of labour at home and in the so-called market.

In Turkey, important limitations to women's participation in the formal labour market arise from the sexual division of labour in the home. In 2012, 61.3 per cent of nonworking women cited housework as a barrier to participation in the labour force. While men reported spending 0.72 hours per day doing housework, working women reported spending 4.32 hours. Combining working and non-working women, the average increases to 5.28 hours a day. Table 21.1 details the sexual division of housework in Turkey.

The same situation applies to care work. In urban areas the ratio of fathers assuming the primary care of their children is 1.4 per cent whereas for the mothers it is 88 per cent (WiS, 2012: 108). The lack and insufficiency of nurseries exacerbates the problem for women. In urban areas nurseries provides only 2.8 per cent of care, and most of these are costly private nurseries. So while neoliberal advocates want female participation in markets, policy makers refuse to take account of the existing unequal division of domestic labour. The result is an intensification of female exploitation. As female paid employment increases, so too does women's total workload, for as long as the sexual division of domestic labour exists (Delphy, 1984; Hartman, 1981).

There also remain barriers and obstacles to women's paid labour that derive from the underlying patriarchal structure of the Turkish labour market. Unemployment figures for women seeking employment remain very high. For

Table 21.1 Household members who do housework, 2011 (in percentages)

Work	Fathers	Mothers	Daughters	Sons
Cooking	5.1	94.7	11.2	0.6
Ironing	3.7	88.5	13.2	0.9
Laundry	2.7	93.8	11.6	0.7
Washing dishes	3.3	93.2	13.1	0.6
Sewing	2.3	93	10.5	0.5
Serving tea in the evening	7.4	89.5	16.9	1.7
Preparing the meal table	9.9	91.2	18.4	2.8
Daily house cleaning	4.4	92.4	15.6	1.2
Weekly/monthly house cleaning	4.7	90.9	15.4	0.9
Daily shopping	41.3	73.6	8.7	4.3
Payment of monthly bills	74.4	25.5	3.6	6.6
Small repairs	70.8	11.6	1.5	6.7
Painting the house	48	14.3	1.8	5.5

Source: Women in Statistics (2012: 107).

instance, in urban areas the female unemployment ratio is 15.5 per cent; the unemployment ratio for young females is far worse at 25.6 per cent (WiS, 2012: 81, 90). Female unemployment persists despite the lower wages paid to women. Men with comparable educational levels earn 16 to 20 per cent more than women (WiS, 2012: 99).

Women's employment in Turkey should be considered in the light of neoliberal flexible employment policies, which deepen gender inequalities by pushing women into precarious working conditions and by taking women's domestic unpaid labour for granted. This is apparent in the 2011 National Employment Strategy document. Women are envisioned as integral to new modes of work that include part-time working, temporary working, and fixed-term employment via private employment offices, teleworking, home-based working, on-call working and work sharing. These modes of flexible working are 'formal' but 'flexible', in a sense of 'flexible security' that benefits employers over women workers. While women often require greater access to social services, these new modes of employment restrict access to income subsidy and other benefits provided through the social security system (Toksöz, 2012: 38). Likewise, the Gender Equality National Action Plan promotes 'female entrepreneurship', a theme familiar from the Family Education Programme implemented by the Ministry of Family and Social Policies in 2012. Women's participation in markets is encouraged through mechanisms such as micro credit and targeted financial support, but these systems do not make allowances for women's continuing family roles.

The 2006 Social Security and General Health Insurance Law is another social policy subordinated to the neoliberal and patriarchal dictates in Turkey. While the law establishes a social security system, rights of access are determined by conditions of formal employment. This institutionally excludes women who are full-time housewives, home-based workers in domestic and care services, day labourers and agricultural labourers, even though all these categories of women require social services. The law also presumes gender neutrality, as it equalises the retirement ages for men and women. Women's unpaid labour in the home is ignored while women's dependence on husbands and fathers in paid work is reinforced. One possible consequence is that single and uneducated women over the age of 18 will be tempted to marry in order to get access to health insurance. At the same time the marketisation, commodification and privatisation of health services is driving up their price. In those families unable to afford the fees, caring for the sick and elderly will again be part of the unpaid work burden on women in the home.

In neoliberal Turkey, therefore, patriarchy and capitalism are reconciled to the detriment of women (Toksöz, 2012), giving rise to a form of women's oppression mediated by the specificity of Turkey's social and familial relations (Acar Savran, 2012). Women's oppression in Turkey has, however, encountered feminist resistance.

Women's Resistance and Socialist Feminist Alternatives in Turkey

While the first wave of feminism in Turkey extends back to the late Ottoman period, the second wave of feminism emerged after the 1980s. This wave of feminist activism started as a movement led by urban, well-educated women in mass democratic and leftist organisations. As in Europe and the United States, demands for birth control and family planning policies constituted the principal feminist discourses, buttressed by claims that 'we are not born but rather become women' and 'the personal is political'. At the same time feminists organised protests against violence, harassment and rape, and started campaigns such as 'Purple Needle' (a needle was distributed to women for use in case of harassment). During this same period, the feminist agenda began to challenge domestic violence, sexual harassment, forced virginity testing, the sexual division of domestic labour and patriarchal family structures.

A third wave of feminism in Turkey in the mid-1990s gave new prominence to questions of identity and difference. The voices of Kurdish, Muslim and lesbian women came to the forefront of the movement. Notably, the Kurdish women's movement embodied both the struggle for national identity and the struggle against the patriarchal family structure. As an evolving struggle, the feminist movement in Turkey has thus considered as a problem a wide range of complex gender roles. Women's struggles have also proposed important alternatives.

With the evolution of feminism in Turkey, distinctions within feminism have become more visible. Socialist feminist women, for example, have sought to break with other feminisms. They organised around the basic premise that women's emancipation can only be realised under socialism, not capitalism. To this end socialist feminist women launched a magazine titled *Sosyalist Feminist Kaktüs* (Socialist Feminist Cactus) in 1988. As was written in the first issue of *Kaktüs*, 'not only can feminism not be realised without socialism, but socialism also cannot be realised without feminism'. The authors of *Kaktüs* criticised more mainstream feminisms for not having a social project targeting political power (Acar Savran et al., 1988: 15–16). Although *Kaktüs* was published only until 1990, throughout the 1990s many socialist feminist women continued to engage politically in trade unions, in mixed organisations and in various feminist communities. This period is referred to as the 'independent feminism period'.

Following the severe 2001 financial crisis in Turkey, new and aggressive neoliberal policies had a profound impact on women. More than ever there was a need for a collective movement capable of considering problems such as the relationship between patriarchy and capitalism, and capable of developing an organised struggle against them. This period can be seen as a precursor to the foundation of the current Socialist Feminist Collective in 2008.

The Collective was founded by a group of feminists in Istanbul, and organised in five cities in the wake of the 2008–09 global crisis and associated capitalist restructuring. To protect corporate profits and bottom lines, managers looked increasingly to exploit women's paid and unpaid labour. Simultaneously, political neoconservatism rendered Turkish women more and more dependent on men and the patriarchal family (*Feminist Politics*, issue 1). Socialist feminism appeared to be necessary, if feminism was to be not merely a movement of resistance and rebellion, but one of offering real alternative futures for women.

Now in its fifth year the Collective has some 300 members. They include some of those feminists who originally published *Kaktüs*, and students, teachers, scholars, trade unionists, activists, paid workers, unemployed women, retirees, Kurdish women, bisexual and lesbian women, and women involved in other socialist–leftist or feminist organisations. In short, the Collective draws together a wide range of women who think that women's liberation can only be achieved by a revolutionary transformation of exploitative labour and production, sexuality and body, and conservative familial relations.

The Collective subscribes to a notion of feminism that does not reify differences and antagonisms between women at the level of identity. Identities are rather considered as constructed forms of femininity related to overarching structures of patriarchy, capitalism and other relations of domination. The Collective is structured as a political and independent organisation that prioritises actions focusing on women's paid and unpaid labour, violence against women, feminism and identity politics. It aims to protect the independence of feminist praxis from the internal dynamics of other male-dominated social movements based on class, ethnicity, religion and so on. The Collective also aims to keep feminist praxis independent of government and international institutions. Finally, the Collective refuses to engage with capitalist 'strategies' for either short or long-term benefits (Çağatay and Kocabıçak, 2012).

In 2009 the Collective began to publish a quarterly magazine, *Feminist Politika* (*Feminist Politics*) – distributed by the Collective's own members, street vendors in big cities, and by subscription – and online bulletins entitled 'Mutfak cadıları' ('Kitchen witches'), which explore current developments in women's labour in Turkey. The Collective has also organised campaigns under the slogans 'Erkeklerden alacaklıyız' (We want our due back from men), 'Aile dişinda hayat var' (There is life outside the family), 'Kadın cinayetlerine karşi isyandayiz' (We revolt against murders of women), and 'Kürtaj haktir karar kadinlarin' (Abortion is a right and the decision belongs to women). The Collective organises meetings and workshops around these themes, and promotes feminist solidarity through regular interaction with the Barış İçin Kadın Girişimi (Women's Initiative for Peace), Halkların Demokratik Kongresi (People's Democratic Congress), lesbian/gay/bi/transvestite/transexual (LGBTT) associations, and some other feminist or socialist democratic organisations.

In challenging patriarchal capitalism the Collective takes solidarity, rather than competition, as a fundamental point of organisation. Together with other feminist organisations, women's organisations, women from trade unions and socialist parties, the Collective is challenging the ruling Justice and Development Party's (AKP's) Women's Employment Law Package, which includes new regulations on women's labour.

In general, socialist feminist struggles target the three main perpetrators of women's oppression and exploitation: male domination, capital, and the capitalist state, around which campaigns revolve. Consequently, the Collective advocates three main socialist feminist policies that aim to move beyond neoliberal patriarchal capitalism: an alternative family structure, an alternative retirement system, and an alternative division of domestic labour and care system.

Alternative Family Structures

The campaign 'There is life outside the family' rejects uniform and patriarchal family structures imposed on women, and militates for the possibility of alternative lifestyles free of gender-based power relations. For socialist feminists, the patriarchal family reproduces gender-based power relations in favour of neoliberalism. The reproduction of the labour force and of new generations is realised through women's unpaid labour, as housework and childcare are understood to be women's duty. Poverty in these circumstances can be especially devastating for women. Prime Minister Erdoğan's discourse around having 'at least three children' and AKP attempts to ban abortion can be interpreted as part of a long-term policy to increase the population as a means of providing cheap labour for capital accumulation.

The 'There is life outside the family' campaign attacks Turkey's patriarchal capitalism in two ways. First, activists challenge the patriarchal family structure, because women's emancipation is impossible within the confines of the current traditional family structure. Advocating alternative forms of family not based on marriage and property might be seen as a radical, even utopian demand. Hence the campaign's slogan 'The family is not an indestructible castle' intends to help women challenge accepted, even imposed, ideas that the existing forms of marriage and motherhood are their sole options in life. Second, activists reject and protest against attempts to control women's bodies, such as government attempts to ban birth control methods.

An Alternative Retirement System

The path of feminist politics is through struggles for social rights. Yet when policies ostensibly meant to protect women are merely temporary and pro-market, these policies serve neoliberalism instead of women's emancipation. In Turkey, the retirement system is such a case. By and large women can only benefit from the social security system if they are dependants of men. At the same time women must make payments to the retirement fund, a fund that mobilises domestic and gendered sources of money in ways that support financialised neoliberalism.

Feminist opposition to public sector cuts on social spending and to the new Social Security Law has had an important effect on women developing new emancipatory demands (see also Chapter 9). As an alternative to the existing neoliberalised retirement and social security system, a feminist system of retirement would have women benefit from social security independently of men. Specific demands include extending women's access rights based on their labour in the home, including care of children, the elderly, the sick and people with disabilities. In this way a feminist retirement system would lead to some basic compensation for women's unpaid domestic labour. For paid working women, feminist demands include formal recognition of the systematic depreciation of women's income based solely on their gender. Corollary demands for just compensation include the payment of lower retirement benefit premiums while employed and the possibility of early retirement with full benefits. To be sure, these measures alone are insufficient, but such specific struggles are necessary components of the overall feminist struggle against patriarchal capitalism.

An Alternative Division of Domestic Labour and System of Care

Strategies seeking to break with patriarchal capitalism in Turkey must also seek to transform the unequal sexual division of domestic labour. Better public services, while vital, are alone insufficient for crafting an alternative organisation of housework and care. Substantive alternatives must pursue a non-gendered system of care, so that domestic and care work ceases to be the exclusive and natural domain of women. In this context, free or inexpensive and well-equipped nurseries for children, and similar care centres for the sick and elderly, would constitute a very real relief to women burdened with care responsibilities. Not only women but men too must be encouraged to work at these centres. In workplaces with more than 50 workers, male or female, feminists demand that accessible nursery services be made available. Because employers would bear the cost of the nursery, part of the cost of social reproduction would become the responsibility of capital. Other feminist demands are non-transferable father-hood leave and having men assume care work. In countries like Turkey, where the unemployment rate is high, the vocational training of caregivers and the formation of suitable conditions to encourage men to choose caregiving as a profession could also serve as a subversive practice.

The persistence of an unequal sexual division of domestic labour makes it impossible for women to have stable employment outside the home and achieve economic independence from men. For this reason, while criticising existing employment and social security policies, it is vital to frame socialist feminist demands as part of an integral whole meant to break the vicious circle of patri-archal capitalism in favour of women and their own choices regarding family, marriage, and the labour market (Acar Savran, 2012).

Women in Turkey and the 2013 Gezi Park Resistance

The Gezi Park resistance, sparked at the end of May 2013, started as a protest against the elimination of public space by the ruling AKP government to create new spaces for capital accumulation. The resistance also arose against the backdrop of the increasingly conservative government intervening in the lifestyles of everyone in Turkey, and it followed many other social struggles in Turkey, such as those against large-scale hydroelectric plants, 'urban renewal' projects, murders of women, and bans on abortion. The awareness generated by these struggles was a significant factor. The Gezi participants included students, service sector workers, white collar employees, artists, academics, lawyers, doctors, activists, environmentalists, organised football team supporters and the unemployed. Trade unions, socialist and leftist parties participated in the resis-tance, but did not lead it. The participants mostly organised via social media.

During the peak 15 days of resistance, the Gezi participants formed a solidarity network in Gezi Park. All people participating in the resistance were invited to take part in the meetings and forums. Their collective aspirations found expres-sion in the 'Taksim Solidarity' group, which included (among others) feminists, LGBTT individuals, Kurds, anti-capitalist Muslims, Kemalists (nationalists), social democrats and socialists. Prime Minister Erdoğan attempted to denigrate the collective spirit of Gezi by calling the resisters a few '*Çapulcu*' (looters). Although an important Marxist academic has argued that Gezi represented a mature class rebellion against the predatory aspects of capitalism (Boratav, 2013), a defining characteristic of the Gezi resistance was that it did not belong to, and was not coordinated by, any overarching party or political organisation. Gezi was and is a grassroots movement. A rainbow of alternative actions developed spontaneously amid the resistance. The cement binding together the disparate Gezi participants was their common antagonism towards the AKP and Erdoğan.

One of the most significant outcomes of the Gezi resistance was that women and the LGBTT community became visible as a political subject. Surveys show that at least half the Gezi resisters were women. No doubt not all the women in Gezi saw themselves as feminists, but all of the women resisters were reacting to the conservative discourses and misogynous practices of the AKP. Gezi became the social forum through which the increasing prevalence of women being murdered, male violence, rape and sexual harassment, and the everyday repression of women (from birth practices to clothing choices) found expression. It was not just feminists pushing back; many non-feminists and women with no political engagement found reason to revolt. This is why the most prominent symbols of Gezi are women (such as the famous woman in red).

Yet the need to organise feminist solidarity, where women do not 'other' each other, also became clear. Socialist feminists, other feminists and other independent women figured prominently in the resistance, united by the idea that the socialisation of peace cannot be achieved without women. Turkish, Kurdish, Laz, Circassian, Muslim, non-Muslim, Alevi and Sunni women struggled together in solidarity in Gezi. The Gezi forums became spaces where everyone had a right to speak. There existed pluralism without representation, while the 'give the right of way' (to consent to another idea even if you do not really accept it) method of feminists came to be used frequently in cases of disagreement. In cases where sexist slogans were used (often by sporting group fans), feminists responded by promoting the slogan, 'Resist with persistence, not with swearing'. Feminists self-organised to remove and erase such sexist slogans written on the walls as a collective political action. As a result, the Gezi resistance evolved into a practice of gathering women around a feminist discourse. Gezi also revealed that discriminatory and repressive practices against women are often closely related to the neoliberal destruction of public spaces.

While the Gezi resistance broke out suddenly, spontaneously, and without the leadership of any particular group, it grew enormously, drawing in the participation of many who had never before mobilised. In parallel manifestations countrywide, millions of people took to the streets. These resisters came personally to experience the struggle for alternative lifestyles, modes of existence, modes of solidarity and politics, which was made possible by the Gezi moment. The Gezi resistance restored hope by showing people that the struggle for freedom and rights is possible through solidarity and resistance.

Many believe that after Gezi nothing will be as it was again. Indeed, the collective solidarity of women in Gezi has prevailed beyond the peak of the Gezi Park resistance. Notably, women's solidarity against war is continuing, especially in Istanbul. Likewise, after the Gezi Park moment the spirit of resistance has moved into the neighbourhoods as yet another form of living, resisting social praxis. The Gezi resistance reminds us that every struggle has the potential to mobilise alternatives against our oppressors.

Select Bibliography

Acar Savran G., Paker B., Akdeniz N., Tura N. et al. (1988) *Sosyalist Feminist Kaktüs* [*Socialist Feminist Cactus*], Issue 1.

Acar Savran, G. (2012) *Feminist Politika* [*Feminist Politics*], 13.

Acar Savran, G. (2013) *Feminist Politika* [*Feminist Politics*], 18.

Boratav, K. (2013) 'Olgunlaşmış Bir Sınıfsal Başkaldırı: Gezi Direnişi' ['A mature class rebellion: Gezi Resistance'], in Ö. Göztepe (ed.), *Gezi Direnişi Üzerine Düşünceler* [*Thoughts on Gezi Resistance*]. Ankara: NotaBene.

Boserup, E. (1970) *Woman's Role in Economic Development*. London: Earthscan.

Çağatay, S. and Kocabıçak, E. (2012) 'Doing materialist feminism under contemporary patriarchal capitalism in Turkey: the Socialist Feminist Collective in Turkey', presentation for 9th Annual Historical Materialism Conference, 8–11 November. Available at: www.sosyalistfeministkolektif.org/aboutus.html (accessed 11 June 2014).

Delphy, C. (1984) *Close to Home*, ed. D. Leonard. London: Hutchinson.

Eisenstein, H. (2005) 'A dangerous liaison? Feminism and corporate globalization', *Science and Society*, 69(3): 487–518.

Feminist Politics (2009–13).

Fraser, N. (2009) 'Feminism, capitalism and the cunning of history', *New Left Review*, 56 (March–April): 97–117.

Hartman, H. (1981) 'The unhappy marriage of Marxism and feminism', in L. Sargent (ed.), *The Unhappy Marriage of Marxism and Feminism*. London: Pluto.

Holmstrom, N. (2003) *The Socialist Feminist Project, A Contemporary Reader in Theory and Politics*. New York: Monthly Review Press).

Socialist Feminist Collective (1988) *Sosyalist Feminist Kaktüs* [*Socialist Feminist Cactus*], Issue 1.

Socialist Feminist Collective (2009–13) *Feminist Politika* [*Feminist Politics*].

Sosyalist Feminist Kolektif website: www.sosyalistfeministkolektif.org/ (accessed 20 November 2013).

Socialist Feminist Collective (2011) Women's Labour Conference Book. Istanbul: Socialist Feminist Collective.

Socialist Feminist Collective website: www.sosyalistfeministkolektif.org/ (accessed 20 November 2013).

Toksöz, G. (2012) 'Ulusal İstihdam Stratejisi Kadınlar ve Gençler İçin Ne Getiriyor?' ['What is there in the National Employment Strategy for women and youth?'], pp. 36–50 in A. Makal (ed.), *Ulusal İstihdam Stratejisi: Eleştirel Bir Bakış* [*National Employment Strategy: A Critical Review*], Ankara: Türk-/İş SBF Sosyal Politika Merkezi Ortak Yayını.

Women in Statistics (WiS) (2012) www.tuik.gov.tr/Kitap.do?metod=KitapDetay&KT_ID=11&KITAP_ID=238 (accessed 20 November 2013).

World Bank (2012) *Women Development Report: Gender Equality and Development*. Washington DC: World Bank.

CHAPTER TWENTY-TWO

Uneven Development and Political Resistance against EU Austerity Politics

Angela Wigger and Laura Horn

In response to the current crisis, European Union (EU) institutions and Eurozone governments have adopted a range of regulatory and treaty-based measures to ensure fiscal discipline through limiting the capacity of Eurozone governments to run budget deficits and accumulate sovereign debt. In addition, almost all Eurozone governments have taken measures to deregulate labour laws, such as easing the conditions for employee dismissals, reducing minimum wages, increasing working time for less remuneration, or introducing new conditionalities and time limits for unemployment benefits, as well as a further decentralisation of collective bargaining more generally.

The imposition of EU austerity packages is essentially premised on regaining investor confidence, while labour market adjustments are meant to re-establish a 'competitive' business climate. Accompanied by a vast suspension of democratic rules, these neoliberal crisis recipes have fuelled considerable social unrest and political protests in many parts of Europe. Hundreds of thousands have demonstrated in Spain, Greece and Portugal against public spending cuts and changes to labour rights over the last few years. Coordination between trade unions and social movements also brought large demonstrations to the streets of Brussels in 2012 and 2013. There were further marches and strikes by health workers, students, teachers, parents, pensioners, and employees in the healthcare, pharmaceutical, automotive, shipbuilding and transport industries in many parts of Europe.

To facilitate concerted actions and new left-wing alliances across borders, several pan-European meetings have been organised over the past three years. Events such as Firenze 10+10, the Alter Summit in Athens, the European Blockupy actions and preparatory conferences in Frankfurt, the initiative for a European Spring, Agora99 in Madrid and Rome, conferences of the Euro Memorandum Group and the Strategy Meeting in Amsterdam, brought together around 200 activists and representatives from NGOs and other civil society organisations. This has led to a series of transnational campaigns, manifestos and petitions, as well as joint strike days and other event mobilisations such as weeks of action against EU austerity policies. New networks coordinating national and local struggles have been established, targeting issues of housing, public health, education, debt audits and the commons. Optimistic voices have consequently praised the reinvigorated 'left', suggesting that a political U-turn breaking with EU neoliberal crisis policies is near. At the same time, sceptical voices are also gaining ground, pointing to the inability of left-wing forces to articulate a coherent set of political demands and viable alternatives that could generate the support of and resonance with wider constituencies.

This raises the question to what extent the context of the crisis constitutes a historical crossroad, marking the beginning of a sustained and enduring pan-European resistance movement capable of translating and generalising local struggles, and pushing them to the EU level. This chapter analyses agents, structures and contradictions in the formation of left-wing resistance against EU austerity politics from a historical materialist perspective. It seeks to gain a class and subject-oriented understanding of social struggles and concomitant power configurations, the logics of action of different agents in articulating dissent and resistance, and particularly the uneven development and timing of the crisis and crisis responses. We argue that the coagulation and consolidation of an alternative agenda is far from being realised, and that the event-based nature of crisis protests provides insufficient grounds to draw conclusions about the composition and internal contradictions of different forces. The common conception that there is indeed a short-lived window of opportunity for 'change' in the context of the crisis, and that whether there will be transformations depends ultimately on the successes or failures of these emancipatory forces, is a dangerous fallacy. Rather, we would argue, we need to understand these developments in the broader context of hegemonic power relations within the European Union and beyond.

Counter/Hegemony – Perspectives on Social Resistance

Some historical materialist approaches tend to focus on the internal fractionalisation of national and transnational capital as the main determinants of neoliberal restructuring at the global or the European level (see e.g. Cafruny and Ryner, 2003). As a result of this elite emphasis, social struggles are frequently reduced to institutional arrangements, while the (re-)production of social power relations is ignored. The hegemonic constitution of the European integration project, supported by the ensemble of European state apparatuses, is implicitly considered to be consistent and relatively stable. Political opposition and dissent from non-hegemonic civil society groups renegotiating hegemonic power, and hence the possibility of a counter-hegemonic project, have remained analytically as well as theoretically marginalised. In order to understand the manifestation of new forms of social mobilisation and the dynamics of resistance in Europe, we need a perspective that allows us to analyse fractures in the emerging European state project. Social forces should be neither marginalised as concrete subjects, nor romanticised or fetishised at the expense of a deeper understanding of their socio-economic structures – as is frequently the case in analyses of 'new social movements' such as Occupy, the Spanish Indignados/M15 and Blockupy.

Based on the Machiavellian concept of the 'prince' and Gramsci's 'modern prince', the 'postmodern prince' typifies a new form of political action by multiple and diverse agents whose radical praxis not only challenges the politics of common sense, but also seeks its transformation. The 'postmodern prince' is not a collective actor, but rather a strategy or agenda of a collective political subject directed at constructing a more ethical, just and sustainable world order (Gill, 2012). Such a strategy or agenda supported by contentious collective action is tied to historically specific political, socio-economic and ecological conditions, without necessarily being anchored in class awareness.

At the same time we would argue that we can only fully grasp the nature of the ongoing developments through a thorough engagement with class – and hence the deeper structures of exploitation, consent and contestation that engender these social struggles. In the context of increasingly authoritative austerity politics, class becomes particularly important when focusing on the strategic relationship between organised labour and social movements which seem to transcend class issues.

Trade unions (as one specific form of worker organisation) here constitute a core, but also a problematic, actor in the European arena. Through institutional co-optation of trade union representation at EU level, organised labour did in effect concede to neoliberal restructuring in the 1990s and early 2000s. It is only in recent years that this complicity has developed into what the European Trade Union Confederation (ETUC), the umbrella organisation of national trade unions representing the interests of workers at the institutional level of the European state apparatus, now calls a 'critical friendship', indicating increasing scepticism about the European Union's social dimension. Moreover, the diversity and divergences of the national and sectoral labour organisations contribute to uneven responses to the crises, and threaten to stymie the potential of solidaristic, class-based struggles.

And yet, as mentioned above, we are witnessing an emerging form of protest, and more importantly, a formulation of alternatives that transcend this uneven dimension by highlighting the shared, combined nature of social struggles. Not being limited by national boundaries, such an emancipatory agenda can become manifest simultaneously beyond and within subnational and national settings. Importantly, conflicts and a certain degree of diversity in demands and identities are inherent. Thus, the agenda of emancipatory forces, or what Gramsci referred to as a 'collective intellectual', is by definition composed of 'a plurality of forms of the philosophy of praxis', because 'critical thought can neither be singular, nor imprisoned by practices of theoretical closure' (Gill, 2012: 519). Crucially, this also addresses the issue of methodological nationalism which is too often still prevalent in discussions of resistance and alternatives. The strategic question of where, on which terrain, these social struggles should be waged and alternatives be formulated, is indicative of this.

Instead of realising the transnational dimension, simultaneous developments and historical precedents of the austerity programmes in the Eurozone, many observers on the left have so far sought recourse in national strategies, taking an increasingly defensive stance against specific structural adjustment measures. This only aggravates the increasing fragmentation of movements and forces, rendering it increasingly difficult to rally in solidarity and on the basis of common interests. But as we argue towards the end of this chapter, it does not have to be this way.

Between the 99 Per Cent and the Avant-Garde: The Divergence and Convergence of Social Struggles in Europe

The discussion of the role and strategies of social movements is frequently unequivocally positively connoted, particularly in critical social science perspectives. In a context where hardly any achievements can be set down, scholars seem reluctant to research the idiosyncrasies and power asymmetries within social movements. Contributions in the media and in scientific analyses alike take as their point of departure the terminology of the 99 per cent, a term borrowed from the Occupy movement. This concept is however notoriously unspecific. Fewer than 1 per cent of people are actively involved in struggles against austerity, implying that 99 per cent still need to be persuaded and mobilised. The terminology of the 99 per cent presupposes moreover that the protesting forces have a monolithic composition and identical ideological orientation.

Historically, left-wing forces have always aggregated a disparate set of struggles, involving a plurality of agents with different degrees of indignation, divergent objectives and rationales for transformative action. Socialist, communist, anarchist, social democratic and environmental justice groups traditionally share a legacy of ideological antagonism. Ever since the gradual fading-away of the alter-globalist 'movement of movements' over the past decade, social movements have been increasingly disparate groups lacking a common strategy or coherent substantive criticism and political demands. Although the plurality of forces are united in a critique of the unequal distribution of wealth and a deep-seated dissent from the existing crisis management, another chasm has opened up with the advent of horizontalist social movements that have organised outside trade union structures and the institutionalised channels of parliamentary representation. Composed of a wide range of participating groups, they bring together previously politically inactive protesters who are far less entrenched in collective identities and common political demands than movements from the past. Although there is an emphasis on consensual politics and grassroots participation, there is no shared understanding of the trenches and fortifications thrown up by hegemonic forces, or an agreement on the tactics of how to overcome them.

The weakness and ideological fragmentation of left-wing forces, and the failure to chart an alternative future for Europe, are striking in comparison with the uprising of the European radical right, particularly the neo-populist and neo-fascist parties which successfully exploit feelings of discontent and insecurity, as well as a growing euroscepticism.

A range of studies situate social movements from the political left as genuine supporters of European integration – in contrast to the growing nationalist far-right sentiments and populist euroscepticism among citizens and political parties. Della Porta and Caiani (2009: 123, 125) for example argue that many left-wing groups within social movements merely criticise the specific political direction of the integration process, while still envisaging another, more social and democratic Europe.

In the past, protests targeting the European Union, such those concerning constitutional referenda and the large protest march in Amsterdam in 1997 against the Treaty of Amsterdam, took place only in domestic settings, and with specific remonstrations against national governments. The current protests indicate that social movements are increasingly addressing EU institutions and raising EU-related issues. Particularly in the context of the fierce austerity imposed on Southern Europe, many left-wing parties are now increasingly questioning the EU dimension, and most of all Eurozone membership. However, so far attempts to transnationalise anti-austerity protests have been rather limited in scope and have showed little success.

The pan-European solidarity meeting 'Firenze 10+10' in November 2012 is in many respects emblematic of the divisions of the left with respect to EU politics. The meeting, ten years after the first European Social Forum (ESF) and at the same location, was intended as a pan-European platform for organised resistance against the authoritarian neoliberal austerity politics of the European Union. Unlike previous social forums, which were committed to social inclusiveness and hence covered a broad spectrum of left-wing groups, Firenze 10+10 was intended to be much smaller in scale, seeking to bring top-level unions into a dialogue with social movements, including new and established political parties and party-affiliated think tanks and non-governmental organisations (NGOs) in the discussions. The idea was that locally isolated or fragmented movements with specific interests ('one-issue' movements) could combine their efforts in a new way and make transnational solidarity come into real existence.

The outcome of the meeting could not have been more disappointing. Vociferous protests by many participants about the procedures of the meeting prevented the issuing of a joint statement against EU austerity politics. Whereas the first ESF in 2002, which had more than 60,000 participants, has widely been considered a success, the Firenze 10+10 meeting, which was attended by fewer than 1,000 people, lacked resonance in the media and attracted little attention from the wider public.

European and transnational NGOs and think tanks are ideally positioned to act as hubs for left-wing alliances, but as relatively insulated avant-garde agents (protesters by profession), they face difficulties in switching between different action levels, and lack the capacity to trigger mass mobilisations. Better networked and better equipped with resources, while speaking multiple languages and travelling frequently, such transnational activists and their organisations tend to be disproportionately located in Europe's North. Their implicit orientation towards the EU terrain, and their limited ability to integrate into local movements, impede not only the formation of alliances but also the crystallisation of a left-wing hegemonic project. Ineligible to speak to people with concrete crisis experiences, they lack the necessary organic articulation and anchoring of alternative projects that would allow them to generate a comprehensive counter-hegemonic movement. As a result, they tend to produce abstract manifestos and position papers attacking neoliberal economic governance at EU level, such as those for the campaigns against the Fiscal Compact or the Competitiveness Pact, which seem doomed to silently abate.

More radical, locally oriented grassroots movements with an explicitly anti-capitalist orientation either stayed away from Firenze 10+10, or gathered at nearby autonomous centres. In the absence of such groups, reformist voices dominated, propagating post-Keynesian crisis solutions in the form of EU investment programmes to promote sustainable green (but still capitalist) growth, stimulated by the European Central Bank as a lender of last resort and a fiscal union issuing eurobonds. The elitist position of participating NGOs and the formalised conference character in which NGO-dominated dialogues took shape contrasted sharply with the disruptive forms of action of street protests and the assembly structures of grassroots organisations.

The increasing 'NGO-isation', which takes the form of a professionalisation and institutionalisation of social resistance through the participation of a politically rather moderate yet growing stratum of transnational activists, has been hotly debated in social movements and academic circles for some time. Similar conclusions can be drawn about the Alter Summit organised in June 2013 in Athens, where a few hundred people, mostly trade unionists and professional activists, gathered in 15 assemblies. They issued a short manifesto stating their most urgent demands. The Alter Summit went unnoticed by the wider Greek public, while the initial domination of Syriza in setting up the framework marginalised other groups. Ultimately, the unequal room for manoeuvre of social groups in the European Union is being reproduced in progressive movements.

The increasingly authoritarian constitutionalisation of austerity, at the expense of the consensual dimension of the hegemony in the EU project, could however be a potential focal point for contentious collective action. The demise of reformist social democratic parties and a growing radicalisation alongside crisis grievances and protest actions opens up new spaces for the left. A rapprochement of trade unions and social movements would be of particular relevance here. The dialogue between trade unions and social movements has traditionally been more conflictual than consensual, however, and remains beset by conflict in many parts of Europe. Unions, organised in hierarchical structures representing mainly the core workforce, frequently collide with the direct-democratic decision-making procedures and prefigurative direct action-oriented politics of horizontalist new social movements. Unions have furthermore been fairly well integrated into hegemonic structures through social partnership agreements, and more recently through revitalised crisis corporatism and new social pacts.

The ETUC has hardly voiced radical positions, although a slight change in position can be observed, particularly after national unions increasingly questioned its stance and associational power (Horn, 2012). Generally the ETUC supports reformist neo-Keynesian proposals for investment and development packages that stimulate demand, capital controls and the protection of labour rights, while falling short of a radical critique of European policies and a politicising of the contradictions and fractions within labour. There are clear tensions between more radical grassroots unionism and the bureaucratised decision-making structures, control of membership activity and agendas of traditional unions. Moreover, national divergence in economic and social conditions complicates the creation of a transnational trade union position.

The joint European general strike of 14 November 2012 did not spark an encompassing pan-European day of action, particularly as ETUC member unions from Europe's North refused to join. The structural weakness of organised pan-European labour within ETUC is however not only the result of internal divisions, but needs to be located in the context of the vast institutionalisation of organised fractions of industrial and financial capital at EU level. To overcome these challenges, the European labour movement will have to not only recalibrate its own position in relation to the European institutions, but articulate a strategy that can overcome the narrow interests of its core constituency and bind a broader coalition of social forces into a class-based, counter-hegemonic project for European integration.

Unequal Development and Political Resistance

The unequal and uneven development of the crisis has generated differences in austerity and crisis measures, which also impact the participation of left groups and unions in a transnational counter-hegemonic movement. Whereas general and wildcat strikes and mass demonstrations have occurred regularly in Southern Europe, no comparable dissent can be witnessed in Europe's North – despite declining real wages, increased precarity and growing poverty. The speed and sequence of EU crisis measures, and concomitantly the deliberate bypassing of democratic processes, have marginalised counter-hegemonic forces considerably, making it difficult to exploit the crisis politically for an alternative project. This raises the question how much room for manoeuvre emancipatory projects have left. Some commentators even suggest a complete reversion to the protection of national welfare state structures as part of a 'progressive' left nationalism or regionalism. The Catalan and Basque independence movements, the Celtic parties and the Irish Sinn Fein are examples of this. However, left-wing initiatives for enhanced autonomy have not led to broad-based support in Europe.

The often defensive nature of current social struggles against EU austerity is rooted in an almost automatic shielding of the status quo of institutional structures, and with it, the existing power configuration in member states. How such structures, including corporatist processes, have contributed to the uneven development in the European Union is frequently ignored in the process. These different positions engender different logics of action with respect to the terrain and targets of social struggles. Such divergences are however highly problematic in the complex power structure in the European realm: without a common understanding of what to target and at what level, social struggles remain isolated, almost arbitrary. In the context of authoritarian competition states, subalterns will have to focus on the transformation of institutional structures (Oberndorfer, 2012: 8). This concentration on the institutional change of EU and nation-state structures contrasts, however, with the contentious politics of social movements, which not only lack access to representative institutions but also seek to disrupt their polities.

The formation of a collective actor in the sense of a 'postmodern prince' and the formulation of a common agenda are impaired by the fact that there is no clarity about the challenges a pan-European movement is facing, and at whom social struggles should be directed. It should also not be underrated that the current developments of the 'new constitutionalism' (Oberndorfer, 2012), and the concomitant isolation of European politics from pressures from below, are flanked by initiatives that ostensibly allow for more democracy in Europe, such as the European Citizens' Initiative and the funding of civil society organisations. It is questionable whether an integration or co-optation of critical social forces into the orbit of the European state apparatus can take place in a context of increasing authoritarian power relations. So far this has not materialised.

Only occasionally do MEPs participate in the dialogues and protests of social movements, and the European Commission has not yet approached protest movements at all. In the European Parliament, the European United Left-Nordic Green Left (GUE/NGL) lack a clear position on how to respond to the crisis, whereas at national level, mainstream left-wing political parties – entrenched in the moderate 'Third Way' rhetoric at best – keep distancing themselves from a radical critique of austerity measures. This moderate pragmatism, which is mainly defending the existing order, has limited the political room for manoeuvre to channel dissent in Europe. At the same time, the institutional argument about the disciplining nature of debt, and the neoliberal crisis rhetoric about an overall belt tightening, and comparing sovereign debt to individual household debt, have become very powerful justifications for austerity measures. This is politically appealing and is widely accepted as common sense in many parts of Europe.

As the inclusion of social democratic demands for a 'European social model' has shown, the ensemble of European state apparatuses enjoys sufficient leeway to appease critical voices in the chorus of the hegemonic project. In particular the widespread call for 'more Europe' can potentially legitimise authoritarian politics, and the legal codification of them, rather than lead to fighting them. This dimension is particularly important with respect to the long-term strategies and tactics of left progressive movements operating outside the confines of representative governments and parliamentary politics.

Counter-hegemonic dissent has mainly been articulated in the streets in the sense of Gramsci's 'war of movement', without consolidating an effective and stable 'war of position' firmly rooted in the organisations of civil society (Scholl and Freyberg-Inan, 2013). So far, alliances have been exhausted in planning large-scale demonstrations, action days and summits. Just as the short-term vision of the crisis management of the European Union can be questioned, so can the social struggles and the capability to formulate medium to long-term alternatives that are not only supported by the networks and alliances of different movements but also organically anchored in the social terrain of European civil society.

Social protests have been slow to translate into left-wing support at the ballot box, with Syriza in Greece, and recently Podemos in Spain, as important exceptions. In Spain, the conservative-liberal People's Party gained an absolute majority in parliament at the height of the occupations of public spaces and protests. In the parliamentary elections in Iceland, voters reinstalled the same centre-right government as had been blamed for the financial meltdown. While the socialist President Hollande in France continues to follow the neoliberal course of labour market deregulation set by his predecessor Sarkozy, and seems to accept the punitive austerity regime without further protest, conservative governments remain stable in Europe's North.

Concerning the European Union and Europe in general, there is no consistent imaginary that exceeds the neoliberal model. Progressive left-wing discourses at European level contain mainly abstract political and economic claims, which do not link up with concrete everyday experiences and struggles of resistance. People may identify with occupying the squares, demonstrations, and acts of civil disobedience taking place at local, regional or national level. Comparable sites of identification in the European realm have not yet become manifest, while common symbols of the European Union, such as the flag, the anthem and the euro, are entrenched by the European state project. New alliances of the left would need alternative collective symbolism, and emblems that become viral and are reproduced in different national contexts.

Uneven and Asynchronous Crisis Development –
Consequences for Emancipatory Projects

The concrete manifestations, frequency and vehemence of the protests against austerity in Europe vary considerably. While protests in the Northern Eurozone have been weak, the situation is different in Europe's Southern and Eastern periphery, whose countries have been affected most profoundly by the crisis and the imposed austerity and structural adjustment programmes. Hitherto non-politicised people have participated in mass demonstrations, square protests and assemblies in neighbourhoods, strikes and actions of civil disobedience, such as encircling parliaments, land squats and supermarket raids. In Spain people organised to block home evictions. At the same time, many of these protesters and grassroots resistance initiatives have been silenced by the disciplinary force of growing unemployment and under-employment, household indebtedness through mortgages, and authoritarian repression by police forces. Moreover, acts of solidarity from the North towards left-wing groups and unions in the South have been weak. In a context in which transfer payments among member states to compensate for (regional) unequal development are hardly possible, there is little reason for optimism that alternative perspectives can gain ground in Europe (Becker and Jaeger, 2012: 111).

To understand social struggles and the formation of a left-wing progressive alliance at European level, a differentiated perspective on the dynamics and contradictions of these processes is necessary. To understand the extent to which social power relations and the fundamental dimensions of the social (re-) production of a counter-hegemonic project can condense at the European level, consideration of the unequal and uneven development of the crisis at the member state level is indispensable. Local and regional events in Southern member states have mobilised the support and sympathy of the wider population. Nonetheless, it remains an open question whether or not the punctual event politics of new social movements have led to sustainable structures that allow for a consistent and enduring resistance of the European left against the authoritarian EU crisis regime. We should therefore not refer uncritically to the European spring. Just as the initial views of the 'Arab spring', which were invariably positively connoted, had to give way to a more pragmatic and more nuanced understanding of social movements, the mobilisations against the austerity course have to be seen as a moment of particular social struggles and potentially a starting point for the development of collective actions, rather than an already existing monolithic block or a concrete and coherent movement.

Even though the agents of the new social movements, their concerns and everyday experiences, are manifold and sometimes contradictory, there are similarities in their objectives and forms of resistance. Scientific debates and knowledge production about the condensation of European integration into a neoliberal and undemocratic project should exceed the limited confines of critical research on Europe and become part of broader social debates. Universities as public spaces for substantive discussions need to be recaptured as part of an alternative Europe project, organically involving social movements, unions, and people working in the media and the cultural domain, governments and the private sector. Critical scholarship can play a pivotal role in demystifying existing beliefs and contesting existing power inequalities, and hence contribute to the organisation of resistance. This also implies that we need to break with the 'strategic silences' of the dominant modes of understanding in economics and political sciences (Gill, 2012: 518). Only through an understanding of the asymmetrical power relations and through a critical confrontation with the institutions of the European Union can we reach a position where we can think about alternatives.

It is on this point that we want to conclude this chapter, by pointing to some of the concrete, and as we would argue, encouraging, attempts to formulate and put into practice resistance and alternatives to the austerity programmes that are being directed at EU level. With all the critical reflections on current social struggles, the very fact that they are taking place at all should of course not be discredited. Moreover, there is a radical and innovative quality to many of these initiatives which needs to be highlighted. In doing so we can transcend the discussion of reformist, pragmatic or utopian perspectives and show the transnational solidarity and common struggles inherent in them. Blockupy might serve here as an example of an initiative that is inherently transnational and targeting EU-level institutions rather than exhausting itself in existing channels of communication with the European Union. It remains to be seen whether and how the initiative will continue, but there is a potential to overcome some of the problematic issues we have discussed in this chapter.

Similarly, the discussion of the commons has become a core dimension in many local and transnational forums, taking cues for example from the struggles against water privatisation in Italy and Greece, and also from previous experiences with structural adjustment in 'developing' countries. Lastly, there is also an emerging transnational cooperation of critical academics who are willing to engage actively in these dynamics of formulating alternatives, for instance through groups of heterodox economists or social scientists. Educational struggles are of great importance for an emancipatory understanding.

While in this chapter we have provided a critical discussion of resistance and alternatives to austerity programmes in the European Union, we would strongly disagree with any forms of defeatism. We therefore stand by Gramsci's appeal, published in the first edition of the *Turin Ordine Nuovo 1*, in May 1919: 'Educate yourself, because we need all your wisdom. Move it, because we need your entire enthusiasm. Organize yourselves, because we need all your strength.'

Select Bibliography

Becker, J. and Jäger, J. (2012) 'Integration in crisis: a regulationist perspective on the interaction of European varieties of capitalism', *Competition and Change*, 16(3): 169–87.

Cafruny, A. W. and Ryner, M. (eds) (2003) *A Ruined Fortress? Neoliberal Hegemony and Transformation in Europe*. Lanham, Md.: Rowman & Littlefield.

Della Porta, D. and Caiani, M. (2009) *Social Movements and Europeanization*. Oxford: Oxford University Press.

Gill, S. (2012) 'Towards a radical concept of praxis: imperial "common sense" versus the post-modern prince', *Millennium Journal of International Studies*, 40(3): 505–24.

Horn, L. (2012) 'Anatomy of a critical friendship: organised labour and the European state formation', *Globalizations*, 9(4): 577–92.

Oberndorfer, L. (2012) 'Hegemoniekrise in Europa' ['A crisis of hegemony in Europe'], pp. 50–72 in Staatsprojekt Europa (ed.), *Die EU in der Krise* [*The European Union in the Crisis*]. Münster: Staatsprojekt Europa.

Scholl, C. and Freyberg-Inan, A. (2013) 'Hegemony's dirty tricks: explaining counter-globalization's weakness in times of neoliberal crisis', *Globalizations*, 10(4): 619–34.

CHAPTER TWENTY-THREE

Crisis, Austerity and Resistance in the United States

David Mcnally

We are living through the fourth great downturn in the history of capitalism. The current global slump originated in 2008 as a financial crisis located in the US banking sector, but it soon developed into a worldwide crisis of the capitalist system as a whole. This chapter provides an analysis of both the immediate triggers of the crisis in the United States and the underlying dynamics that have made it so deep and prolonged. It then analyses the austerity agenda introduced in the aftermath of the global bank bailouts, and concludes by discussing alternatives to a system fraught with such crises and the human suffering it wreaks.

More than five years since the March 2008 collapse of the Wall Street investment bank Bear Stearns, whose meltdown precipitated the acute phase of the crisis, there are no signs of a return to sustained growth. Global capitalism continues to limp through a protracted period of high unemployment and exceptionally sluggish growth. Whereas an ordinary downturn in the business cycle is followed in a year or so by a quick return to robust expansion, the US and global economies remain mired in one of the great slowdowns in the history of the capitalist economy, on the scale of those of 1873–96, the Great Depression of the 1930s, and the crisis period of 1971–82.

The Financial Crisis of 2008–09

When banks started to collapse in 2008–09, former US central banker Alan Greenspan declared that he was in a state of 'shocked disbelief'. Yet, all the warning signals had been flashing for at least a year. In July 2007, investment bank Bear Stearns had shut down two multi-billion-dollar hedge funds after they lost a whopping US$1.6 billion on mortgage-backed securities gone sour. Such securities are created when financial institutions bundle up hundreds or thousands of mortgages and then chop these bundles into smaller packages that investors can purchase. So long as people are paying their mortgages, these investments will pay off. But if economic troubles lead large numbers of people to default on mortgage payments, then investors in mortgage-based financial products will be hit by losses – precisely what happened in the summer of 2007. And since hedge funds, major banks and pension funds had been buying such 'securities' for years, it should have been clear that big troubles were afoot. Yet, in the summer of 2007 the International Monetary Fund (IMF) proclaimed that 'global economic risks have declined.'

Nothing could have been further from the truth. Within a matter of months (March 2008), Bear Stearns disintegrated. But it was the collapse of the much larger Wall Street bank Lehman Brothers in September of that year which unleashed a full-scale panic. It is not hard to see why.

Five days before it imploded, the venerable Wall Street bank had been valued at $635 billion – making it ten and a half times larger than the previous record US bankruptcy, that of Enron in 2001. As Lehman crumbled, gut-churning panic gripped the world's financial markets. After all, if a major US investment bank of Lehman's rank was actually stuffed full of worthless financial assets such as mortgage-backed securities, who else might be in similar straits? So interconnected are the world's banks that no one could be considered immune. By the fall of 2008, therefore, 'Every major firm on Wall Street was either bankrupt or fatally intertwined with a bankrupt system,' as one former central banker explained. Worried they might never get their money back, bankers and financiers around the globe effectively stopped lending to one another.

Short-term lending, sometimes for as little as 24 hours, is crucial to keeping the wheels of the economy turning. Every day banks and corporations lend and borrow billions of dollars in order to make payments to suppliers and creditors. So when lending halts, the day-to-day operations of capitalism quickly seize up. This was precisely what happened in September 2008, as the financial tsunami generated a global credit crunch.

As banks went under, stock markets crashed. Before the end of 2008 global markets had lost half their value – wiping out around $35 trillion in financial assets. Worse, the financial crisis was spreading, with banks melting down in France, Britain, Iceland, Germany, Spain and Ireland. Then, as 2009 began, the crisis spread beyond the financial sector, hitting renowned US-based manufacturing corporations such as General Motors and Chrysler. By this point, the slowdown was hitting the economies of the Global South, especially those – from China and Brazil to India and Bangladesh – that are tied into global production chains. As manufacturers tottered on the edge of collapse – and required government bailouts to stay afloat – it became clear that the crisis was not confined to the financial sector or to the Global North. Capitalism was in the throes of a general and system-wide slump.

A Systemic Crisis of Capitalism

To characterise these events as a generalised crisis of capitalism is to fly in the face of conventional wisdom. Mainstream commentators prefer to tell a story of severe disturbances in the banking sector having been caused by faulty financial policies. Yet serious analysis reveals that the crisis has to do with fundamental problems in the very workings of capitalism.

Consider that during the Great Recession of 2008–09 world industrial output fell by 13 per cent. International trade plummeted a stunning 20 per cent. The production of goods and services – not just financial transactions – was in terrible convulsion. Moreover, stabilisation of global finance, via a massive wave of government-led bank bailouts throughout 2008–10, has not brought the slump to an end. Because the problems are more deeply rooted, bailing out finance has not been enough to solve capitalism's troubles.

The global slump since 2008 thus conforms to Marx's observation that 'At first glance ... the entire crisis presents itself as simply a credit and monetary crisis' (1981 [1867]: 621). The reason is straightforward: the banking system is the nerve centre of capitalism, the place where all the flows of money that drive the economy come together. As a result, this is where all great economic shocks are most concentrated. It does not follow, however, that there are no deeper causes at work. Indeed, if the crisis becomes a prolonged and generalised one, it is obvious that there must be such deep causes. And that is exactly what a proper look at the evidence reveals.

As a starting point, we need only observe that total corporate profits in the United States had stopped growing by mid-2006, and then began a three-year decline (documented by the Bureau of Economic Analysis). As critical political economists have shown, profits are the fuel that drives a capitalist economy. After all, massive corporations and their ultra-wealthy owners do not invest hundreds of millions of dollars just for the good feelings that come from producing useful goods or services. They invest their wealth in order to make a gain. As the former CEO of US Steel put it, 'U.S. Steel is in business to make profits, not to make steel.' Thus, if profits start to shrink, so will the capitalist enterprises that live and grow off them. Just as a human heart seizes up when the flow of blood is constricted, the capitalist economy goes into its own version of cardiac arrest when the flow of profits slows down.

It is this – the decline in total profits beginning in 2006 – that laid the basis for the global slump. As profits contracted, corporations had less money to put into the banks. The banks, in turn, found themselves with fewer funds to lend out. They tried to compensate by seeking out even riskier lending opportunities, which are meant to deliver higher returns. Yet they did that just as the economy was turning down, following the downward trend in profits. Meanwhile, the profit decline led firms to cut back investment and lay off workers or reduce their hours. Inevitably, millions of workers soon found themselves unable to make mortgage payments, triggering a crisis in mortgage-backed securities, which only stoked the fires of the banking crisis.

Again, note the timing here. The downturn in corporate profits preceded the financial crisis. To be sure, unique problems in the financial sector made a bad situation worse, but these were not the exclusive cause of the slump. Indeed they might have been contained, as had other banking crises, if the corporate sector had been healthy and robust.

The crisis since 2008 thus bears significant similarities to all great slowdowns in the capitalist economy. As we have seen, capitalism is a profit-driven economy. It is also a system of rivalry, of intense competition between corporations – for sales, market share and profits. The proven way to win sales and profits is for a firm to find more efficient ways of producing a given good or service. And the sure-fire way of becoming more efficient is to introduce new technologies and production systems that speed up labour and, in so doing, reduce production costs. This is why capitalists are always gathering intelligence on the technologies, research plans and marketing strategies of their competitors. Whoever can gain an edge should be able to garner more profits – and profits are what make possible large new investments in state-of-the-art machines and production facilities.

However, if every firm is engaging in frantic strategies for new investments – in machines, research, factories, buildings and more – eventually a situation of *over-accumulation* will develop. Put simply, frenetic competition among capitalists leads to the building of more factories, mines, office towers, machines and shopping malls than can profitably be utilised. In such circumstances, the average returns on investment plummet. By over-investing in the heat of competition, corporations inadvertently undermine the conditions for secure profit making. This compels them to cut back investment and lay off workers, which causes the whole economy to contract – all because competition led to over-accumulation and a profits crisis.

By 2006–07 just such a situation had developed, signalling the end of the neoliberal economic expansion that had started in 1982, in the aftermath of a decade of crisis. The foundations of neoliberalism have been dealt with elsewhere in this book. Suffice it to say that crushing unions, reorganising work processes, using new technologies to speed up labour, reducing social benefits, allowing less efficient firms to go under, relocating production facilities in low-wage zones, and introducing reforms favourable to capital – all this and more restored the profitability of capital around the world. The result was a prolonged boom, from 1982–2007, punctuated by partial crises in 1997–98 (East Asia and Russia) and 2000–01 (the collapse of the 'dotcom boom' in the United States). In response to those partial crises, central banks, led by the US Federal Reserve, repeatedly slashed interest rates (borrowing costs) each time the economy faltered. While this stimulated the economy just when it showed signs of slowing down, it also meant that more and more economic growth, especially after 2000, rested on debts taken on by banks and consumers in particular. When profit growth ground to a halt in 2006, debt bubbles in both the real estate and banking sectors burst, signalling the acute phase of the crisis.

The global slump since 2008 thus demonstrates all the classic features of a crisis of over-accumulation – and not merely a financial convulsion. In response, the capitalist class around the world has used all the classic weapons in their arsenal. In so doing, they have ushered in the Age of Austerity.

Bailouts for the Banks, Austerity for the People

As the world economy stumbled into 2009, things just kept getting worse. Before the first month of the year was over, the US government would have to bail out Citigroup, Bank of America and AIG, the world's largest insurance company. With world capitalism now in freefall, governments went into damage control. They began by throwing a few trillion dollars into the financial system, giving banks real money in exchange for toxic asset such as mortgage-backed securities. But a few trillion was not going to do the trick. Still the banks kept falling. Before the end of 2009, eight US banks and 20 European financial institutions had collapsed.

And so governments pumped trillions more into financial institutions – to be followed by yet more trillions. By mid- 2010, something in the order of $27 trillion had been injected into the system, by way of bank and corporate bailouts and 'stimulus' programmes meant to kick-start growth. And the bailouts have just kept coming, especially in Europe, where massive operations continue to rescue faltering banks.

But having spent unheard-of amounts to save capitalism from itself, governments were confronted with a dilemma. In borrowing trillions on money markets to prop up banks and corporations, governments had gone into significant debt. Sooner or later, they needed to find some way to pay off these huge new debts – and before global investors began to doubt their ability to repay (precisely the problem that has confronted Greece and other European nations recently). Being good neoliberals, they had one sure-fire strategy: make working class people pay for the bailouts. Thus began a new Age of Austerity, in which public education, health care, food aid, old age security payments and more would be sacrificed so that large shares of state revenues could be used to pay for the bank bailouts. Even the governor of the Bank of England admitted as much, when he remarked that 'the price of this financial crisis is being paid by people who absolutely did not cause it'.

Let's be clear about what this means in fundamental human terms. Austerity equals greater suffering, poverty, unemployment, stress and hardship for millions upon millions of people. Schools are being closed, Medicaid programmes slashed, old age security reduced – all to protect banks and the investments of the rich and powerful. Millions of people will be less healthy; many of them will have years cut off their lives. As the New York Times reported on 17 March 2013:

> A cut of $350 million to the Centers for Disease Control and Prevention will mean 25,000 fewer breast and cervical cancer screenings for low-income women; 424,000 fewer H.I.V. tests; and the purchase of 540,000 fewer doses of vaccine for flu, hepatitis and measles. Community health centers will be cut by $120 million, meaning about 900,000 fewer patients lacking insurance will receive primary care.

A $350 million cut is just the tip of the austerity iceberg.

Predictably, cuts to health and education are having devastating effects on children. The state of California has eliminated the Healthy Families Program, which provided medical insurance for 900,000 children. The state of Michigan has ordered Detroit to close half of its schools, while the City of Chicago plans to close 57 schools of its own – overwhelmingly in poor and predominantly African-American neighbourhoods. Other cuts will remove access to early childhood education for 70,000 children. Astonishingly, more than one in five US children lives in poverty – a rate of child poverty worse than that found in countries like Bulgaria and Latvia. The data for food aid are even more shocking. Fully half the children in the United States will rely on food aid stamps at some point in their childhood – a figure that rises to 90 per cent where African-American children are concerned.

Next, consider higher education, which has been hammered by cuts. Forty-nine US states have slashed support to public colleges and universities – by a whopping 28 per cent on average. As tuition payments have soared in consequence, so have student debt levels. As of 2010, total student debt in the United States exceeded $1 trillion, for the first time surpassing total credit-card debt. And given a tepid job market, with diminished prospects for young people, millions will be haunted for years by these debts.

Then there are the dampening effects of austerity on the overall economy. Remember that cutbacks to government spending eliminate jobs – for teachers, nurses, sanitation workers and millions more. Just the $85 billion cut imposed in early 2013 (as a result of what is known as 'sequestration') will cause 1 million jobs to disappear. And people who are out of work, just like those whose wages or social benefits have been reduced, spend less on everything from food and housing to cars and appliances. The inevitable result is reduced consumer demand, less economic activity and slower growth.

Not surprisingly, there has been no sustained recovery from the Great Recession of 2008–09. The International Labour Organization reports that as of 2013 there were 50 million fewer paid jobs in the world than in 2008. And while the official unemployment rate in the United States has come down below 8 per cent, these figures are highly deceiving. After five years of slump, millions of people have simply given up looking for work – and are thus removed from the jobless figures. If there had been no drop in labour force participation, the official US jobless rate would be around 12 per cent. Add in those who are underemployed – able to find only part-time employment even thought they seek full-time work – and the rate of unemployment would be about 17 per cent. For African-Americans and Latinos it would be over 25 per cent – a level last reached during the depths of the Great Depression of the 1930s.

It is worth reminding ourselves that things are even worse in parts of Europe, where the *official* jobless rate in countries like Greece and Spain exceeds 25 per cent, and surpasses 50 per cent for young people. 'Call it a depression', as the *Economist* magazine pointedly declared on 2 May 2012.

Understanding the Economics and Politics of Austerity

Because austerity reduces economic growth, many commentators have described such policies as irrational. These analysts subscribe to John Maynard Keynes's view in *The General Theory of Employment, Interest and Money* (1936) that the central obligation of government is to sustain employment by ensuring an adequate level of demand for goods and services. When the private sector is flailing, they suggest, government should spend to pick up the slack. On these premises, austerity clearly is irrational, as it pushes down economic activity and employment. That line has been taken by celebrated economist and *New York Times* columnist Paul Krugman, and by Robert Skidelsky, biographer of Keynes, who contends that austerity during a slump is 'economic madness'.

Keynesian economists are right that unemployment and lower incomes are bad for the economy, but they forget that the driving force of capitalism is profits. Corporations do not invest millions in order to create jobs and stimulate growth. Their objective is not the well-being of the economy; it is to maximise their gains. Consequently, unemployment and reduced incomes for workers can be useful to capital if they help to boost profits. And that is just what happened after 2008: US corporate profits rose by 20 per cent a year, easily surpassing their previous peak, only to level off by 2012. In short, as US workers have gotten poorer, corporations have prospered. In that respect, the austerity agenda makes sense – capitalist sense, that is.

The profit recovery has been driven principally by four things: speedup (squeezing more work out of every hour on the job), declining real wages, unemployment (which pressures workers to accept jobs for less pay) and reduced hours and job security. This is why average US incomes have been falling even as workers have become more productive. In fact, wages as a share of US gross domestic product (GDP) are now at their lowest share ever. Until 1975, wages always made up more than 50 per cent of GDP. In 2012 they hovered a hair above 43 per cent. This is the context in which the median income of US households has fallen to its lowest level since 1995. And it explains why a new measure of poverty introduced by the Census Bureau found that that fully one-third of US citizens are living in poverty or are desperately close to falling into it.

Austerity has thus reinforced the neoliberal trend towards increased poverty and social inequality. In so doing, it has served the interests of corporations and the rich, while making life worse for millions. The result has been a boon for profits. Yet rising profits have not translated into big jumps in corporate investment and economic growth. These remain sluggish. And all indications are that they will remain that way for quite some time to come.

The reason for this is that boosting profits is not enough to kick-start a wave of capitalist expansion. For that to happen, the problem of over-accumulation – of too many factories, machines, mines, retail outlets, office towers and so on – must be resolved. And the classic capitalist 'solution' is widespread corporate bankruptcies. As the least efficient and least profitable companies are driven out of business, the surviving firms are able to grab a larger share of the market, which gives them an incentive to expand by hiring more workers and introducing new technologies. What Marx called 'the destruction of capital' – a wave of corporate bankruptcies – is essential for a crisis to prepare the ground for a new period of expansion. Ironically, in propping up the banking sector governments have limited the scale of bankruptcies. For by flooding the system with money and pushing interest rates close to zero, central banks have enabled even the least profitable firms to borrow funds, virtually for free, in order to stay afloat. In the absence of destruction of over-accumulated capital, rising profits have not been ploughed into new investments. Instead, corporations are holding on to their profits, salting them away in banks or in short-term financial instruments, or distributing them as dividends to stockholders.

As of 2013, US corporations were sitting on nearly $2 trillion in cash, the highest amount ever recorded. Companies in Europe are awash with similar amounts. So long as money remains super cheap and over-accumulation persists, it is difficult to see why this will change. And since large-scale business investment – in constructing new factories and buildings, in equipping their businesses with new machines, and in hiring extra employees – is what creates economic growth, companies will continue to hoard their profits and the economy will continue to stagnate.

But amidst stagnation, austerity marches on. In consequence life will get worse for millions – unless mass resistance changes things.

Social Resistance and Alternatives to Austerity

While the austerity juggernaut has ridden roughshod over people, this is not for lack of resistance. Unfortunately, the opposition that has flared up is typically episodic, short-lived and disconnected from other fronts of resistance. But it is there, and it could be built upon.

Before looking at some critical moments of resistance to austerity, let us address a common misapprehension. The weakness of organised workers and socialist movements in the United States is frequently cited as proof that radical social change in the United States is simply not possible. While it would be foolish to ignore the effects of patriotism and individualism on the wider political culture, it is equally wrong to dismiss the vibrant history of mass protest in the United States – from the sit-down strikes and labour struggles of the 1930s and 1940s to the more recent civil rights and anti-war movements. Furthermore, popular opinion in the United States is frequently much more progressive than is presumed. An April 2013 Gallup Poll, for instance, found that six out of every ten people in the United States favour a more equitable distribution of wealth, with a majority also supporting a 'Robin Hood' tax on the rich to that end. That aspiration for a more equal society is clearly visible in a wave of recent struggles to change the course of US social policy.

Among the earliest and most inspiring responses to the Great Recession was the December 2008 factory occupation by the largely immigrant workforce at Republic Windows and Doors in Chicago. These workers, many of them veterans of the May Day 2006 strike by a million immigrant workers, seized their plant when management announced its closure. The Republic workers initiated a stream of factory occupations that ran through Canada, Ireland, Spain and beyond. Then, just over a year later, a mass uprising in Wisconsin demonstrated the potential power of coordinated action by workers, students and others, who occupied their state legislature, inspiring rallies of up to 100,000 people to preserve social services and defend union rights. Unfortunately, officials in the unions and the Democratic Party directed this magnificent struggle into the demobilising channel of electoral politics.

Yet barely six months later hundreds of people seized a Manhattan park and launched the Occupy Wall Street rebellion. Within weeks, Occupy movements had emerged in hundreds of cities and towns in the United States and far beyond, mobilising tens of thousands in direct actions. Targeting an economic system that serves the '1 percent' at the expense of the '99 percent', Occupy articulated an economic justice agenda that fundamentally questioned capitalism. Notwithstanding its lack of deep pockets, slick public relations campaigns and the like, Occupy's message electrified large numbers of people, garnering majority support in one opinion poll after another – and particularly high levels of support among youth.

While it was unable to sustain effective organisation, particularly after police evicted occupiers from one park after another, the spirit of Occupy has continued in struggles to block foreclosures against people unable to pay mortgages, and in a wave of spirited protests by some of the lowest-paid workers in the United States – including actions against Walmart and several fast food chains.

But perhaps the most inspiring anti-austerity struggle in the United States was the September 2012 mass strike by Chicago teachers, a group that is 87 percent female and nearly half African-American or Latino. While many commentators were caught off guard by the militancy and self-organisation of the teachers and by the enormous support they received in working class communities, it should have come as no surprise. All of this was the result of years of dedicated work by the Caucus of Rank and File Educators (CORE), which had long mobilised in solidarity with neighbourhood groups to stop closures of local schools. In 2010 CORE candidates won a majority of positions on the executive of the Chicago Teachers Union (CTU) and then produced a superb document, *The Schools Chicago's Students Deserve*. There, they made the case for adequate funding, smaller classes, enriched curriculum and for challenging 'the apartheid-like system' in Chicago that privileges schools in wealthy white neighbourhoods while starving those in poor and predominantly Latino and African-American communities. In so doing, they positioned their union as a champion of class and racial justice.

By taking a stand on behalf of the city's working class students and their families, the CTU broke the confines of the corporatist model of trade unionism, which focuses exclusively on the wages and conditions of union members. They made the quality of education, opposition to racial and class apartheid, and the participation of parents in their children's education central to their vision for schooling in their city. It thus came as little surprise when, on day three of the strike, huge demonstrations of support took place in largely African-American and Latino neighbourhoods in Chicago's South and West sides. This public support was crucial to the considerable gains made by the CTU, notwithstanding its inability to beat back all concessions.

Democratisation was also a key to the transformation of the CTU. The revitalised union created House of Delegates meetings where teachers elected from every school would discuss, debate and shape union policy and action. Delegates also convened open-air meetings at schools to directly involve rank-and-file teachers in the running of their strike and in deciding its course of action. In so doing, they demonstrated that the ideas of assembly-style democracy often associated with Occupy, and with struggles like the Québec student strike of 2012, can play a central role in a revitalised labour movement. Nevertheless, also like these other struggles, the inability to create a sustained and ongoing oppositional movement, meant that the austerity agenda surged forward once the picket lines were down and the demonstrators had left the streets.

In spite of the setbacks, these struggles in the United States against social inequality, in defence of public services, for immigrant rights and the rights of unions are proof positive of a growing search for alternatives to neoliberal austerity. Especially significant is the idea that public services such as education ought not to be for profit, or for the interests of the wealthy, but should serve working class people. Implicit here is the notion that public resources should be used to make life better for people – by providing housing, healthcare, schools that promote human development, and so on. In short, these struggles suggest that society should be oriented to meeting human needs, not promoting corporate profits. Equally important are ideas of radical, participatory democracy of the sort that animated the Wisconsin protests, Occupy and the Chicago teachers' strike.

Moreover, struggles in the United States have stimulated resistance movements in the rest of the world. This was particularly clear in the case of the Occupy movement, whose tactics and slogans quickly spread to dozens upon dozens of countries. At the same time, Occupy and other movements in the United States drew inspiration from powerful protest elsewhere. The great uprisings of the 'Arab spring' in Tunisia and Egypt electrified protesters internationally, as did the predominantly youth-based movement of 'the indignants' in countries like Spain, where tens of thousands occupied city squares to protest austerity and unemployment. Anti-austerity struggles in the United States are thus drawing energy from movements elsewhere, just as upheavals in the United States inspire protesters around the world.

Struggles that aim to radically democratise society and to assert the priority of human needs, not profits, clearly challenge the fundamental logic of neoliberalism. They are sources of hope and inspiration in difficult times. More than this, they point beyond capitalism itself, demonstrating the need to develop alternatives to a system of crises, austerity and hardship for the majority in the United States and worldwide.

Acknowledgement

This chapter draws heavily on McNally (2011a, 2011b).

Select Bibliography

Marx, K. (1981) [1867] *Capital*, Vol. 3. Harmondsworth: Penguin.

McNally, D. (2011a) *Global Slump: The Economics and Politics of Crisis and Resistance*. Oakland, Calif.: PM Press.

McNally, D. (2011b) 'Slump, austerity and resistance', in L. Panitch, G. Albo and V. Chibber (eds), *Socialist Register 2012*. London: Merlin Press.

Contributors

Baba Adebola Ayelabola Jr. is head of the Education, Planning, Research and Statistics Department of the Medical and Health Workers' Union of Nigeria (MHWUN), and doctoral fellow in global social policies and governance in the Social Science Department at the University of Kassel. baba_aye@yahoo.com

Pietro Basso is professor of sociology in the Philosophy Department of the University of Venice Ca' Foscari. He has published extensively on working hours, migration, racist theories and state racism. He is director of the Master's in immigration, and engaged in anti-war and anti-racist activities. pbasso@unive.it

Dae-oup Chang is senior lecturer in development studies in the Development Studies Department at SOAS, University of London. His current research investigates the impacts that the rise of East Asian capitalism and the emerging social movements of labour in East Asia are having on global neoliberalism. dc13@soas.ac.uk

Adam Hanieh is a senior lecturer in the Development Studies Department at SOAS, University of London. His research interests focus on processes of state and class formation in the Middle East, with a particular emphasis on the states of the Gulf Cooperation Council. He is author of *Capitalism and Class in the Gulf Arab States* (2011) and *Lineages of Revolt: Issues of Contemporary Capitalism in the Middle East* (2013). ah92@soas.ac.uk

Rohini Hensman is an independent scholar who has published extensively on issues related to the impact of globalisation on workers' rights and trade unions in India; women workers, domestic labour and feminism; and minority rights, identity politics and the right to self-determination in the context of India and Sri Lanka. She is currently working on re-imagining the Marxist notion of socialist revolution. rohinihensman@yahoo.co.uk

Laura Horn is associate professor in international relations and European integration in the Department of Society and Globalisation at Roskilde University, Denmark. Her main research focus is on the critical political economy of European integration. lhorn@ruc.dk

Jerome Klassen is a postdoctoral research fellow in the International Development Studies Programme at Saint Mary's University (Canada). He has published two books on the political economy of Canadian imperialism and several journal articles on transnational corporate interlocking. He is currently working on a study of US President Barack Obama's foreign policy practices. jerome.klassen@smu.ca

Andreas Malm is in the Human Ecology Division, Lund University, Sweden. His research focuses on the role of fossil fuels in capitalist development, as well as the political ecology of climate change adaptation and mitigation in the Middle East and North Africa region. andreas.malm@hek.lu.se

Abelardo Mariña-Flores is professor of political economy, Universidad Autónoma Metropolitana-Azcapotzalco, Mexico City. His main research focuses on Marxist political economy, the theory of labour-value, prices, economic fluctuations and crises, and Latin America within the structure and tendencies of the world market. abmf60@me.com

Thomas Marois is a senior lecturer in the Department of Development Studies, SOAS, University of London. He works in the field of comparative political economy researching problems of finance, development, privatization, and alternatives to neoliberal capitalism. He is the author of *States, Banks and Crisis: Emerging Finance Capitalism in Mexico and Turkey* (2012). tm47@soas.ac.uk

David McDonald is professor of global development studies at Queen's University, Canada, and co-director of the Municipal Services Project. dm23@queensu.ca

David McNally teaches political science at York University, Toronto, Canada, and actively supports numerous social justice movements in that city. His research interests include the theory and practice of democracy, Marxism and anti-racism, socialist-feminism, classical and Marxian political economy, Hegel and dialectical social theory, and the history of anti-capitalist movements. dmcnally@yorku.ca

Sarah Miraglia is a doctoral candidate in sociology, and Master of public administration, Maxwell School of Citizenship and Public Affairs, Syracuse University (Syracuse, NY, USA). skmiragl@syr.edu

Lucia Pradella works at the University of Venice, Ca' Foscari, and is a research associate in the SOAS Department of Development Studies. She is conducting research on the working poor in Western Europe, globalisation, and the history of political economy. She is the author of *L'Attualità del 'Capitale'* (2010) and *Globalisation and the Critique of Political Economy* (2014). luciapradella@hotmail. com

Tim Pringle is a senior lecturer in labour, social movements and development at SOAS, University of London. His current research interests focus on the nexus between labour unrest and trade union reforms in post-socialist countries and the emergence of collective bargaining in China. tp21@soas.ac.uk

Hugo Radice is a life fellow of the University of Leeds, where he taught economics and political economy from 1978 to 2008. He has just published *Global Capitalism* (Routledge, 2014), a collection of essays written between 1984 and 2011. He is currently working on class theory and socialist politics, and recently rejoined the Labour Party. H.K.Radice@leeds.ac.uk

Alfredo Saad-Filho is professor of political economy at the School of Oriental and African Studies (SOAS), University of London, and was a senior economic affairs officer at the United Nations Conference on Trade and Development. He has published extensively on the labour theory of value, the political economy of development, neoliberalism, democracy, alternative economic policies, and Latin America. as59@soas.ac.uk

Benjamin Selwyn is senior lecturer in international relations and development studies, International Relations Department, University of Sussex. He is author of *The Global Development* Crisis (2014), and is currently writing a critique of the academic discipline of development studies. b.selwyn@sussex.ac.uk

John Smith is in the Faculty of Art and Social Sciences, Kingston University London. His current research interests include imperialism, outsourcing and theories of value. johncsmith@btinternet.com

Susan Spronk is associate professor in the School of International Development and Global Studies at the University of Ottawa (Ontario, Canada). Her research focuses on critical approaches to development, social movements, and state and class formation in Latin America. Susan.spronk@uottawa.ca

Leandro Vergara-Camus is lecturer in development studies at SOAS, University of London. His research has focused on the Latin American left, peasant movements, peasant agriculture and alternative development, and he is currently working on the internationalisation of the Brazilian sugarcane ethanol industry. His book *Land and Freedom: The MST, the Zapatistas and Peasant Alternatives to Neoliberalism* was published by Zed Books in 2014. lv6@soas.ac.uk

Jeffery R. Webber is a senior lecturer in the School of Politics and International Relations at Queen Mary, University of London. He sits on the editorial board of *Historical Materialism* and is the author most recently of *Red October: Left-Indigenous Struggles in Modern Bolivia* (2011). j.r.webber@qmul.ac.uk

Angela Wigger is a lecturer in global political economy and international relations in the Department of Political Science at Radboud University, Nijmegen (the Netherlands). Her current research focuses on analysing the root causes for the global economic crisis and the power configurations driving and contesting it, as well as resisting crisis responses in the advanced capitalist world from a historical materialist perspective. a.wigger@fm.ru.nl

Demet Ozmen Yilmaz is assistant professor at Ondokuz Mayis University, Samsun, Turkey. She works on development, women, and gender and family policies in Turkey. demetozy@omu.edu.tr

Index